RESTLESS QUIETISTS

RESTLESS QUIETISTS

Muslim Forms of Life in
Russia's Volga Region

Matteo Benussi

CORNELL UNIVERSITY PRESS   ITHACA AND LONDON

First published 2025 by Cornell University Press

This book was written with the support of the EU's Marie Skłodowska-Curie funding scheme, grant number 843901, project name MeMuRu.

Librarians: A CIP catalog record for this book is available from the Library of Congress.

ISBN 9781501784408 (hardcover)
ISBN 9781501784415 (paperback)
ISBN 9781501784422 (epub)
ISBN 9781501784439 (pdf)

Contents

Note on Treatment of Terms

Throughout this volume, words in Russian are marked in italic, vocabs in Tatar are italicized and underlined (except honorifics attached to names, unmarked), and words in Arabic, a language of spiritual relevance and prestige among Muslim pietists, are underlined. Thus, the noun "person" would be rendered as *chelovek*, _keşe_, or <u>shakhs</u>, respectively. This does not apply to words that are of common usage in English, such as "intelligentsia" or "sharia." Romanization of Russian and Arabic follows a slightly simplified version of the BGN/PCGN system and the ALA-LC system, respectively, while Tatar is written in the modern (Latin) alphabet (zamanälif). For the sake of readability and uniformity, people's names (Russian and Tatar) are given in their international, Anglicized form; but in keeping with a decolonial ethos, I adopt Tatar toponyms for sites located in Tatarstan. The Russian toponym Povolzhye for the broader Volga River basin is used as the default form considering the term's breadth, conciseness, and official status, though its synonyms—Volga region (English) and Idel-Ural (Tatar)—are used as well. English toponyms are used for places of wide renown.

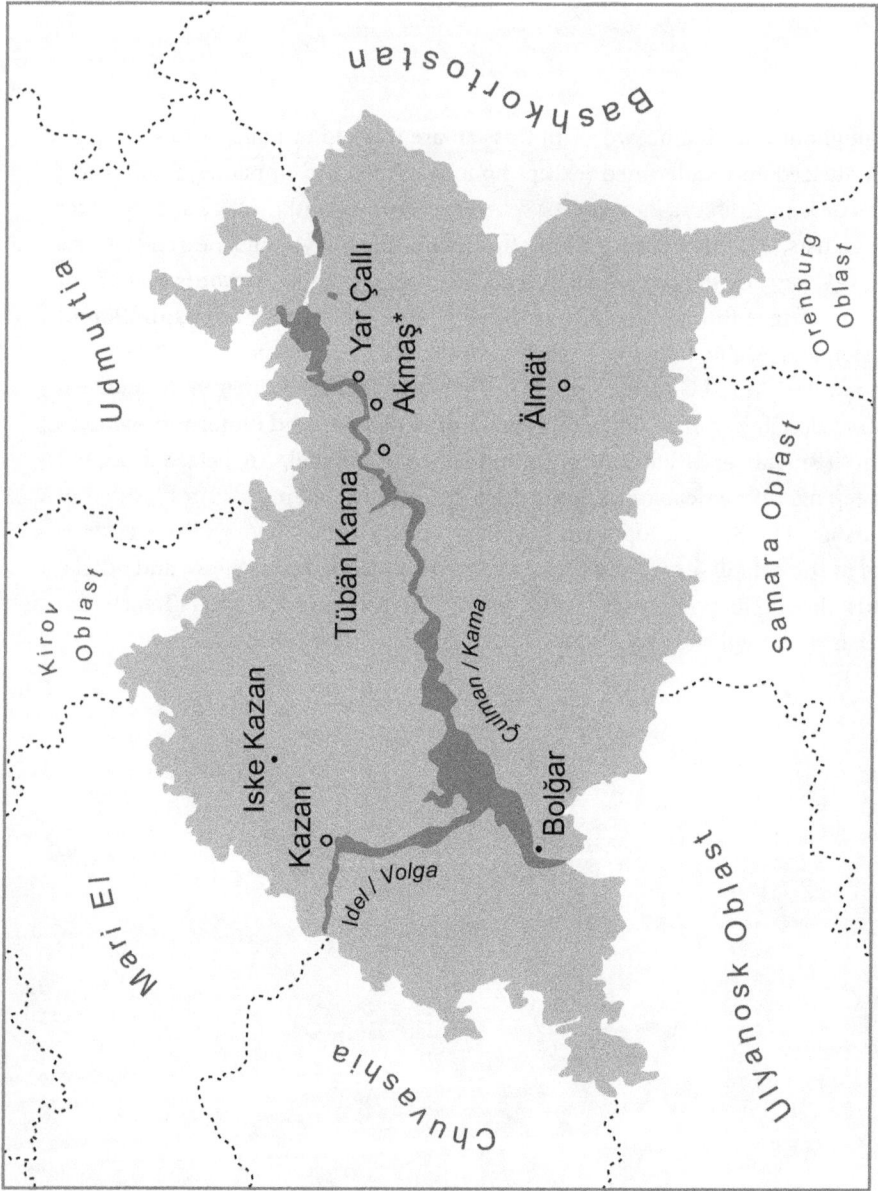

MAP 1. The Republic of Tatarstan in the Russian Federation and the broader region. The shaded area indicates areas densely and/or historically inhabited by Muslims. The asterisked pseudonym indicates the approximate location of a research site.

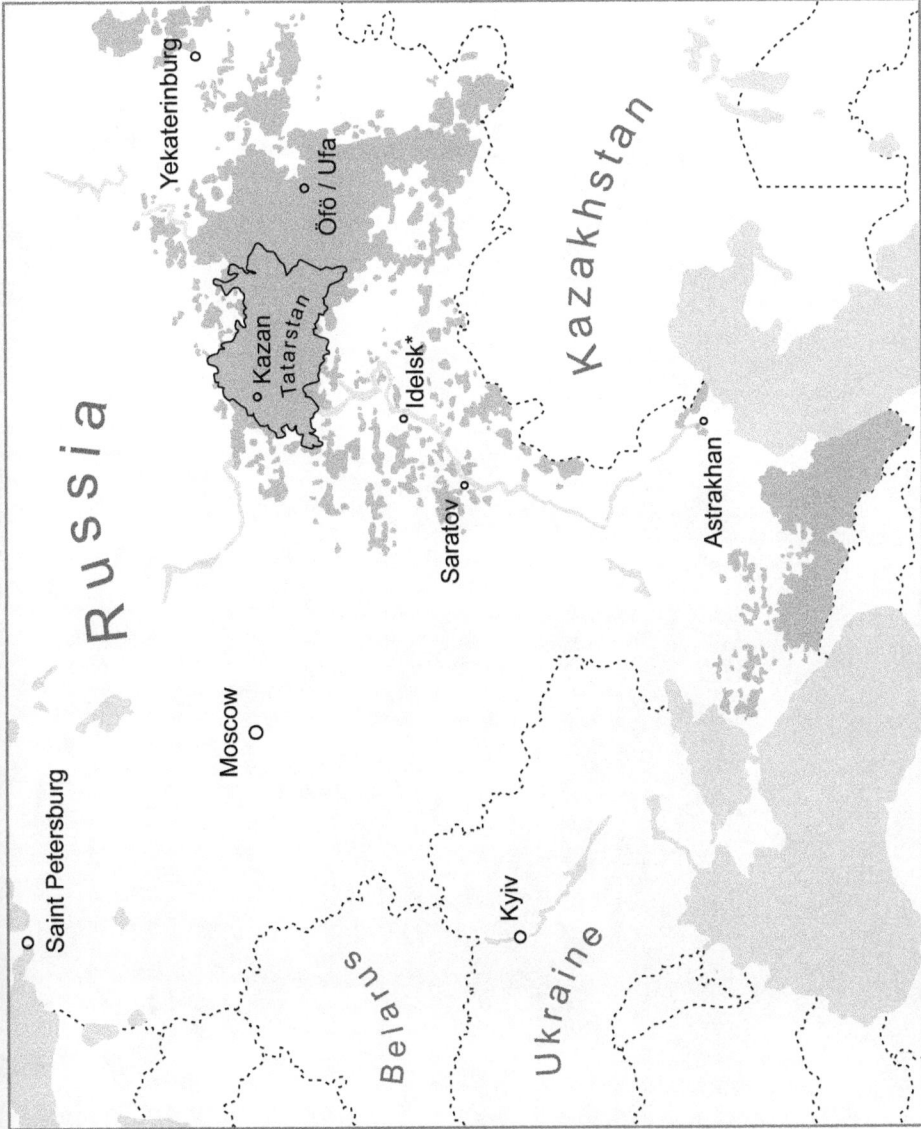

MAP 2. The Republic of Tatarstan and its main urban centers. The asterisked pseudonym indicates the approximate location of a research site.

RUSSIA'S HALAL MILIEU AND AN AUTONOMIST ANTHROPOLOGY OF ETHICS

Amir and I sat at a halal café on the ground floor of a glass-paneled high-rise in central Kazan, the capital of the multiethnic Republic of Tatarstan in the Russian Federation. Now lying within Moscow's orbit, even boasting the title of Russia's "third capital," Kazan prides itself on being the northernmost historically Muslim metropolis and has long been a hub for Islamic piety movements in Eurasia. The post-Soviet transition rekindled that vocation, though the atmosphere of the halal café my interlocutor had selected for our meeting was more hipster than Islamic. Amir, an articulate thirty-year-old IT entrepreneur, cosmopolitan traveler, father of two, and passionately committed Sunni, shared with me his views on life as a Muslim millennial in Russia in the mid-2010s.

> For Russia's Muslims, the main obstacles to overcome are conformism and a lack of courage. You are told to think a certain way. It's like Steve Jobs said: you are taught that the world has a given structure, and you shouldn't think outside the box. You're not given a different path. You go to school, go to work, put the "good student" or "good citizen" mask on, and wear it all your life. Society imposes you to do that. But sometimes people realize that society is man-made, that people can have different ways, that you can change something, create something new. People realize it and wear a new kind of glasses, see more clearly. Understand that what surrounds us has been created by somebody, by God, and with His help it can be changed. You can do something. You can be part of something.

Like many of his pious peers, Amir comes from an irreligious Tatar family, both his parents having been raised in the ultrasecularist Soviet Union. Despite his worldly upbringing, in his teens Amir became a Muslim by conviction rather than mere ethnic background upon encountering an Islamic piety movement booming among the Tatarstani youth. In our conversation, Amir did not shy away from voicing, with seraphic nonchalance, scripturalist opinions that would perturb many of his secular neighbors, including his own parents (concerning, for instance, the permissibility of polygamy or the virtues of censorship). However, his words during our interview captured something more—the existential urgency, optimistic impatience, and spirit of defiance common among young Muslim pietists in postsocialist Russia. His reference to Steve Jobs, a symbol of capitalism as well as maverick innovation, speaks to both his Muslim circle's middle-class aspirations and pietists' proclivity for breaking the conventions of a social order perceived as stagnant and stifling. The nonconformist, aspirational attitude encapsulated by Amir's words is a key theme of this book, as are the political ramifications of such an attitude. Pietists' undocile discipline—their steadfast, self-willed adherence to Islamic principles while running counter to mainstream societal expectations—corresponds to a pronounced capacity for social change. The post-Soviet era is rife with transformations, aspirations, and visions of a better life. In Putin's Russia, however, when a spirit of defiance converges with Islamic piety the very real possibility of repression appears on the horizon.

A few weeks after my conversation with Amir, I found myself in Akmaş, an East Tatarstani industrial city built by the Soviets in the 1960s. I was in the company of a local acquaintance named Rustam. "I'm telling you, if things keep going this way, *they*'re gonna wage *war* on us," Rustam gloomily told me as we drove in his family-size minivan through the concrete-flanked streets of Akmaş. A longbearded, muscular man in his early forties, Rustam was the co-owner of a small but successful halal café. "Things cannot carry on this way forever," my interlocutor continued, lamenting what he perceived as the hostility that "the organs" (*organy*)—that is, the Russian state's security apparatus—harbored toward "sincere Muslims" who followed the "true religion." He complained about nosy bureaucracies, Federal Security Service informants, and unwarranted perquisitions or fears thereof being an unavoidable part of the life of Russia's Muslims—especially those who sought guidance in theological sources not approved by the Kremlin-affiliated Islamic officialdom. The things he said, the way he prayed, the books he read, even the length of his trousers—all these things were frowned upon by "them," because they identified him as a "Wahhabi" (in Russia and other former Soviet territories, the term "Wahhabi," originally indicating a Saudi reform movement, has acquired the negative and even derogatory meaning of foreign-bred fanaticism). To Rustam, a hardworking father of four, such a conceit was ridiculous. Yet its potential implications were no laughing matter. As our conversation progressed, however, Rustam's tone became more and more sanguine. At one point we drove past Akmaş's new, imposing, brutalist-style mosque, lit by the evening sun. My host beamed at me: "You've seen how well our community is doing? Come back again in five, ten years—you'll see we'll be doing even better, if the Most High so wills: more numerous, wealthier, more steadfast in our faith."

Rustam's seemingly contradictory statements—evoking conflict and thriving in nearly the same breath—sum up the paradoxical dynamics that affect the political life of Islamic piety in Putin's Russia. On the one hand, Muslim pietists are faced with moral disapprobation, surveillance, and, in some cases, repression at the hand of state authorities. On the other hand, grassroots Islamic piety networks have been on an upward trajectory of demographic expansion, social and cultural dynamism, and economic prosperity.

Maneuvering between imperial legacies, resurgent authoritarianism, and newfound economic opportunities, this community oscillates between subalternity and success, anxiety and hope. Amid this ambivalence, committed Muslims have proved capable of forging robust, self-determining, independent subjectivities—both individual and collective—while altering the religious, moral, and political landscape of the postsocialist society. This book investigates the making and thriving of such subjectivities. Its goal is threefold. It aims to fill a gap in the English-language ethnographic archive by providing a granular yet broad account of scripturalist Islamic piety in post-Soviet Tatarstan—and Russia's Volga region at large. It advances a novel, politically attuned reconceptualization of halal living. Lastly, it articulates a radical theoretical framework for thinking anthropologically about religious ethics, drawing on autonomist and postanarchist ideas and syncretizing them with long-standing conversations in the anthropology of religion. Through this combination, I hope to capture a facet of the experience of religious commitment that is often undertheorized: its emancipatory dimension.

Restless Quietism

Since the collapse of the institutions of state atheism and its postsocialist transformation, Russia has witnessed the resounding success of transnational Sunni piety trends of different theological orientations. These trends bring together mostly young, upwardly mobile urbanites attracted by new and "alternative" forms of subjectivity. Within the piety network, devotion and strict spiritual discipline are bound up with coolness, urbanity, entrepreneurship, cosmopolitanism, and a keenness for self-legislation.

Soon after arriving in Kazan in September 2014, I became aware of the pervasive presence of the Islamic concepts of halal ("permissible") and haram ("forbidden") across many of the city's social and physical spaces. Commitment to what my friends and acquaintances called a "halal form of life" implies being mindful of spiritual purity, pursuing maximum religious exactitude in both ritual and everyday conduct, and accumulating Islamic theological knowledge. Throughout this volume, I refer to post-Soviet Muslim pietists as Russia's "halal milieu": a dynamic, grassroots community, unified, despite internal doctrinal nuances, by the common goal of following the truths—my use of this term will be clarified in a moment—of the Quran and the Sunna in pursuit of piousness and avoidance of anything sinful.

While the post-Soviet era ushered in a surge in Tatar ethnic pride and nationalist activity, the halal milieu tends to prioritize Islamic universality over ethnic particularism and customary solidarities. As Amir put it, "Sometimes people emphasize nationality over religion. This is common in Russia, but is wrong. It should be the other way round. Different peoples exist, and there is nothing wrong with it. You see, I am happy to be a Tatar, I like to have this Eastern 'streak.' But religion should always come first. Through religion, we can develop our selves, develop our community, develop as an ummah. Cultural traits are a completely separate thing. Religion is more important. Eternal values are above national values. They should be taught to children first." In addition to the universality of Islam's "eternal values," this quote effectively captures the halal milieu's vitality and future-orientation. The quote's emphasis on "development" suggests at once middle-class aspiration, the striving toward self-perfection, and a readiness to challenge received norms, all of which resonate with the existential needs of young and cosmopolitan post-Soviet urbanites. However, halalists' commitment to the truths of Islam and orientation toward alternative futurities can, and often do, chafe against the region's hegemonic moralities, based on ethnic particularism, identitarian conservatism, and the state's cautious stewardship of the present. Both the conservative moral expectations of the nominally Muslim but secularized Tatar public, and the biopolitical norms of the nominally pluralist but increasingly reactionary Russian state, which strives to co-opt Islam for its neo-imperial purposes, stand in tension with grassroots pietism. The halal milieu's ethical "courage" and rejection of "conformity"—to return to Amir's earlier quote—are often perceived as "unsettling" (Fernando 2014) by outsiders, nonpietists and state actors alike.

Such a perception is not unwarranted: High-intensity ethical movements, such as Russia's halal milieu, do defy conventions and unsettle the social situations in which they move. The Islamic piety boom has disrupted taken-for-granted moral and political presuppositions, shifted the balance of power dynamics, and forced all players on the field, including dominant secular ones, to update their strategies in accordance with this unexpected development. This affects the social situation at all scales, forcing institutions to either ostracize pietists as "Wahhabis" or cautiously accept them as interlocutors. The experience of this young, headscarved pietist from Kazan encapsulates such dynamic:

> One year ago [in 2014], I struggled with my school administration. They forbade hijab at school, wanted to expel me, called my parents, who nearly moved me to another school . . . there was a great deal of commotion [*skandal*]. But because of my good grades, they eventually decided to leave me alone. It was tough though. But now, things are changing. There is a lot of girls like me. I have personally talked to the minister of education [of Tatarstan]. Although dress codes are down to individual school [administrations], the minister pledged that hijabs will be permissible in schools in Tatarstan.

Ethical intensity may not take the form of what is normally labeled "Islamism" or "political Islam": Indeed, the halal milieu can be described as overwhelmingly quietist. Yet its Islamic quietism remains intrinsically, and intensely, political.

Even before the dictatorial turn of 2022, inaugurated by Russia's invasion of Ukraine, the suffocating setup of Putinist Russia left little room for anything that smacked of political Islam, a category usually applied to coordinated projects and movements aiming to bring about a top-down Islamization of society. Such projects are looked at with suspicion in many countries, but the Kremlin has been particularly ruthless in policing grassroots actors perceived as Islamist. As we shall see in detail, organized Islamist networks are banned in the Russian Federation, including programmatically pacifist ones. The ban extends to most transnational Islamic groups and organizations, including many that operate legally in other countries. Even though the presence of Islam in the lands between the Volga River and the Ural Mountains long predates the Russian conquest, ethnic and confessional parties are prohibited in all of Russia's territory, as, de facto, are independent Islamic organizations, citizens' groups, think tanks, and so forth. Since the eighteenth century, the Russian state has equipped itself with institutions called "Muslim Spiritual Directorates," or Muftiates, tasked with acting as middlemen between the sovereign center (be it Orthodox-tsarist, Soviet-atheist, or illiberal-conservative) and indigenous Muslim populations. But expressions of Islamic faith emerging without these structures have long been and remain tightly policed.

Nonetheless, even in the face of authoritarianism, my use of the concept of quietism in reference to the halal milieu does not imply state-forced, passively endured resignation, but a positive ethical-spiritual attitude that emphasizes virtuous conduct, self-reform, and the bottom-up realization of pious Muslim lives over grand societal transformation. Quietism prioritizes inner religious commitment over outer duties and rights, hic et nunc communities over utopias. Terms such as "post-Islamism" (Bayat 2013) or "apoliticism" (Alagha 2016), or qualifiers such as "moderate" (Bustanov 2017; Kovalskaya 2024), have been offered to describe this inflection of the Islamic revival, but they risk relying on a narrow conceptualization of the political or lack thereof. "Quietism," by contrast, retains a thick aura of political potentiality (Olidor 2015) that, as we shall see in a moment, is central to this book.

Framed this way, quietism is antithetical to apathy or indifference. Muslim pietists in Russia might be careful not to cross the moral and political red lines that are imposed on them, but they do engage with, participate in, and transform the public sphere. A detachment from worldly matters might be cultivated, but this is an active ethical stance rather than a form of inertia. In November 2015, for example, I met with Umar, a thirtysomething father of three close to the quietist scripturalist teachings of sheik al-Albani. In those days, Tatarstan was reeling from a diplomatic crisis with Turkey following a lethal confrontation between Turkish and Russian forces in Syria. The media arena was filled with acute feelings—especially intense in Tatarstan, owing to the Turkic-majority republic's special ties with Ankara. When our conversation touched the crisis, Umar seraphically declared ignorance of the matter ("Crisis? What crisis?"). As I protested that this news was making the headlines across continents, Umar replied that he lived without television and newspapers and used the internet sparingly. He looked deliberate about his cluelessness and did not show any interest in being filled in. Even in 2022, as his country was rocked by the Kremlin's war against Ukraine, Umar sought to preserve a similar semblance of imperturbable detachment during our online conversations—he only went so far as acknowledging that "the situation is not among the simplest" before moving on to spiritual topics. Yet my interlocutor is anything but a recluse: He is one of the most active members of his community, a fine speaker and sagacious mediator, including with local state actors, and a man curious enough to cultivate his acquaintance with an anthropologist.

In performing detachment from state politics, Umar was adhering to a specific ideal of pious personhood valued among his circle. His behavior might not be representative of all pious Tatarstani Muslims in the specific cases of Turkey and Ukraine (Sidło and Benussi 2020, 134–137), as there are plenty of pietists in Russia who follow the news, comment passionately, and so on—though many keep a low profile to avoid repressive backlashes. Rather, Umar is illustrative of the ideal of quietism as an active ethical stance. Such a stance does not preclude, and indeed often generates, ripple effects well beyond one's immediate circle and into the political domain. Umar had cultivated self-discipline to the point of resisting the call of the worldly fray and preserving imperturbability in the face of turmoil: It is not surprising that over time he should go on to become a city-level leader of his scripturalist faction, with the ability and agency to influence the environment of Akmaş both within and outside his community. This book seeks to provide an anthropological framing for the politics of this undocile discipline.

Forgotten No More: Russia's Muslims and the "Halal Milieu"

Sunni Islam has been practiced in the Volga region, also called Povolzhye (in Russian), Idel-Ural (in Tatar), and Volga-Ural, from at least the early tenth century (Ibn Fadlan 2012). For centuries, this part of Eurasia at the crossroads of the steppe and the forest—an ethnic and confessional mixture of Turkic, Slavic, and Finno-Uralic elements—had been controlled by Muslim-ruled Turkic polities such as Volga Bulgaria (eighth to thirteenth centuries), the Golden Horde (thirteenth to fifteenth), and the Khanate of Kazan (fifteenth to sixteenth), before falling under the suzerainty of the Russian tsars in 1552. The Volga region has maintained strong cultural, economic, and religious connections with the Kazakh steppe, Transoxiana, and Khorasan, forming the northernmost corner of Central Eurasia's Persianate-Turkophone-Chingisid koine. But on account of nearly five centuries of uninterrupted Russian rule and settler colonialism (Rorlich 1986; Kappeler 2001), Povolzhye is arguably the most Russified subdivision of this Muslim-majority ecumene.

Once called the "forgotten Muslims" (Benningsen and Lemercier-Quelquejay 1981), the Sunni populations of formerly socialist Eurasia have been attracting a growing amount of interest from Anglophone anthropologists over the past two decades (McBrien 2006; Pelkmans 2006, 2009, 2017; Abashin 2007; Khalid 2007; Ghodsee 2009; Sultanova 2011; Rasanayagam 2011; Borbieva 2012; Sagitova 2014; Montgomery 2016; McBrien 2017; Henig 2020; Féaux de la Croix and Reeves 2023, to mention but some titles). Compared to those in Central Asian regions such as today's Uzbekistan and Kyrgyzstan, however, ethnographic studies of Muslim lives in the Volga region remain few and far between.

This is regrettable considering that Povolzhye is a part of the historical Muslim world. Ancient Islamic centers such as Bolğar and Kazan lie within its borders. The five-million-strong, predominantly Sunni Volga Tatars are Russia's largest ethnic minority (of them, two million live in Tatarstan—53 percent against 39 percent of Russians—and one million in neighboring Bashkortostan). The overall Russian Muslim community, which also comprises Bashkirs, several Cauca-

sian peoples, growing numbers of immigrants from the former Soviet republic, and a small but dynamic group of Russian converts, is projected to reach
between one third and one half of the Russian Federation's total population by
2050 (Laruelle 2016a)—and piety movements have been steadily expanding for
two decades. Thankfully, scholarship on Islam in Russia is gradually losing its
niche status and being recognized as crucial to understanding the fast-changing
Eurasian great power. Historians and political scientists have recently produced
valuable scholarship on Islam in Russia's past and present (Suleymanova 2009;
Graney 2009; Bustanov and Kemper 2012; Kefeli 2014; J. Meyer 2014; Campbell
2015; Tuna 2016; DeWeese 2016; Bustanov 2017; Sibgatullina and Kemper 2017;
Ross 2020; Bekkin 2020a; Dinç 2021; Bustanov and Usmanov 2022; Boterbloem
2023; Kovalskaya 2024). Excellent fieldwork-based anthropological works have
started being produced as well (Faller 2011; Rabinovich 2017; Schmoller 2020;
Di Puppo 2019; Kaliszewska 2020).

Within this fledgling area field, this book breaks fresh ground by providing
a wide-ranging yet fine-grained investigation of scripturalist piety among young
urbanites in the Volga region/Tatarstan and considering its interlockings with
state apparatuses, the nonpious Tatar population, and the capitalist market. By
framing my subjects of research in terms of a "halal milieu," I hope to capture
the this-worldliness (to put it in Weberian terms) of post-Soviet pietists' *askesis*.
During my ethnographic visits in Povolzhye, I was often struck by the emphasis
on the bottom-up "halalization" of several aspects of experience—from nutrition
to business, leisure, body care, and beyond—resulting in a flourishing of Mus-
lim-friendly establishments and the proliferation of discourses concerning halal
and the practicalities of Islamic permissibility (Maevsky 2014; Benussi 2020a,
2020b, 2021a, 2021b). One of my acquaintances, a veteran of the Islamic reform
in Tatarstan, used the expression "halal movement" (*khalyal'noe dvizhenie*) to
describe this moment of heightened awareness and determination to bring Islam
to bear on the minutiae of everyday existence. Other acquaintances and friends
often insisted that halal, far from pertaining uniquely to food, defines the entire
"form-of-life" (*obraz zhizni, tormış rävese*) of Muslim pietists. My choice to use
the expressions "halal milieu" and "halalists" to encompass several expressions of
Islamic piety in this region, while not beyond criticism, acknowledges a specific
idiom through which the piety boom is vernacularized in Russia's Volga region.

This term allows me to escape the prickly issue of defining post-Soviet pietists
in theological-juridical terms. The Tatars have historically followed the Hanafi
school of Islamic jurisprudence (madhab), but the recent piety boom has been
spearheaded by scripturalist revivalism—or Salafism—and other transnational
trends that emphasize purity, doctrinal competence, and vigorous, thought-
through faith at the expense of madhab affiliation (Wiktorowicz 2006). Scrip-

turalist revivalism has left an indelible mark on post-Soviet piety milieus, even among those who might not identify as Salafi (Kovalskaya 2024). Different doctrinal positions (and sometimes debates) exist across this demographic—within which Salafi-Hanbali, rigorist Hanafi, orthodox Sufi, and other influences overlap—but this loose network shares an emphasis on leading lives defined by Prophetic example and hadithic guidance.

Rather than dissecting what is, in fact, a multifarious and changing galaxy of theological nuances, this volume aspires to take the reader into the lived experience of Tatarstan's halalists and through that experience explore the political life of Islamic piety in Povolzhye: its unsettling ethos, its complicated relationship with the forces of sovereign power and capitalism, and its ability to engender change both within and outside the worlds of committed halalists.

Autonomist Encounters

To grasp the political scope of the halal milieu's restless quietism, *Restless Quietists* pursues encounters and exchanges between the anthropology of Islam and a fuzzily defined region of the post-Marxist galaxy that may be captured by the term "autonomist theory." For the purpose of this book, by "autonomism" I mean the heretical strands of leftist thought that emerged from the social and intellectual turmoil of the 1970s in Italy and France, blurring the boundary between Marxism and anarchism and exploring political subjectivities autonomous from both the conditioning of state and capital, on the one hand, and the institutional monopolist of the revolution, the Party, on the other. In particular, I engage with styles of political thinking that, through a variety of approaches, emphasize the actualizing of autonomy in the present, within immanent power dynamics, over programs for a future palingenesis (Virno and Hardt 2006; Treiber and Christiaens 2021).

My relationship with autonomism and its intellectual implications are discussed in the next section. Now, it is important to emphasize that my exploration of possible intertwinements between autonomism and Islamic piety is not framed as a direct comparison (Candea 2016), and even less as the unilateral imposition of a Western heuristic framework on raw ethnographic explananda. Rather, I attempt to contribute to what Mohamed Abdou, in his recent work on Islam and anarchism (2022), envisions as a "hospitable space" where scholars, activists, and free (but rigorous) thinkers may encounter and interact with each other as well as with ideas or praxes derived from Islam and radical politics. According to some radical Muslim voices (Abdou 2022; see also Shariati 2002, [1979] 2011), Islamic piety has long, if not always, had much to do with emancipation, potentiality, and autonomy. Auspiciously, Russia's Volga region is the birthplace of the man who more than a century ago opened the path for a dialogue between leftist and Islamic un/orthodoxies: the Tatar revolutionary and anticolonial thinker Mirsaid Sultan-Galiev (Soltanğaliev 1998).

My search for points of interweaving between Islamic and autonomist praxes aligns with Bruno Reinhardt's (2015, 407) idea of "contrapuntal" juxtaposition of seemingly incommensurable ethical-philosophical traditions, accommodating consonances as well as discordances and hesitations. I explore this juxtaposition because for me, at this juncture, this is the most intellectually authentic and generative way to attend to the existential correspondences that emerged with the people and ways of living I encountered in the field. It is, in other words, the only honest piece of anthropology I could write. Of course, there might be something speculative in such a contrapuntal experiment. Yet, in anthropology, a degree of speculation—counterbalanced by one's best attempts at rigor—is perhaps something not just to acknowledge but to treasure (Ingold 2017), for it allows the truth of the ethnographic encounter to surface while at the same time enabling the emergence of fresh possibilities for cross-fertilization. Naturally, such a reflexive, open-ended exercise opens the door to a transformation and decolonization of autonomism itself, away from Christocentric and/or secularist prejudices.

While strands of autonomism have become popular, even influential, in conversations on globalization, labor, and political organization (Federici 1998; Dyer-Witheford 2015; Hardt and Negri 2017), autonomist thought on ethics has been less thoroughly explored by social theorists and anthropologists (see below). In this work, I rely particularly, though not exclusively, on the oeuvres of three voices in radical theory: the Italian philosopher Giorgio Agamben, the French radical collective Tiqqun, and the French post-Maoist thinker Alain Badiou. The choice of grouping these voices under the (slippery anyway) label of autonomism might be questionable. While not everybody will agree on this choice, for the purposes of this volume I contend that all these authors' works point in the direction of a theory of self-cultivation centered on the autonomization of human subjects and the liberative potential of ethical discipline.

Agamben, of *Homo Sacer* fame, is renowned for his theorization of heteronomy through the figure of "bare life" (1998, 2000). In this book, I primarily engage with bare life's less-known counterpart—emancipated life or "life that coincides with its form" (2013a, 99)—which Agamben studied through a genealogy of autonomy in Western Christian asceticism (2013a, 2013b). The Tiqqun collective, a more niche voice, can be introduced as Agamben's bolshy disciples: Stridently anarchical, at the turn of the 1990s and 2000s the anonymous outfit issued a series of ferocious if erudite pamphlets fusing theory and praxis to delineate an approach to ethical life as inherently insurgent and irreducibly inimical to Empire and Spectacle (Tiqqun 2010, 2011a, 2011b, 2012). Although Tiqqun's identities remain unknown, it is believed that members of the collective later founded the equally controversial Invisible Committee (2009, 2015, 2017). Badiou, on account of his Maoist background, can be seen as an outlier vis-à-vis the former voices, more directly influenced by Italian autonomism. However, the bulk of Badiou's work has been defined by the search for an unorthodox communist philosophy autonomous from the party-state, and the formulation of a theory of ethics and subjectivity well beyond classic Marxism (2002, 2003, 2011, 2019).

Departing from the staunchly materialist Marxian mainstream, all these authors have in different ways engaged with religion. Agamben has devoted several works to medieval monasticism and the early-modern church. Tiqqun took their moniker from Jewish mysticism, explicitly advocated an "enchantment" of radical struggle, and defined their project as "critical metaphysics," oscillating between anticlericalism and fascination for nonconformist faith groups. Badiou, despite his wariness of including religion in his theory of ethics, dedicated an entire book to Saint Paul's radically innovative universalism.

Even though the following chapters foreground specific concepts in accordance with the argument's unfolding, for the purpose of this introduction it might be useful to outline the main intellectual keywords associated with the authors mentioned above. These keywords form a constellation of concepts that recur throughout the book. My reading of Agamben's biopolitical theory of asceticism rests on two main ideas: the notion of *Rule*, whose dialectical counterpart is *Law*, and an idiosyncratic rereading of the Wittgensteinian concept of *form-of-life*. Rule indicates a subjectively embraced ethical principle that gives a (self-chosen) order to life: the nomos of autonomy, which stands in structural tension with the regimenting, heteronomous principle of Law. Ethical forms-of-life are the realization, for instance as ethical communities, of human existence given shape by Rule.

Tiqqun further explores this avenue by positing ethical intensity as the opposite of, and antidote to, political alienation and numbing conformism under sovereign power and neoliberal capitalism. They frame the field of the social as the interplay of forms-of-life of various, even inimical, ideological and philosophical orientations: It is only through this interplay, however conflictual, that the "line along which power grows" can be pursued (Tiqqun 2010, 25). The task of the state and its moral-ideological apparatuses, in this interpretation, is that of preventing such threatening growth by dampening forms-of-life interplay and keeping ethical intensity within sovereign-approved limits.

Badiou frames ethics as fidelity to a universal, innovative, singular truth. To qualify as such, truths ought to have certain characteristics, such as being extraneous or even contrary to a fidelious subject's individual or corporate interests. Truths do not exist objectively, nor do they correspond to verifiable statements: Rather, they exceed the ordinary domain of situations in which the subject (being a human animal) is ontologically tied. As such, verities manifest themselves through their capacity to disarticulate the premises of a situation and bring about a new one (an "event")—it is in this extraordinary potentiality, which also makes them dangerous and contentious, that truths show their truthness. Events occur at all scales, from global (revolutions) to subjective (falling in love).

To complete this thematic glossary, I should mention the handful of neologisms that I have coined in the process of placing autonomist thought in conversation with the anthropology of religion. I have appropriated a concept by James Faubion, a respected nonautonomist anthropologist, to advance the concept of themitical apparatus, which combines biopolitics in the Agambenian sense with Faubion's notion of the themitical (from the Greek *themitos*, the laws of gods and men), indicating the governmental or repressive implications of dominant moral order. Another neologism is *ákesis/áketic*, from the Greek *akos*, "healing, cure," which I propose as a counterpart to *askesis/ascetic* to discuss the remedial religiosity of the human animal. Lastly, I use the notion of fideme/fidemic speech, derived from "fidelity" and "phoneme," to indicate illocutionary utterances that express ethical fidelity.

Myself About the Truth

Commenting on an early draft of this book, a wise reader pointed out to me that its pages seem perfused with a "sense of mission"—which is not necessarily a compliment, as anthropologists must be careful not to impose their own intellectual priorities onto the voices of their interlocutors. Yet the reader's observation is true, and I can only embrace it and make it my own: This book is written by a restless subjectivity entangled in a distinct knot of political, intellectual, and existential fidelities.

Autonomism came into my field of vision relatively early on, when, as I was easing into my fieldwork, I happened upon what struck me as family resemblances between the piety milieus I had started to acquaint myself with and some of the extraparliamentary formations that I had acquired direct or indirect familiarity with during my formative years in the Italian Left (as well as in punk and punk-adjacent subcultural milieus).

Alain Badiou wrote that the highest form of thought, *real* philosophy, is not (just) solid reasoning, elegant argumentation, or compelling abstraction but militant thought-in-action that emerges as intellects grapple with and are transformed by the encounter with a truth. One of my earliest exposures to such philosophy-in-action happened in a setting that Badiou would find familiar: the lectures organized by a far-left formation whose meetings I attended during my student years in Italy. The speakers, hailing from decades of militancy, had razor-sharp minds; they delivered dazzling lectures to motley handfuls of blue-collar workers, students, and assorted misfits and could switch from erudite dissections of Feuerbach to ingenious analyses of labor relations in developing countries. Even though I was a bit put off by their doctrinarian overtones, I could not help but find these lectures as invigorating as the university classes I attended. However, the premises and goals behind them were not those of the academy (producing case studies with individualized authorships, experimenting with ideas within a pluralist space, forwarding debates, etc.): The objective was to produce revolutionary subjects. Ethnographic work in Povolzhye brought back to me unexpected but vivid memories of that and similar experiences. Although the context and contents differed widely, I felt I had encountered a comparable form of thought-in-action in my interactions with Sunni pietists, whose conduct and speech can be seen, in itself, as a materialization of Badiousian "pure" philosophy. It should be clear that this is not the kind of speculative reasoning that historical Muslim voices such as al-Ghazali criticized as <u>falsafah</u>, thinking for its own sake, but a transformative convergence of intellect, speech, and praxis anchored by commitment to a higher order of truth and clarity—in my interlocutors' case, the Islamic revelation.

I had not anticipated such a sense of recognition during my fieldwork, especially because religious movements tend to be more readily likened to right-wing activism (see Gambetta and Hertog 2016). As mentioned earlier, however, Povolzhye's halal milieu cannot be pigeonholed as stricto sensu Islamist: Its restless, ethically intense quietism is undoubtedly political, but not in the sense commonly attributed to political Islam. At the same time, the resemblances I sensed could not by any stretch of the imagination be interpreted as a direct ideological affinity, considering the gulf separating my interlocutors' scripturalist religiosity and the left radicalism of my (often staunchly secularist) comrades at home.

I came to feel I needed a conceptual and terminological scaffolding capable of accounting for what I experienced as points of resonance—the halal milieu's undocile discipline, its emphasis on strong, self-willed subjectivities, its recalcitrance vis-à-vis heteronomy, and of course its truth-driven, disruptive philosophy-in-action—at a meta-level, while avoiding crude comparisons and direct juxtaposition. Autonomist theories of ethics, whose scope of applicability far exceeds the remit of autonomist leftist politics and ab origine applies to the field of religion, furnished me with such a scaffolding.[1] The process of bringing such theories in conversation with Islamic piety also implied a critical reassessment of their authors' Eurocentric or secularist blind spots—which, hopefully, may contribute to a decolonization of the Western leftist tradition itself.

I do not see my engagement with autonomism as a normative or proscriptive project for anthropology, which must remain a pluralistic domain: The cross-fertilization, convergence, and divergence of multiple intellectual, philosophical, and political strands is beneficial to the advancement of the discipline. Yet this move does come from and with a distinct positionality—hence the "sense of mission" mentioned above. By looking for radical pathways within the ethical turn in the discipline, my ambition is to offer a concrete answer to the late David Graeber's (2004) call for an "anarchist anthropology," to which I return in the book's conclusion. If this volume makes even one step in the direction of an autonomist anthropology of piety, as I hope it does, it will have been far from the first time that an "awkward relationship" between anthropology and a radical political praxis proves generative (Strathern 1987).

The next section expands on what an autonomist take can contribute to wider debates in the field. For now, however, let me dwell on the risks that such an operation may entail. Both dyed-in-the-wool empiricists and ideologically or religiously conservative readers may worry that my theoretical framework could misportray Sunni pietists to advance a partisan agenda. As said earlier (and I hope the following chapters will bear me out), this is not the case. This book does not endorse an anti-authoritarian, anti-capitalist interpretation of Islam or religion in general: Others have done so (Abdou 2022), but that is not this text's mission, and it would not have the authority to do so anyway. I never argue that Povolzhye's Muslim pietists are "actually" leftist radicals. Not only are they not—though I have had occasional encounters with anti-authoritarian and anti-capitalist opinions in the field—but some of my interlocutors would feel uncomfortable, even outraged, at such a suggestion, given a context in which memories of Soviet antireligious persecutions are still vivid. What I am arguing is that autonomist theories can be put in conversation with high-intensity ethical movements, including Islamic ones, and the resulting resonances can help us grasp something important about them. I do not ask readers to embrace the politics of autonomism but to appreciate what it does in the context of an anthropological endeavor—that is, compellingly frame the emancipatory and biopolitical dimensions of religious *askesis*.

Coming from a different place, leftist readers may be unimpressed by my appropriation of radical thought for the purpose of an anthropological study of religion. Some may resent my "domestication" of an insurrectional praxis into a defanged academic argument. Such a risk exists. Nonetheless, using theory is better than leaving it untapped in the name of purism. The "university discourse" has limitations, but its interstices still afford radical possibilities (Rousselle 2012). Some may object to my associating autonomism—a rebellious, often joyously anticlerical praxis—to a religious milieu. As mentioned, however, thinkers like Agamben, Tiqqun, and even the atheist Badiou, as well as many others (Tomba 2013; Žižek 2014; Eagleton 2018), already have an engagement with religion— although not, or only superficially (Iqbal 2021), with Islam.[2] Some have spoken of a "theological turn" in Marxist/left thought (Youzhuang 2012), with anthropology joining in the pursuit of critical, prefigurative political theologies (McAllister and Napolitano 2021; Breherton et al., forthcoming). I sympathize with these developments. Anthropology offers means to recognize and overcome the latent Eurocentrism that lingers in radical theopolitics: Even the theological turn can be deprovincialized.

To skeptical comrades, I suggest thinking of this book as an invitation to look at faith and piety differently. Dominant attitudes to religion on the left tend to range from scathing dislike ex principio, to humanist toleration-cum-detached-curiosity, to superficial conflation with one or another oppressed-minority or identity-politics causes. Restless Quietists proposes another way to approach religious piety—which, to be sure, is not the entirety of religion—on its own terms and discover deeper-level points of contact through the optics of emancipatory askesis. If, in the course of this rethinking, some of the secularist and Christian-centric assumptions of the left are unsettled, well, that is one of the strengths of anthropological thinking: to force us to reconsider what is often taken for granted. Anthropology is "secularism's doubt," as Joel Robbins (2020, 163–164; see also Furani 2019) has pointed out, quoting Bruce Kapferer: This "fifth column status" must play out in relation not only to state-enforced, colonial, or hegemonic secularity but also to the intellectual habits of the left.

In the end, this is the only book I could have written on my ethnographic work in Povolzhye without doing terrible injustice to either my interlocutors' subjectivities or my own. The experience of resonance between pietists' philosophy-in-action and forms of ethical intensity and emancipatory praxis that I had known at home in militant contexts, and have contributed to making me into the person I am today, could only result in this anthropological experiment. The result is a delicate act of triangulation between an epistemologically pluralist academic discipline, a leftist activist theory-cum-praxis, and a Revelation-based philosophy-in-action. I consider my interlocutors' verbal and practical deeds as a philosophy in their own respect—a manifestation of higher-order thought that lends itself to juxtaposition to the more conventional philosophical texts produced by autonomist militant thinkers.

Toward a Political Anthropology of Ethics

Even without advancing a normative agenda, this book's intellectual mission translates into a set of theoretical urgencies and goals, especially the outlining of a distinct framework for the investigation of the politics of (Islamic) virtue. I consider this book as a radical, anarchistic contribution to the kaleidoscopic "ethical turn" in the anthropology of religion, and I engage extensively with the conceptual repertoire developed within the anthropology of ethics. At the same time, this book seeks to recast in original ways several themes—such as emancipation and the politics of virtue—that have been underexplored or have become crystallized in recent anthropological conversations.

Anthropologists of ethics and moralities have turned to autonomist authors, as have some anthropologists studying Christian life (Bialecki 2010; Handman 2015). Naisargi Dave's masterful study of the ethics of queer activism in India (2012) appears saturated by autonomist sensibilities about prefigurative politics and radical potentiality. Caroline Humphrey (2018) has borrowed from Badiousian theory to describe radical shifts in individual subjectivities, while renouncing Badiou's "transcendental" revolutionariness and scaling down the scope of his philosophy of truth to the micro level of personal biography. The phenomenologically inclined ethicist Jarrett Zigon (2007, 2017, 2018) has engaged with Badiousian and Agambenian concepts, synthesizing a compelling theory of moral life, without, however, exploring what I see as core dimensions of autonomist ethics— that is, the notions of fidelity and an ethics of Rule. This volume is thus more explicit than the works above—which, however, I see as belonging in a shared lineage—in its attempt to imagine an autonomist anthropology of religious piety.

Thanks to the interplay of multiple theoretical approaches (and subsequent debates), the anthropology of ethics has achieved exceptional insight into subjects such as religion and piety. Particularly in the case of Islam, conversations in this field have been powered by the vital intellectual rivalry between what I have elsewhere called "communitarian" and "liberal" philosophical approaches or "families" of theories (Yadgar 2015; Benussi 2022a).[3] However generative, though, this interplay has also had a polarizing effect (Mittermaier 2012; Fadil and Fernando 2015; see Fassin 2014; Laidlaw 2014, 2018), limiting in part the ways in which the concepts of emancipation and the politics of virtue are, or are not, mobilized.

Animated by the urge to look beyond academia's secular-modernist, post-Enlightenment assumptions, thereby gaining insight into non-Western ethical traditions, a pioneering generation of anthropologists of piety have downplayed the concept of emancipation, seen as synonymous with Berlinian understandings of negative freedom (freedom from the shackles of external imposition, including of moral nature) and Western-progressive takes on agency (Mahmood 2001, [2005] 2012; Hallaq 2014). In different ways, studies in this vein have fore-grounded the poietic power of obedience, docility, and passivity vis-à-vis ethical traditions and their other-than-human agents (including God). Partly as a reac-tion to this development, other scholars have focused on religionists'—and par-ticularly Muslims'—ability to navigate multiple moral registers (Marsden 2005; Lambek 2010, 2012; Schielke 2015a; Louw 2018; Henig 2020). This "family" of scholars foregrounds an everyday rife with contradictions and accommodations. While praised for its realism, this latter approach has also been criticized for smuggling back in a bland, secular-Western understanding of the individual as picking and choosing, syncretizing and compromising, free-riding in a Haber-masian pluralist landscape. The pragmatic, disenchanted model of late-modern bourgeois personhood is thus confirmed not only as normative but as altogether inescapable, and once again we find ourselves on square one (Fadil and Fernando 2015).

I argue that at the core of this dynamic is a rather too narrow, and not radical enough, conceptualization of emancipation and autonomy, either suspiciously avoided or reduced to its tame, hegemonic liberal version. It is an unruly, ethi-cally incandescent paradigm of emancipation that autonomist thought allows me to recuperate.

A similar dichotomy can be detected in conversations about the politics of (Islamic) virtue, and especially the power friction around piety. The anthropolo-gists most committed to debunking the West's post-Enlightenment certainties have often displayed a keenness to frame the politics of Islamic ethics in terms of an antagonistic dichotomy between piety and secularity, placing the latter at the receiving end of a robust process of critique (Hirschkind 2006). This approach has cast the modern secular order as a power arrangement bound to alienate, exclude, and sometimes racialize the religious other, especially in the wake of colonialism (I. Ahmad 2017). This scholarly current has framed secularity as genealogically, if not ontologically, opposed to an ethics of virtue, casting the pockets of piety—especially in Muslim settings—as counterforces antagonistic to secular arrangements. By contrast, anthropologists working on "everyday moral-ities" have investigated religionists' ability to navigate secularized lifeworlds and draw on diverse moral repertoires. Without altogether denying religion's potential for friction, the latter studies outline a less polarized picture, where "religious" and "nonreligious" domains blur into each other and other arenas of potential conflict are highlighted.

Once again, I would argue that the rivalry between these approaches origi-nates from the framing of the politics of ethics around an a priori secularism-ver-sus-religion civilizational dichotomy. This risks foreclosing analytical openness to political potentialities (Zigon 2018) and power dynamics beyond those terms. This book does not deny that the relationship between pious milieus and secularist temporal authorities may and often does become tense—in fact, it documents a case in which this happens a lot—but neither does it posit secularity as the fundamental frame of reference to explain such conflict. Instead, that axis of contradiction is explored as one of the possible declinations of a more general pattern of antagonism between alternate forms of power and normativity, which can be glossed as the autonomizing force of self-Rule and the heteronomous imperium of the Law.

Tensions between ethical communities and sovereign institutions predate the Enlightenment: One might think of the fraught relationship between monastic orders and the medieval church (Agamben 2013a) or the chronic dearth of pious men willing to serve as state-appointed judges in the Golden Age of Islam (Bulliet 1994). Even today, political tensions exist within the same religious landscape rather than across the religion/secularity fault line. The post-Soviet Russian state, for example, is ostensibly secular but, uniquely among post-Christian European countries, relies on official Islamic institutions that date back to the theocratic imperial age and are staffed by Muslims. The rivalry between pietists and the spiritual officialdom, now or in the past, cannot therefore be easily framed through the lens of secular modernity. Conversely, the repressive apparatus of the Putin regime may be just as keen to harass irreligious ethical movements as it does religious ones (Dinkevich 2014). A civilizational religion-secularity dichotomy keeps key dynamics and vectors of enmity out of focus. Furthermore, modernity has proved to be more than a postvirtuous moral desert, instead turning out to be a reenchanted ecumene seething with emancipative self-reform projects, alternative asceticisms, and incipient ethical potentialities often clashing with moral hegemonies (Van der Veer 1996; Keane 2006; Sloterdijk 2009).

In light of this, the theoretical questions behind this book are, Is there room for radical subjectivities and approaches in the ethical turn? What does, or can, the relationship between emancipatory politics and virtue ethics look like? What ramifications does all this have vis-à-vis anthropology? By placing emancipation and the power dynamics around it at the front and center of my project, I hope to offer workable answers to these questions.

Rather than a sociological abstraction or a philosophical ideal, this volume takes emancipation to mean not negative freedom in the liberal sense but the meta-individual cultivation of affirmative, discerning, and vigorous subjectivities, well equipped for self-rule (see Castoriadis 1991, 163–164). Relatedly, potentiality indicates an orientation toward an(y) ethical difference irreducible to a heteronomous moral/political status quo: not mere utopia but concrete, historically specific ethical projects susceptible to disorganizing existing arrangements. A radical-progressive anthropology of ethics, then, ought to foreground these emancipatory, future-oriented, and politically disruptive aspects of *askesis* that are manifest in the modern ecumene. To do so will illuminate the power relations that coagulate around high-intensity ethical movements and milieus, religious or otherwise, thereby foregrounding the dialectical relationship between the self-legislative dimension of voluntaristic ethics and the heteronomous hegemonic forces that shape and regiment ordinary subjects.

Within this analytical framing, the ideological content of given ethical projects—quietist or interventionist, religious or secular-humanist, conservative or revolutionary—albeit relevant, is not self-explanatory. What is central is the extent to which said projects foster autonomous subjectivities (individual and collective) that exceed the biopolitical grid of dominant mores. Such a framing is not antithetical to either communitarian or liberal approaches. It does not deny that ethical projects—or "traditions"—have a past and an authoritative scriptural basis. It admits that late-modern individuals operate in a pluralist moral landscape and exercise their freedom of choice. Thus, this book's aim is not to replace existing paradigms or launch a new "ism" (Pina-Cabral 2010) but to add to the discipline's polyphony by exploring fresh vantage points. At its most generative, an emancipation-focused optics may complement both positions by revealing the ethical subject as endowed with a specific power to transform not only themselves but also the political arrangements they inhabit—and in the process destabilize the interests of hegemonic power wielders.

The Setting: Methodological Observations

Restless Quietists rests on ethnographic material collected over eight years of active research in the Volga region (2012–2019), including sixteen consecutive months of fieldwork (2014–2015). I have engaged with a wide array of interlocutors: mainstream sources, officials, and networks, as well as politically and theologically sensitive, hard-to-access circles, from reformed ex-mafiosi turned Salafi autarkists to secretive Sufi brotherhoods. Ethnographic material is anonymized or pseudonymized throughout, including some place names. My main working languages were Russian, of which I have good command, and Tatar, which I speak at a conversational level.

This book photographs a certain phase of Putinist Russia, in which, despite growing authoritarianism, it was still possible and relatively uncomplicated to carry out ethnographic fieldwork (I made my presence known to the religious authorities very early in my fieldwork). The coronavirus pandemic (2020–2021) and then the war in Ukraine (2022–ongoing), with its nefarious radicalizing effect on the Russian regime and society, have severely impacted my access to the field, though not my commitment to the region and its people.

The Republic of Tatarstan is the Volga region's most economically and infrastructurally advanced subdivision, as well as the main focus of my research. Kazan—Tatarstan's capital and Povolzhye's largest city—was my base and one of my main research sites. I also conducted research in Tatarstan's industrial east, particularly in the Soviet-planned town I pseudonymize as Akmaş, which has a reputation as breeding grounds for Tatar nationalism and Islamic scripturalism. Outside Tatarstan, I visited Muslim communities in lower Volga region cities, such as Saratov, Astrakhan, and the place I pseudonymize as Idelsk, noticeable for their Salafi leaning and composite ethnic makeup. I also traveled to Bashkortostan, Perm *krai* in the Urals, and western Povolzhye, including the oblasts of Penza and Ulyanovsk and Chuvashia, where sizeable Muslim rural enclaves exist. During fieldwork, I recorded dozens of individual semistructured interviews as well as countless informal conversations. I attended public seminars, conferences, and lectures or gatherings organized by religious bodies (from Muftiates, to mosque communities, to informal faith-based groups). Written materials, including reformist pamphlets, Islamic self-help best-sellers, and social media posts, also served as valuable sources. I carried out ethnographic observation in a plurality of contexts, from formal events to spontaneous friendly meetings and family meals.

Despite its ambition in terms of ethnographic insight and breadth, this book is not an exhaustive picture encompassing the entire tapestry of lived Islam in Volga region. It explores the representative, but partial and not generalizable, experiences of an unavoidably limited number of grassroots pietists in depth, while proposing new ways to interpret those experiences in both their local context and the broader intellectual horizon of the social theory of religion. Gender-mixing rules are stricter within the halal milieu than in broader Povolzhye society, and as a result, my status as a male researcher granted me greater access to male religionists. In light of this limitation, and even though I do include the voices of female Muslims whenever possible, this book's main ethnographic focus is on Muslim men. Even within that demographic, and although I may have accessed hitherto misrepresented or hard-to-access milieus, I am sure that there are communities, circles, or cliques that fell below or beyond my radar. As always, ethnography reflects the unique and subjective dynamic of fieldwork, providing the unrepeatable snapshot of a certain place, at a certain moment in time, from a certain, idiosyncratic, angle. It will prove, I hope, a valuable and enlightening snapshot, able to inspire further research.

Chapter Outlines

The first chapter sets the scene by discussing the emergence of what I call the "halal milieu" in perestroika-era Tatarstan in conversation with insights gleaned from Alain Badiou's theory of ethics. Through the voices and life histories of pietists, these pages chart how a novel ethical subjectivity, bound by a fidelity to Islam's universal truth, emerged from the chaotic void of 1990s Russia: Lawlessness and crime begot an aspirational, discipline-seeking Tatar middle class but also high-intensity ethical projects that unsettled the secularist foundations of the post-Soviet world. I proceed to frame the consolidation of Islamic piety milieus and their antagonistic relationship with the state and the moral mainstream through a reinterpretation of Giorgio Agamben's concept of "form-of-life" and the attendant Rule/Law dialectic. This chapter acquaints readers with the conceptual coordinates and tools that recur throughout the volume.

Chapter 2 takes readers deeper into the book's exploration of the Tatarstan Republic's halal milieu by placing Islamic conceptualizations of sincerity in resonance with Badiousian notions of fidelity. A discussion of my ethnographic materials shows the difficulties and rewards of enacting the ethical-theological principle of sincerity in the piety-unfriendly context of Tatarstan, while also shedding light on how an ethos of sincerity has driven a moral wedge between scripturally minded pietists and secular-minded Tatars, locally called "ethnic Muslims." The tension between halalists and ethnic Muslims finds expression in the sphere of ritual, which is illustrated through an examination of how Islamic prayer and life-cycle ceremonies, such as weddings, have become fiercely contested grounds in the region.

The third chapter takes the argument further by zooming in on the Russian state's response to the unexpected event of Tatarstan's post-Soviet piety boom. I outline a genealogy of the governmental techniques deployed by Moscow to harness and control Islam in Russia's inner provinces. These political strategies, many of which hark back to colonial and Soviet times, have led to the post-Soviet expansion of neo-imperial official Islamic apparatuses and nationalist discourses aimed at cementing state control over religious truths. Through an engagement with Tiqqun's theory of "civil war," these pages discuss the extent to which the Russian state's often contradictory moral interventionism is (or is not) capable of intercepting and taming grassroots Muslim forms-of-life at a time of resurgent authoritarianism. In doing so, this chapter also reflects, self-critically, on some limitations of autonomist theory vis-à-vis some Russian Muslims' openness to being co-opted by the state.

The fourth chapter delves further into the relationship between halalists and their ethnic Muslim neighbors by contrasting the former's orthodox approach to

Quranic medicine and the latter's devotional practices of spiritual healing and pilgrimage to sacred springs. This examination reveals that, despite a shared Islamic matrix, different understandings of human suffering, Muslim subjectivity, and other-than-human agency are at play between the two communities. To interpret this contrast, I propose to differentiate the "*ascetic* principle" of scripture-based Islamic medicine, based on a stronger transcendentalism, from what I call the "*aketic* principle" underlying Tatar vernacular devotions, which is oriented toward the wholeness of the body in all its creatural fragility.

Chapter 5 returns to the halal milieu's bad reputation as an unsettling, and even outrageous, phenomenon by focusing on the domain of language. These pages chart the moral and political life of high-intensity speech events, advancing the notion of "fidemic speech" to illuminate the extent to which language is an arena in which Russia's Muslim pietists pursue forms of political autonomy. Originating in pietist circles, fidemic speech events exceed the boundaries of ordinary Russian language and, as a result, regularly perturb secular onlookers and engender the knee-jerk reaction of paranoid temporal authorities. To appreciate the ethical content of such speech events, the twin problems of (religious) belief and (doctrinal) knowledge in Islam are considered through a framework that combines autonomist theories of truth with classical theories of locution and veridiction.

Chapter 6 addresses the complex political economy within which the halal milieu operates. It emphasizes regional class dynamics and the challenges posed by Russia's market environment to Muslims' aspirations to achieve the good life in both the material and the spiritual domains. Tatarstan has benefited from Russia's transition to capitalism, but the republic's postsocialist economy is also rife with spiritual and ethical dangers, from corruption to selfishness to sheer financial crime. To foreground how Islamic forms-of-life navigate the turbulent waters of capitalism, I draw on autonomist thinking, Georges Bataille's philosophy, and Weberian motifs to advance the idea of "moral chrematistics"—that is, the rules defining the boundaries of Islamically legitimate pursuit and enjoyment of wealth. The limits of autonomy, and the spiritual risks incurred by pietists, are discussed with reference to halal business practices.

The volume's conclusion emphasizes how thinking about Islam, in Putin's Russia and elsewhere, in dialogue with autonomism can help us appreciate in full the emancipatory, liberative aspects of ethical discipline while also taking us a step closer to what David Graeber has called an emancipated, liberated—in a word, anarchist—anthropology.

PHARAOH'S CONVERSION

From Void to Form-of-Life

I met Azhar-abzıy at a café in Edilsk as I was doing research in the Volga region city's Salafi-oriented community, led by the influential preacher Ilyas-xäzrät. Uncle Azhar was a stout, energetic, middle-aged man with a lupine face and—as it turned out as I pieced bits of his story together—a checkered biography.[1] It was common knowledge in town that Azhar-abzıy had moved to Edilsk from the lower Volga in his early twenties and became a gangster in the stormy 1990s. According to common acquaintances, he was involved in racketeering, gambling, and prostitution. He owned a casino in downtown Edilsk and had faced down several rivals and enemies in the middle ranks of the local underworld, gaining a rather fearsome reputation.

In the tumultuous years after perestroika, Islamic piety movements had just made their appearance, and the then-young, charismatic imam Ilyas was building his fame as a fiery preacher. Ilyas-xäzrät's specialty was mobilizing the power of aurality (Hirschkind 2006): Cassette tapes with his vibrant sermons quickly became popular with Edilsk's Tatar, Kazakh, and Caucasian youths, fascinated by these "strange" new things—Islam, the Quran, the Sunna—that seemed at once so resonant with and yet so unlike their childhood reminiscences of grandmotherly devotions. Despite being a proud Tatar man, Imam Ilyas addressed listeners in Russian, not in the old mullahs' "village tongue," and spoke of everyday problems: how to navigate money and relationships and how to keep one's sanity and dignity in a disintegrated country. Young, wolfish Azhar was an uncommitted listener and paid but fleeting attention to Ilyas-xäzrät's injunctions. Still, he liked the sermons and would sometimes donate some of his questionably gotten money to pious causes, as mafia types would often do.

One morning, Azhar lowered his guard—a mistake that, in a way, saved his life. He came out of his apartment block absentmindedly listening to a Ilyas-xäzrät tape, his cassette player secured at the belt—and got shot at. One bullet whizzed past; one hit its target. Azhar collapsed on the street. Luckily, he was picked up and whisked to the hospital before it was too late. The story now takes a turn that sounds a bit like a Russian gangster drama and perhaps over the years has been romanticized by Azhar's informal biographers: The bullet that should have taken his life was intercepted by the cassette reader with which he was listening to the sermon. Islam had saved him.

After a long convalescence, Azhar turned up at the mosque a changed man, thirsty for guidance on how to mend his ways. To mark his commitment to a pious life, I was told, he even tattooed a Quranic verse on his chest. When somebody cautiously advised him that tattoos are not welcome in Sunnism, all the more so if they feature Quranic quotes, Azhar did not say anything and pensively absorbed this new information. A few days later, he showed up again, his chest wrapped in bandages—he had scratched away the tattoo with a knife. Clearly he was not willing to give up his reputation of toughness together with his vices.

Azhar-abzıy dropped his haram businesses, got married, and refashioned himself as a respectable if tough entrepreneur. His newly found faith community was composed of (mostly) observant but rugged, streetwise, mosque-going men who did not need external protection and would know how to fend off attempts to impose it on them. At the time of our meeting, Uncle Azhar ran a large furniture store, reportedly on the premises of his old casino. He had been on hajj more than once and was a regular at Edilsk's mosque. On the streets of Edilsk, the mosque guys—collected, assured, ever-sober—were looked up to with respect.

This story is remarkable, and likely exaggerated, but not unique: In the post-Soviet era, many Muslim pietists in Tatarstan transitioned from villainy to virtue, from delinquency to discipline, and from haram to halal. Tatarstan's piety boom is inseparable from the post-Soviet moment, and not just because of the end of the USSR's institutional atheism. This historical juncture—from the hopeful perestroika years, to the wild 1990s, to the start of Vladimir Putin's regime—was haunted by the biopolitical, institutional, imperial, and affective remains of the grandiose Soviet edifice. It was a space of ruin, nostalgia, and resentment that, though defined by what was "no more" (Yurchak 2005), was still rife with possibilities. The end of the socialist experiment ushered in novel possibilities for moral personhood (Zigon 2010a), as well as new ways to imagine what "religion" could mean and what its place in private and public life could be (Pelkmans 2009; Karpov 2010; Benussi 2021b).

As French philosopher Alain Badiou (2002, 68; see also Humphrey 2018, 44) has argued, ethical projects based on the pursuit of a truth are more likely to emerge from "voids" than from "plenitudes." In his theoretical system, plenitudes are stable, albeit complex, sociopolitical and moral arrangements—coherent, self-satisfied, easily ossified. Voids by contrast are crucibles of crisis—mercurial and volatile, hence fecund and transformative, in existential as well as structural terms. Since its emergence from the void of post-Soviet crisis, the truth of Islamic piety has proved to be a force capable of attracting scores of restless seekers like Uncle Azhar—predominantly young, cosmopolitan, urban, and aspirational people, mostly of Tatar background but also hailing from other ethnic groups. By fostering novel forms of ethical selfhood, Islamic piety trends have generated new collective subjectivities, which in these pages I bracket together as the halal milieu. Albeit quietist, these subjectivities have revealed a significant potential for disrupting biopolitical arrangements and hegemonic moral codes by contradicting common-sense values and ingrained assumptions about Muslimness.

This chapter describes the rise of the Volga region's halal milieu from the tumult of the early post-Soviet period and retraces its course up to the time of my fieldwork. By engaging with Badiou's autonomist theory of ethics, Giorgio Agamben's politically attuned reframing of the concept of form-of-life, and Kierkegaardian existentialism, it contextualizes the troubled biographies of pietists—both the hardened first guard and the younger generation of aspirational ethicalists—as the unfolding of a "truth-process" capable of transforming individual subjectivities and altering the broader social, political, and moral landscape.

The Post-Soviet Void

Islam's long history in the Volga region dates to the Middle Ages (Rorlich 1986; Campbell 2015; Ross 2020). Yet it would be problematic to adopt a continuity reading in trying to understand the post-Soviet surge in Islamic piety trends. We may interpret the "halal boom" as an iteration of the global Islamic revival (Schielke 2015a)—but only with the caveat that the term "revival" here does not indicate the reemergence or intensification of religious traditions stably enshrined in an Islamicate civilizational plenitude. Too many things today are profoundly different from what we know about Povolzhye's prerevolutionary "Muslim domain" (Tuna 2016). Contemporary pious milieus flourish without relying on the pedagogical, ideological, and cultural institutes of tsarist-era Islamicate Eurasia—Sufi brotherhoods, Quranic schools, sharia experts, religious foundations, elder councils, and so on—of which, indeed, little has survived eighty years of state atheism that could be "revived." Today's halalists live their faith in ways, and in a world, that would appear extremely unfamiliar to their prerevolutionary ancestors.

Perestroika upended many things. Buckling under the weight of its own contradictions (Yurchak 2005), the exhausted Soviet project gave way to a time of upheaval and chaotic attempts at reconstruction that chaotically reverberated throughout the 1990s. In the Volga region, this epochal breakdown revealed a gaping cavity at the heart of the socialist-atheist civilizational plenitude that had replaced the Muslim domain, giving the cue to a large-scale search for replacement plenitudes. Building on grievances that had been simmering since the socialist period, a mass political and civil movement combining Tatar ethnonational pride with demands for republican autonomy swelled in Tatarstan during the perestroika era. "Sovereignty" (*suverenitet*, *suverenlık*) became a much-used buzzword (Yakupova 2000) that captured many Tatars' dream to replace the pulverized real-socialist project with a new, "truly" modern, liberal-democratic but also ethnolocalist plenitude: a robustly self-governing, or perhaps—some dared to dream—even independent, Tatar Republic. At the same time, across the broader Russian Federation, a multipronged drive to restore the plenitude of imperial might began to pick up steam, paving the way for the return of autocratic politics.

Despite managing to stall the republic's formal accession to the Russian Federation for a decade, the Tatar national movement (*milli xäräkät*) was ultimately unable to achieve its autonomist dreams. Tatarstan was eventually corralled into the Russian Federation's progressively more centralized administrative and political order, coming to share—at least officially—the latter's visions of neo-imperial Eurasian greatness (Iskhakov 2006, 2010; Friess and Kaminskij 2019).[2] Ideological disunity within a weakening national movement meant that several currents advanced competing visions of the past and the future.[3] While positions labeled "Islamo-nationalist" existed within the national movement (Mukhametshin 2010, 41), the use of "Islamic" motives and imageries by nationalists was not taken very seriously by the pietists I asked about this, who viewed it as a merely instrumental strategy aimed at advancing a de facto secular agenda. In their view, the key concern of "Islamo-nationalists" was that of replenishing the Tatar nation through an atavistic, romantic understanding of spiritual heritage rather than embracing Islam as an individually binding universal truth.

The national movement's overwhelmingly nonreligious stance resonated and still resonates with majoritarian sensibilities. During my fieldwork, numerous interlocutors expressed the view that the Tatars are the most "Europeanized" (*evropeizirovannye*) among the world's Muslim peoples, by which they meant the most removed from Islam's world-ordering influence (see Humphrey et al. 2009, 208). Today's Tatar public culture is profoundly secularized, a hardly surprising fact in light of over four and a half centuries of Russian domination, the erosion of Islamic institutions autonomously regulating juridical and political life (Campbell 2015), and the antireligious campaigns carried out by the Soviets (Froese 2010; Usmanova et al. 2010; Luehrmann 2011). The ruling elite of post-Soviet Tatarstan has kept a firmly secularist course, limiting their engagement with religion to measures of symbolic value, such as investing in the region's Islamicate cultural heritage, while embracing the federal state's logic of "moderation," managed pluralism, and tight control over religion by temporal authorities (Benussi 2021d).

Beneath mainstream public discourses on sovereignty, culture, and heritage, however, the post-Soviet void was fizzling with energies set to transform the situational balance of the region. Young men and women (though I have had more access to the experiences and points of view of men), feeling betrayed by the elusive plenitudes of both real socialism and ethnic nationalism, unconvinced by the mainstream moral registers of postatheist secularity, encountered something else: Something at once familiar, redolent of half-forgotten childhood memories of uplifting stories or invocations passed on from elderly relatives and caregivers, and yet utterly unlike anything they had learned from their parents, educators, or authorities—something that heralded an altogether "new way of being" (Badiou 2002, 42). They encountered Islamic piety.

This encounter happened in a broader historical conjuncture marked by the global success of the twentieth-century Islamic revival and the partial liberalization of Russia's public sphere. New media outlets and technologies had appeared. International traveling had become easier, if one could afford it. Several madrasas, some of which were allegedly funded by Saudi "Wahhabi" agencies, opened in the Volga region. A number of Tatar students emigrated to pursue religious knowledge in countries such as Turkey, Pakistan, and the Gulf States. Eight "Tatar-Turkish Lyceums," connected to the transnational Hizmet network, transformed Tatarstan's education system.[4] Yet it is important to clarify that Islamic piety trends are not just an exotic import or an irresistible force predetermined to gain traction among specific social categories. Determining quite what happens, and why, when large-scale historical transformations occur is a formidable challenge to social theory's continuity thinking (Robbins 2007a), one that will forever frustrate any pretense of ultimate clarity (Rancière 1994). This is particularly true in the case of innovations that radically disorganize preexisting setups, like Povolzhye's halal boom.

The relevant sociological variables—age, ethnicity, social mobility, and so on—must be considered, but they cannot explain what makes piety compelling, why certain people heed the calling to spiritual reform and others do not, and how a religious revival can affect the social, moral, and political environment in which it takes place. In this respect an engagement with autonomist theory can be both enlightening and liberating for a radical anthropology of religion, as autonomism suggests that reality, at all levels, is open to an "excessive otherwise" that resists sociological determinism and other forms of reduction. Left-Lacanians might call this excess "the Real" (Stavrakakis 1999, 2000), radical democrats "the Political" (Mouffe 2005), Badiousians a "truth" (Badiou 2002), the Christian proto-autonomist Kierkegaard a "paradox" ([1946] 2016). Pious people might call it God's Revelation at work. Radical theory can, to an extent, account for this excess, and, above all, it can help us comprehend the biopolitical disquiet that surrounds forms-of-life based on "excessive" truths.

A Truth

Islamic ethical trends found receptive ground in Povolzhye, where a significant number of people proved ready to enter the composition of a new subjectivity, "excessive" vis-à-vis both the secular-conservative state and a conformist ethnic majority adhering to a Muslim social identity yet invested in the state's secular vision (Benussi 2020a, 2021c). Different visions and ideologies fed into the burgeoning halal milieu throughout the 1990s, including purist scripturalism (Salafiyyah), orthodox Hanafism, educational revivalism (the Hizmet movement), transnational Sufi confraternities,[5] missionary movements (Jamaat Tabligh), and elements of political Islamism (Muslim Brotherhood, Hizb ut-Tahrir). Transnational organizations were soon outlawed and persecuted, as we shall see in chapter 3, but looser networks such as Hizmet, certain Sufi groups, and especially Salafism—not an organization but rather a broad school of thought—maintained an influence on different segments of the pietist milieu. Despite the theological and ideological dissimilarities between them, these various tendencies share a common attitude toward Islam as a universal and binding verity.

Alain Badiou's theory of ethical truth can help us grasp some aspects of Islam's "truth-ness." A key starting point is that Badiousian truths are not factual. They are not empirically verifiable statements but a special category of existence that exceeds the domain of facts and comes into being through human action. Badiou identifies four types of truth: political (a vision or yearning, like the idea of communism), artistic (a demanding aesthetic or stylistic ideal, such as cubism or punk rock), intellectual (a soaringly ambitious paradigm or theory, for example psychoanalysis), and amorous (the love that one feels for another person). Truth is, at heart, something that people *do* in a certain way—chiefly, by showing commitment to it. This commitment underpins what Badiou calls a "truth-process," the manifestation of a verity through sustained conduct that has real-world reverberations. All genuine truths, according to Badiou, are universal—that is, applicable and urgent to all humans irrespective of historical, cultural, or ethnic background. To unswervingly embrace a truth and hence inhabit the world in a "new way" means to be seized by a principle that Badiou calls "the Immortal"—something that transcends the limited faculties and scope of an individual. Though Badiou does not linger on religious truths, Islam's universal message fits the bill: As the guiding light of pietists, it possesses them; it commands their commitment, molds their comportment, and overrides to a significant extent other considerations, including personal opinion or interest, social harmony, sovereign will, and so forth. Pietists come to see themselves as the bearers of immortal souls but also members of a vast collective subject, the ummah, that far exceeds the limited lifetimes of its individual components.

What, then, are the core contents of the halal milieu's truth? They may be sketched out as follows: Humans inhabit a coherent, orderly cosmos endowed with material and spiritual dimensions. Both realms are regulated by God in just if sometimes inscrutable ways. Humans' worldly existence is the prelude to a second, augmented, and eternal life (ākhirah). During our brief sojourn in the worldly domain (dunyā), we are tested by God through a range of temptations and difficulties, and our eternal abode is predicated on our performance on this test. To pass the test, humankind has been endowed by God with a set of eternally valid instructions that cover all aspects of life: the Quran and the Sunna. These determine what is permissible and what is forbidden, halal or haram.

By summarizing my interlocutors' truth in a few pithy sentences, I have, in fact, done an injustice to their actual experience. While truth is eo ipso coherent with itself, it cannot be explained through reduction to terms external to itself. Despite amounting, for its adherents, to the highest degree of thought (see chapter 5), a truth resists any attempts to be explained, defended, or vindicated through rhetorical or empirical means. A truth can only be subjectively encountered, experienced, and embraced—or rejected (Badiou 2002, 50). Badiou here appears to channel Kierkegaard's ([1946] 2016, 409) understanding of "the absolute" in religion: In matters of faith, any "determinant of truth" lies so to speak "inwardly" and therefore cannot be objectively captured. What can be grasped by an observer, however, is the outward manifestations of a truth: in the case of Povolzhye's halalists, their pious ways of comportment, as well as the political and social reverberations of such comportment across Russia.

At the everyday level, the pursuit of piety—a truth-process in Badiousian lingo, the path of Islam or dīn in theological terms—unfolds through a Weberian rational ethic of everyday life based on what Marsden and Retsikas (2013, 10–11; see Parsons [1964] 2023, xliii; Weber [1964] 2023) call "systematicity." As one of my interlocutors, Uncle Amir, put it, "Believers must live according to a plan" (*veruyushchie dolzhny zhit' po planu*): "This material world [*dunya*] is like a computer program. We are like pixels living in a computer program. Quantum physics says that matter is in fact made of energy—this is how God created us, from his breath into matter. Everything is already prearranged [*predupreleno*], like in a program. Through prayer and sincerity [*iskrennost'*] we can interact with the programmer. But He has set clear rules that we are to follow if we want to succeed." In Tatarstan, a growing community of young converts has emerged—and was still emerging at the time of my fieldwork—from an encounter with Islam's truth. My use of the word "converts," which might appear out of place in a historically Muslim setting, is deliberate. A phrase often heard among halalists is that "Russia's pious Muslims are all converts [*neofity, novoobrashchennye*]." Again, it is fruitful to put pietists' words in resonance with Badiou's characterization of truth-processes as ever-emergent, future-oriented trajectories, born of radical rupture, and that produce hitherto unexpectable subjectivities (see Humphrey 2018; Robbins 2020, 49–55; see also Marcuse [1964] 1972, 60–61).

Despite the plurality of trends innervating the multifarious Muslim network that took root in the post-Soviet era, scripturalist and purist Islam, glossed as Salafism, emerged as a particularly dynamic and influential force within this truth-process, even after becoming the main target of the state's demonization campaign. This literalist trend in Sunni reformism, in particular its quietist branch (sheik Muhammad al-Albani's school), came to hold sway over sizable sectors of the halal milieu—even many Muslims who do not identify as Salafis are exposed to, are interpellated by, and may selectively appropriate teaching derived from that current (Kovalskaya 2024). What makes scripturalism's demanding, stern approach so contagious and resilient? Some critics of Salafism point their fingers to the financial support that scripturalists worldwide obtained from Saudi funding bodies (such as the Ibrahim bin Abdul Aziz al-Ibrahim, Taiba, and the Al-Igatha foundations; see Mukhametshin 2010, 41). While it would be unwise to ignore transnational missionary and financial fluxes, this kind of explanation does not address the existential and affective pull of scripturalism—what makes this supposedly inauthentic "foreign import" so compelling—and fails to explain why scripturalist piety kept thriving even as financial influx from the Gulf dried up.

A Badiousian interpretive framework can cast a brighter light on the success of scripturalist Islam among Povolzhye's mostly young and urban population. Its vitality becomes apparent if we approach Muslim piety not just in terms of organizations or groupings based on contingent, situational, geopolitical interests but as a truth that affords an ethical grounding to ever-emerging individual and collective subjectivities. Ethical truth-processes gush forth spontaneously and horizontally as long as receptive subjects exist on the ground. Scripturalism offers answers to "the problems of life" to receptive individuals—the dissatis-fied, the ambitious, the "young toughs" at the margin of the capitalist metropolis (Hobsbawm [1965] 2012, 61)—by equipping them with concrete, actionable tools for ethical self-fashioning (Sloterdijk 2009; Foucault 1997a, 2010, 343–354; 2011; Mahmood [2005] 2012). Historian Richard Bulliet (1994, 27) has observed that it has long been the case, in Islam, that the most successful configurations of the faith are those that give actionable guidance on how to deal with concrete ethical issues. Scripturalist trends emphasize precisely this: the individual pursuit of reli-gious knowledge and its unmediated operationalization into virtuous practice.

Badiou suggests that ethical truths eo ipso exceed the established moral order of a situation—which is also a balance of power—and therefore expose the limi-tations of the guarantors of that order, revealing their obsolescence and forcing said order to change. Albeit quietist, Islamic piety was seen as an "excess" capable of disorganizing the dominant state of affairs and forcing even its opponents to play by new rules: Recall the hijabi student mentioned in the introduction, who not only prevailed on her school administration but even confronted Tatarstan's minister of education, contributing to greater toleration of Islamic veiling. Radi-cal innovations that override social etiquette, moral consensus, and sovereign order are bound to create alarm—and to be sure, this sudden surge in ethical fer-vor was experienced by Russia's state actors and secular majority as a traumatic, potentially unmanageable turn of events. The halal milieu came to represent an unpredictable spanner in the works of state-enforced secularity. This prompted Moscow to wage a relentless ideological and governmental war against "nontra-ditional Islam" (see chapter 3). However, ethical truths do not rest on or require formal affiliations that can be traced, physical headquarters that can be stormed, structured organizations that can be outlawed, or a media presence that can be censored. All these things happened, but scripturalism did not disappear. A con-nection to the internet, or an informal conversation with an acquaintance, can be enough to gain exposure to Islam's verity, be "seized" by it, and establish a con-nection with God and fellow pietists.[6] It is such interstitial, individual, horizontal encounters with the pietist option that have powered the growth of Povolzhye's halal milieu. In this sense, Islamic piety was from the start beyond the reach of the watchdogs of Russia's state-engineered, anxiously regimented, conservative secularity.

Observing Islamic scripturalism as a truth-process rather than as culturally inauthentic, imported "fundamentalism" (Yemelianova 2010) allows us to appre-ciate that its success is predicated on a subjective orientation toward ethical disci-plines and solutions among the grassroots. Salafism and other ambitious Islamic self-transformation projects resonate with the existential needs of individuals, both within and outside historically Muslim ethnic communities. But how do we explore the void that produced the existential demand for ethical discipline and new technologies of the self among post-Soviet pietists-to-be? A good way to answer is by following Povolzhye Muslims' biographical trajectories into the halal milieu.

A Generation of Pharaohs

Tatarstan has a reputation as a former hub of gang crime. Bouts of street violence raged from the late Soviet era through the early 2000s (Belyaev and Sheptitsky 2015; Stephenson 2015; R. Garaev 2020), later to provide fodder for internationally successful TV shows such as *The Boy's Word* (2023). East Tatarstan's industrial city Akmaş has a place in this story that almost rivals that of the capital city Kazan. Despite being comparatively small, between the late 1980s and mid-2000s the town became notorious as a hotbed of gangs (*brigady*)—the most famous of which went under the name of "Mongols"—running protection rackets and profiteering from prostitution and drugs. Romantic tales about homegrown outlaws and "bandits" still enjoy some currency among the residents.

My friend Usman, born in Akmaş in 1979, thus grew up in an environment where juvenile delinquency was rampant. As a teenager, he liked electronics, listened to techno and hip-hop, practiced weight lifting and martial arts, and above all wanted *things*—computers, cars, clothes, sunglasses. One of the few people he looked up to was his neighbor, a stylish, business-minded young man a few years his senior, with a somewhat shady past but who was known to attend the local mosque. Among those whom Usman despised the most were his father and his generation of worn-out, conformist, prematurely aged Soviet factory workers. Usman was sure he wanted his life to be better off—much better off, in fact. The most obvious way to obtain the life he wanted was by going into violent entrepreneurship. The "Mongols" surely could put a sharp (*rezky*), athletic guy like him to some use. To make a long story short, he became involved in Akmaş's criminal underworld as a rank-and-file brigade thug and spent a few exciting years moving from one basement (*podval*) to another, through night patrols and knife fights. I don't know much more—Usman is quite buttoned-up about this part of his existence; only a couple of scars bespeak the roughness of that life.

But he told me that when he was a young man, he had harbored strong sentiments for a girl. One of the reasons behind his thirst for money was the dream of securing a good life for himself and his sweetheart. They somehow managed to keep their relationship going despite Usman's unstable life, until the day she left Usman and Akmaş for good. "I cannot stay with you anymore, always fearing for the day you get killed. You are a dead man walking," she told him as they parted.

This happened in the early 2000s as mafia wars were intensifying in Akmaş, along with police activity. Usman, distraught, quit the business shortly afterward. His brigade disbanded, and he stayed put for a period, during which he made contact with his former neighbor and started attending the mosque.

Akmaş's mosque had a reputation as a den of "extremists": Rumor had it that its basement housed a training center for jihadists. Usman found nothing more than a gym frequented by "sharp guys" (*rezkie rebyata*) whose background was quite like his own. For a while he worked as a security guard for a large chemical company, but as his religiosity deepened, Usman found the job painfully limiting—he could not grow a beard or leave his post to pray, and he was expected to wear a suit. Encouraged by his boss, who had taken to him, he decided to set up his own business as an electric appliance technician. By the time we met, Usman had become a respected self-employed and happy father of four who raised his kids under strict Salafi observance. He had restored a loving and respectful relationship with his father.

Stories such as Usman's and Azhar's—at the beginning of the chapter—featuring thuggish existences halted by a loss, a life-threatening injury, or an illness, are representative of many others I heard in the field. These are stories of men's lives lived in the void of the early 1990s, when the pursuit of personal interest had dethroned the hollowed-out socialist morality of collectivism (Humphrey 2002). Yet this void created favorable conditions for young toughs to be seized by the advent of subjectivities "which they did not know themselves to be capable of" (Badiou 2002, 49). This is, of course, not the only possible avenue toward piety. Some early post-Soviet pietists had moved away from a past militancy in (and relative disillusionment with) the *milli xäräkät*—a journey out of the void of political disappointment. Others, a minority, had long been spiritually inclined, "idealist" truth-seekers.

However, several interlocutors told me that a majority of male pietists aged between thirty and fifty have a criminal or semicriminal past (the touchiness of the subject gives little hope that this piece of anecdotal information could be verified quantitatively). The imam of Idelsk's mosque, Ilyas-xäzrät, opined that in his congregation, believers "out of pure ideal" (*ideinnye lyudy*) were but a minority, while most of his male community members had embarked on redemption and self-reform after experiencing what Jarret Zigon (2007) may call "moral breakdowns" and Caroline Humphrey (2018) "decision-events": existential crises that jolted them out of brutal, crooked existences. The imam of one of Kazan's best-attended mosques also told me that many of the longest-standing members of his community had awkward pasts. Not all my interlocutors were ready to share their experiences with late- and post-Soviet criminal underworlds (*priblatnennost'*, *zhulichestvo*). Some had been, according to their accounts, not quite full-fledged criminals but simply "hooligans" and "thugs" (*khuligany, patsany*), undisciplined youths always "spoiling for a fight" (*lyubily drat'sya*). One of my acquaintances told me that he still felt emotionally incapable of carrying out animal sacrifice on the Islamic festival of Kurban Bayram as he "could not forget, after years, the feeling of a sharp blade against his throat." Although he had not been too deeply involved in criminal activities, the 1990s were such a period that "one had to quickly learn how to defend himself." Others were loath to share details about their past, responding to my cautious inquiries with uneasy silences and nervous dodging. It was obvious that some of these people's biographies were rife with haunting, traumatic memories.[7]

Criminal chronicles of that era (R. Garaev 2020) depict masculine juvenile milieus bound together by a proneness to violence, an oppositional attitude, and the at least perfunctory adherence to a well-defined code of conduct, which albeit devoid of ethical content foreshadowed the strict and uncompromising religious discipline of the first guard of Muslim converts. It is not coincidental that notions of Islam as a "salvation factor" (*spasatel'ny faktor*), for both society and individuals, and "repentance" (*täübä*) are common among this group of Muslim men who converted in the early post-Soviet era after a brush with street violence and crime. Abdullah-abıy, a portly Salafi man in his early forties, described that collective condition using a powerful, theologically laden metaphor:

> We were a generation of Pharaohs. When we were kids, we fought each other for the sake of Komsomol medals. Pieces of plastic . . . but how we wanted them! Then, as young men, we fought each other for money and Mercedes. Then, for power. We would destroy each other. It was actual bloodshed [*istreblenie*]. Some of us drunk ourselves to death [*spivalis'*], others are still in jail. My [Muslim] brothers and I have been through a lot, a`ūdhubillāh [I seek refuge in God]. But Islam is our salvation—not only for Russia, but for the whole world. I think all that evil brought us closer to religion.

Uncle Abdullah's dim picture of the early post-Soviet generation—self-destructive, incontinent, and rapacious men, driven by a yearning for something more and better—is made more ominous by his theological reference to Pharaoh. In Islamic tradition (Halverson et al. 2011), Pharaoh is depicted as a paragon of evil, a tyrannical and ruthless ruler as well as an arrogant, greedy man who amasses riches by exploiting others, and who even likens himself to God. Within Islamic discourse, in the Volga region as elsewhere (Kefeli 2014, 92–93), the figure of Pharaoh has long been associated with villainy and loathsomeness, and its use exemplifies Abdullah and his peers' ethical and emotional uneasiness with their pasts. Pharaoh stands for an individuality "obstinately dedicated to the cruel desires of his own power" (Badiou 2002, 59). In Kierkegaardian terms ([1845] 1988, [1843] 1994, [1843] 2004), the Pharaoh metaphor stands for, simultaneously, an intensely amoral incarnation of the "aesthetics life," driven by hedonistic principles, and a figure of "despair," embodying a condition of "not wanting to be oneself," a state of diminished subjectivity enslaved to desire ([1946] 2016, 352–353).

A Changing Situation

Earlier, I suggested that trying to explain the fact of conversion and the appeal of religious discipline solely through extrinsic societal, structural, or geopolitical factors would occlude from our view the imponderabilia of lived faith (I. Ahmad 2017, 10–14). Jacques Rancière (1994, 37) observed that scholarly approaches to historiography risk diluting the radicality of ruptures and revolutions by reducing them to their "social causes," thereby foreclosing the possibility that phenomena and subjects may emerge that transcend preexisting sociological determinants. Rancière's observation resonates with radical theory's framing of the event[8] as a singularity "founded in itself" (Eagleton 2018, 29), which "exceeds" its causes (Žižek 2014, 5, 121–135) and cannot be reduced to the predictable outcome of preexisting situational causes, be those societal, political, or cultural. Events, in this framework, are unanticipated innovations that might not have happened— but once they happen, they change everything.

If we are to frame Tatarstan's Islamic effervescence through this lens, as this book proposes to do, it is appropriate to distinguish a "higher-order event" ever unfolding at the global, macrohistorical (perhaps metahistorical) level—that is, the Quranic revelation in the seventh century—and a "lower-order" event subordinated to the former: the conversion surge in post-Soviet Povolzhye. The latter is situated in a specific historical and geographic setting, but it would not have taken place without the transhistorical and deterritorialized truth-process called Islam. In turn, what this book frames in collective terms as the "halal boom" is in fact a myriad of subjective "decision-events" (Humphrey 2018) transforming uncountable individual lives. By engaging with some of these individual decision-events, these pages try to account for the historically and geographically situated lower-order event, tiptoeing between autonomist theory and social analysis.

Although an event is not *of* a situation, it is *in* it (Hallward 2002, x): The process inaugurated by an event unfolds within a specific situational domain, and, while altering its state/composition, it is simultaneously affected by it. Let us take a classic example: love (Badiou and Truong 2009). Love can open a brand-new chapter in a person's life, potentially turning it upside down—yet that chapter will still be part of that person's biography, and earlier chapters will influence how the new course unfolds. The advents of cubism, or punk rock, or psycho-analysis, can be counted as events too (Badiou 2002; Žižek 2014)—radical inno-vations that forever alter the rules of their respective games, while nonetheless remaining deeply entangled with preexisting mainstream cultures, communities, markets, institutions, and so on. The evental, in sum, can and should be consid-ered in its meaningful interconnections with the situational (Badiou 2002, 105). This principle holds true in the halal boom case too: Attending to the historical circumstances and social dynamics in the background is enlightening, as long as we avoid a determinist outlook. What meaningful connections, then, can be detected between the evental and the situational? How are we to frame the politi-cal economy and dominant ethos of the situation in which people like Azhar, Usman, and Abdullah converted out of a life of violence and into one of piety?

To begin with, let us consider what violent entrepreneurship and Islamic vir-tue movements may have in common: Both can be seen as avenues toward a "better life," and both furnish individuals with tools that can be used to achieve success in a landscape rife with opportunities and risks. The two projects, how-ever, operate under radically different "spirits of capitalism"—the former rapa-cious, the latter ethically inclined (Boltanski and Chiapello 2002, 2; see Yurchak 2003).[9] Russian activist and public intellectual Marlen Insarov (2003) has pointed out that across Russia, the early post-Soviet criminal underworld swelled thanks to swathes of young and disenfranchised members of the impoverished laboring class turning to violent entrepreneurship to fulfill their aspirations. Oblivious to class solidarity and collective solidarity, otherwise regular, decent guys started exploiting their fellow victims of market reforms through racketeering and theft. In Tatarstan's case, many tough, headstrong youths ignored not only political commitment (unions, rights movements) but also nationalist ideologies and col-lective projects of ethnic emancipation. This emerging demographic was bent on little else than getting its share in the fledgling capitalist order. This nascent, amoral protobourgeoisie was the mainspring of the post-Soviet "criminal revolu-tion" (Ivanets 2015). Alienated from the proletarian frugality of the older socialist generations, they were also deprived of legal avenues to social advancement, for Yeltsin's privatization had mostly benefited the country's elites. As a result, they resorted to extortion, illicit trade, and illegality as alternative means of pursuing their goal of building a good life (Ivanets 2015, 39).

Sociologist Vadim Volkov has extensively explored the emergence, (mis)deeds, and culture of Russia's violent entrepreneurs of the 1990s. Drawing on the radi-cal social theorist Thorstein Veblen, Volkov considers post-Soviet *bandity* as iterations of the "predatory man"—rational economic agents that pursue success through exploitative violence rather than planning and discipline (Volkov 2002, 23–26). With the progressive restoration of institutional order, however, sectors of the Russian criminal world became faced with the issue of legalization. Successful violent entrepreneurs climbed the social ladder, while others relapsed into an amorphous underworld (125). The most successful violent entrepreneurs, who had emerged from the ruins of the state as late-modern versions of the "ennobled predators" of the past (chevaliers and warriors), subsequently embarked on an accelerated "civilization process" that turned them into "economic men," or respectable businesspeople, within a generation (23, 163). Taking Volkov's cue, the success of Islamic reform movements among segments of Povolzhye's rapacious underworld can be collocated within a broader situational background characterized by the gradual transformation, across Russia, of a class of uprooted, materialistic predators into a new, "civilized" bourgeoisie. This trend encouraged the pursuit of novel ethical dispositions and moral registers and a different capitalist spirit.

In other words, religious reform offered the prospect of a materially, relationally, and spiritually fulfilling existence through means other than predation. To many secular Tatars, Islam was a (then rather vaguely) familiar and culturally viable option, which could endow an emerging middle class with the ethical instruments and dispositions of a responsible bourgeoisie. Crucially, the purposeful embrace of an ethical fidelity, however demanding, was experienced as invigorating, empowering, in line with the converts' drive for autonomous self-affirmation, while the uplifting force of a divine truth opened new trajectories of self-actualization that surpassed worldly ambitions. Proclaiming exclusive obedience to the universe's ultimate Sovereign, besides, allowed converts to preserve a sense of self-worth in a world teeming with would-be authorities and bosses.

It is perhaps not a coincidence that, my ethnography suggests, Islamic piety appealed particularly to the lower and intermediate levels of Povolzhye's emerging predatory class. Extreme, violent competition and restoration of state order frustrated low- and mid-ranking "Pharaohs" such as Azhar, Usman, and Abdullah, who could not realistically aspire to climb the social and economic ladder or even preserve their gains. Hankering for the good life, these flailing Pharaohs were both ill at ease with the harshest aspects of criminal life—constant strain, exposure to alcohol and substance abuse, physical risks, and emotional deprivation—and unlikely to rise in the criminal hierarchy above a certain level without incurring unsustainable danger. We return to the void experienced by them and many others like them—a void that had both structural and existential dimensions.

Traces of an ennobled-predator ethos dominant in 1990s criminal culture are still visible among members of the first generations of male Muslim pietists, who are frequently described as *rezkie* (brusque, gruff), *burnye* (impetuous, wild, rough), and *goryachye* (hot-headed). Even years later, these qualities and macho mannerisms are to an extent still prized or at least accepted. At the same time, these traces are gradually fading: For example, Usman told me he had been consciously working on himself to become "softer" (*myagche*), "amiable" (*druzhelyubny*), and more smiling, since gentleness is one of the virtues of the Prophet.

Of course—I reiterate—far from all violent entrepreneurs embraced piety: A "decision-event" such as conversion is never the predetermined outcome of a unilinear trajectory. Furthermore, the doctrinally ambitious forms of Islamic piety that gained traction in the post-Soviet era exceeded the locally available conventional repertoires about Islam: Rather than merely buying themselves a new bourgeois respectability through religion, converts encountered and committed to an ideal that defied moral norms and put them at odds with the mainstream. Embracing a life of piety thus may have resolved certain existential tensions, but it also brought about new ones.

Upward, but Hollow Inside?

Since the turn of the millennium, younger generations of pietists have swelled the ranks of the halal milieu via avenues other than the "Veblenesque" transformation undergone by the ex-thugs. As the appeal of Islamic lifestyles made inroads among better-educated, cosmopolitan, and aspirational urban youths, Russia's Muslim milieus grew increasingly removed from the early post-Soviet (un)ethos of toughness and rapacity. Young Tatar Muslims had spent most or all their adult lives in Putin's Russia. Despite crises, setbacks, and resurgent authoritarianism, this regime has been striving to leave the chaos of early postsocialist times behind, lift the standards of living within the framework of a relatively "tamer" capitalism, and achieve a degree of normalcy, at least until the war in Ukraine. This is particularly true of Tatarstan, an infrastructure- and resource-rich republic whose leadership succeeded, through a managed entry into the market economy, in establishing it as a competitive business hub within the Russian Federation. While Tatarstan's economic landscape is not free from corruption and scandal, the region enjoyed years of steady growth, attracting international investments, and sustaining the burgeoning of embryonic (and often state-engineered) civil-society structures (Bikbov 2016; Brunaska 2017).

Younger pietists tend to represent a particularly entrepreneurial slice of the Volga region's population, with much in common with the "Muslim yuppies" roaming other corners of the Islamic world—idealist yet pragmatic "saints/merchants," whose natural playing field is Islamized neoliberal modernity (Rajaee 1999, 222; Rouhani 2003). The blossoming of practices and discourses related to a halal economy (Benussi 2021a, 2021b; Kaliszewska 2020; see chap. 6) testifies to pietists' eagerness to positively engage with a regulated, predictable marketplace. Young halalists often associate Islam with notions of progress, innovation, and development (*razvitie*).[10] By contrast, especially compared to the priorities of the old guard, the trope of salvation/redemption seems to have somewhat decreased in importance—or shifted in meaning to include a collective comeback from postsocialist destitution.

If perestroika ushered in an aggressive capitalist form marked by the Pharaohs' Veblenesque, predatory spirit, the following decades witnessed the popularization of more sustainable avenues toward a good life, including the search for novel moral repertoires. The consolidation of a capitalist order proved an ideal environment for the bourgeoning of religious-ethical projects, especially those that feature a calling to prosperity (Zigon 2008, 41–42; see Coleman 2000, 2011) and a Weberian *bürgerlich* spirit suitable for navigating Russian capitalism (Yurchak 2002, 2003). This new capitalist spirit intertwined with Islam both in Russia's Volga region (Benussi 2021a; Sagitova 2014) and elsewhere in Eurasia (Botoeva 2018). It is not a surprise, then, that fewer of the young pietists have a history of violence, while many embody cosmopolitan, global-middle-class aspirations of respectability and success. Nonetheless, in its glamorous aesthetics and fascination with the immaterial sphere of *biznes*, this fledgling bourgeoisie appears to retain a Veblenesque disdain toward factory work, menial occupations, and Soviet-era proletarian rusticity (see chapter 6).

However, middle-classness remains a site of anxiety for young Russians, Muslim and non-Muslim alike, rather than a taken-for-granted condition. Life in many corners of Russia remains tough, full of subterfuges and rough edges. Terms such as "middle class" and "bourgeoisie" in this context indicate more a set of aspirations than a defined social stratum. In terms of income, cultural capital, and suchlike indicators, the halal milieu is diverse, including big-time businessmen, petty self-employed entrepreneurs (drivers/deliverers, repairers, shop owners, etc.), members of the cognitariat, small-town contractors, gig economy workers, and so forth. By pointing out the pietists' aspirations, thus, I am not trying to conjure up scenarios of boundless bourgeois plenitude.

Although the spiritual biographies of young halal milieu members tend to be less rife with trauma than those of older Muslims, preconversion life is often referred to as a time of disorientation, unhappiness, even self-abuse. A cavity, an existential void persisted at the heart of many existences even as Russia lifted itself from the chaos of the 1990s. The choice of embracing Islam frequently followed a period of disquiet, spiritual frustration, and experimentation that, albeit perhaps less acute than the spiritual-moral malaise of the Pharaohs' generation, was described by my interlocutors as a combination of hedonism and spiritual despair (see Kierkegaard [1946] 2016; Harding 2001, 44). Some acquaintances had dabbled in religious-spiritual experimentalism (a few of them mentioned Buddhism, Hare Krishna, or New Age practices) before encountering the truth of Islam, but most just told me they had felt existentially lost. Consider the words of these interviewees, young fashion designer Fatima and thirty-year-old web entrepreneur Marat:

> Several factors led me toward religion. Before Islam, I had been conducting a life full of haram. Hung out with the wrong people, did stupid things. But I didn't like it, I was disgusted with myself. So I went to a mosque, started to observe, read about prayer. I remember how deeply in turmoil I was . . . praise be to God! Plus, there was this acquaintance of mine—a girl from a very wealthy family. She was very pious and I was like, "How come somebody who's so well off decides to live like this, constraining herself, keeping such a strict code?" I was curious, and we started to hang out together. She took me to [Quranic] school, Friday prayers . . . ultimately, I too decided to wear the veil too, and through her I got closer to Islam. (Fatima)

> We used to drink alcohol and eat pork in my family. Nobody would ever think about keeping halal, praying, or any of these things. I went to university in the mid-2000s, and some university friends of mine performed prayer [namaz]. They were older than me, cool guys. I admired them, but was reluctant to join their crowd. I liked partying, and liked girls above all. Well, let's say I liked partying too much. At some point I went off the rails. That was in 2008. It was a critical turning point in my life. I got seriously scared. I realized I needed to change something in my ways, to drop certain dangerous habits. So, things changed. I started praying—at first just a little bit, then five times a day, then I ruled out certain foods from my diet. Now I live in a halal way. Which I like much better. (Marat)

Such stories of teenage rudderlessness may pale in comparison to the Pharaohs' wild, brutality-ridden biographies. But it is worth recalling that Kierkegaard's aesthetic despairer is not necessarily engaged in immoral, or amoral, conduct but rather leads a life that is not "ethical" because it is not articulated around a truth. While embracing the truth of Islam entails the abandonment of the inadmissible habits hinted at by Fatima and Marat, such as partying, drugs, and casual sex, going halal does not mean becoming less cool. In fact, one thing that struck me during fieldwork was that the sociality of halal cafés, mosques, and piety circles was surrounded by a definite atmosphere of coolness. Let us take a closer look at this "halal cool," as this will help us bring into sharper focus the connection between ethical discipline, self-mastery, and existential autonomy.

Halal Cool

Consider the mentorship mechanism at work in the stories of Usman, Fatima, and Marat, whereby the role of spiritual guide and exemplar is played not by traditional or institutional figures but by peers who stand out thanks to their social capital, credibility, and aura of self-empowerment. Forms of coolness run through the life stories of many of my interlocutors. "Hooliganism" enjoyed a lot of social appeal in late Soviet and early post-Soviet Tatarstan, and it is still glamourized decades later by TV shows like *The Boy's Word*. Some younger pietists had flirted with popular juvenile countercultures, such as gangsta rap, hardcore punk, or heavy metal. A small number of interlocutors, committed halalists, still identified with the punk-derived, drugs-and-alcohol-free straight-edge scene, mixing sobriety, extreme music, and spirituality (see Stewart 2019). A couple of friends played in a punk rock outfit—in their opinion, the merit of promoting the Islam-compatible straight-edge message counterbalanced the faith's much-debated prohibition on music. This may not exemplify a broad trend, but it illustrates how, in the eyes of these young men, both punk rock and Islam were cool things to do: "A mosque and a rehearsal studio is all I need in life," one of them told me.

The semantic spectrum of the Russian word *kruto*, "cool," which I have often heard uttered by my interlocutors, runs the gamut from smart and fashionable to transgressive and edgy. As we have begun to see, part of the story is that post-Soviet Islamic piety is germane to a middle-class Weltanschauung that incorporates stylishness, glamour, and prosperity.[11] An ethos of self-worth and success, which may contribute to the allure of piety, runs through the halal milieu—I explore it in more detail in chapter 6. Another factor likely to generate a buzz of interest about Islam is its cosmopolitanism, which links individuals and groups with transnational communities and evokes compellingly romantic geographies (Hirschkind 2020). Many interlocutors mentioned an "Oriental craze" that took place among Povolzhye's Tatar youth between the early 2000s and 2010s: an eclectic pop-culture mix of arabesque melodies, Eastern fashion, belly dancing courses, Turkish or Central Asian cuisine, and exotic TV shows such as *The Clone*, credited with kindling a fascination with Islam across the post-Soviet world.[12] Although there was little specifically Islamic in this Oriental craze, it helped create affective bridges between Tatarstan and a fashionable, more-or-less imaginary Muslim elsewhere (Sidło and Benussi 2020).

Transgressiveness and nonconformity are relevant dimensions of the halal milieu's Muslim cool as well. As we have begun to see, pietists' standing in the eyes of the conservative political mainstream and its agencies is ambiguous at best. Official apparatuses, including security structures, official Islamic organizations, and media outlets, take a dim view of any religious milieus regarded as bearers of eccentric convictions (Kravchenko 2018). Significant portions of Tatarstan's secular public, too, regard observant Muslims with apprehension, even antipathy, and I have heard words such as "fanatical" or "obscurantist" being thrown at them. What is striking is that several people in the halal milieu appear to enjoy the bad press. Of course, pietists are conscious of the risk incurred by those who fall foul of the state and its repressive "anti-extremism" apparatuses. As one friend told me, "Our country has little patience with those who pursue alternative ways of living." Yet there was something gleeful in my friend's awareness of standing out of the ordinary and being "alternative." In part, halalists act on the Islamic principle of <u>ghurbah</u>: the enjoinment to keep removed from all things sinful, thereby drawing scripturally informed lines between those who get Islam right and the rest (see Elridge and Iqbal 2022). This apartness is cherished by some Muslims—as one interlocutor worded it, pious folks ought to "buffer themselves [osteregat'sya] from what is out there [okruzhayuschee]."

Yet alongside theological reasoning, I observed a sort of defiant jouissance stemming from being visibly, Islamically, different. Countless details—the use of language (peppered with expressions in Arabic rather than Tatar), attire (trimmed beards, headscarves, and a range of more-or-less overt sartorial statements), diet, and so forth—mark halalists' difference from the mainstream. I have had many opportunities to sense the mood with which pietists exchange literature that is disapproved or arbitrarily banned, pray in ways that diverge from the recommendations of state-controlled Muslim organizations, gather in their universities' dusty basements to perform prayer between classes, or surreptitiously empty liquor bottles down the drain at parties. These are acts of piety but also transgressions of mainstream norms, and they set pietists apart from the stifling conformism of the "grey mass," to use the words of one of Russia's most prominent incarnations of "Muslim cool" (Alyautdinov 2013a, 30). They are lived as statements of existential self-sufficiency and autonomy. For all the entrepreneurialism and social aspirations that animate Povolzhye halalists, there remains much in religious piety that exceeds and defies bourgeois common sense and mainstream respectability (see Kierkegaard [1946] 2016, 7–9). This unsettling edge may put halalists at odds with the broader context (Fernando 2014), but it contributes to making ethical discipline feel rebellious and cool.

It is well established that religious—especially Islamic—revivals generate what Charles Hirschkind (2006) has called "counterpublics" standing in tension with

Habermasian configurations of the public arena, which, since the Enlightenment, has been framed as religiously neutral, pluralistic, and dominated by secular reason. In recent years, some studies have attempted to explore Muslims' "counter"-positionality from a slightly different angle, foregrounding the interconnections of restlessness, coolness, sociality, and alternative lifestyles in the lived experience of young Muslims (Bayat and Herrera 2010; Tarlo 2010; Herding 2013; Khabeer 2016). Rather than the frictions and discontents of the Enlightenment's (colonial) legacies, these approaches highlight the similarities, connections, and borrowings that (mostly) Euro-American young Muslim communities display with secular underground scenes based on music and style. This, to a degree, is also true of Russia's halal milieu, though music appears to be less important in Russia than in Western settings.[13] Some interlocutors described pious circles in "subcultural" terms as *tusovki* (social scenes, informal networks): As a friend put it, "something that people deliberately [*osoznanno*] choose, rather than something one is born into." Like in underground circles, pietists' belonging stems from volition rather than the perpetuation of received cultural norms. Like nonreligious *tusovki*, piety milieus are marked by a distinct "sub-ness": horizontal sociality, specific semantic codes, self-organization, discontinuity vis-à-vis dominant social mores, and so on. And yet, also like underground scenes, piety milieus remain bound up with the mainstream from which they claim discontinuity. Restless quietists exist, as Alexei Yurchak (2005, 128) put it discussing Soviet-era informal youth networks, "simultaneously inside and outside" the dominant systems: doing, uttering, wearing, thinking nonconformist things, without, however, being militantly "anti."

Studies of Muslim "subculturality" and youth scenes take us a step away from civilizational understandings of Islam, thus complexifying the concept of "revival." They bring to the fore the empowering coolness of transgression as well as the analogies between late-modern piety milieus and other forms of nonconformist togetherness. These analogies do not, however, have explanatory power in and of themselves: It is important to avoid flat comparisons that risk awkwardly mixing incommensurable domains—ethical commitment/virtue and pop culture/style—doing an injustice to both in the process.[14] Muslim pietists are focused on self-discipline and ethical consistency rather than aesthetic self-expression and cultural subversion. How, then, are we to account for pietists' existential swag, the aura of self-affirmation they project?

This book's dialogue with radical theory may enable us to envision a metaframework apt to rethink the family resemblances between "transgressive" milieus of different stripes, ethical-religious as well as aesthetic-subcultural, from religious counterpublics to underground youth scenes. Consider Badiou's concept of truth-process as "the real process of a fidelity to an event" (2002, 42–43): Under this light, the phenomena called "subcultures" or "underground scenes" qualify as aesthetical truth-processes whose participants hold true to a given aesthetic or "style," constituting themselves as fidelious aesthetical subjects. The apparent family resemblance between piety milieus and at least some underground cultures, then, can be framed in terms of both forms of community being shaped by truth-processes, one ethical-religious and one aesthetic-stylistic.[15] Another author associated with autonomism, Giorgio Agamben (2013a), has proffered a rereading of the philosophical trope of "form-of-life" that resonates with many of the most striking characteristics of the halal milieu: its "sub-ness," its emphasis on self-chosen discipline rather than received civilizational norm, and the coexistence of a quietist positionality with an unsettling ethical-political potentiality. In the remainder of this chapter, I thus turn to the Italian philosopher in the pursuit of a new way to reimagine the political dimensions of ethical self-fashioning. Agamben's proposal attunes us to the hidden tensions between close-knit ethical communities and the moral mainstream and allows us to reconsider the emancipatory force of coherence and self-discipline—in the sphere of piety but also, arguably, in other domains, including militancy and creative expression.

Another Form-of-Life

I first encountered the notion of "form-of-life" applied to Islamic piety in conversation with friends in the field. Ideas about "halal form of life" (*khalyal'nyi obraz zhizni*, *xäläl tormış räveşe*—literally "image of life") enjoy ample currency among Povolzhye's Muslims, in whose parlance the term implies a binding, systematic life choice. Indeed, in Russia's alternative circles (not just piety milieus), the idiom of "form-of-life" conveys nuances such as discipline, commitment, and sincerity, which stand in tension with terms such as "lifestyle" (*layfstayl*), the frivolous connotations of which my pious interlocutors in the Volga region prefer to avoid: "'Form of life' stands for something deep and substantive. As for 'lifestyle,' well, that feels like it is just a bad imitation [of the former], at best. At worst, it is something totally superficial, ephemeral, and non-binding. This is your lifestyle for today; tomorrow you will have another one. The idea of changing your form of life is much more complicated, even just by the sound of it" (Dinkevich 2014, 7).[16] Accordingly, many observant Muslims with whom I discussed the matter would insist that following Islamic precepts half-heartedly, superficially, or out of conformism would be a diminished way to be a Muslim. The holistic concept of halal, therefore, is central to ethically meaningful, properly "shaped" Muslim lives. Theological notions of halal and haram apply to most spheres of life. Existential domains encompassed within halal *obraz zhizni* include food and drink, money and finance, social relations (intimate, amical, and professional), language (control over one's speech, avoiding voluntary or involuntary falsehood), fitness (practicing sport and looking after one's health), free time and leisure (pursuing spiritually sound entertainment), space, place, and time management, decorum and beauty, and even naming:[17]

> Halal is a complex of rules for life [*zhiznennye pravila*]. It encompasses all aspects of the life of a Muslim. For this reason, I call halal the Constitution of the believer. (Mansur, thirty-three, entrepreneur, Kazan).

> If Islam is a form of life [*obraz zhizni*], then halal refers to food, employment, relationships . . . it's everything permitted by Allah. Halal is a global thing, it has to do with a Muslim's mental activity, nutrition, professional sphere, and way of living in general. (Dinara, twenty-two, Akmaş).

> Halal is a form of life [*obraz zhizni*]. Year after year, I delve deeper into it [*vnikayu v eto*]. Year after year, I pay more and more attention to prohibitions. To what is forbidden and what is not [*na zapretno I ne zapretno*]. To haram and halal. I am more aware of the minute actions that expose me to sinfulness, I am more watchful. I try to really pay attention to how to live a halal life [*zhit' po khalyal'nomu*], to stay farther away from haram [*ot kharama derzhat'sya po dal'she*]. (Rustem, forty-four, businessman, Yar Çallı).

Halalists' use of the concept of *obraz zhizni* has both analogies and differences with Western iterations of this concept, especially the notion of *Lebensform*, made immensely popular by Ludwig Wittgenstein and his followers ([1953] 1986, 226e; Kishik 2008; Tonner 2017). It is hard to do justice to the manifold ways in which this idea has been developed since via sustained debates on issues such as relativism, rationality, and science (Lukes 1982; Nielsen and Phillips 2005; Salazar and Bestard 2015). Some thinkers envision *Lebensformen* as essentially coherent worlds of practice resting on internal criteria of appropriateness, unanswerable to external "rational" parameters (Winch [1958] 2003; Gier 1980; Taylor 1989; Phillips in Nielsen and Phillips 2005). Others frame them as sociohistorical formations liable of critical engagement from a rational-humanist standpoint (Gellner 1960, 1986; Nielsen in Nielsen and Phillips 2005; Jaeggi 2018). Over the course of many decades, the philosophical contours of *Lebensform* have remained vague—even contested—and its potential declinations near endless. Attendant debates have influenced anthropology's "ethical turn," from reflections on piety (Asad 2020; Moad 2022) to "ordinary ethics" approaches (Das 2012, 2015; Tayob 2017; see also Deutscher 2016; Clarke 2023). Albeit generatively open-ended, the idea of form-of-life has thus proved slippery as an analytical tool and manipulable as a framework.

Wittgensteinian philosophy tends to put a premium on the conventions that tacitly shape *Lebensformen* into hidebound entities, defined by habit and custom. This has points of overlap with anthropological concerns with cultural continuity and discursive tradition but partly chafes with my interlocutors' emic framing of *obraz zhizni*, which as we have seen emphasizes self-chosen rules that may disrupt norms and rock the boat of common sense. Indeed, the Wittgensteinian commandment to "leave the world as it is," with its disarming conservatism, appears to be worlds apart not just from the evental dimension of the piety boom but from any rupturing, transformative, or nonconformist thoughts and praxes (McLennan 2015). Not by coincidence have champions of emancipation from Marcuse ([1964] 1972, 141) to Badiou (2019) vigorously rejected Wittgenstein's philosophy. Yet those critiques, however incisive, have rarely been constructive. Other radical thinkers have engaged with Wittgenstein more nuancedly, recasting *Lebensformen* as spaces of discipline and rupture, fidelity, and autonomy. A whole liberative epistemology of ethical intensities has developed around this intuition, according to which "everything is political that relates to the encounter, the friction, or the conflict between forms of life, between regimes of perception, between sensibilities, between worlds *once this contact attains a certain threshold of intensity*" (Invisible Committee 2017, 62, emphasis in the original).

Hailing from the autonomist intellectual/political tradition and equipped with keen concerns about the conditions of possibility for other communities, Agamben (1998, 2000, 2013a, 2013b; Kishik 2012; Smith 2013) has offered an idiosyncratic and uniquely generative conceptualization of form-of-life, laden with ethical and political connotations. It is this iteration of form-of-life that I invite to read in tandem with Muslim pietists' idea of a halal *obraz zhizni*. Unlike Wittgenstein, Agamben does not conceive of "life" as a given. Life always unfolds within political entanglements and power relations: Life and power must be considered together. Sovereign power entails the capability of extricating *zoé* (biological existence) from *bios* (socialized life), thereby isolating "bare life," making it heteronomous. Located on a slippery surface between *zoé* and *bios*, bare life is "life exposed to death" (Agamben 1998, 88): Threatened by monopolists of violence, alienated by market forces, or subtly subjugated by the guardians of the law (Agamben 2000). I will not rehearse Agamben's well-known argument any further, except to point out that, to him, form-of-life is the structural opposite of bare life. Form-of-life describes an existence in which encroachments by sovereign, judiciary, or economic power are kept in check, a condition by which *zoé* and *bios* cannot be extricated at (sovereign) will: "Human life . . . removed from the grasp of the law, . . . [characterized by] a use of bodies and of the world that would never be substantiated into an appropriation. . . . [Life that] is never given as property but only as common use" (2013, xiii). Form-of-life is, in Agamben's framing, life in the process of emancipating itself.

In a volume that expands prefigurative politics beyond a familiar secular-modernist family album, Agamben (2013a) develops his concept of form-of-life (1998) through an investigation of medieval Christian monasticism. Such a religiously attuned framing of ethical form-of-life, underpinned by the concept of a Christian *regula*, resonates with Tatarstani pietists' emphasis on Islamic halal normativity as a reflexively chosen "plan for living." By pursuing this analogy, I am not advancing any direct comparison between Christian monasticism and Islamic piety;[18] rather, I am interested in using form-of-life as a higher-order analytical tool to shed light on family resemblances between seemingly incomparable milieus, religious and nonreligious.

Form-of-life comes into being as individual and collective human life is given shape through the adoption of a Rule—here, a more specific term than in Wittgensteinian philosophy, and no longer synonymous with custom or tradition.[19] In an autonomist reading of Rule, the implementation of Rule depends on subjective volition—for example, through the willful pledge of a vow, an ethical transformation, which is "an unconditional and indivisible promise of the rule and of life. . . . Through the concept of 'form [of life],' rule (*forma regulae*) and life (*forma vivendi*) enter into a threshold of indistinction" (Agamben 2013a, 60–61) where life and ethical code are neutralized and transformed into one (107). As exemplified by monastic *regula* as well as halal normativity, ethical Rule encompasses virtually all aspects of life, including day-to-day bodily conduct, timing, labor, speech acts, finance, and affective or mental states. Self-chosen Rule-following, in this paradigm, is emancipatory because it enhances the subject's mastery over the nooks and crannies of her own life. Sovereignty, in Islam, is ultimately God's, but it is humans' responsibility—both a choice and an opportunity—to enforce it during worldly existence. Halal thus equips pietists with an actionable framework to exercise their free will and establish self-mastery in everyday life.

Form-of-Life and the Political

To venture a working definition (always a risky move), I would frame ethical form-of-life as a socially codified, collectively experienced, reflexively chosen way of living, defined by fidelity to a Rule or code of conduct, which applies to bodies, minds, actions, temporalities, and so on, and transcends and relativizes the moral, juridical, and political-economic norms (Law) of a situational order. Forms-of-life strive toward states experienced as self-affirmatory, thereby actualizing or prefigurating emancipatory potentialities. To put it in Badiousian terms, form-of-life is the composite, supra-individual subject of an ethics of truth.

This notion of form-of-life can be applied to a variety of social phenomena, including Islamic pious milieus in Inner Russia. Halalists embrace a Rule enshrined in Islam's truth, a code regulating disparate areas of experience, from temporality to bodily care, including labor and economic life. Povolzhye's pietists follow halal norms on a voluntary basis, without coercion and even going against societal norms, to build a fidelious relationship with God, the source of their truth. Even though all this is done quietistically, there is no escape from the political ramifications of this kind of ethical fidelity. The autonomist theory of ethics casts the ethical and the political as deeply interconnected. While this connection is spelled out in more detail in the following chapter, it is worth concluding this section by highlighting how this approach may contribute to anthropological conversations on the politics of Islamic piety (Hirschkind 2006; Mahmood [2005] 2012; Fernando 2014).

It is telling that, rather than the specialistic, institutional semantic domain of sharia, it is the terminology of halal that has gained the upper hand in my interlocutors' quotidian usage. Of course, the concept of halal belongs to and is predicated on the broader juridical domain of sharia, which remains a resonant category among Povolzhye pietists. However, the repertoire of halal is the predominant one in everyday language. While this may be in part due to concerns about the Islamophobic connotations that the term "sharia" has acquired among secular publics in Russia, I would argue that the discursive centrality of halal among Povolzhye pietists can primarily be understood in light of this terminology's existential, experience-near connotations (Rule) vis-à-vis sharia's more legalistic and impersonal ones (Law). Halal captures the subjective, workaday, bottom-up ethical praxis of discernment of, and fidelious adherence to, what is divinely permissible. Halal is, in short, the vernacular idiom for the self-chosen Rule that informs Tatarstani pietists' form-of-life.

The autonomizing potentiality of Rule underpins what Michael Herzfeld describes as "alternative polities" (2021, 99–100)—"modes of existence" that inform biographies as well as communal histories, "spaces of freedom" animated by an "ordered" discipline that "liberates the soul instead of caging it," thereby unlocking radical potentialities (104). In the following chapters, we shall see, ethnographically, how this applies to countless quotidian instances. Rule stands in a complex relationship with what Agamben calls Law—namely, dominant juridical as well as moral norms, the type of heteronormed polity that Herzfeld associates with the word "*politia*" (2021, 101).[20] In Badiousian terms, Law can be seen as the internal regulative forces that stabilize a situation, limiting its multiplicity. This framing of Law is close to what James Faubion has defined as "the thematical"— that is, the "regnant normative order[s] . . . that include *values, ideals and exemplars* as well as imperatives" (2011, 24; emphasis added; 104–115).

Rule and Law imply different patterns and modes of obedience, and their inter-play should not be envisioned as a zero-sum game. Whereas Rule adheres to the complex biographical reality of each individual, subjection to and through the Law drives toward conformity, enabling the production of heteronomous selves and regimented bodies under asymmetric power relations. If a liberating potential had long been discerned in self-discipline by thinkers of different backgrounds (Weber 1946, [1964] 2023; Flathman 2003; Newman 2015), Agamben casts fresh light on this dimension through a novel, nondichotomous dialectic of subject formation.

It may be added that Law, in Tatarstan, emanates not solely from temporal appa-ratuses but also, as we shall see in chapter 3, from official Islamic institutions that cloak themselves in shariatic legitimacy. Yet the state's appropriations of Islamic norm-making are met with resistance and skepticism at the grassroots. A pietist friend once complained about what is sometimes called *mechetsky islam*—"the Islam of [institutional] mosques"—referring to anodyne sermons made up of plati-tudinous injunctions to "be good to one another and respect authority." During a public lecture on Islam I attended in Kazan, a spokesman for the state-backed Islamic bureaucracy defined Muslims as "those who respect our elderly." While filial piety is an Islamic virtue, some halalists in attendance later expressed dissat-isfaction at a statement smacking of generic humanism. Every decent person can respect the elderly. Pietists do so too, but this is done in the context of their fidelity to the Quran and Sunna and out of a personally binding God-awareness. Of course, pietists are, by and large, decent people who would respect their elders anyway, but they strive to be more than that: an ethical form-of-life defined by a chosen fidelity. In the pietists' eyes, the spokesman's remark "diluted" what Islam really is about—subjective commitment to a truth—into reassuring, mainstream morality.

Through the dialectic of Rule and Law, the concept of form-of-life allows a renewed understanding of the power dynamics within which ethical projects unfold. Rule enables autonomous forms of subjectivity and eccentric collectivi-ties; it is emancipatory in the literal sense of enabling forms of self-mastery from below. Vis-à-vis the homogenizing, top-down, constituent power of Law, Rule amounts to the power of those who, without wielding worldly power, manage to bring to fruition, however fleetingly, other forms of subjectivity and together-ness. As postanarchist theorist Saul Newman (2015) puts it, radical discipline actualizes the prospect of an "exodus" from existing orders of sovereignty. In radical scholarship, the notion of destituent power has been advanced (Aarons and Robinson 2023). Yet a slightly different conceptual nuance can perhaps be proposed, which may be termed *trans*tituent power: the power to make lives and communities *beyond* established norms and dominant power relations.

We have seen that, in Badiousian terms, an "ethic of truth" displaces the order of a situation and unveils the possibility of novel political configurations. Furthermore, Rule establishes a binding, personalized link between individuals and their ethical truths without the need for heteronomous apparatuses, thereby relativizing sovereign claims to moral authority and a monopoly of "the good" and the avenues thereto. In other words, an autonomist framework reveals the degree to which becoming a fidelious subject is an emancipatory process. As we will see, encroachments by external sovereign, economic, and judiciary powers do not disappear from a pious believer's everyday experience—far from it. Yet Rule buffers these influences, at least within the form-of-life.

Beyond the Secular-Religious Divide

Being a manifestation of ethical intensity, form-of-life resonates with Asadian notions of praxis and subject formation under Islam's discursive tradition. However, there are points of difference. First, whereas Asadian approaches emphasize engagement with the past and surrender to its moral-religious authority, autonomism foregrounds the future-orientation of ethical life as an actualization of potentialities. Rule is the nomos of autonomy: Embracing it prefigures a "life that coincides with [its form]" (Agamben 2013a, 99), enabling the fulfillment of human potentialities. In Badiou's (2002) thought, the ethical subject coparticipates in the processual, in(de)finitely unfolding *advent* of a truth, which in itself is temporally "infinite," for a truth's emergence is by definition a breach in situational temporality, under the imperative to "keep going!" This is not to deny the temporal trajectory of Rule but to capture an important facet of ethicalists' experience: For all their reverence for the Prophetic age, Tatarstani pietists commit to Islam's timeless truth in light of the future possibilities it discloses, its transformative power and salvific promise that actualizes in Muslim life.

Second, the concept of form-of-life maintains analytical purchase across the religious-secular divide, applying to piety movements such as Tatarstan's halal milieu as well as nonreligious scenes and forms of praxis characterized by fidelity, coherence, and "unsettling" subjectivity. The notions of form-of-life and Rule might help us visualize the relationship between Povolzhye's halal milieu, the secular mainstream, and the state, and reimagine a comparative framework encompassing religious, aesthetic, or political countersubjectivities existing in an agonistic relationship with, yet enclosed by, broader societal and moral structures. The family resemblances and points of contact between piety movements and other, religious or irreligious, underground milieus can be approached in light of a shared method of autonomous subject formation based on fidelity and commitment to a truth.

While autonomist theory helps us account for the emancipatory potential of pious Rule-following, then, it does not romanticize Islam—or secular humanism, or any religious or political revelation or doctrine—as *in itself* subversive, liberative, or unsettling. Rule may be turned into Law, truths risk ossifying into dogmatic simulacra, and fidelity can lose steam and fade into opportunism. Perhaps all radical forms-of-life are haunted by their authoritarian reversals, as the history of twentieth-century social utopias has shown (Badiou 2010). This, in the abstract, might also be true of Povolzhye halalists' truth. The halal milieu is quietist. However, to the extent that they are animated by a universalist, missionary drive, some pietists might as a matter of principle embrace the assumption that an indefinite expansion of their form-of-life would cause, indeed even guarantee, collective emancipation under God—that is, the highest state of human existence. Trying to engineer such an outcome through the means of Law, as Islamist movements and regimes do, would risk producing a new sovereign order, with all the related societal and theocratic accretions, thus betraying the purity of the original event (see Ali Shariati's [1979] distinction between "red," revolutionary and liberative religion, and its "black," oppressive and conformist mirror image). This, anyway, is not what my Rule-embracing interlocutors in Tatarstan do. The politics of Islamic virtue in Putin-era Tatarstan are not the same as they would be in other countries under other regimes. Autonomism invites us to approach the politics of ethics, including religious virtue, through the analysis of concrete situations and context-specific power relations.

Form-of-life sits at the intersection of a situational epistemology concerned with power dynamics, historical transformation, political economy, and sociocultural shifts, on the one hand, and an evental dimension concerned with imponderabilia that resist sociological reduction—a fundamental aspect of existence that "cannot be digested or converted into a common syllogism" (Kierkegaard [1946] 2016, 392; see Marcuse [1964] 1972, 60)—on the other. Form-of-life is a social form caught in the immanent forcefield of a certain setup (post-Soviet Tatarstan/Russia with all its economic, cultural, and moral tumult), but it is also the expression of an "excessive subjectivity" (Finkelde 2017) fueled by a suprahistorical truth: the Quranic revelation.

This framework has allowed us to attend to the structural factors enabling or facilitating the emergence of a halal milieu without casting any of these factors, individually or collectively, as determinant for the irruption of new Muslim subjectivities or sufficient to explain the spread of the piety movement. But what does fidelity entail in the context of halal living? Who makes a fidelious Muslim in Povolzhye, and how does this subjectivity differ from locally available moral discourses on Muslimness? The next chapter tackles these questions as we take a closer look at the debates of Islam in post-Soviet Tatarstan.

BECOMING FIDELIOUS MUSLIMS
Sincerity and Ritual

In 2011–2012, Tatarstani media outlets brought a controversial case of religiously motivated marital desertion to the public's attention. The controversy allegedly unfolded in the East Tatarstani city of Akmaş, whose mosque community had already been beleaguered by charges of extremism.[1] According to a series of media reports, a handful of local Tatar women, indoctrinated by "Wahhabi" preachers, had deserted their husbands on the grounds of the latter's negligence in worship and conduct. Immediately afterward, new Islamic wedding ceremonies had been celebrated—but not civilly registered—between the eloping women and other men, suitably righteous and God-fearing. The protesting husbands were allegedly intimidated into silence by muscular, bearded men.[2]

To grasp the rationale behind this alleged incident, it must be considered that under certain interpretations in Islamic jurisprudence, one's status as a Muslim is assessable based on heart, speech, *and action*. Visible misbehavior thus impinges on the invisible realm of faith (īmān): Grave sins—such as systematically skipping ṣalāh (prayer, *namaz*)—generate a condition of major disbelief (kufr ākbar). Professing belief without following up with action is not enough to rectify this situation. Inadequate conduct impinges, to use the local expression, on one's status as a "full-fledged" (*polnotsenny*) Muslim and may even constitute grounds for expulsion from the faith according to rigorist interpretations, which today may be found in association with the Salafi movement. Here comes the marital problem: Under Islamic jurisprudence, being Muslim constitutes a necessary precondition for men to lawfully access Islamic marriage. If a lack of īmān can be detected, one's marital tie to one's Muslim spouse becomes null.[3] To evoke

British philosopher of language J. L. Austin (1962), īmān is a "condition of felicity" underpinning the validity of an Islamic marital alliance. The problem is that there is no agreement on the boundaries of īmān.

"Who counts as a Muslim?" thus is a tricky question, for students of Islam as well as Muslims faced with incidents such as the one above. This chapter explores the question of Muslimness by considering the intertwined dimensions of conduct and ritual. Concepts of "fidelity" and "commitment" are discussed through a Badiousian conceptual prism and an engagement with Roy Rappaport's theory of ritual (1999), before I return to J. L. Austin and venture an update on his classic conceptualization of performative utterances.

But for the moment, let us remain in Akmaş. The town's _cämäğat'_—religious community—is a composite one. Its fulcrum is charismatic Imam Musa-xäzrät Mukhammetshin, who was once enthusiastically described to me as "Akmaş's Steve Jobs" for his ability to infuse the mosque community with a "capitalist spirit" of honest entrepreneurship. Despite the admiration of his followers as well as a formal role within the republican Islamic bureaucracy,[4] Musa-xäzrät is disliked by some in the Islamic officialdom for his reputation as a "Wahhabi." In fact, although Musa-xäzrät is socially conservative and receptive toward orthodox Islamic reformism, he is more of a champion of the Tatar spiritual legacy—which, as far as theological labels go, is historically Hanafi/Maturidi—than a pro-Saudi Hanbali doctrinarian.[5]

Most Akmaş pietists share this broad orientation. Under Musa-xäzrät's tenure, however, Akmaş's mosque community did come to include a Hanbali/Athari-oriented fraction, animated by a small number of young Saudi-trained preachers. Sheikh Abdulmalik, one of the key religious leaders around whom this fraction coheres, is an energetic, brawny man in his mid-thirties who frequented Akmaş's turbulent criminal underworld as a teenager before setting off to Medina and enrolling at the Islamic University of al-Madinah al-Munawarah,[6] where he focused on the science of Prophetic sayings at the faculty of Dar ul-Hadith. At the time of my stay, several dozen men would gather twice a week at Abdulmalik's courses, held in the city's second-largest mosque. His classes were held in Russian, and this group tended to place little stock on ethnicity.[7] Other components added to the community's theological and ideological diversity. Owing to the presence of a Tatar-Turkish Lyceum in Akmaş, Musa-xäzrät's mosque catered to a number of "liberal" Muslims influenced by the teachings of Fethullah Gülen's Hizmet movement. Last, an important group within the _cämäğat'_ was the _babaylar_ or elders, devout retirees who have invested their time in the religious community. Their custom-infused vernacular religiosity was frowned upon by the most zealous modernist youths, but Musa-xäzrät exercised his influence to defuse any potential conflict between generations.

Albeit not altogether implausible, extreme occurrences such as the alleged marital scandal are thus not representative of this variegated community's everyday life. At the time of my visit (2014–2015), the facts behind media sensationalism were already very difficult to verify. Some of my local acquaintances appeared embarrassed at my mention of the incident, and I did not press the issue. Sources from Sheikh Abdulmalik's entourage were displeased with the unwanted publicity that politicized media attention had brought to their milieu, while representatives of the mosque leadership would not dwell on the specifics, instead insisting that "their community is not extremist." In retrospect, it seems possible that tensions over different interpretations of Islamic marriage did erupt, though not necessarily with the severity alleged by the media. The (alleged) "Wahhabi" wedding woe, however, raises important analytical questions that are addressed in this chapter: How should one account for the diversity and pluralism within as multifarious a grouping as the halal milieu? How differently do pietists and nonpietists understand Muslimness? What are the emic "conditions of felicity" that afford one the status as a "full-fledged" (*polnotsenny*) Muslim?

Halalists and Ethnic Muslims

In 2009, a Tatar-language pamphlet titled *Am I a Muslim Because I Am a Tatar?* appeared on the shelves of Islam-themed shops across Tatarstan. Its author, Niyazetdin-mulla Minleakhmat al-Hanafi, had chosen his onomastic attributions (title and nisba) strategically: By declaring himself a "Hanafi mullah," he claimed continuity with a time-honored legacy of Tatar spiritual leadership, thereby preempting any accusation of being an extremist, foreign-brainwashed "Wahhabi sheikh." This legitimized the otherwise stern message delivered through the booklet, which, by making theology, jurisprudence, and quotations from the Quran and hadith understandable to a nonspecialist readership, set about to convince its readers that no, one is not a Muslim just because one is a Tatar, however commonplace that statement is held to be by many people in Tatarstan.

The pamphlet declares that today's Tatars have lapsed into the "evil of disbelief" (*käferlärneñ yavızlığı*) due to the pernicious influence of "the Russians and other infidels (*käferlär*)" (Äl-Xänäfi 2009, 5). Niyazetdin-mulla then explains that the "concept of a Muslim" is predicated on submission before God: A Muslim is anyone who puts one's heart and soul into following God's guidance and decrees, arranged in an all-encompassing and rational system of regulations. The pamphlet has an ethnocentric tone—a feature that distances it from more cosmopolitan Salafi literature—and remarks on the importance of Islam in Tatar cultural history. Nonetheless, Niyazetdin-mulla affirms that being a Tatar and being a "proper" Muslim are distinct things, the latter being predicated not just on the utterance of the profession of faith but also on dispositions of the heart and the body: assiduous worship (prayer, fasting, pilgrimage, etc.) and sincerity (*ixsan*)—that is, acting "as if you can see [God], even if you do not see Him, because He sees you" (Äl-Xänäfi 2009, 17–18).

None of this, stresses the author, has anything to do with one's national background: Any ethnic Tatar is susceptible to falling into disbelief, which constitutes not just a "betrayal" (*xıyanat*) of the nation but also, spiritually speaking, a condition close to animality. Pamphlets like this reveal the extent of the gulf between Tatarness and Muslimness, an undefined area rife with anxieties for Povolzhye's secular majority as well as for pietists concerned about the spiritual fate of their co-ethnics.

Halalists often remark that "proper/full-fledged" (*polnotsennye*), "practicing" (*soblyudayushchye*) Muslims in Tatarstan are but a fraction of those who call themselves Muslims or declare belief in God. A trope that circulated among my pious interlocutors would have it that observant religionists make up just 2 to 5 percent of the overall Tatar population. Such folk statistics are likely based more on self-representation as a select spiritual elite than on sociologically accurate calculation. Contradictorily, some interlocutors—sometimes the same individuals, in the same conversation—stressed the vitality of Islam in post-Soviet Russia by pointing out that "our mosques are swarming with believers on Fridays."[8] There is factual validity to both claims: The halal milieu, however expanding, lively, and aspirational, remains a minority—an unsettling form-of-life within an overall secularized and state-engineered moral landscape. Assessing the demographic strength of the halal milieu against the secular majority would be maddeningly complex. The inherent slipperiness of counting human beings on the basis of orientations and behaviors is compounded by the fact that the picture is ever-changing: Piety trends have been expanding steadily, but the country's downward authoritarian spiral may limit their visibility. Post-Soviet accounts suggest that between 60 and 90 percent of Tatars consider themselves "believers" (between two and three times as many as in the late Soviet era) and that the number of officially registered mosques and Islamic associations has skyrocketed since the collapse of state atheism (Furman and Kaariainen 2000; Sulakshin et al. 2006, 679–682). But these figures are not necessarily illustrative: As we have already begun to see, one's status as a pietist is based on more than self-affiliation, ethno-confessional background, or generic claims of belief in a benevolent deity.[9]

"Ethnic Muslims" (*etnicheskye musul'mane*) is the emic concept used in Povolzhye in reference to people of Tatar/Bashkir descent who do not observe Islamic practices yet consider themselves Muslims by virtue of an ancestral essence shared by all members of the national community (Dannreuther 2010). It is widely accepted in Tatarstan that a difference exists between pious halalists and ethnic Muslims: Even representatives of ecumenist, state-backed Islamic institutions have publicly declared, in a mournful tone, that these two groups are "worlds apart" (Mukhamedov 2011). At one level, thinking in dichotomous absolutes is patently unhelpful. Life is much messier than any simple binary. Yet these polarities are more than mere ideal types: They are rooted in people's experiences of Islam and of very intensely felt fault lines in Povolzhye's religious tapestry.

To the best of my judgment, the term "ethnic Muslim" is not derogatory, and it is sometimes used as a self-descriptor ("Do I abstain from alcohol? Nah, I'm an ethnic Muslim"). It does, however, carry a somewhat mournful note, maybe a tinge of contrition, and may be uttered with disapprobation by pietists. I have heard a joke that takes aim at ethnic Muslims by branding them *pokhoronno-pominal'nye musul'mane*, "funerary-commemorative Muslims." The joke borrows from the stuffy jargon on folklore studies—namely, the expression "funerary-commemorative ritual"—to convey the sense of a conformist, veneer religiosity that finds expression only through life-cycle rituality, such as funerals and memorial banquets. However, ethnic-Muslim religiosity may carry powerful existential attachments. Let us look at it ethnographically through the example of two Tatar women.

Milausha-apa was a well-educated lady in her sixties, who quietly embraced Catholicism in the early 1990s, a time of liberalization and religious ferment in the post-Soviet space. Her move, back then, was motivated by her fascination with the meekness of Christ and the charisma of John Paul II, and by the appearance of a new way to explore Christianity without having to embrace the "Russian religion," Orthodoxy. Her choice was of an intellectual nature, and in fact, the Soviet-raised Aunt Milausha never became very observant or prayerful. Only irregularly would she attend Sunday services, read the Gospel, or say Hail Marys. On many accounts, she maintained a secular outlook. Still, in Catholicism she claimed to have found her path to spiritual fulfillment. On one occasion, I paid Milausha-apa a visit at her place to record one of our oral history sessions and was taken aback upon finding her clothed in full Islamic attire, headscarved, and holding a prayer mat. "You're here early today—you disturbed my namaz," she casually remarked. "Your namaz? But you asked me to bring you Pope Francis postcards from Italy last month," I replied in puzzlement. Ah, true, but that day, Milausha-apa explained to me, was the anniversary of her mother's death. Her *äni* (mother) had been a devout Muslim, like her *däü äni* (grandmother)—a mullah's daughter—before her. Therefore, Aunt Milausha commemorated her mother by performing Islamic prayer. "But you are not a Muslim any more, right?" I challenged her. "Of course I am a Muslim, like all Tatars! I'm a Catholic Muslim, or a Muslim Catholic. Perhaps [when I die] half of my soul will go one way, and the other half somewhere else," she laughed. In fact, I was to learn later, Milausha-apa had never stopped cooking celebratory dishes on Islamic Eids and giving alms to mosques.

As far as her embrace of Catholicism is concerned, Milausha-apa's biography is not representative of widespread conversion trends: Only a minority of ethnic-Muslim Tatars change religion, for reasons that will soon be clear. However, this episode of ambivalence and filial loyalty powerfully illustrates the moral, indeed existential, implications of ethnic Muslimness. Ethnic Muslims live Muslimness as something jealously bodily, viscerally intimate (Benussi 2018), that at the same time links one with something greater: the bygone generations and the moral community of the Tatar *natsiya*.

On one occasion, my failure to understand the depth of these obligations got me in trouble with my Tatar landlady in Akmaş, Guzel, a retired math teacher in her mid-fifties. From the moment we first met, Guzel struck me as a vivacious and outspoken woman, proud of her Soviet background and her internationalist outlook. Like many Soviet-bred Tatar parents, she had given her children European-sounding names (Rafael and Marcel) so they would not be mistaken for Russians but not sound too "Oriental" either. She stayed clear of mosques and religious institutions. Rather than reading "obscure" Tatar national authors, she preferred "world-famous" Russian writers, like Pushkin, and felt uncomfortable with "old-fashioned" Tatar female honorifics such as *apa* ("just Guzel is okay"). In short, during my period of tenancy, little in her lifestyle struck me as particularly Islamic or even Tatar: Indeed, she was happy to define herself as "quite Russified" (*obrusevshaya*).

One night, upon returning after a meeting with the mosque community, I mentioned that I had had a chat with some local Russians and Jews who had embraced Islam. This information provoked an unexpectedly emotional reaction from my interlocutor. Guzel was aghast at the idea that someone could change his or her religion. I politely proposed that anyone should be free to choose their spiritual path according to individual inclinations. She rejected the notion, looking nauseated. Guzel was adamant that conversion would amount to disgracing one's parents and was, in her opinion, the ultimate offense one could commit against one's kin. When I pointed out that she could hardly be called a Muslim anyway, Guzel erupted in a fiery monologue in which she contended that however Russified, she had married a Muslim man, taught her children Islamic invocations, and would be buried "the Muslim way" (*po musul'manskomu*). She pitied those Russians and Jews I had met, adding that "they'd better go back home and talk to their poor mothers as soon as possible." Guzel claimed that I, too, had a perverted understanding of religion, urging me to discuss the issue with my own parents. When I woke up the morning after, I found a Bible on my bedside table, alongside a spiritualist book by a Russian new-age author, evidently intended as a stimulus to rekindle my hereditary Christianness. When I quizzed Guzel about what other religious literature furnished her library, it turned out she did not possess a copy of the Quran, only the Bible she had given me—but again, that did not make her any less Muslim.

These episodes illuminate a central component of the mainstream themitical order among the Tatars: Acknowledgment of Islam as one's ancestral religion and recognition of the primacy of the Tatar language as one's "mother tongue" (*tuğan tel*) are determinants of personhood. Failure to respect these basic tenets carries the risk of being branded a *mankurt*—an actually derogatory term among post-Soviet Turkic-Muslim groups, whose meanings include blind submission to Russification, the betrayal of one's community, the disregard of shared memory, moral bankruptcy, and, in literature and mythology, unthinkingness (Toshchenko 2012), "idiocy" in the literal sense of separation from the social (see Mazzarella 2017, 67).

Muslimness as a Birthright

My ethnic-Muslim interlocutors emphasize Muslimness as an ancestral birth-given essence, consubstantial with the "stuff" one's most intimate self is made of, rather than bearing explicit connections to a coherent body of precepts, ritual practices, and scriptures. It must be emphasized that within the post-Soviet region, this understanding of religion is not unique to Povolzhye. Ludek Broz (2009), echoing David Schneider, has identified comparable tensions between notions of religion as "shared substance" and religion as "code for conduct" among Evangelical converts in a Siberian province, while other ethnographic studies show that essentialist understandings of Muslimness as "shared substance" are widespread across the former USSR's Muslim-majority countries (Privratsky 2001; Borbieva 2009). The term *mankurt*—ethnic deserter—is itself of Kyrgyz origin (Toshchenko 2012).

The idea of religion as essence is not necessarily devoid of a spiritual aspect. My ethnography corroborates the picture offered by post-Soviet statistical analyses of Tatar religiosity: Despite varying degrees of distance from the doctrinal foundations of Islam, most ethnic Muslims, if asked, would identify themselves as Muslims and declare that they believe in God. A common way in which many ethnic Muslims elaborate on their understanding of God implies the idea of carrying faith in one's heart (*vera v serdtse*), a formulation consistent with Mikhail Epstein's notion of Soviet "minimal religion" (1999a, 1999b). To an extent, these secularist Tatars' understanding of God appears consistent with a widespread human tendency to find the supernatural plausible and reassuring—a tendency that some cognitive anthropologists have described as a cross-cultural, near-universal psychic phenomenon (Boyer 2002, 2008; Whitehouse and Laidlaw 2007) but that, as Laidlaw (2007) noted, "ethicized" and scripturally oriented religious traditions tend to look down on as mere superstition.

Ethnic Muslims' experience of belief—especially for the most spiritually inclined—can in fact carry sophisticated existential and cultural dimensions to which we return in chapter 4. However, faith is located by most ethnic Muslims "deep down" in their souls, sealed within the innermost tabernacle of the self.[10] Charles Hirschkind (1996) has argued that the idea of a private God one should worship within the depths of one's heart stems from a Western tradition of separation between the worldly and the sacred, state and church, which took shape during the Enlightenment through the work of John Locke and his followers. Locke believed that "divine worship was essentially a matter of inner disposition of the believer towards God, and therefore the actions of the body were without consequence with regards to salvation" (Hirschkind 1996, 470). Historically, this notion enabled the transformation of Europe's potentially explosive sectarian "differences" into conceptually manageable "diversities" within a pluralist (secular) landscape (McClure 1990, 376; see Hallaq 2013)—a dynamic that has innervated Russia's approaches to modernity from the Catherinian age onward. In the next chapter, we shall see how autonomist theory casts fresh light on the "taming" of ethical intensities at the hand of the state, exploring aspects of governmentalization that cannot be summarized as just a matter of secularism versus religion. Nonetheless, it is undeniable that a recognizable modernist genealogy has influenced Russian and Soviet secularism, thereby affecting ethnic Muslims' Weltanschauung.

Still, despite its genealogical links with broader patterns of European modernity, ethnic Muslimness is to a significant extent a phenomenon idiosyncratic to the post-Soviet world (Dannreuther 2010, 13). Ethnic Muslimness is similar but not identical to "Muslimness by heritage" or similar expressions used by scholars of secularity to describe people who identify with Islamicate cultural traditions and communities but may not observe the faith's precepts (Amiraux 2006; Suleiman 2013, 2015). Heritage implies a cultural-immaterial dimension that is shared, communal, and public (Benussi 2021d). Essence, by contrast, is something that runs in one's blood—something private and intimate, inborn, inalienable, and inheritable, which undergirds public narratives on collective heritage and belonging but cannot be reduced to them. This emphasis on identity as a quasi-bodily substance is the outcome of the essentialist approaches at the core of Soviet and post-Soviet paradigms of ethnic personhood (D. Anderson et al. 2019). These approaches, which Victor Shnirelman has called "primordialist," hold that "a conscious or unconscious attachment to one's primary group is formed on the basis of blood relations, language, religion, . . . characteristics that make for highly durable, if not permanent, groups" (Shnirelman 1996, 8; also see Slezkine 1994; Suny and Martin 2001). Under this paradigm, in the Soviet era, hereditary Muslimness—as distinct from the practice of Islam—became Tatarness's fundamental bastion. In today's Povolzhye, it is still widely assumed that Muslimness is the most constitutive and inalienable element of the Tatar *etnos*, having "protected" the Tatars from Russification for centuries.[11]

This scenario is the outcome of the combined effects of Soviet antireligious campaigns and ethnopolitical engineering. On the one hand, the Soviets dissolved the political, juridical, and moral institutes that upheld a "traditional" prerevolutionary order infused with norms derived from Quran and Sunna. On the other, their project of forging discreet ethnic cultures based on set traits that included historical religious affiliation "enshrined" the position of Islam in the Muslim-majority regions of the USSR (Khalid 2007, 99). As a result, "by the end of the Soviet period, national identity was intimately tied to Muslimness, but a Muslimness that had been stripped of much of its 'spiritual' content and was thereby made compatible with Soviet ideals. . . . These processes allowed for an environment where self-avowed atheists could actively claim to be Muslims" (Pelkmans 2017, 94). The Putin-era process of "desecularization from above" (Karpov 2013) reintroduced religion into the public sphere—including Islam—in a managed fashion to capitalize on its "identity" potential and engineer a socially conservative moral order.

Sincerity and Ritual

The halal milieu on one side, ethnic Muslims on the other, and Islam in the middle. Is there an "Islam proper," and who if anybody is getting it right in Tatarstan? One relatively safe way to handle—or to eschew—this supremely thorny question would be to emphasize the multiplicity, fluidity, and multifariousness of Islam, as some, legitimately, do (Montgomery 2016, 61–63). However, the notion that there may exist as many "Islams" as Muslim social contexts has been criticized for missing one of the most dearly held spiritual certainties of Muslims worldwide: "The unity of a single Islam is a consciously theological aspect of what Muslims believe, despite the fact that Muslims are at least as aware of the diversity of interpretation and practice of Islam as are Western anthropologists" (Anjum 2007, 658; see Asad [1981] 2009; Secor 2007; Marsden and Retsikas 2013, 21). Faced with the question of how to account for multiplicity without dismissing unity, scholars working in the path opened by Talal Asad have relied on the notion of discursive tradition, understood as "a religion-cum-worldview with a relatively clearly defined set of foundational texts and an established history of reasoned arguments based on these texts" (Anjum 2007, 662). Studies in this vein (Hirschkind 2006; Mahmood [2005] 2012) have attracted praise for their subtlety in rendering the richness of Muslims' ethical self-fashioning as well as criticism for advancing a somewhat monolithic picture of Islamic virtue (Fadil and Fernando 2015; Schielke 2015b; Tayob 2017).

In a context such as Tatarstan, the issue with an Asadian approach is that Islam's foundational texts—the Quran and hadith—are hardly a meaningful component of the lived experience of many of Povolzhye's ethnic Muslims. Some, like Guzel, may not entertain any consequential relationship with them at all. In most cases, an engagement with scriptural sources is relegated to special occurrences such as life-cycle ceremonies and to the domain of ritual specialists—the official Islamic "clergy" and some categories of individuals, especially the elderly and in particular older women—expected to engage with scripture on behalf of the broader community. Only indirectly, if at all, do scriptural sources feature in the moral registers that guide ethnic Muslims' everyday conduct. A strictly Asadian framing of Islam would not leave us with much choice other than describing ethnic Muslims, to paraphrase Morten Pedersen (2011), as "Muslims without Islam."

It is therefore not surprising that many ethnographic studies of Islam in the former socialist space have avoided such risk by adopting the optics of "ordinary" Muslimness. In an influential monograph on Islam in Uzbekistan, Johan Rasanayagam (2011, 206, 231) has advocated an approach that, by privileging quotidian moral experience, avoids "dichotomies between scriptural and everyday ways of being Muslim" and abstains from making "theological" claims as to whether or not certain practices are Islamic or not. Post-Soviet Uzbeks, he argued, draw on multiple, Islamic and non-Islamic, moral repertoires, all contributing to the formation of Muslims' subjectivities. Noor Borbieva (2009, 9–10) formulated a similar point by stressing the plurality of sources and the interplay of discourses and counterdiscourses about Islam among Kyrgyz Muslims, while David Henig (2020) has detailed the nonscriptural "ethics of proximity" that regulates the communal lives of Muslim villagers in Bosnia. However, this approach is not without drawbacks either: By "diluting" Islam into a pluralist and nonbinding moral order, the specificity of Islamic living is denied, while the secular norm—by which religion should come in small doses—is implicitly reinforced (Fadil and Fernando 2015). This means sidelining Islamic forms-of-life and potentially even reproducing a state-driven exclusionary discourse framing pietists as culturally inauthentic and abnormal.

A Rule-bound form-of-life like the halal milieu can hardly be understood in terms of "ordinariness" and "multifarious" moral repertoires: The Law of mainstream morality may encroach on the lived experience of halalists—who are not hermetically sealed off from broader themical and biopolitical regimes—yet precisely for this reason pietists make a strong, *extra*ordinary effort on the path of Islam's truths, thereby revindicating the existence of a difference between "correct" (*pravil'ny*), "proper" (*polnotsenny*) engagements with Islam and more ambiguous, "weaker" relationships with the faith.

To analytically reframe the different claims to Islam made by halalists and ethnic Muslims, I propose to start by attending to emic categories and taxonomies of Muslimness and placing those in conversation with the insights afforded by autonomist theories of ethics. We have seen that a shared ancestral essence is vital to "ethnic" paradigms of Muslimness. We have also begun to see that pietists, such as pamphletist Niyazetdin-mulla, distance themselves from such understandings, instead placing individual dispositions and conducts, from the observance of rituals to righteous conduct, at the front and center of their experience as Muslims. Consider Akmaş's Salafi-leaning Sheikh Abdulmalik, who exemplifies the emic taxonomies of Muslimness widespread among scripturalists:

> Some people do not know how to properly worship Allah the Most High. . . . First, there are some people who sincerely [*iskrenno*] love Allah but fail to properly worship Him—they follow all sorts of abominable innovations. They are erring Muslims [*zabludshchye*]. Second, some other people show off their righteousness, always show up at the mosque for prayer, but they do it only as a façade. They are the hypocrites [munāfiqūn]. Third, there are those who not only ignore how to worship properly, but neglect their obligations towards their Creator altogether. This is the majority. Lastly, there are those who sincerely love Allah the Most High and follow the right path of the Prophet (Allah bless Him and His family and grant Him peace) and his Companions [*Spodvizhniki*].

Abdulmalik organizes his model around two key parameters that identify "proper" Muslims: sincerity (righteousness, steadfastness) and ritual correctness (worship). According to this model, there are those who live their faith with zeal but fail to appropriately adhere to the "best practices" of worship due to incorrect interpretations (by which Abdulmalik likely meant Sufi and, in general, non-Salafi Muslims). Then, there are those who appear assiduous and precise in fulfilling their ritual duties but are not sincere in their day-to-day life (opportunists and show-offs). The best Muslims are the "happy few" who combine high sincerity and high precision in ritual (the group in which my interlocutor feels he belongs), while most Tatars/ethnic Muslims are, to him, both remiss in their conduct and neglectful of ritual.

Despite carrying a specific theological baggage, Abdulmalik's words are illustrative of sensitivities that are as widely held among pietists, even beyond Salafi circles. Consider the following words by Izmail-abıy, a cadre of Russia's Association of Muslim Entrepreneurs—a state-approved organization aiming at fostering halal business, solidly ecumenist and "moderate" in outlook—and note the recursive mention of the themes of prayer and conduct: "When the Association of Muslim Entrepreneurs wants to identify sincere brothers [*iskrennykh brat'ev*] in a new city or district, we begin by looking into about who prays regularly [*kto chitaet namaz*] and embraces an Islamically permissible way of life [*kto veded razreshenny obraz zhizni*]. Then we make contact with them."

When I picked the mind of Aynaz, a financial consultant who lives between Tatarstan and Turkey, he too mentioned prayer and halal discipline as the main preconditions for becoming part of the community: "A Muslim is somebody who follows certain rules. This is because as a believer you have certain obligations . . . primarily, with regards to our Creator. And our Creator has established rules, which you are to follow. What are these rules? First of all, to perform *namaz*. Second, to stay clear of anything forbidden. Abstain from alcohol. Look away from provocative women. In general . . . avoid anything haram. It is a matter of self-discipline." Of course, the specifics of righteous conduct and ritual correctness are hotly debated in Povolzhye, as in other theologically diverse regions of Russia (Yarlykapov 2010, 111–115). In 2016, a gathering of clerics of Sufi orientation, predominantly from the Caucasus, issued a document aimed at defining the "truly correct" (*istinno pravil'ny*) way to be a Muslim. The document, sometimes referred to as "the Grozny fatwa" after the Chechen city where the gathering took place (Shagaviev 2020), also places great emphasis on ritual and sincerity. However, the theological-juridical references and exemplars singled out as paragons of righteous conduct by the Grozny fatwa are Sufi masters such as Junayd al-Baghdadi, al-Gilani, and al-Naqshbandi, rather than Muhammad's Companions invoked by Salafi-leaning Muslims like Sheik Abdulmalik. In the Grozny fatwa, predictably, it is the "Wahhabis" who are branded "erring" Muslims. Different theological-juridical orientations play out at the grassroots level too. During prayer, for example, followers of the Hanafi school stand (<u>qiyām</u>) with their feet close to each other and their hands folded over their navels, while followers of Salafi teachings keep their feet wider apart so that they can touch their neighbors' feet, and they place their hands over their chests. Following Sheikh al-Albani's "Prophet Prayer" canon, Salafi-inspired worshippers raise their arms in salutation three times during <u>rak'ah</u> (prayer unit), move their index fingers during silent invocations while kneeling (<u>sujūd</u>), and chant "ameen" aloud. Remembrance (<u>dhikr</u>, <u>zikr</u>) performed with prayer beads, by contrast, tends to indicate adherence to Sufism or Hanafism. These nuances can be seized on to explicitly make a theological point, and during my research, Salafis were sometimes criticized by other halalists for ostentatiousness and pushiness in displaying their orientation. A Hanafi friend told me how he had once found his right foot squarely and painfully squeezed underneath his Salafi neighbor's left foot during a congregational prayer. After several attempts to free his aching appendage, he resolved to leave the row mid-prayer, despite this being a serious breach of Islamic etiquette.

Yet, despite everything, a broad consensus exists within the halal milieu that prayer, carried out with regularity, and sincerity, expressed through halal-mindful choices and disciplined behavior, constitute the main criteria defining "proper" Muslimness. This allows for the accommodation of theological differences. Salafis and Sufis may disagree on a great many points of theology and jurisprudence and trade accusations of "error," but both groups agree that full-fledged Muslims are defined by *iskrennost'* and engagement in Islam's foundational ritual actions. The same friend who had his foot squeezed told me how, on a separate occasion, he showed up at the mosque of a predominantly Salafi community—where he had been invited for business purposes—carrying with him a string of prayer beads (*disbe*). After namaz, he pulled out his beads and started performing remembrance with them, raising a good deal of eyebrows: The use of prayer beads is frowned upon as a harmful innovation (bid'ah) among many scripturalists. My friend's move was calculated. Performing namaz in congregation was intended as a collective enactment (and mutual recognition) of belonging in the same spiritual space. Using prayer beads, on the other hand, was intended to signal to the community that, despite the amicable relations he entertained with some members, he followed a different theological school. To the extent that his zealous conduct and ritual assiduousness were never in doubt, his status as a full-fledged (albeit perhaps "erring") Muslim was not cast into question, and the business meeting was a success.

Ikhlāṣ, Iḥsān, and an Ethics of Truth

Having identified the centrality of sincerity and ritual (first and foremost prayer[12]) to the halal milieu, let us consider the insight autonomist theory may offer into pietists' ethical discipline vis-à-vis ethnic Muslims' Islam-as-essence. Alain Badiou's reflections of the ethics of truth, specifically, capture key aspects of Islamic *askesis*, while his category of plenitude can cast fresh light on ethnic Muslims' identarian relationship with Islam. Such a move may help us avoid the normativities of both Asadian and "everyday" approaches to Islam; furthermore, Badiou's philosophical concern with how verities shape human conduct allows us to take seriously—and respectfully—Islam's claim to truth, without reproducing categories of Islamic theology or metaphysics. Of course, doing so requires pushing Badiousian thought beyond its original Euro-secularist matrix. Rather than a betrayal, however, I see this move as an example of how an open-ended correspondence between autonomist, anthropological, and Islamic praxes can open up novel spaces of possibility in the domain of theory itself.

In Islamic theology, the virtue of sincerity (ikhlās, locally glossed as _ixlas_ or _iskrennost'_) is accompanied by a privileged, hard-to-achieve state of God-awareness (ihsān): Earnest worshippers enact righteous conduct not only before their peers but also before God "as though one could see Him, and even if one cannot see Him, then indeed He always sees His creatures." In the words Giorgio Agamben used to describe the monastic form-of-life, sincere pietists keep track of "'every action, great or small' . . . with care, because [they are] conscious in every instant of doing the will of God" (2013a, 23). Ihsān is a quintessentially intimate and personal aspect of spiritual life. As has been observed (Lambek 2007, 69), it is very hard to assess something like religious seriousness "objectively," even within ourselves. Thus, unsurprisingly, the specter of hypocrisy (_nifak_, nifāq) is omnipresent among pietists. Charges of _nifak_ are both made (with varying degrees of gravity) and rejected (with varying degrees of vehemence). Entire religious pamphlets are dedicated to the importance of avoiding the spiritual risks of "showing off" (_pokazukha_) (Galyautdin 2011). Akmaş's Sheikh Abdulmalik was adamant that pious action must be carried out "for the sake of God, for the sake of God alone" (_radi Allakha, tol'ko radi Allakha_). On the other hand, in conversations I was also met with the optimistic notion that Povolzhye Muslims—that is, the halal-minded minority—might be on average "more sincere" than Muslims elsewhere in the Islamic world. Theologians distinguish greater nifāq, or hypocrisy in faith (falsely proclaiming conviction in religious matters), from lesser nifāq, hypocrisy in deed (workaday inconsistency). In a secularized context like Povolzhye, the argument goes, there is no societal compulsion to become pietists: In fact, doing so runs counter to the mainstream and might get people into trouble. Therefore, if the halal milieu grows, the reason lies mainly in adherents' own conviction: Halalists do not have any reason to commit greater nifāq.

Although sincerity might be impossible to measure objectively, it can still be comprehended subjectively; and as Kierkegaard ([1946] 2016, 231) remarked, subjectivity is what counts the most in religious matters. Badiou (2002, 41, 42) insists that the condition of being an ethical subject is acquired through the encounter with that "surplus of reality" that is an ethical truth and preserved by henceforth relating to the situational domain from the perspective of that verity: "Under the effect of a loving encounter [with a truth], if I want to be really faithful to it, I must completely rework my ordinary way of 'living' my situation." Consider the following excerpt from a conversation with my acquaintance Ayub, a young man who had embraced a deeper commitment to Islam a couple of years earlier and was eager to revisit his conversion and its domino effect in his life:

> You start to look at things through the lens of Islam [*cherez prizmu Izlama*] and experience a sort of upsurge [*pod'em*]. Through this upsurge, a movement begins, like a chain reaction in your life. Now I want to have more kids, learn more, and inshaAllah find my place in this world [*naiti svoe mesto v zhizni*]. Now I know why I am alive. I know that anybody can become a president, and that a president can become a beggar, too. But no bad weather can now prevent me from seeking self-perfection. In Islam, everything—how to conduct your family life, how to treat other people, and how civilizations develop—everything proceeds from one single starting point. You must bear in mind that *there is another life*. And that the Hereafter is more important than anything here. A pious Muslim does not confine himself within this life . . . he also bears on himself responsibility for the other life. And tries to work for both. It is like discovering that the city you were born in is not, after all, as big as you thought—and that there is a whole country around it, a whole world around it—a new continent, and you can't wait to explore it. And once you're back, you will have learned new ways to fix those problems [*reshat te voprosy*] that, in the narrow scenario of your native town, seemed so big, but they are not, after all. And now you can fix all those problems you couldn't fix before.

The "single starting point," a truth; the "chain reaction in your life," an embodied truth-process; and the new outlook on life, a renewed relationship with one's situation. Ayub's description of the "decision-event" of conversion (Humphrey 2018) resonates with Badiou's notion of entering a new subjectivity. It links the individual, the collective (from "other people" to "whole civilizations"), and the cosmo-ontological levels. The event of conversion, the universal truth it manifests, bears directly on quotidian life. Thus, objectively mundane things, like having children, are in fact "extraordinary" in a subjective sense, as they reveal a thoroughly revolutionized relationship with the situation (A. Ahmad 2017, 20–21). Fidelity is a "necessary" consequence of this transformative event. Only through fidelity can a subjectivity be sustained: To Badiou, an ethical subject is inseparable from a concrete truth-process, and a truth exists only insofar as fidelious practice manifests it. Hence, conversion is better understood in terms of an ongoing, dynamic, recursive practice of becoming (A. Ahmad 2017), to which iḥsān and ikhlāṣ are central. In a similar fashion, Ayub's words can be read in dialogue with Cornelius Castoriadis's framing of autonomy as a process (1991, 163) inaugurated by self-reflectiveness and "unlimited interrogation . . . that has its bearing not on [mere] 'facts' but on the social imaginary ... and [its] grounding." This moment of reflectiveness—which, Castoriadis notes, "ushers in a new type of individual"—enables the positing of questions that are both political ("Are our laws good? Are they just?") and ontological ("What is it that we ought to think? What ought we to think about Being?"). This opening allows one to "give to oneself one's own law ... knowing that one is doing so" (164), which, in Ayub's case, means his proud and deliberate choice of making halalness a guiding principle.

My interlocutors insisted that a great deal of effort should be invested in policing one's inner self to minimize any discrepancies between event and exteriority, conviction and conduct. Ihsān is achieved by consistently adopting a series of technologies of the self, from veiling (Mahmood [2005] 2012), to listening to sermons (Hirschkind 2006), to consuming halal and leading a halal way of living (Benussi 2021a). Consider the case of my acquaintance Alsu. She and her husband Mansur are "intellectual" pietists—cosmopolitan and highly educated—exploratively engaged with Salafi theology. Alsu was born in a Northern Tatarstani town to a family of secular Tatar nationalists. At school, Alsu discovered the performing arts, and she rapidly made a name for herself as one of the republic's most promising Tatar-language actresses. After high school, Alsu moved to Kazan to study Oriental studies in the faculty of Tatar studies at Kazan State University, while she kept perfecting her acting skills in preparation for a professional career with one of the republican capital's prestigious theater troupes. During her university years, she became involved with the halal milieu, acquainting herself with the subtleties of halal and growing increasingly disillusioned with her family's secular nationalism, which she came to recognize as spiritually "empty" (buş) despite its ostensible concern with "Tatar spiritual heritage."

As Alsu explored orthodox Sunnism during her university studies, she became uncomfortable with her career as an actress, since rigorist theological schools discourage singing, performing before strange men, masquerading, and dancing. Alsu came up against a painful choice: If she were to be true to her ethical project, she must renounce her career as a thespian and give up her passion. And that Alsu did, in a decision that testifies to this young woman's strength of will. Her husband Mansur loves to jocularly remark how she is the decision-maker in the family, overturning a "traditionally" patriarchal Tatar family model. She subsequently embarked on a "halal" career as a pedagogist.

Alsu's ideal of Muslimness is a painstaking lifetime endeavor to create an ethical form-of-life, a "life which coincides with its form," through the processual pursuit of Islam's truth. Her secular self has had to be remodeled, taking on new (halal) habits and unlearning old (haram) ones. To live *po khalyalnomu*, in a halal way, the haram must be identified as such—as an obstacle in the path to God—and pruned away with "consistency" and "perseverance" (Badiou 2002, 48–49), distancing from what Badiou identifies as the principle of interest. The fidelious subject has the unique capacity to escape the dominance of "animal" (that is, ordinarily human) priorities and repurpose her capacity for interest toward her ethical goal (49–50; more on this below). This shift away from self-interest is visible in Alsu's ability to renounce a source of gratification and recognition, a potential career, in the name of her commitment to a truth.

All halalists are faced with the challenge of the principle of interest: It might be a lucrative but Islamically illegitimate business deal, or the pleasures of hedonism, or simply the comfort or normalcy of secular life. The ethical subject's disinterestedness might be "unmeasurable" strictly speaking, yet *askesis* can be appreciated—and comprehended—ethnographically, by looking at the concrete choices that individuals make in their lives. In the process, autonomist theory furnishes us with conceptual equipment that allows us to attune our sensibilities to iḥsān and ikhlāṣ without replicating these categories of Islamic theology.

One point must be clarified: While I use the concept of *askesis*, this term is not to be understood as mere renunciation in an exclusively negative sense as limiting limitation (which, incidentally, Badiou does not endorse—nor, indeed, does Islamic theology, which warns against extreme asceticism and self-mortification[13]). What the pursuit of a truth implies is the avoidance of what interferes with said verity: Thus, a cubist will renounce classical mannerism (however popular), a loving monogamist will renounce occasional flings (however alluring), and a conscientious activist will renounce backroom deals (however expedient). A fidelious subject redirects her interest toward her ethical goal; hence, cutting back on situational interests is not experienced as a sacrifice—to the contrary, her engagement with a truth guarantees "unequalled intensities of existence" (Badiou 2002, 53). As Niyazetdin-mulla put it, faith means "to remove from the path any obstacle, anything that hinders the traveller" (Äl-Xänäfi 2009, 17). Halal living may involve the renunciation of haram things and practices, but this is lived as an enabling limitation, unlocking the kind of existential intensity that we have encountered in Ayub's word and that makes choices like Alsu's worth their while.

A Secular Plenitude

Where does this leave us with respect to the other facet of Tatar Islam, "ethnic Muslimness"? We have seen that ethnic Muslims' Islam is cherished as an essence, the inalienable property of a discrete group. Islam-as-essence is experientially different from Islam-as-fidelity, though the two realms might be connected and overlapping. Islam-as-essence points in the direction of an imagined plenitude that as such, from a Badiousian viewpoint, stands at variance with an ethics of truth. Any idea of essence, based on the "absolute particularity of a community" rooted in soil, blood, ethnicity, or custom, is inescapably situational and "works directly against truths" (Badiou 2002, 72–73, 76). The French philosopher warned that when the particularist moralities of plenitude become mixed up with the militantism of an ethics of truth—or its "simulacrum"—unpleasant things can happen: This is the genesis of supremacisms and nationalisms of various stripes.

This may not directly apply to the colonial setting of Russia's inner borderlands. As a left-leaning Tatar cultural activist told me, Tatar nationalism belongs to the family of "nationalisms of the oppressed": While some may dream of one kind or another of ethnic plenitude, for the most part Tatar ethnic campaigners frame sovereignty in self-defensive terms. A Badiousian return to this compelling argument may be that, nonetheless, when a universal truth-process becomes ancillary to a particularity, a fundamental shift may take place, and the ethical drive of the endeavor risks losing intensity—which, perhaps, resonates with the decline of Tatar nationalism under Putin's tenure and the co-optation of what is left of the post-Soviet ethnolocalist impulse under the state's plenitudinous Eurasian supremacism.

Be that as it may, their qualitative difference does not rule out that an ethics of truth and a particularist morality of community can be related, even intertwined. Badiou would not deny the *fil rouge* linking, say, the anarchist movement in 1968 France and the activities of a local trade union in the same context. However, he may argue that their respective relationships with the truth of social revolution are different, in the former case articulating a universalist truth-process, in the latter cohering around the interests of a particular subset of people (Badiou 2009). Moving back to the roots of this book's genealogical tree, Søren Kierkegaard made a similar argument nearly two centuries ago when he highlighted the ambivalent relationship of sameness and difference between the passionate, subversive, intense Christianity of a restless minority and the placid, tame "Christendom" embraced by swathes of respectable burghers ([1946] 2016, 193–256, 436–468). An analogous ambivalence can perhaps be seen as linking and separating halalists' and ethnic Muslims' approaches to Islam, with the caveat that accepting a distinction between Islam-as-fidelity and Islam-as-essence is not tantamount to alleging that Islam lived as a shared essence is in any way "less moral": To the contrary, such an essence appears germane to the kind of everyday morality of "proximity" (Henig 2020) that anthropologists have recognized in rural Muslim communities across Eurasia. Nor does it diminish the richness of ethnic Muslims' spiritual lives: As we shall see in chapter 4, these lives abound with historically layered identities, interpersonal solidarities, and existential quests. Accepting this distinction simply affords us an advantageous vantage point to contemplate the tensions between two groups that stake competing claims to Islam.

One way to look at this tension is, once more, through the Badiousian prism of interest, as Islam-as-essence does not require or invite a conduct that runs counter to a person's immediate lifestyle benefits. As we have begun to see in the previous section, the term "interest" in this context does not necessarily mean personal gain or advantage over others but, more broadly, the set of entitlements that people have come to be vested with—and take for granted—under Russia's postatheist secularity, which has made the ethical-jural demands of Islam non-binding, indeed even irrelevant, to many Tatars. This entitles people to a broad set of lifestyle options, from cheaper groceries at regular (non-halal) supermarkets to a daily schedule free from the demands of prayer, from more flexible opportunities to socialize (drinks, clubs, etc.) to not having to worry about anti-extremism legislation. It is chiefly in this sense that ethnic Muslims enjoy the benefits of Russia's secular plenitude.

In this model, engagement with Islam, where still present, may work by addition rather than subtraction (enabling limitation or *askesis*). One of my ethnic-Muslim sources, a socially active woman named Gulnara (roughly in the same age cohort as former actress Alsu), explained to me what it meant for her to be a "believer": She told me that, even though she does not pray five times a day and does not observe halal norms, she often utters the invocation *bismillah*, endeavors to be generous and kind to others, and respects her ancestral faith. Borrowing from Ulf Hannerz's model (1992, 247), one could argue that Gulnara's ideal of Muslimness is construed as a "secularity plus" mechanism: a secular lifestyle plus *bismillah*, a secular lifestyle plus "shared essence," a secular lifestyle plus faith in her heart, a secular lifestyle plus kindness to others, and so forth. However important these additions might be to Gulnara—and they are—they do not add up to a fidelity comparable to that of Alsu, whose halal mindfulness overrides other interests such as the comforts and opportunities of the secular plenitude. Even the devotional practices we shall explore in chapter 4 are, in a "secularity plus" paradigm, "at best incidental to a good, or pious, or virtuous, or enlightened life" (Laidlaw 2007). Of course, other intense ethical commitments are possible, for Alsu as for any other ethnic Muslim. But the organizing principles that orient everyday conduct differ from those of halalists in ways that social analysis can, if not measure, at least appreciate.

Ritual (and) Commitment

Having discussed the tensions between an ethics of Islamic truth and the secular plenitude that underlies Islam-as-essence, let us delve a bit deeper into the topic of ritual, aided by anthropologist Roy Rappaport's influential theory (1999). Let us begin by considering these snapshots:

Dialogue one—Akmaş, publishing company office

EMPLOYEE: Foat, sir [*äfände*], that Ramil fellow gave me a call this morning. He offered to find new distributors in Moscow for us. Do you reckon we can trust him?

FOAT-ÄFÄNDE: Uhm, I know him. He's a prayerful lad [*namaz ukığan malay*].

EMPLOYEE: Ah, all right then. I'll get in touch with him after lunch.

Dialogue two—Kazan, at home

ME: I need to get a hold of that guy, Timur, for an interview. He seems to be everywhere.

FRIEND: You should. He is really active in town; last month he organized a Tatar hip-hop contest.

ME: I know, he's a legend. But . . . what sort of person is he, anyway?

FRIEND: Yeah, he's all right. Does namaz [*namaz ukıy*]. Just give him a call, don't worry.

Dialogue three—Kazan, café

GIRL 1: I heard you went on a date with Rustem, uh?

GIRL 2: Yes, he's very nice, but . . .

GIRL 1: But what? He's a serious person, nice-looking, with a good job and all . . .

GIRL 2: I know, I know, but he prays [*on na namaze*]. It never works between practicing and nonpracticing [Muslims], right? We're just too different.

The centrality of daily prayer emerges as a recurrent theme, and indeed, we have seen that prayer is a central concern to the halal milieu, alongside sincerity, with which it is deeply intertwined. Expressions such as *namaz ukuğan keşe* / *chitay-ushchy* (a person who prays [regularly]) or *namazda* / *na namaze* (on [constant] namaz) are used to make statements about one's relationship with Islam and hence one's position in the ethical, social, and existential worlds. As the owner of a halal café in the city of Idelsk explained to me, "In our community, many maintain that meat produced by [ethnic] Muslims who don't pray [*ne chitayut namaz*] cannot be halal. These brothers think that those who don't pray are not Muslims at all. So, my business partner and I have decided to play it safe. In the Idelsk environs, we know only one farmer who prays regularly. Only one person . . . so it happens sometimes that we do not have enough poultry or enough beef." In the illiberal and only selectively tolerant context of Tatarstan under Putin, practicing Muslims in business or prominent administrative positions may adopt a religiously neutral/secular public image. In such situations, one may discreetly code-signal one's prayer habits to those who can decipher the message, to the exclusion of others. For example, a cadre or business leader may strategically place a folded prayer rug (_namazlık_) in a visible spot of his office. While untrained eyes are likely to overlook a piece of cloth casually hung on a seatback, fellow _chitayush-chye_ may pick up on the clue.

Ritual is experienced differently among nonpious Muslims. As a rule, people in this group turn to Islam's ceremonial repertoire on three types of ceremonial occasions: life-cycle events such as weddings, circumcisions, and funerals; eth-nonational festivals; and, for spiritually inclined nonpietists, vernacular devotions. Life-cycle rituals are considered "basic Muslim rites" (Bekkin 2020a, 276) that even nonspiritual or religiously indifferent ethnic Muslims regularly turn to (recall the joke about "funerary-commemorative Muslims"). Take for instance Aynaz, one of my ethnic-Muslim acquaintances. Thoroughly irreligious, Aynaz is a candid Islamophobe who holds piety in contempt (as he once told me, "I'm a Muslim who hates Muslims: Funny, isn't it?"), yet his positions did not prevent him from marrying (multiple times) in a mosque with full nikāh ritual, proudly wearing his embroidered skullcap. Another acquaintance, an elderly ethnic-Muslim woman, recounted how she convinced her ill husband, on his deathbed, to undergo an Islamic funeral despite his being a convinced atheist, on the grounds that that was "the way of our ancestors." Life-cycle rituals add a public, visible, stipulative dimension to the concept of Islam-as-essence: Without a chance to ritually manifest one's ancestral Muslimness, one would be indistinguishable from a _mankurt_.

As regards national festivals, the main example is the Holy Bolğar Gathering (_Izge Bolğar Cıenı_), a national day of celebration that takes place every year to commemorate the official adoption of Islam by Volga Bulgaria's rulers in 922. Attending the gathering is seen as de rigueur for a "good Tatar" and a great way to celebrate the start of summer. While collective namaz and the "prayer of repentance" feature prominently, the festival's main elements are public speeches by authorities (both religious and temporal), "cultural programs" featuring folk performances and concerts, and convivial moments in an effervescent atmosphere. The gathering has attracted criticism from some rigorist Sunnis who consider it unscriptural (Abu Ibrakhim Tatarstani [2012?]; Urazmanova et al. 2014, 139–141). At the time of my research, however, some scripturalist leaders had agreed to participate on the condition that the gathering be framed not as a religious event but as a mere celebration of Tatar religious heritage. While both pietists and ethnic Muslims converge at the Holy Bolğar Gathering to proclaim their allegiance to the region's ancestral Islamic legacies, I observed that namaz generates a split between those who perform the prayer and those who, as the sequence unfolds, stand aside in small groups or disperse among the crescent-topped ruins and Islamic souvenir shops.

Vernacular devotions are discussed in chapter 4. For now, let us ask, How are we to interpret the discrepancy between an approach to Islamic ritual practice based on namaz and one oriented to life-cycle rituals and national celebrations? In his monumental study of ritual, Roy Rappaport recognized that, within a society, rituals build onto one another within hierarchically organized liturgical orders featuring foundational and contingent rites (1999, 270–279). Contingent rituals are predicated on foundational ones: For instance, being knighted is predicated on the monarch's coronation, while the coronation is in turn predicated on the Sunday service, where the existence of the God in whose name the monarch rules is celebrated. This notion brings into focus an aspect of Austin's theory of performativity that the British philosopher had left underexplored: the fact that a ritual utterance's felicitousness is not validated solely by correct execution in the moment or along a sequence ("horizontally") but also by correct position within a more complex, "vertical" ceremonial hierarchy. For example, a Catholic wedding would not be valid without the prior ordainment of the officiant, nor, of course, without the foundational ritual of the mass. What makes foundational rites foundational, then? According to Rappaport, foundational rites index a commitment to what he calls the "ultimate postulates" undergirding a cosmological, philosophical, and/or moral order (Rappaport 1999, 27; see Bowen 2012, 50–58; Benussi and Manzon 2023). Returning to the Catholic wedding, a young couple cannot be ritually wedded in the name of a deity if the existence and might of the deity have not been ceremonially accepted by the parties involved through the mass. Put in Badiousian terms, a foundational rite expresses, ceremonially, one's commitment to a verity in the form of an (implicit or explicit) enunciation of postulates that encapsulate that truth.

In scriptural Islam, the foundational ritual is daily prayer, namaz (see Clarke 2013, 211–212), and the truth-postulate is the shahada, Islam's First Pillar and central creed, uttered multiple times during the worship routine: "There is no God but God, and Muhammad is His prophet." We are nearing full circle: The word "shahada" means to bear witness, and that is done both ritually and through conduct. Fidelity to Islam-as-truth is simultaneously indexed by *askesis* (halal living) and worship (namaz), with the two reinforcing each other. Prayer becomes part of everyday ethical routines, innervating daily *askesis* with moments of reflection and communication with the Divine, while halal mindfulness infuses prayer with meaning and, quite literally, reinforces its validity: According to hadith, the prayers of one who breaks halal will not be accepted for forty days, despite remaining obligatory. Let us dwell for a moment on the fact that ritual formalizes one's commitment publicly (Rappaport 1999, 120–124). In Islam, though worshipping in congregation is encouraged, namaz can be and often is performed in solitude. However, as we have seen, a fidelious pietist versed in iḥsān is never really alone, for she knows that God is always "closer than one's own jugular vein" (Quran 50:16), and that is the audience that counts the most.

From the halal milieu's viewpoint, based on Islamic theological reasoning, life-cycle rituals and collective ceremonies are contingent on namaz: Weddings, funerals, commemorative banquets, and festivals like the Holy Bolğar Gathering are liturgically meaningful inasmuch as one's commitment to the foundational order is demonstrated through namaz and pious conduct. In the case of ethnic Muslims, by contrast, it appears that life-cycle rituals assume a foundational character of their own, as they have come to index one's allegiance to the Tatars' "shared essence" and the kinship ties that connect Tatars to their illustrious and demanding ancestors. An emphasis on blood and community risks, in the eyes of pietists, subordinating Islam's universal truth to the plenitude of a particular Muslim ethnos, contradicting the faith's universalism and disturbing its liturgical order. This also applies to ceremonies such as the Holy Bolğar Gathering, an event that is entirely dedicated to celebrating, invoking, and making a commitment to a worldly plenitude—the Tatar nation with its illustrious Islamicate history—while subordinating prayer into a position that many see as ancillary. While Muslim pietists, too, enjoy celebrating Tatar resilience in light of a long history of oppression, many are wary of this ceremony's simulacral potential. The ultimate sacred postulate on which the ethnic-Muslim ritual system rests appears to be the very statement that Niyaezetdin-mulla's pamphlet endeavors to refute: "We are Muslims, because we are Tatars."

Naturally, Islam occupies a central part of the Tatar ethnic plenitude. It is often through an engagement with and assessment of Islam-as-essence that many people gain their first exposure to Islam-as-truth. Life-cycle rituality and communal liturgy may and do act as gateways to namaz and virtuous conduct—as Alsu's life story exemplifies, and as the pietist leaders who endorse the gathering recognize. But the existence of fundamental, unresolved opacities about Islam's liturgical order and ultimate sacred postulates will likely keep feeding a troubled relationship between Povolzhye's halal milieu and its ethnic-Muslim neighbors for the foreseeable future. How are these tensions negotiated, justified, amplified, or softened through theological and moral discourses? How do pietists relate to those who, in Sheikh Abdulmalik's words, "not only ignore how to worship properly, but neglect their obligations towards their Creator altogether"?

(In)felicitously Muslim? Rereading Austin in Akmaş

As we near the conclusion of this chapter, let us return to the marital desertion scandal mentioned at the beginning. Long ago, the philosopher J. L. Austin compellingly observed that performative utterances—such as a wedding rite—are felicitous to the extent that they are accompanied by a series of conditions (authorizing actions or procedures) preceding or accompanying the ceremony itself (1962, 8, 14–18; see Bowen 2012: 50–51). Austin's theory can help us frame the failure (at least in the eyes of some of the parties involved) of the wedding ritual, but this argument must be expanded and adjusted to account for the significance of ethical consistency, or the lack thereof, to determine the felicity of an Islamic marriage ceremony—and, even more consequentially, the felicity of Islam's foundational ritual, the utterance of the shahada.

Austin identified several cases in which an utterance or ceremony fails: when it is performed inappropriately (e.g., in an unsuitable context, under unsuitable circumstances, with an unsuitable command of conventions and implication—for example, without people's understanding that they are participating in a wedding, or with the understanding that it is a mock wedding), when it is performed incorrectly (e.g., the wrong formulas and ritual sequences are carried out, thereby invalidating the ritual), or when it is performed fraudulently (e.g., the wedding is performed by imposters or officiated without the authority to do so). Austin described those misfires as, respectively, misinvocation, misexecution, and insincerity. However, Austin admitted his inability to find a name for a fourth case, that in which felicitousness is voided by the utterer's inconsistent conduct.

It can be argued that Austin's focus on the formal, procedural aspects of performative/illocutionary acts, and especially religious ritual, prevented him from including ethical intensity in the picture as one of the authorizing parameters. Even though he was aware of the importance of commitment (1962, 137) and occasionally used the concept of disloyalty, with the related implications of diachronic consistency (Falkenberg 1988), Austin's vantage point as a logician of everyday language did not afford him a great deal of insight into the domain of pious conduct, which arguably weakened his grasp of the pragmatics of conviction, or the lack thereof (Lambek 2007, 69–73). Having engaged with Badiou's terminology, we are now in a position to expand Austin's original argument by identifying and naming a fourth type of illocutionary infelicity—caused by inconsistent conduct—as *infidelity*.

The media reports about the scandal might have been sensationalistic, but they captured an Austinian tension that exists at the intersection of the two faces of Povolzye's Islam. One's Islamic wedding might be correctly executed by a legitimate imam, with all the parties involved "sincerely" voicing their belief in God. But without a disinterested, steadfast fidelity that manifests in halal-conscious conduct post factum, a spouse would still risk falling short of the high standards of fidelious subjectivity that make one eligible for a felicitous Islam wedding—at least from the point of view of rigorist pietists.

From the point of view of the halal milieu, infidelities can engender an array of possible responses. Excommunication (takfir), the formal charge of disbelief, is an extreme position hardly contemplated outside a rigorist minority, but it can be intellectually justifiable. The Salafi school, drawing on Hanbali jurisprudence and Athari theology, holds that faith resides not only in one's hearth and tongue but also in one's body. Infidelities thus directly affect one's Muslimness, potentially rendering it null and void. However, while some people in the most "autarkist" segment of the pious milieu may occasionally refer to pork-eating, namaz-shunning ethnic Muslims as "disbelievers," this is rarely taken to its extreme consequences— the marital desertion incident being an infrequent exception. Excommunication not only would imperil relationships with secular co-ethnics but also may lead to spiritual counterblows in the afterlife. It is not coincidental that Niyazetdin-mulla's strong-worded pamphlet, despite evoking the "evil of disbelief," uses the epithet "disbelievers" in a direct way only with regard to the Orthodox Russians, sparing lapsed Tatars.

A less risky position likens infidelity to jāhiliyyah: a condition of "ignorance," lack of knowledge or understanding of God's commands. As one interlocutor explained, "There is no such thing as non-practicing Muslims. One either is a Muslim or is not. So-called ethnic Muslims are simple jāhili [ignorant people]." In Islamic traditions, the term "jāhiliyyah" is used with regard to Arab tribes before Quranic revelation (609–632 CE). Within certain schools of thought, though, this category can be stretched to cover virtually all locations and eras in which people are unaware of Islam's religious truths, including "nominal" Muslims who live removed from sharia. As one acquaintance told me, "Any jāhili is a potential Muslim." Within this missionary view, ethnic Muslims are recognized as potential truth-bearers who need to be reminded of the divine message. The word "jāhili" carries a less ominous sense than the word "disbeliever," but, due to its negative connotations,[14] it is rarely employed directly. In my experience, people tended to use it in a self-reflexive manner, to describe their own former secular selves before conversion.

At the most diplomatic end of the spectrum, ecumenist Muslims champion an accommodating, come-as-you-are approach. They justify this religious inclusivity by appealing to Hanafi-Maturidi theology, which, in this interpretation, states that faith lies in the believer's heart and finds expression in speech but is not necessarily reflected in one's actions. This makes anyone who professes themselves a Muslim a member of the ummah, regardless of their deeds. In addition, Maturidi scholars maintain that faith in one's heart does not increase or decrease according to the righteousness or sinfulness of one's conduct, and judgment about one's behavior lies in the hands of God alone and will take place in the afterlife. In the meantime, Muslims do not have a right to banish anyone from the ummah, however sinful, as long as they claim to be Muslims. One of my ecumenist sources, a cadre in the Islamic officialdom, explained this though a civic metaphor: "Once you utter the profession of faith, it's done—you get your passport for the ummah, you are a citizen of the ummah with all the advantages of this status, as well as the obligations before God the Most High. You cannot be expelled. Now, whether you are a patriot, or you aren't—this isn't important. This is a personal problem between yourself and God. People's inner world [*vnutrenny mir*] is known by God alone, and He will establish who is a true believer [*iskrenny*] and who is not. What I mean is that Maturidism made excommunication impossible." In a similar vein, a programmatic document by the Tatarstani Islamic officialdom states that "practicing Muslims must acknowledge that non-practicing Muslims are Muslim as well, and they have a right—even more so, an obligation—to feel part of the ummah" (Mukhamedov 2011). But even this position, however ecumenical, does not consider Muslimness a birth-given essence, as it still requires a minimum of commitment—the utterance of the oath of faith. Lacking that, even the most welcoming ecumenist might give up.

To quote Roy Rappaport's elaboration on Austin's theory of speech acts, we may say that Maturidis consider the Islamic profession of faith "factive"—that is, unconditionally felicitous and thus capable of permanently changing the existential and social status of the novice. Hanbali-Atharis, by contrast, appear to consider the shahada "commissive"—that is, conditionally felicitous, an utterance geared to "bring[ing] into being the commitment of those performing [it] to [act upon it] in the future" (Rappaport 1999, 115; see Hirschkind 2001, 640; cf. Ahmed 2016, 137–140). Infidelities are especially consequential in a commissive mode: Muslims who renege on their commitment risk retrospectively invalidating their initiation into the faith. Even a shahada uttered in a factive mode, however, would not shield an unrighteous Muslim from charges of sinfulness, hypocrisy, or ignorance. For ecumenists, infidelities are not irrelevant: According to Maturidi theology, wrongful conduct may not lead to excommunication but could still condemn the sinner to hellfire. Therefore, pietists have a missionary duty to encourage ethnic Muslims to remember their obligations—becoming "patriots" of the ummah—to felicitously reach their potential as full-fledged Muslims.

Remaking the Situation

In the summer of 2015, I was doing fieldwork in Akmaş during the holy month of Ramadan and the Feast of Breaking the Fast (*Uraza Bäyräm*), which marks its end. Islamic norms make it incumbent on every able Muslim to give alms on that day. This compulsory charity is called <u>sadaqah al-fitr</u> and is customarily directed toward fellow Muslims in financial need.[15] I had the opportunity to witness the process of <u>sadaqah</u> collection in the mosque community and observe the deliberation process that determines to whom the significant amount of money collected by the mosque was to be bestowed. Before Ramadan, a cluster of Tatar villages in the vicinity of Akmaş had been stricken by a violent storm that flooded fields, killed livestock, and damaged buildings. One village in particular, Syerly, had borne the brunt of the tempest, resulting in several houses' roofs being ruined. Some of Akmaş's alms-collectors proposed to allocate <u>sadaqah al-fitr</u> to this community in need. But a handful rigorist-minded committee members stalled the proposal: The Syerly populace was not known for its religiosity—to the contrary, this rural, working-class community was mostly composed of ethnic Muslims, negligent in performing namaz and inclined to dilute the hardship of toilsome lives in alcohol. Doubts were raised, questioning the theological soundness of donating to people whose Muslimness could not be vouched for. Some feared that, if <u>sadaqah al-fitr</u> were to be allocated to this community, criticism would follow to the effect that resources were squandered while more deserving (i.e., observant) people were also in need of support. After lengthy considerations, however, the committee unanimously decided to donate <u>sadaqah al-fitr</u> to the stricken village.

This decision was based on a series of considerations. Failing to help Syerly would leave the mosque open to criticism and possible charges of extremism by outsiders; conversely, a generous gesture would convey the image of an ecumenical, inclusive community. More importantly, the committee agreed that even though Syerly inhabitants by and large could not be described as "good" Muslims, they still "considered themselves Muslims" (*schitayut sebya musul'manami*), they mastered notions of the oneness of God and the prophethood of Muhammad, and their local customs (*ğoref-ğadätlär*) carried Islamic echoes. Giving alms to this village could be seen as a way of doing <u>da'wah</u>—that is, sharing the truth of Islam with a community as much in need of spiritual enlightenment as of material aid. In this light, the decision to donate alms to the not-quite-pious Syerly populace became a form of missionary action, based on the idea that ethnic Muslims live in a state of ignorance and represent, as such, potential Muslims.

This episode indicates two things. First, despite their being described as "world apart," the chasm between pietists and ethnic Muslims is not unbridgeable. The uncertain status of ethnic Muslims in the eyes of their observant neighbors generates both otherness and commonness. Solidarities can be formed on the grounds of shared histories, identities, and destinies as well as in the name of a simple "morality of proximity," the principle of helping your neighbor when needs arise. Second, the halal milieu as an ethical form-of-life is not removed from its sociohistorical context; it is in its context, by engaging with it, that it upholds its ethics of truth. Commitment to Islam's Rule, even "secession" from the forcefield of Law, does not mean detachment from the situation but rather its reorganization under fresh premises. The halal milieus' situation includes the legacies of seven decades of antireligious campaigns, the aggressive manipulation of religion by the Putin regime, the dominance of essentialist understandings of religious identity, and the demographic prevalence of ethnic Muslims, but, also, a widespread curiosity for more ambitious forms of engagement with the faith. Within this situation, reaching out to nonpietists might unlock latent potentialities, perhaps—the mosque community hoped—enabling a further expansion of Islamic forms-of-life. "The good" for halalists amounts to any modus operandi that may forward their verity (Badiou 2002, 60).

Thus, Muslimness in Povolzhye is not just a point of contention but also an arena for pragmatic situational work, fidelious diplomacy, and fraught yet promising encounters. This shifting terrain is one of the most important fronts on which pietists must "keep going." A tension between pietists and nonpracticing Tatars is inbuilt in the situation. Pietists cannot undo this, but they can reorganize the situation by bringing their disruptive truth to bear on it.

(NOT QUITE) MANAGING MUSLIM MORALITIES
Pietists, Muftiates, and the State

During Vladimir Putin's tenure, Islam consolidated its official role as one of Russia's four legally recognized "traditional" (*traditsionnye*) heritage faiths, along with Orthodoxy, Judaism, and Buddhism.[1] On September 23, 2015, the "largest mosque in Europe" opened in Moscow with great fanfare under the auspices of Putin—a move saluted with enthusiasm by Muslims in Povolzhye and all across Russia. A few months later, in April 2016, the very same people who had rejoiced shuddered in fear as the government passed a draconian antimissionary bill, the so-called Yarovaya Package (of amendments). This legislative measure targeted grassroots religious groups and preachers and sought the regimentation of religious communities under the purview of state structures (Bekkin 2020, 58, 223–230). In this volume's terminology, the Yarovaya Package might be called an "anti-forms-of-life bill."[2] This development shrouded in law is a policy of repression of independent religious voices that had long been applied to Muslims.

The opening of the Moscow Cathedral Mosque and the Yarovaya Package highlight the contradictory relationship with the state that characterizes the political life of Russia's Muslim community. Contradictory is not the same as schizophrenic: In fact, this contradictoriness is revelatory of what has been called Russia's "managed" pluralism (Gvosdev 2001/2002; Warhola 2007). As discussed in chapter 1, Law may have an openly repressive dimension, here manifested in the surveillance and policing of Muslims, as well as a "pastoral" side, embodied in what might be called the state's themitical apparatuses. Russia's current regime, bent on engineering a cohesive moral hegemony in line with the state's ideological stance policies, has met a perceived ethical-biopolitical threat in the halal milieu.

While the post-Soviet moment presents unique challenges, the state's posture is consistent with a governmental style dating back to Soviet and tsarist times (Poe 2003), according to which spontaneous ethical phenomena must be considered dangerous if left undealt with—that is, not repressed or co-opted.

For its part, the halal milieu is constitutively prone to outrageousness, in the etymological sense of "outrage" as a "going beyond" (Latin: *ultra*) the pale of the accepted and the familiar. As Kierkegaard noted, ethical intensity is often "offensive" to "bourgeois intellect, aesthetic nature, herd instinct, [and] prudential common-sense" (Bretall [1946] 2016, 373). During my ethnography, several pious participants admitted that the habits of toughness and uncompromisingness of the halal milieu's "old guard," forged in the violent 1990s, have led to impolitic choices. Bold statements of religious superiority such as the notion that only the path (dīn) of the Quran and Sunna can lead to salvation, not uncommon within some segments of the milieu, cause shock in the Soviet-educated, religiously pluralist secular majority (Minnullin 2014; Sagitova 2014, 476). As James Faubion noted, ascetical movements' transgressions of the themitical order are "very likely to provoke the good member of society's rage and disgust" (2011, 260, see 2001). Such feelings are indeed often hurled at pietists in Tatarstan, as exemplified by the words of my acquaintance Ilshat, a Kazan-based ethnic-Muslim shop owner: "I hate them. They behave aggressively. They are fanatics. Plus, they even dress stupidly. Women hide their faces—which are unsightly anyway, just look at them!—and get the rims [of their long dresses] soaked with mud. Look, I even tried to hire a [practicing Muslim] once, and the slacker kept skirting his duties to go pray or something. And seriously, what is that nonsense about a right way to wipe your arse?"

Needless to say, incidents like the Wahhabi wedding woe discussed in the previous chapter, amplified by Islamophobic media campaigns, do not help assuage the fears of secular citizens. Less publicized conflicts happen also at the micro level. During my fieldwork, the household of some friends found itself divided over "proper" Islamic burial practice. This led to bitter, heartrending fights between the mother, Fauziya-apa, an ethnic Muslim and follower of "local folkways," and daughter Gulnaz, a pietist committed to scriptural exactitude, during the father's funeral. Instances like this show that the "disorganizing" potential of form-of-life emerges at all levels and can be perceived as profoundly disruptive by pietists and nonpietists alike. At the aggregate level, these tensions are simultaneously tapped into, exploited, and tamed by the Russian media structures. However, it must be emphasized that societal feelings of mistrust are not directed only against Islamic pietism: A survey from the early 2000s indicates that the general Russian public was even more likely to dislike Adventists, Baptists, and Jehovah's Witnesses than homegrown Muslims (here, including secular ethnic Muslims),

again suggesting a heightened sensitivity around religious forms-of-life characterized by ascetical intensity and cosmopolitanism (Warhola 2007, 84–85).

In this scenario, the Russian state initiated a sophisticated, multipronged biopolitical maneuver aimed at curbing and regimenting the intensity of Islamic
piety milieus while preserving Islam within the public morality campaigns—or
"religious political technologies"—directed at its Muslim ethnic populations
(Kemper 2019). While of course the idea of "domesticating" Islam is anything
but unique to Russia (Sunier 2012), the Russian case is quite singular compared
to other non-Muslim-majority countries considering the presence of indigenous
Islamic legacies, strategically utilized by the state in pursuit of its strategies,
and of a centuries-long experience of governmentalization of Muslims through
state-loyal apparatuses. This chapter discusses the entanglements of temporal
institutions and Islam in Russia by exploring the effects of repression (bans and
blacklisting), desecularization (the top-down management of religion), institu-
tionalization (the themitical apparatuses of Muftiates), and discursive regimentation (the elusive but omnipresent vision of "Russian traditional Islam").

Quietism and Biopolitical Irreducibility

One of the striking characteristics of the Kremlin's attitude toward Muslims
is its inability or unwillingness to distinguish between Islamist threats and
quietist Islamic milieus (Dannreuther 2010; see Bayat 1996, 2013; Hoesterey
2016; Montgomery and Heathershaw 2016). Povolzhye's halalists place greater
emphasis on individual religiosity and subjective conduct than on public cam-
paigning or militancy. At the time of my research, even the most theologically
uncompromising segments of the halal milieu sought to stay away from parti-
sanship and avoid trouble with temporal institutions. For example, insurance
is frowned upon under Salafi jurisprudence in light of the Islamic prohibition
of interest/credit, gambling, and mistrusting God in planning one's future.
However, the Saudi-educated Abdulmalik, leader of the "autarkist" circle in
Akmaş's mosque community, explained to his congregation that although
Muslims must be mindful of such prohibitions, they are nonetheless obligated
to insure their possessions whenever doing so is a legal requirement, such as
if they own a vehicle. Abdulmalik explained that individuals will not be held
accountable for a sharia violation forced on them by third parties. Second, and
no less importantly, violating the state's legislative order may sinfully provoke
fitnah, "strife, unrest," which constitutes a more serious religious offense than
insuring one's car, for it risks disrupting Muslims' quiet, meticulous, steadfast
pursuit of virtue.

Despite keeping to themselves and avoiding trouble, quietist Muslims in Russia at the time of my research were often cast as dangerous "extremists," "Wahhabis," or "fifth columns" in the press and, even more disquietingly, by some experts on Islamic matters (Alexeev and Ragozina 2017, 93; Ragozina 2018; Kravchenko 2018; Shterin and Dubrovsky 2019). This oppressive atmosphere is not an invention of the Putin regime: The Russian state has long tended to produce public discourses on Islam and Muslims that misrepresent them as inherently dangerous. In the late imperial period, for instance, unfounded but rampant paranoia over "pan-Turkism" and "fanaticism" in the Volga region caused waves upon waves of heavy-handed repression (J. Meyer 2014; Campbell 2015; Tuna 2016). In post-Soviet Russia too, harmless individuals are at risk of intrusive surveillance, suspicion, and harassment. Consider, by way of example, the testimony of Fatima-abıstay, a spirited, elderly Tatar woman, cherished by halalists for championing pietist women's rights in the post-Soviet era. Teacher Fatima is credited with obtaining, after years of patient, quiet, but stubborn negotiation with local and federal authorities, a right for Muslim women to appear headscarved in Russian ID photographs: "We wanted to appear veiled [*yaulık belän*] on official documents. That was in the late 1990s and early 2000s, and it was really hard at first. There were about thirty of us. Only the bravest women were there—state organs would scare us; they'd say we were crossing a red line. Some of us got fired from our workplaces. People would tell us [in Russian], 'You are destroying Russia [*Rossiyu vy unichtozhayte*]! You are breaking Russia up [*Rossiyu vy narushayte*]!' They were afraid of us." The veil stirs controversy in Western counties as well (Bowen 2008; Bracke and Fadil 2012; Fadil 2011). But while in Western Europe veiling-related anxieties are inseparable from issues of migration and xenophobic fears of "invasion," women's veiling in Povolzhye elicits anxieties related to Russia's ancestral body politic. Fatima-abıstay and her quietist companions—respectable, Soviet-bred women, with a stable position in society—sparked outrage because, by making their faith visible through their bodies rather than keeping it "in the depths of their hearts," they violated a national pact, their fidelity being interpreted as a threat to the moral organism of Russia.

Antipietist feelings do not spare the upper echelons: One respondent told me that Tatarstani civil officers who happen to live piously sometimes must stay in the closet, hiding their religious commitment from bosses and other associates or downplaying it to the extent that they can. Sovereign harassment can reach unbearable levels, as testified by the plight of thousands of escapees from Russia ("new *muhajirs*") who throughout the 2000s sought refuge in Turkey after experiencing persecution at home (Sal'vadore 2014; BBC 2015; Nefliasheva 2018).

How are we to frame the Russian state's attitude toward quietist Muslims (which is harsher but not incomparable with that of liberal democracies)? I submit that it is not sufficient to frame the state's enmity toward pious milieus in terms of a stark genealogical incompatibility between post-Enlightenment secularism and (discursively) traditional counterpublics. Although it might successfully illustrate political dynamics in other settings (Asad 2003; Hirschkind 2006; cf. A. Ahmad 2017 for a subtle, insightful critique), such a binary appears less useful in a context such as Putin's ultraconservative/"traditionalist" Russia—whose relationship with the Enlightenment and secularism, contradictory from the beginning (Karpov 2010), has become more and more antagonistic over time. Furthermore, the Putin regime's intolerance for "alternative" forms-of-life is not limited to Islamic ones, extending as it does to other underground milieus, religious and secular alike, on the left (anarchists, liberals, etc.; see Merzlikin 2019) or the right (rogue warlords, disloyal ultranationalists, Christian "sectarians," etc.; see RFE 2020).

An autonomist reading allows us to explore an alternate reading by fore-grounding the inherent biopolitical dimension of ethical intensity—including quietist piety—and reactions thereto. While quietist forms-of-life might not engage with "politics" understood in the limited sense of the situational jockey-ing of partisan interests and identities, the ethical excess that they manifest lies at the heart of "the Political" in the term's vaster meaning (Stavrakakis 1999). They represent something that "surprises" onlookers, throwing the sovereign mecha-nism "out of joint" (Zupančič 2000, 235), exposing the limits of its civil and the-mitical arrangement. By merely existing, pious milieus constitute an unsettling element in the regnant order. Yaacov Ro'i made this argument about Muslim qui-etists during the Soviet era: Despite not actively criticizing the regime or oppos-ing it, "Homo islamicus . . . represent[ed] by his very existence the refutation of uniformity within the system, the failure of the Soviet endeavour to create a new prototype, to change not only the structure of society but also the thought pro-cesses and sentiments of its citizenry" (1984, 41).

To turn Michel Foucault's well-known maxim (1997b, 25; see Butler 2001) on its head, we might claim that "there is something in *virtue* that is akin to *critique*." Intriguingly, Foucault traced his Western genealogy of "arts of voluntary insubor-dination" to medieval Christian pietism's indocility vis-à-vis ecclesiastic authority (1997b, 29–32). Following the same lead, Agamben's work on monasticism (2013a, 110–122) also foregrounds the friction between grassroots Christian milieus and ecclesiastic juridical authorities. These milieus were "quietist" in the sense that they did not try to overtake or deny the juridical authority of the Church of Rome; how-ever, they sought spaces of autonomy—"extraneousness to the law" (122)—and through this process of implicit critique they forced the church to rethink itself. In premodern Islamic contexts, a well-documented pattern existed by which pious men systematically refused to serve as qāḍīs (judges) for rulers and military leaders in light of their unwillingness to subordinate to worldly powers (Bulliet 1994, 59,

122). In a similar vein, before the Russian Revolution, eminent Muslim spiritual leaders in the Volga region would criticize, disavow, or refuse to join the official Islamic state institutions (Bekkin 2020a, 110–115).

These examples suggest that tensions between ethical projects and themitical authorities lie within religious traditions themselves, predating the emergence of secular modernity (Shariati 1979). A critical and emancipatory potential is inherent in ethical intensity, not a mere by-product of religion's marginalization at the hand of the secular state. As the French situationist collective Tiqqun has argued (2010, 2011b; see Weber 1946, 327), "civil war" between ethical projects and sovereign authorities—of which Russia's Muftiates are an instantiation—is inherent in statecraft dynamics. State-making, in Tiqqun's theory, requires the large-scale regimentation of ethical forms-of-life, framed as "sects," fringes, "fifth columns," extremists, and so forth. Twentieth-century totalitarian states have tried, without success in the long run, to achieve a complete eradication of ethical forms-of-life. The political purges and ruthless antireligious policies that took place in the 1930s USSR can be seen as a textbook example of this approach, as to some extent is the Yarovaya Package in its repressive effects vis-à-vis unregistered religious communities. More subtle governmental approaches, such as the desultory attempts at reform by the Russian autocracy under "liberal" rulers in the long nineteenth century (Campbell 2015) and the more sophisticated project of "sovereign/managed democracy" under Putin, operate instead through the attenuation and co-optation of forms-of-life, with the goal of preventing ethical differences from attaining a politically threatening level of intensity. The interplay of attenuated forms-of-life, the expression of normalized difference, may be even encouraged by mature governmental regimes, which "tolerate all transgressions, provided they remain soft" (Tiqqun 2010, 141; see also Marcuse [1964] 1972, 25, 52–53, 57).

This irreducibility translates into a peculiar stickiness when it comes to demanding loyalty of quietist ethicalists. Caroline Humphrey has contended that being loyal

> means responding to a particular call for allegiance and at the same time it implies the activity of forsaking—the cutting out of the alternatives to the object to which loyalty is given, i.e. the cost of relegating other aspects and leanings. . . . The loyal subject is a . . . simplified version of the subject. True, loyalty does not have to be exclusive . . . ; but nevertheless it must involve prioritising: it consists in having a commitment to X *in some agreed respect* at the expense of ties of that same kind to Y and Z. (2017, 499)

In the previous chapter, we explored "fidelity" in the making of pious Muslim subjectivity, and it is easy to see how actors that "see like a state" (Scott 2008) might come to apprehend Islam as a dangerously competitive project, particularly in light of the Putin regime's ambition to corral Russia's populations under a uniform themitical landscape (Caldwell 2011, 2014; see Pryce 2013). Yet the quietist halal milieu, including its "autarkist" sectors most concerned with self-legislation, does not frame piety and Russian citizenship in zero-sum terms as mutually incompatible loyalty projects: While fidelity to Islam is pursued in and through Rule, loyalty to the state is a matter of Law, and pietists are skilled at situationally navigating these two levels, as the abovementioned instance of conforming to citizenship obligations (insuring one's vehicle, paying taxes, etc.) illustrates. From an analytical standpoint, we observe that fidelity to ethical Rule does not eo ipso exclude forms of loyalty to state Law; therefore, we may reconsider the idea that Islam's ethical-juridical tradition and the authority of the modern state necessarily compete for the same conceptual "space" in Muslims' experience (Asad 2003, 251). That said, "seeing like a state" often does imply a binary and exclusive understanding of loyalty, steeped in governmental paranoia. Ethical intensity remains, in Russia as elsewhere, a biopolitical sticky point fraught with consequences.

Pars Destruens: Bans and Disbandments

Let us turn to the governmental tools used by the Kremlin to deal with this stickiness, starting from the "negative" tactics of repression and intimidation. Russia's draconian legislative apparatus on "religious extremism" that culminated with the Yarovaya Package (not considering wartime censorship measures) began developing more than a decade earlier, with the 2002 "anti-extremist" law marking the beginning of the country's authoritarian turn (Aitamurto 2021, 284). By the early 2010s, Moscow had embraced a strategy based on "suppress[ing] fundamental civil rights and liberties through an intentional confusion between extremely dangerous behaviours (such as terrorist attacks) and harmless ones (such as statements of religious superiority)" (Verkhovsky 2010, 35; see Sagramoso and Yarlykapov 2013; Akhmetkarimov 2020; Kovalskaya 2024). State-critical Muslim voices and Islamist organizations, even programmatically nonviolent ones such as Hizb ut-Tahrir, were the first to fall under the state's axe (Aitamurto 2021, 288–289), but the process did not stop there.

Banning religious literature became a preferred technique to police the boundaries of Islamic discourse and, in the process, turn large swathes of pietists into potential felons: "The list of banned Islamic literature burgeoned within a short period [2002–2004], and [as early as 2010] include[d], in addition to leaflets of banned groups, the books of prominent Islamic preachers and theologians"

(Verkhovsky 2010, 35). During my stay in Povolzhye, I often came across Law-abiding pietists anguished by their possession of harmless religious treatises, or even just prayer books, deemed illegal by state apparatuses. This is true even of followers of the twentieth century's Turkish-Kurdish pedagogue Said Nursi, an early post-Islamist scholar whose work specifically elaborated forms of piety compatible with a secular setup. Nursi's book had become popular among sectors of the piety movement through Fethullah Gülen's Hizmet movement in the 1990s. By the mid-2000s, however, all books by Nursi had become "extremist propaganda," and in 2008 Hizmet was formally outlawed—which is noteworthy considering the movement's commitment to moderation, dialogue, and maintaining a low profile in the public arena.

In May 2015, in my capacity as a Kazan State University visiting student, I had a chance to participate in a series of seminars on Russia's "nontraditional"—that is, undesirable—Islamic groups (more on this term below), hosted by the Faculty of Islamic Studies. The seminars were run by a security specialist working for the republic's official Islamic bureaucracy. Our meetings had a matter-of-fact, practical slant, as they were intended as a glimpse into the job of a security analyst (among the most plausible professional paths for academically trained Islam experts in Russia). The seminars' goal was to acquaint students with "extremist" groups. To me, these classes ended up being more informative about the idiosyncrasies of the Russian state in the mid-2010s than about Islamic extremism. Our instructor was sometimes disarmingly candid. In discussing the ban on Said Nursi's work, he noted (I paraphrase),

> Admittedly, Nursi's ideas of Islam would fit our [Russian] secular society well. However, his books still ended up on the list of forbidden literature. I must say that they were banned out of sheer obtusity [*glupost'*]; the peculiar obtusity one can frequently detect among our civil officers [*chinovniki*]. Around 2013, the FSB raided the headquarters of the Gülen Movement in Orenburg . . . shortly afterwards, they banned *all* books they found in the office. Regardless of their authors: If they were there, they must have been evil. Sixty-three books got banned, including classic stuff like [eleventh-century Persian Sufi scholar] al-Ghazali . . . they might just as well have banned the Quran.

Our instructor's admission about *chinovniki*'s stupidity and nescience carries striking echoes of David Graeber's argument about the "direct relation . . . between the level of violence employed in a bureaucratic system, and the level of absurdity and ignorance it is seen to produce" whereby officials and functionaries "can wander about largely oblivious of what is going on around them" (2016, 65, 81). The process of blacklisting itself was, according to our instructor, strikingly intricate. First, a special, Moscow-based federal commission is designated to blacklist "extremist" literature:

> This team of experts includes an Orthodox priest who is also a religious studies specialist [*religoved*], a linguist, and a psychologist. As far as I know, the priest didn't voice any criticism towards Nursi and Gülen's works . . . I'm not so sure about the linguist and the psychologist though; I guess they could find something suspicious in almost any text, if they wanted to.

Apparently, no Muslim representatives had a say in the process. Besides this central "expert board," literature could become "extremist" through a further avenue—namely, the opaque decisions of local courts in any Russian province. Ironically, the paperwork was so intricate that even the bureaucrats might risk losing their way in it:

> One of the banned books, the *Fortress of the Muslim* [ḥiṣn al-muslim] was rehabilitated recently, but not long ago one court in the Russian Far East banned it again. Now [in 2015], if the FSB finds the *Fortress of the Muslim* in any mosque, they can charge mosque community members with extremism. An imam in Ekaterinburg was fined 50,000 Rubles a few months ago. The system is completely unpredictable . . . any local court has the power to ban any book, which in turn affects the whole country. If a Siberian court bans a book, you can be prosecuted for its possession in Kazan. Even if they are just average prayer books.
>
> Another problem we face is that the list of forbidden literature is immense . . . thousands of nonindexed pages; even specialists have a hard time trying to get a handle on it. The list lumps together all forms of extremisms; you could find *Mein Kampf* alongside Jihadi pamphlets and all sorts of other stuff. . . . Moreover, the list changes endlessly. Once it took us [the Islamic officialdom] weeks of work to locate all the Islam-related forbidden books and list them separately. When we were done with it, we found out that by then the original list had been changed once more.

Bans on books represent only one side of the question. The official list of outlawed organizations raises perplexities as well. As part of the debarment of the Gülen network, "the authorities unleashed a campaign of closing all [Hizmet-inspired] Tatar-Turkish lyceums as part of criminal prosecution against Said Nursi's followers—even though the lyceums are not even religious schools" (Verkhovsky 2010, 35). Other groups, while different in their outlook and goals, shared a similar fate. The pacifist, apolitical Islamic renewal network Tablighi Jamaat was disbanded. Salafi literature and groups were of course prohibited, "Wahhabism" being the archvillain in the Russian "anti-extremism" discourse. However, as we have seen in chapter 1, the Salafi milieu was comparably less affected by Kremlin policies, Salafism in Povolzhye being more a do-it-yourself ethical project than a concrete organization that can be located and disbanded.

Antiterrorism prophylactics are the most frequently voiced reason the authorities put forth to justify the ban on faith-inspired groups. As our lecturer explained to us, even though banned organizations are not a threat in themselves—being programmatically nonviolent—they are feared to facilitate their adherents' shifting toward more "extreme" formations. Still, this explanation hardly makes sense vis-à-vis the most moderate or ecumenical groups, such as Tabligh and Gülen's movement. Our lecturer ventured a further, geopolitical reason for the Russian government to ban harmless transnational movements:

> State organs fear that such groups might take root, grow powerful, infiltrate local religious institutions, and eventually carry out the orders of masterminds from abroad. Tablighi Jamaat has its roots in Pakistan. Gülen's movement is originally Turkish, but its leader lives in the US. State organs don't want our Muslims to be under the influence of foreign powers. In fact, the problem is that Turkey and Pakistan are NATO countries.[3] Our intelligence probably thinks that religious activists from these countries might disclose valuable information to Washington. To put it bluntly, state organs fear that the West, through foreign *jamaats*, could meddle in the domestic affairs of Tatarstan, or indeed the whole of Russia.

These words suggest that decision-making sectors in the Russian vertical of power have been unable to abandon the entrenched, paranoid mistrust of "pan-Turkism" that wreaked havoc on Povolzhye Muslims at the turn of the last century (J. Meyer 2014; Ross 2020). As Tatar revolutionary and anticolonial intellectual Mirsaid Sultan-Galiev ruefully observed a hundred years ago, the specters of Tatar fanaticism separatism, pan-Islamism, and other "isms" seem to haunt the chambers of Russia's power, rendering it blind to the actual circumstances of its Muslim citizens (Soltanğaliev 1998, 103, 123, 438, 449). Sultan-Galiev himself was persecuted by the Soviet regime for his unorthodox (by Soviet standards) views on Islam, which he considered a potentially progressive force, and decoloniality (Soltanğaliev 1998, 363–365, 546)—and he was eventually executed in 1940. Although history never repeats itself unchanged, one can detect a sustained dysfunctional pattern at play between the Russian state and its Muslim populations (Kovalskaya 2024, 9). In the early twenty-first century as in earlier phases of Russian politics, the state's gaze misconstrues Muslim pietists' ethical fidelity to a higher-order Sovereign as ideological loyalty—an "ism"—to one or another of the Kremlin's rival worldly rulers. The regime's clampdown on dissent following the war in Ukraine, though not directly aimed at Islam and Muslims, has rendered the political atmosphere in the country even more suffocating, forcing Russian citizens of all faiths to toe the patriotic line, at least in public settings.

Pars Construens: Governmentalizing Russian Islam

Having discussed the "negative," repressive strategies for policing Islam in Russia, let us turn to the "positive," pastoral sovereign interventions aimed at managing Muslim moralities. Since the early 2000s, the Kremlin has been robustly investing in morality as a tool for statecraft. It is not a coincidence that Vladimir Putin's patriotic rhetoric is replete with explicit catch-all moral and spiritual motifs (Sharafutdinova 2014), with the all-Russian values including "belief" in "God," a normative emphasis on the nuclear heterosexual family, respect for organized religion and authority in general, and the promotion of sober lifestyles (Laruelle 2016b, 291). On account of their generic conservatism, these values are expected to harmonize with the expectations and views of Muslim-background citizens and demonstrate that Russia's temporal authority is the best guarantor of Muslims' ethical lives.

While its engagement with Islam might be instrumental, it would be problematic to depict the Russian state as consistently Muslimophobic or indeed even as "secularist"—though its foundations remain largely secular, and Russia has no official state religion. It goes without saying that secularity can take different forms: France, (post-Kemalist) Turkey, (post-Gandhian) India, the United States, or the old USSR, to name but a few examples, represent widely different models (Fernando 2014; Ozyurek 2006; Göle 2015; Bellah [1970] 2010; Luehrmann 2011). Post-Soviet Russia, however, occupies a unique position in this landscape for being a Christian majority, formerly atheist conservative regime endowed with organic, age-old governmental mechanisms for the management of a large native Muslim population (Matsuzato and Sawae 2010; Sibgatullina 2025). These mechanisms include the semiautonomous republics established by the Bolsheviks in the early twentieth century—which, despite not having a confessional character, offer an institutional scaffolding for Muslim-majority regions in Povolzhye and Northern Caucasus—and above all the Muslim Spiritual Directorates (*Dukhovnye Upravleniya*) or Muftiates. These state organs came into being in the Russian Empire; survived, albeit in a diminished role, during the Soviet period; and were resurrected with renewed thematical functions and powers in the postsocialist period as a pillar of secularism "with Russian characteristics." To comprehend their role in the current scenario, it bears briefly recapitulating this history.

The establishment of the first directorate for Muslims—the Orenburg Spiritual Assembly, founded in 1788 as the Islamic equivalent of the Orthodox Christian Holy Synod—came as a watershed in the Russian Empire's relationship with the native Muslim populations residing in Povolzhye. On the one hand, this development coincided with the official discontinuation of direct antagonism, which had included several waves of forced Christianization and other discriminatory economic measures against Muslims (Rorlich 1986; Campbell 2015, 22). Islam became recognized as a tolerated imperial religion.[4] Conversely, the foundation of Muftiates signaled the ramping up of efforts intended to bring the Volga Muslims under tighter control by the imperial autocracy (Garipova 2013, 265–361; Tuna 2016, 38). However, the establishment of a governmental-administrative structure meant for Muslims and staffed by Muslims enabled the existence, throughout the nineteenth century, of a "mediated distance" between the state and the Muslim population, which retained a certain degree of cultural independence (Kefeli 2014, 86; J. Meyer 2014; Tuna 2016).[5]

Governmental ambiguity was inherent in the Muftiates as institutions: Being the result of the co-optation of already-existing Muslim elites as well as ex nihilo administrative engineering by the imperial center (Ross 2020), they sat at the intersection of forces moving from the top down and the bottom up, from the outside in and the inside out. Muftiates played the role of "intermediary bodies" in the tsarist monarchy, sometimes acting, locally, as brakes on the emperor's unbridled autocracy but also becoming "sources of social power [that] could do things that, in the course of modernization, became necessary to the state" (Poe 2003, 61). Even without wielding effective executive power, the Orenburg Spiritual Assembly vetted and appointed imams, settled disputes over family and inheritance issues, kept civil registries, issued fatwas, and handled communications between Muslim communities and the tsars. The Islamic officialdom gave institutional stability to the social world of Muslims as well as buffering it from the outside (Soltangaliev 1998, 368). Still, the Muftiate was not the only wielder of legitimacy, as the Volga region teemed with preachers, elders, scholars, and reformers of various stripes.

If the long buildup to the Revolution contributed to wearing this world's moral fabric thin, the Soviet experiment led to its unraveling. The postrevolutionary antireligious campaigns attacked all levels of religious authority, including itinerant preachers, Sufis, village mosques, Quranic schools, and modernist circles, as well as Muslim leftists. This fatally disrupted the circulation of religious knowledge and moral teachings across localities and generations, effectively ending the

"Muslim domain" and pushing Volga Muslims, now identified by ethnic labels as Tatars or Bashkirs, into the mold of Soviet modernity. Islam de facto disappeared from public life. New, pervasive state institutions—schools, the pioneer corps, workplace organizations, labor brigades, Komsomol, houses of culture, local Communist Party branches, mass media, and so on—promoted Soviet ideals of socialist personhood and morality from a very young age throughout one's productive life (Kharkhordin 1999; Yurchak 2005; Golubev and Smolyak 2013).

The Muslim Spiritual Directorates survived, but in a diminished and marginalized guise, and only after painful internal struggles over survival strategies. The Soviet authorities, especially during the totalitarian phase of the socialist experiment in the 1930s, could not tolerate external nuclei of moral authority, all the more so if religious in inspiration. However, the Soviets realized that the Muftiates could be useful as state-controlled institutions (Bekkin 2020a, 147–184), and to this end they modernized and expanded the administrative-territorial structure of Spiritual Directorates. In the international arena, Muftiates came in handy as tools of diplomacy with the Muslim world, being brandished as proof that Islam was tolerated in the USSR. Domestically, they propagated state-compliant messages among the fraction of the population that still gathered in the few active mosques, an aging group that, the authorities hoped, represented the demographic leftovers of unenlightened eras and would die out within a few generations.

Postatheist Russia witnessed a return of Muftiates to the landscape of Russia's Islam. But whether or not these institutions can legitimately claim the mantle of their imperial predecessors and credibly claim to speak on behalf of the Russian ummah is a debated question.

Post-Soviet Muftiates: Contracting for the State

Despite—and partly because of—the turmoil of perestroika and the 1990s (Bekkin 2020a, 182–183; Sibgatullina 2025), which led to schisms and settlings of accounts in the Muslim officialdom, Russia's Islamic institutions mushroomed in the post-Soviet era: At the time of my research, there were numerous local and several all-Russian Spiritual Directorates, chief among them two competing federal Muftiates based in Moscow and Öfö (Bashkortostan). The powerful Muftiate of Tatarstan, albeit regional, was also seen as a heavyweight owing to its size and prestige (Kemper 2012; Bekkin 2020a, 233–236). While all these institutions are politically subordinate to the Kremlin, they have shown ideological differences, with Moscow being more inclined to experiment with forms of Islamic modernism, Öfö staunchly traditionalist, and Kazan juggling the different theological forces converging in its sphere of influence.

The growth of the Islamic officialdom is not just a sign of territorial-administrative fragmentation during the breakup of the USSR (though that, too, is a factor); it is also an expression of the process of Putinist Russia's desecularization from above: "The (re)introduction of religion into the . . . institutions, its return to the public sphere, restitution of [religious bodies'] properties and state-sponsored rebuilding of [places of worship], and the propaganda of the ideologies of ethnodoxy and religious nationalism" (Karpov 2013, 259; see Turoma and Aitamurto 2016; Sibgatullina 2025). Russia's desecularization is piloted by "an alliance of state-secular and religious élites" (Karpov 2013, 259) jointly invested in using religion as a state-making tool: Through the Islamic bureaucracy, Islam can be tapped into as a source of legitimacy and a themitical resource. Although in Tatarstan some tension exists between the secular principle embraced by parts of the Tatar nationalist intellectual elite and the theological principle expressed by the Muftiate (Laruelle 2007), the Tatarstani institutions overall support the Muftiate's claims to moral authority over the republic's Muslims and, accordingly, its legitimacy to define the scope of "proper" Islam for the republic.

In a vivid historical analysis of Russia's Spiritual Directorates, aptly titled *People of Reliable Loyalty*—echoing the formula first used by the Catherinian-age Russian administrator who first recommended the establishment of these institutions—Renat Bekkin (2020a) has described the Muftiates as suspended between the needs and expectations of the Muslim population, on one side, and those of the secular-illiberal state, on the other. Following a "marketplace of religions" theoretical model originally developed in the context of North American pluralism, Bekkin tentatively describes Muftiates as religious "firms" selling goods and services to two sides: rituals and guidance to the Muslim populace, and an "ideological concept, a version of Islam which . . . correspond[s] to the goals of state religious policy," to the Kremlin (2020a, 56). While there is no doubt that it is in the Muftiates' best interest to cater to the ideological needs of its temporal patrons, particularly Russia's presidential administration, it might be problematic—as Bekkin himself acknowledges (356)—to cast the asymmetrical relationship between structurally dependent Spiritual Directorates and the authoritarian Kremlin as one of free marketplace horizontality. In its dealings with the Muftiates, it is the state that calls the shots (Sibgatullina 2025, 120, 126–127), commissioning and overseeing the creation of desirable discursive items destined for Muslim consumption. Tweaking Bekkin's metaphor, then, Muftiates may be framed as contractors for the state; and in that capacity, their job is to inculcate state-approved ideological packages to the very same populace they sell ritual and moral instructions to, while vying for the Kremlin's approval and patronage.

The proliferation of pastoral Islamic bureaucracies in post-Soviet Russia, especially under Putin's tenure, therefore reveals the expansion of a themitical apparatus aimed at shepherding Muslim subjects. Agamben defined apparatuses as objects endowed with the "capacity to capture, orient, determine, intercept, model, control, or secure the gestures, behaviours, opinions . . . of living beings" (2009, 14). During the Putin presidency, this effort to "capture, orient, etc." Muslims into a "managed civil society" framework (McCarthy 2020) has gained momentum and coherence as the Kremlin attempted to realize its ideal of a stable and harmonious conservative society in Russia. However, Muftiates' role as the Russian state's "themitical contractors"—a source of guidance shrouded in, and invested in propagating, the *themitos* or the "Law of men and God"—comes with a lot of headaches.

Muslim Apparatuses or Passionate Muslims?

It has been observed that the Muftiates' goal to position themselves as a credible "church" for post-Soviet Russia's Islam—institutions on which the state can depend and the ummah can trust—has not been met: The internal diversity of Russia's (and Tatarstan's) Muslim population is too great, and these new bodies' reputation too compromised (Sibgatullina 2025). In Tatarstan as elsewhere in Russia, Spiritual Directorates' monopolistic pretenses are regularly thrown into doubt by pietists. Far from all intended "buyers" are interested in the ideological merchandise that the Islamic officialdom peddles, and in fact the most prized customers, those whose loyalty is most often doubted, tend to be the most reluctant ones.

In autonomist theory, the political dimension of virtue lies in ethicalists' ability to circumvent, displace, or hack moral, political, and ideological apparatuses. If Agamben's dialectic nuancedly contraposes ethics forms-of-life to sovereign moral *dispositifs*, Tiqqun more radically frames ethics itself as an insurgent "science of apparatuses" aimed at busting the machines of moral discipline. Even more, Tiqqun and its later incarnations envision ethical and political life as the tumultuous, untrammeled interplay of forms-of-life of different shape, orientation, and intensity (Tiqqun 2010, 53–58; Invisible Committee 2017, 62). Such interplay may take the form of enmity or amity, or any station in between, but is anyway opposed to Empire's pretenses to mold tame citizenries. Against a statist idea of politics as the recomposition of ethical differences through repression, co-optation, or a mix thereof, Tiqqun frames the political as fundamentally disharmonious—ab origine open to the ever-lingering chance of conflict (Stavrakakis 1999; Mouffe 2005; Laclau 2007). High-intensity forms-of-life are associated with the capability to "unsettle" the situational order (Fernando 2014). Low-intensity forms-of-life, while also potentially unsettling, are more co-optable and hence compatible with the governmental ideal of maintaining ethical differences at a manageable level (Tiqqun 2010, 2012).

Within this dialectic of apparatus versus form-of-life, Russia's Muslim Spiritual Directorates find themselves in a paradoxical position. As contractors for the state, whose existence depends on the satisfaction of their secular patrons, they function as thematical apparatuses. Yet as assemblages of practicing Muslims, they partake in the same truth and ethical Rule as grassroots piety movements and therefore can be considered, in Tiqqunian terms, low-intensity forms-of-life. There can be no doubt that many in the Islamic officialdom are committed to Islam and genuinely believe that by working within the system they can benefit Russia's ummah. During my fieldwork, I had the opportunity to observe the employees of Tatarstan's Halal Certification Committee, a Muftiate agency, at work; many of them struck me as committed pietists who not only appear assiduous in their ritual practice and earnest in their conduct but also do their best to protect Muslim consumers in the republic and serve God in the process. I observed a similar enthusiasm in the ranks of Tatarstan's Muslim Youth Organization and the Association of Muslim Entrepreneurs, institutional platforms that bring under the aegis of the Muftiate swathes of the piety-leaning civic society attracted to the networking, sociality, and economic possibilities that these infrastructures enable.

As far as leaders are concerned, the Islamic officialdom is a mix of enthusiasm and establishment at all levels. Öfö-based Chief Mufti Talgat-xäzrät Tadzhuddin, the Soviet-bred doyen of Russia's Islamic clergy, often gets chastised for his apparatchik mentality and theological gaffes (Bekkin 2020a, 253–277) but is also credited with formidable organizational efforts spent on behalf of Muslims. The charismatic Mukaddas-xäzrät Bibarsov, provincial mufti of Saratov and affiliated to the more modernist-friendly Muftiate of Moscow, is respected by pietists nationwide for his openness to scripturalist approaches (and hence criticized over alleged "Wahhabi" sympathies by outsiders) yet has publicly extolled patriotism as a Muslim value and put his weight behind ecumenical initiatives. At the local level, I observed how two of the leaders of the Salafi faction of the Akmaş mosque community, known for its dynamic scripturalist contingent, were co-opted by the local branch of the Tatarstani Muftiate and given official leadership responsibilities—and, one can assume, the related rewards—without being asked to compromise on key theological points.

Muftiates derive their legitimacy from both temporal power (the power that makes them "Directorates") and Islam's doctrinal tradition (the power that makes them "Spiritual"). From the viewpoint of pietists, this makes them suspicious on doctrinal and moral grounds, as well as potentially dangerous in their coppish meddlesomeness. On the other hand, Muftiates can also provide helpful institutional scaffolding to the form-of-life's ethical intensity, as demonstrated by civil-society initiatives, the erection of mosques, and the managerial efficiency of leaders whose integrity is acknowledged by the grassroots.

Their ambiguous positionality finds expression in the irony that I heard some pietists direct at the Muftiate. Calling the Islamic bureaucracy "Ministry of Jinn Affairs" (*Ministerstvo po Delam Dzhinnov*), for example, makes light of both its institutional character (it is a "ministry," but not a serious one) and of its pretense to embody moral-spiritual authority. "Jinn affairs" sounds inherently ridiculous, but there is a deeper layer of irony here: Islamic theology teaches that jinns are a spiritual reality, but one that should bear no relevance to human affairs. This mocking moniker thus seems to echo the oft-repeated (by pietists) complaint that the official clergy can harp on endlessly about religious topics without making them even remotely relevant to religionists' actual lived experience. Another joke I have heard is dubbing Muftiates "*Dukhovki*," a wordplay on the Russian *Dukhovnoe Upravlenie* (Spiritual Directorate) and *dukhovka*, which means "oven"— while nonsensical, this appellative has an affectionate tinge to it and seems to indicate that these institutions are simultaneously useless and harmless. In short, this irony suggests that the halal milieu has adapted to live "alongside," "with," and in some cases even "within" these institutions, which offer the possibility of bringing bureaucratic efficiency to bear on issues that matter to halalists.

A Treacherous Terrain

Another factor that complicates post-Soviet Muftiates' positionality is the demographic, moral, and cultural landscape in which they are supposed to carry out their governmental mission. Since perestroika, the Muslim Spiritual Directorates have been confronted with a split constituency, divided between a secularized ethnic-Muslim majority under no real obligation to acknowledge the Mufti's authority and an ethically autonomous minority inclined to systematically challenge it. Furthermore, the postsecular order of late modernity has severed the connection between ethnic and religious identities. Piety movements frame Islam as a universal truth rather than an ethnic confession, yet Muftiates remain anchored to a logic of ethnic particularism and saddled with the Kremlin's expectations over nation-building and Russia's identity. These headaches are, of course, specifically postsocialist ones: In the late imperial period in which Muftiates came about, openly irreligious Muslims were a rarity, while in the socialist period, openly religious Tatars were.

When it comes to speaking to ethnic Muslims, the Muftiate's formal task is not just to provide life-cycle ritual services to Tatar families (though that is undoubtedly important) but also to reconnect a thoroughly secularized population to its spiritual and cultural "roots," while balancing two potentially contradictory sets of Kremlin-approved values: religious conservatism and religious moderation. Ideally, Tatars are supposed to practice Islam in a way that implies obedience to the temporal and state-approved spiritual authorities, does not call into question the illiberal-secular foundations of the state (including the segregation of religious confessions along ethnic lines), and does not morph into autonomous forms-of-life. In 2014 I attended a series of classes held at Kazan's Muftiate-aligned Russian Islamic Institute, which gave me insight into how this balancing act works out in practice. The classes, directed to ethnic-Muslim adults, included Foundations of Islam, Tatar Language, and Tatar History. While the Foundations course, taught by an imam, offered a basic Islamic catechism tailored for people who had been "distant from religion" for all their lives, the Tatar History course, taught by a secular professor, offered a Eurasianist take on the past, mixing ethnic pride, all-Russian patriotism, and a territorial nationalism that extolled the civilizational symbiosis of Turkic and Slavic elements in opposition to the decadent West.

In order not to alienate the Muftiate's secular constituency, Spiritual Directorate personnel often opt for a "soft" line that downplays commitment and self-cultivation. In the summer of 2018, I attended a religious gathering at the fourteenth-century Hussein-Bek Mausoleum (Bashkortostan), a historical site popular with heritage lovers, New Age "energy" tourists, and Sufis honoring the local holy man. The gathering was not open to the general public, and two mild-mannered imams from the Öfö Muftiate were tasked with keeping visitors at bay. At one point, as we waited for the ceremony to begin, a trio of scantily dressed female Tatar tourists approached, causing a worried expression to appear on the imams' faces. A brief exchange revealed the trio's ethnic Muslim positionality. After explaining that the mausoleum was temporarily closed, one of the imams added, coyly pointing to one of the women's short dress, "And in addition to that, you know, this is a holy place. It would be better to enter it with more suitable clothes on." "Oh, of course," the woman replied with a mildly embarrassed smile, "I get that. I'll bear that in mind next time." The imams reacted to this exchange with striking enthusiasm. "There is hope," one of them repeated several times after the tourists left: "Deep down, they [ethnic Muslims] care about religion. They are good people; they just need to be reminded." In my eyes, nothing suggested that the tourist's polite reaction was motivated by a spiritual awakening rather than, say, a generic humanist understanding of "holy place" etiquette. This, however, is beyond the point; what is significant is that (a) the imams saw that exchange as one instance of their "moral mission" of reminding secularized ethnic Muslims of Islam, and (b) they had set the bar of success notably low, in a spirit of ecumenism that struck me as starkly at odds with the piety milieus' emphasis on self-reform and doctrine-compliant conduct.

When it comes to dealing with pietists, by contrast, the Islamic bureaucracies' goal is to harness the latter's ethical impetus and reconcile it with the state's securitarian, patriotic, and ethnically segregated frameworks. Discursively, this means making a theological case against "Wahhabism" and using the bureaucracy's resources to press it far and wide (see next section). But Muftiates being far from the only source of theological guidance, and hardly the most reputable one from the viewpoint of autonomous forms-of-life, active ideological stewardship may sometimes be beyond reach. In such cases, their tasks are surveillance, monitoring, and if possible co-optation. Muftiates are thought (known) to closely cooperate with security agencies such as the FSB to keep tabs on what goes on in and around mosques. During my fieldwork with the scripturalist-leaning—and hence "problematic"—community of Akmaş in 2015, I once witnessed a Gogolian "general inspection" in the course of which a party of controllers from the Kazan Muftiate audited the local mosque to detect signs of "Wahhabism": long beards, ankle-length trousers, and the Salafi prayer routine, which, unlike in Hanafism, includes loud <u>amīn</u> chants and the raising of hands before bowing. Many of such signs were, predictably, identified. This, however, did not to my knowledge lead to disciplinary action; rather, as mentioned earlier, key elements of the Salafi group were subsequently (and wisely) incorporated in the formal leadership, thereby expanding the Muftiate's sphere of influence. Needless to say, there are limits to such a big-tent strategy: The open circulation of materials banned as extremist (legitimately or paranoidally) and recruitment on behalf of outlawed groups (radical or quietist) would hardly be tolerated, and mosque leaders are expected to prevent, suppress, and/or denounce such phenomena.

Part of the "harnessing" carried out by the Islamic officialdom concerns avoiding, or stemming, the disruption of Russia's ethno-confessional setup by Muslim forms-of-life that ignore not only external national boundaries but also internal ones—namely, by proselytizing among the Orthodox Christian Russian population (Bekkin 2020a, 326–328, see 264–265). In 2016, Tatarstan's mufti announced that Friday sermons across the republic should be delivered exclusively in the Tatar language (Nazarova 2016; Mukhametrakhimov 2020). The status of Tatar is a debated issue in Tatarstan: On the one hand, it is extolled, including by many pietists, as the precious "mother tongue" (<u>ana tele</u>) that must be cherished and defended. On the other, Tatar's actual currency is dwindling, and many urban pietists are more fluent in Russian (Bustanov 2017). To some Russophone pietists, the decision to ban Russian from mosques felt not like an innocent move to boost the mother tongue but like a cynical move to thwart pedagogical communication about Islam.

Ethnomusicologist Elise Anderson (2020) has used the term "compelled sound" to describe how, in the Chinese province of Xinjiang, state campaigns targeting Muslim Uighurs altered the soundscapes of communal life by ejecting religiously or ethnically connoted sounds from the public sphere and injecting Mandarin sounds instead. In the Tatarstani case, the state's Muftiate-mediated soundscaping strategy—which could be defined as "compelled code"—is subtler. Rather than altogether prohibiting religiously or ethnically connoted sounds, the Muftiate's decree cages Islamic universalism within an ethnically particularistic aural medium, which has the extra advantage (from the state's viewpoint) of being opaque to many even within the titular ethnic community. If successful, this strategy could prevent or at least hinder the universalist "spillover" of the Islamic truth-process without recourse to repression and indeed with the pretext of ethnic survival.

This strategy is consistent with what Karpov et al. (2012) have dubbed "ethnodoxy"—that is, ethno-confessional segregation under a division of labor between Russia's Islamic and Orthodox clergies. The extent to which "compelled code" policies are enforced on the ground, however, is hard to assess: As of 2019, some mosques in Kazan continued to use Russian, combining sermons in both languages. It might be too late for a policy rooted in nineteenth- and twentieth-century nationalist sensibilities to alter a landscape defined by the postethnic tide of late modernity. In any case, the need to compromise with the secular public and the state exposes the Islamic officialdom's vulnerabilities in the eyes of their most crucial, yet more reluctant, pious interlocutors.

(Non)traditional Islam and Its Discontents

The Muftiates' last headache concerns the very "ideological constructs" that these bodies are supposed to pitch to their constituencies. In the Russian state's bid to domesticate Islamic piety, no political technology has proved as influential and controversial as the trope of "traditional Islam" (*traditsionny islam*). At the time of my research, the mid-to-late 2010s, this term was saturating public conversations about Islam in Tatarstan. These two words embodied a reassuring idea of Islam that mirrors Tatarstan's carefully crafted image: moderate, patriotic, steeped in ancestral custom yet in step with modernity. The terminology of traditional Islam conjures the idea of a faith that is at once nonsectarian, placidly progressive (in historical terms—i.e., compatible with a modern setup, not ideologically liberal or leftist), and infused with quaint folkways and echoes of "Oriental" mysticism. Traditional Islam has a dark twin in "non-traditional Islam" (*netraditsionny islam*)—that is, the embodiment of the specific brand of treachery, foreign influence, and radicalism that unshepherded Muslims, according to the Russian state's paranoid view, are liable to fall for (Bekkin 2020a, 192–193). Consider the following excerpt from a conference talk held at Kazan State University in April 2015, part of a panel devoted to the analysis of "Challenges and Prospects of Russia's Islam":

> You shall find two polarized [*bipolyarnye*], mutually confrontational [*confrontatsionnye*] structures among Russia's Muslims. On the one hand, you have official, pro-state structures. They advocate separation of state and religion. They advocate mutual respect and non-interference between state and religion. I would call this all-Russian [*rossiisky*] Islam or state [*gosudarstvenny*] Islam. The second camp relies mostly on the Internet to produce and circulate propaganda videos and sermons. This is what we call non-traditional Islam. Some criticize the term "non-traditional Islam," but no one can deny that Russia witnesses the appearance of new religious currents, fundamentalist currents. If traditional Islam means Islam adapted to long-standing local customs [*obychai, kotorye byly zdes'*], non-traditional Islam resembles that of Saudi Arabia or other Muslim countries. New Islamic currents are getting a foothold in Russia now, and they deny traditional Islam and its values. They promote such approaches through Internet propaganda, publications of all sorts. I think that over 90% of the observant Muslim youth gather information by watching online materials. This makes it increasingly difficult to work with young people. It's a form of globalization. People reject their state, territorial borders are lost, traditional boundaries are lost [*steryayutsya territorial'nye granitsy, stereayutsya traditsionnye granitsy*], and even kinship boundaries [*rodstvennye granitsy*]. People are torn apart from their families—family connections don't matter to them anymore.

Much of this aligns with the anti-"Wahhabi" policies of suspicion discussed above: nontraditional Islam is a spontaneous, uncontrollable, fundamentalist, and globalist fifth column that threatens "territorial borders" and is intolerably similar to Islam as it is practiced in "other countries." Muslim pietists are not the only form-of-life caught in this type of rhetoric: in a similar vein, for example, Siberia's transnational Tibetan Buddhist milieus are vehemently opposed by the state-backed official Buddhist clergy (Bernstein 2013, 80–81). Yet Muslims have been singled out as uniquely in need of surveillance. The quote above reveals a moral dimension added on top of the securitarian argument: "Traditional" boundaries get lost alongside territorial borders (what exactly is meant by this remains open to interpretation, as *granitsy* covers both meanings), kinship loses meaning, families are broken. In an overalarmist way, these words testify to the disruptive potential of the extrasituational ethical intensity of pietistic forms-of-life, their refusal to be constrained within identities based on local/ethnic solidarity and ancestral allegiance through "shared essence." The quote contraposes such disruptiveness to *traditsionny islam*, a themitically acceptable way of being Muslim, one that is state-approved, suitably "all-Russian" (the adjective *rossiisky*, meaning "pertaining to Russia," is more inclusive than *russky* in having no ethnic connotations), and congruent with the long-standing customs of the Tatar moral community.

The foundations of *traditsionny islam* can therefore be summed up as (a) loyalty to the nation-state-regime (and its president), (b) connection to an essentialized ethnonational community, and (c) an acceptance of the regnant balance of power, illiberal but "harmonious," and legitimized by an anti-Western ultraconservative ideology meant to represent the "traditional" orientation of Russia's populations, including Muslim ones (Laruelle 2007, 2016b; Kaylan 2014). Fittingly, the emergence and consolidation in the public sphere of the *traditsionny* versus *netraditsionny islam* conceptual pair, from the late 1990s through the 2000s, coincided with the legislative clampdown on grassroots piety movements and intensification of the state's managed desecularization.

While some authoritative observers seem to accept the idea of *traditsionny islam* as heuristically meaningful (Mukhametshin 2010; Yemelianova 2010; Malashenko and Starostin 2015), discussions around the loaded politics of "traditional Islam" have recently begun among scholars of the region (Müller 2019; Akhmetkarimov 2020; Almazova and Akhunov 2020; Bekkin 2020a; Yarlykapov 2017; Ragozina 2018, 2020; Shagaviev 2020; Yusupova 2020; Sibgatullina 2025).[6] Even contributors who choose to suspend disbelief over this term's scholarly legitimacy do so with subtlety and awareness of its ideological implications (Di Puppo 2019; Schmoller 2020).

At the heart of traditional Islam's success lie its polysemy and its superficially neutral, even benign connotations. Its terminology has been used in association with different, if adjacent, phenomena and political-ideological projects. A key interlocutor, Ruslan-xäzrät, assisted me in this unpacking (see Benussi 2020a). Ruslan, an energetic Novgorod-Tatar man in his early forties, is a former imam and religion expert who held a high office in Tatarstan's Muftiate until just a few years ago. He received religious training in Moscow and secular education at the Russian Presidential Academy of National Economy and Public Administration, the goal of which is to train high-ranking civil servants. By virtue of his background and public role, at the time of our meeting he could be considered a veritable personification of Russia's state-Islam entanglement under the banner of *traditsionny islam*.

Ruslan was not liked by everyone in the halal milieu, but he was a well-read, subtle, intellectually honest man, endowed with a social-scientific sensitivity that I could not but relate to. I first met him during a talk he delivered to a crowd of Muftiate-rallied Tatar youths. The topic of the talk was "traditional Islam," and, instead of delivering the trite anti-Salafi sermon I had expected, Ruslan-xäzrät delved into a lucid, thorough dissection of the various meanings carried by this trope, culminating in a programmatic explication of the Muftiate's objectives of ideological policing. Weeks later, during a one-on-one conversation in which we explored the issue in further detail, he mentioned four major interpretations of *traditsionny islam* in Tatarstan, which I would arrange as follows: At a foundational, prepolitical level, *traditsionny islam* indicates (a) customs and devotional practices attributed to Muslim-background people in Russia. At a purely ideological level (extraneous to the actual cultural or spiritual life of Muslim communities), this term stands for (b) the Kremlin's themitical vision of a state-loyal Muslim population. Between those two levels, *traditsionny islam* has been used in association with (c) nationalist attempts to frame the "ethnic spiritual heritage" of Inner Russia's Muslims and (d) the Spiritual Directorates' theological project of a "domesticated" but scripturally sound Islam. Schematically, (c) and (d) may and often do gesture toward, or at least claim some connection to, (a), while in fact being subordinated to (b).

Drawing clear-cut lines between these categories is impossible, and it would obscure the inherent fluidity of political technologies about Islam in Russia. There might be, of course, other ways to analytically unpack the Muftiates' ideological production.[7] However, if taken with a pinch of salt, Ruslan-xäzrät's perspective affords emic insight into a post-Soviet political technology through a critical insider's sophisticated and self-aware viewpoint.

Folk Islam

In an "ethnographic" sense, *traditsionny islam* describes vernacular practices such as pilgrimage to local shrines. While not always or necessarily scripturally based, local devotions have long existed among Central Eurasian Muslims, including among Tatars and their Bashkir neighbors. Historically, such practices have been reinforced and legitimized by folk Sufism's emphasis on saintly figures and their burials as repositories of spiritual "force" or *baraka* (Schmoller 2020).[8] Some of these practices are discussed in detail in chapter 4. "Pure" vernacular spirituality may well be the most state-independent iteration of *traditsionny islam*: As we shall see, such practices concern the primal domain of the "human animal," operating at a level "below" ethics and politics. On the other hand, vernacular spirituality can become a site of ideological intervention as "traditional" customs or sites are co-opted by nationalist intellectuals or religious bureaucracies.

Sovereign Islam

During our conversation, Ruslan-xäzrät recounted an anecdote from the time Dmitry Medvedev was standing in for Vladimir Putin as Russia's president (2008–2012). During a meeting with Islamic religious leaders and rank-and-file Muslims, Medvedev gave a speech on state-Islam relations generously peppered with the expression *"traditsionny islam."* During a pause in the proceedings, one of those present, an uncomfortable-looking imam from Northern Caucasus, approached the president and awkwardly squealed, "I beg you, respectable Dmitry Anatolevich, could refrain from using that expression? You know how contentious it is!" Medvedev was reportedly taken aback: "But how, then, am I supposed to describe a Russian Islam that supports the Russian state?"

The line attributed to Medvedev encapsulates how Russian authorities view *traditsionny islam*: a religiously tinged ideology of statist patriotism, homegrown and anticosmopolitan, placing greater emphasis on loyalty to worldly authority than fidelity to an ethical project: as an Orthodox Christian commentator put it, "Islam that teaches Muslims to be law-abiding citizens of Russia and respect the Christian majority" (Roman Silantyev in Bekkin 2020a, 222). Fittingly, another label I have encountered with reference to this declination of *traditsionny islam* is "sovereign" (*suverenny*) Islam (Aslamova 2011; Benussi 2020a), where sovereignty is not God's but the Kremlin's. As themitical contractors for the state, this is the "product" that Muftiates are supposed to peddle among their constituencies, but the Medvedev episode illustrates the pressure that the Islamic officialdom is under when it comes to aligning themselves with a political technology that many pietists find indigestible.

National Islam

A range of ideological visions for the mobilization of religion in the context of Tatar nation-building within the overarching ethnic framework of the Russian Federation have been explored, often by secular thinkers. The goal is to forge a "Tatar national religion" loosely based on Islamic motifs to shield ethnic Muslims from cultural assimilation into the Russian majority while also enabling them to harmonically blend in the broader Russian social order. Ruslan-xäzrät pointed out that "Tatar intellectuals of various orientations have used the term *traditsionny islam* in very different, sometimes diametrically opposite ways to legitimize their preferred, idealized projects of spiritual renewal for the Tatar people." Some of these projects hover closer to the universalist principle of Islam, others to the state's temporal needs.

In the late Soviet period, a school of thought that has been called "Mirasism" (Bustanov and Kemper 2012) emerged among Tatarstani academic elites. Mirasism framed the Tatar spiritual "heritage" (_miras_) as inherently tending toward "progress," replacing the ethical and juridical components of Sunnism (prayer, fasting, keeping halal, observing sharia) with an intellectualized and identarian theism (Benussi 2022). In the post-Soviet era, this school of thought evolved into a conversation about "Euro-Islam," the idea of a nondenominational ethnic "civic religion" supposedly representative of the inner needs of the "Enlightened"—that is, secularized—Tatar population (Khakimov 2003, 2004; Bustanov and Kemper 2012). Despite the buzz Euro-Islam generated among secular intellectuals, its nature as an ideological abstraction lacking in actionable ethical content prevented it from picking up among the rank and file. The 2020 news of the retirement of Euro-Islam's main ideologue, Rafael Khakimov, and the concomitant downscaling of the academic institution he chaired, was interpreted by some as the project being put to pasture after proving "too secular" to succeed (Religiya Segodnya 2020).

More recently, a new and less secularist ideological experiment has been making ripples in Russia's erudite Islamosphere, championed by the "Renovationists" (_obnovlentsy_), also known as Quranic humanists or Quranists (_Koranity_) (Bekkin 2020b). Although compared to Euro-Islam they are closer to "theological" _traditsionny islam_ (see below), Renovationists prioritize "progressive"/humanist interpretations of the Quranic text at the expense of the Sunna, minimizing the authority of the hadith corpus that forms the basis of orthodox Islam's ethical discipline. The motley Renovationist contingent includes academy-related figures such as the Moscow-based Syrian scholar Taufik Ibragim, alongside more recognizably "religious" thinkers such as the imam and Moscow Muftiate figurehead Damir Mukhetdinov, as well as the ex-Tatarstan Muftiate affiliate Rustam Batrov.[9] This ideological experiment occupies a sort of middle ground between the secular intelligentsia and the more doctrinally aware Islamic officialdom. It is a fragile synthesis, and Renovationism has proved to be a hard sell among both pietists and sections of the state-loyal Islamic officialdom, concerned about a watering down of Sunnism's Prophetic traditions. As a result, its long-term political viability has been cast into doubt (Kemper 2019; Kemper and Sibgatullina 2021).

Soviet-era Mirasism, Euro-Islam, and Renovationism can be seen as related on three levels: genealogical, structural, and ideological. Genealogically, all three projects rest to some extent upon the "Jadid myth" (Benussi 2017, 11–13). "Jadidism" is a term used to describe a phase of modernist, reformist ferment that spread among the Tatar and Turkestani Muslim youth at the turn of the twentieth century. Never a coherent, organized front, the Jadids had much in common with the reformists active across the Muslim world at the same time. Despite their small demographic base, the Jadids' activities sent shockwaves across the Russian Empire: Among their goals were the "purification" of Islam from custom and clericalism—much to the disapprobation of the established Muslim authorities of the time (Garipova 2016; Ross 2020)—and the deprovincialization of Russia's Muslims through cosmopolitan education. The Jadid saga did not survive Stalinism: even Jadidism's prorevolutionary fringe was wiped out. In the late-socialist era, however, a Frankenstein creature made of pieces of Jadidism was reanimated by some Tatar intellectuals, who developed a Sovietified retelling of the Jadid adventure as a secularist national palingenesis shorn of its Islamic components (DeWeese 2016; Sartori 2016). In this retelling, Jadidism had brought a centuries-long indigenous trajectory of religious freethinking to its logical conclusion, propelling the entire Tatar ethnos into a golden age of enlightenment (Almazova and Akhunov 2020[10]). The Tatar religious heritage, in this narration, was inherently, natively imbued with a secular rationality that apexed under the Jadids' watch. During one conversation with an older, Soviet-educated Mirasist activist, she enthusiastically explained to me that "the Tatars have never been Sunnis or Shi'a: we are Jadid*ists*!" meaning "modern," secular, and different from the "sectarians" in the Middle East. Needless to say, the Jadid myth has little to do with historical fact: not only had Jadidism never become a mass movement, but its proponents were for a good part Sunni scripturalists who hardly thought of themselves as secular. However, the idea of a Tatar national religion vaguely connected to Islam but championing freethinking and secularity was bound to catch on in the context of ethnic Muslims' pursuit of a "national spiritual tradition." Both Euro-Islam propagandists (Khakimov 2013) and prominent Renovationists have cast themselves as the heirs of Jadidism (Kemper 2019; Kemper and Sibgatullina 2021; Bekkin 2020b).

The structural commonality connecting Mirasism, Euro-Islam, and Renovationism is their "revolutionariness" in matters of religious legitimacy and continuity. While affirming to embody the timeless genius of Tatar exceptionalism, these three positions advocate a clean break with Islam as a scripturally defined discursive tradition, which to them amounts to obscurantist, sectarian detritus. While Mirasism and Euro-Islam are the brainchildren of secular intellectuals who have never been invested in <u>kalām</u> or <u>fiqh</u>, the Renovationists' case is a bit different. Although the principle of discontinuity is openly expressed in their moniker, Renovationists tend to have a more substantial engagement with Islamic theology via the Quran, whose authority is at least in principle retained; hence, this position has at least to an extent found receptive ears in the Moscow

Muftiate. According to critics, however, Renovationists' theology verges on (or, to some, falls straight into) unorthodoxy.

Ideologically, Mirasism, Euro-Islam, and Renovationism share a conservative outlook and deference to the Kremlin's reactionary politics and "sovereign" domestication of Islam. This may seem counterintuitive given these groups' "revolutionary" religious aspirations and identification with the "progressive" Jadids. But Soviet-era Mirasism was the product of accommodation between ethnolocalist elites and the USSR's authoritarian order, while Euro-Islam's champion Khakimov has long been a vocal Kremlin loyalist, and eminent Renovationists have expressed far-right Eurasianist views and eagerly embraced the Putinist rhetoric about Russia's "traditional values" (Kemper 2019; Bekkin 2020b, 109–110; Sibgatullina and Kemper 2019). By all indicators (economic policies, minority rights, and attitudes to democracy, nationalism, and imperialism), these narratives belong to the extreme right both at the level of ethnic nation-building and at that of the federal setup. The reason is clear: From a themitical viewpoint, these accommodationist projects explicitly coincide with the Kremlin's view of social harmony as premised on socially conservative, patriarchal moral order sans excesses of ethical intensity—in other words, Law over Rule.

Theological Traditional Islam

The last iteration of *traditsionny islam* refers to the project of mass pedagogy advanced by most segments of Russia's Islamic officialdom and endorsed by the Tatarstani Muftiate; it may be called "orthodox" or "theological" traditional Islam (Benussi 2020a, 127–130). This project is to an extent contiguous with the above-described "national Islam" experimentations of Tatar intellectuals, and it is not always easy to draw a line between them—all the more so considering that some individual ideologists have moved from one category to another (such as Rustam Batrov, who switched to Renovationism after having championed "theological" *traditsionny islam*: Almazova and Akhunov 2020, 50; Bekkin 2020b), and others, like the mercurial Damir Mukhetdinov, cannot be pigeonholed into one or another category (Kemper 2019). Like its more secularist analogues, "theological" *traditsionny islam* tries to strike a balance between national particularism and accommodation with Russia's political and themitical setup. For example, Tatarstan's Mufti Kamil Samigullin, a champion of Tatar language and identity, has often extolled patriotic pluralism and religious moderation (Kamalova 2015; Tatar-Inform 2019), as well as the primacy of natural science and classical philosophy—that is, the intellectual foundations of the modern secular order (Alimov 2018).

There are, however, important divergences: While national projects' connection to Islamic scriptures tends to be either weak (Mirasism, Euro-Islam) or discontinuous (Renovationism), "orthodox" *traditsionny islam* locates the resources for national renewal in the Volga Muslims' prerevolutionary theological horizon. Instead of perpetuating the "Jadidist" myth, Spiritual Directorate ideologists are committed to scripturally defined Sunnism, Maturidism (in kalām), Hanafism (in fiqh), and (optionally) Sufism—casting them as the most "rational" and "progressive" theological-juridical currents in Islamic thought (Di Puppo 2019). The argument is that Tatars have "always" followed these schools of thought—therefore delegitimizing alternative theological currents such as Atharism and Hanbali fiqh—and this has "always" guaranteed interethnic peace, harmony, and neighborliness in Inner Russia (Alimov 2018).

Practically, this translates into encouraging apoliticism—which should be distinguished from quietism by its lack of emphasis on ethical intensity—using Islamic arguments. As one of my pietist friends lamented, "Official Islam is all about being good and respecting the authorities," while offering little in the way of ethical content. I could appreciate what he had in mind when, during a Foundation of Islam class organized by the Kazan Muftiate, our imam instructor described the experience of Muslims as divided into multiple concentric spheres. The innermost, one's relationship with God, should receive the most attention. After that, there were the spheres of family and community life. The outer sphere was that of society and politics. On these theological grounds, our teacher bluntly told us that Muslims are supposed to "let the professionals deal with politics and this kind of complicated, dirty things: Our duty as believers is to mind our own business [*zanimat'sya svoimi delami*]."

"Theological" *traditsionny islam* is not devoid of aporias. Some are logical and ideological: Hanafism is extolled as intrinsically dialogical, tolerant, and predisposed to friendly relations with the Russian state, seemingly forgetting that hardline Islamist movements such as the Deobandi and the Taliban, which are also Hanafi, have been seen as extremist by the Kremlin (though in 2025 Russia suspended the terrorist status of the Taliban). Conversely, prerevolutionary religious leaders who were Hanafi, Sufi, and generally ticked all the boxes of *traditsionny islam* were considered "fanatical" by the imperial authorities (Kefeli 2014; Ross 2020). More recently, as we have seen, the secularism-compatible "soft" movement Hizmet was banned despite its Maturidism and Hanafism.

The deepest aporias, however, are moral. The task of Tatarstan's Muftiate as a themitical contractor is to raise ethical intensity among the ethnic Muslim population while simultaneously curbing it among "nontraditional" pietists. Trying to balance the principles of scriptural exactitude and ethnic particularism, commitment and moderateness is not easy, even by figures whose theological literacy and sincere devotion cannot be doubted. The late Valiulla Yakupov, one of the foremost authorities in the Muftiate, attempted to "domesticate" Hanafism into a specifically Tatar "madhhab culture" (Yakupov 2011; Bustanov and Kemper 2013; Almazova and Akhunov 2020, 38). After Yakupov's tragic and untimely death, his mantle was picked up by Mufti Samigullin. The position of Kamil-xäzrät about the precise framing of *traditsionny islam*, however, remains to this day ambiguously suspended between ethnicity and piety, the ethical imperatives of Islam and the biopolitical ones of temporal power (Almazova and Akhunov 2020, 44).

A Challenge to Theory

In autonomist terms, *traditsionny islam* can be described as a discursive apparatus for the de-intensification of Islamic forms-of-life (see Bekkin 2020a, 277). By leaning on the Jadid myth, its secular-nationalist iteration seeks to preserve the disruptive potential, future-orientation, and radically innovative semblance of an Islamic truth-process, but divorced from an ethical Rule. None of its secularist incarnations are premised on fidelity to a truth: Instead, the subject that is envisioned is attached to ethnoreligious identities, state-loyal, and ultimately Kantian in its moral outlook, with ethical discipline ruled out as a precondition for salvation (Kemper 2019, 223–224). By contrast, "theological" *traditsionny islam* maintains a more explicit engagement with the scriptural-ethical content of Sunni tradition, but they cage it within the situational constraint of local custom, conventional morality, and sovereign expectations. In their attachment to a prerevolutionary Muslim world that they idealize but cannot resuscitate, its ideologists try to keep the truth but downplay the process. The tension between the universalist principle of Islam and the particularistic principle of *traditsiya* means that the *traditsionny islam* terminology was, at the time of my research, increasingly recognized as polarizing and problematic. Despite that, it may still be too early to proclaim *traditsionny islam* a thing of the past (Alimov 2018; Schmoller and Laruelle 2025).

Terminology apart, the strategy behind "theological" *traditsionny islam* appears to have greater mileage than most of its secular counterparts, thanks to its ability to tap into genuine ethical trends that have been on the rise for decades. The apparent failure of Mirasism, Euro-Islam, and Renovationism to take root beyond intellectual circles testifies to these experiments' lack of resonance with ethical strivers. By contrast, Muftiates' ability to just about manage to juggle patriotism, ecumenism, and scripturally based morality allows the Islamic officialdom to preserve its alliance (as junior, dependent partners) with the federal and republican state organs, maintain a degree of legitimacy in the eyes of ethnic-Muslim nonpietists, and keep a porous interface with the halal milieu. In this sense, the Muftiate's "calculated conformity"—as Kaarina Aitamurto (2021, 285), channeling James Scott (1985), put it—results in what in Tiqqunian terms might be called a low-intensity form-of-life. This might not quite be a space of "subversion," as per Aitamurto, but it is indeed one of partial, conditional ethical autonomy.

In Tatarstan and elsewhere in Russia, Islamic Spiritual Directorates have proved capable of creating social and discursive spaces around issues of genuine importance for halal-conscious pietists—for instance, through the Tatarstani Muftiate's Halal Standard Committee, the Association of Muslim Entrepreneurs, or the Muslim Youth Organization. The co-optation of individuals and groups of "nontraditional" orientation is one of the strategies that keep these themitical apparatuses viable, alongside their ongoing investment in Islam as a vital theological tradition. Muftiates have not (yet) achieved success in absorbing or liquidating autonomous Islamic forms-of-life. But in order not to alienate pietists and/or entirely lose legitimacy in the eyes of their intended constituencies, the "people of reliable loyalty" need to keep Rule in sight alongside Law.

The case of Russia's Muftiates reveals the strengths as well as some blind spots of this book's engagement with autonomist theory. Its strengths show, as I hope the above discussions exemplify, in the analytical insight that the concepts of "themitical apparatus" and "(low-intensity) form-of-life" allow in discussing the politics (and concrete policies) of the Islamic officialdom in Russia. However, this framework becomes more problematic once we try to define Spiritual Directorates: Are Russia's Muftiates *apparatized* forms-of-life or *ethicized* apparatuses? Each formulation would tell part of the story; each would be insufficient in isolation. Analytically impervious and hard to research ethnographically, Muftiates will perhaps continue to puzzle analysts, pietists, and nonconfessional state actors alike as long as they remain operative. To Russia's Muslims, however, the continuous existence of these tsarist-era institutions contracting for an authoritarian state is undoubtedly preferable to open oppression: there may be spaces of opportunity within institutional machineries trying, but never quite entirely succeeding, to manage Muslim moralities.

SEEKING HEALING

Tatar Nonpietists Between *Askesis* and *Ákesis*

In previous chapters, I have discussed the halal milieu and its ethical approach to religion as standing in tension with ethnic Muslims and their secularized, nationalistic understanding of Islam. As we have seen, a scripturalist joke brands ethnic Muslims as "funerary-commemorative Muslims," castigating them for a limited, conventional engagement with Islamic life-cycle rituality, devoid of day-by-day fidelious conduct or theological awareness. In the eyes of *praktikuyushchie* Muslims, this is barely (if at all) sufficient to qualify as a Muslim. Certain rituals, such as postmortem commemorative banquets (*pominki*), are even considered harmful innovations by some scripturalists (Schmoller 2020).

Like all clear-cut distinctions, however, a black-and-white contrast of pietists and secularists does not do justice to the shades of gray in the picture. In this chapter, I discuss the vernacular devotions practiced by many nonpious Tatars in addition to life-cycle ceremonies, in particular the pursuit of spiritual healing through special prayers/ceremonies (*tselebnaya molitva* or *öşkerü*), and the visiting of holy sites (*ziyarät*), which often, in Tatarstan and the broader Idel-Ural region, take the form of sacred springs (*izge çişmälär*). The post-Soviet era has ushered in a lively revival of exorcistic practices and local pilgrimage. Not all ethnic Muslims practice such devotions, which are not regimented into rigid liturgical scripts and allow for a variety of interpretations (Seligman et al. 2008). Yet they are popular, and, inasmuch as they retain a spiritual dimension and a doctrinal connection to Islam, they complicate the black-and-white opposition between practicing and ethnic Muslims. These ritual forms are, to an extent, shared by halalists and nonpietists. Scripturally grounded spiritual healing is practiced across the halal milieu, while *ziyärät* to the burials of religious masters, while mostly shunned by Salafis, is often performed by devout, sharia-abiding Sufis.

However, the existence of a gray area of partly shared ritual activity does not overcome all tensions or annul the difference in approaches to faith. In what follows, I argue that whereas halal milieu religionists tend to approach spiritual healing and pilgrimage from the ethical premise of *askesis*, their nonpious neighbors tend to do so from what I call the situational principle of *ákesis*. The latter involves the pursuit of relief from affliction, the mending of a broken situation, or, to put it in the words of Italian anthropologist Ernesto De Martino ([1959] 2015), the overcoming of a "crisis of presence." As a result of this difference in premises, the actual manifestations of ritual often differ between the two groups, and there is little intermingling when pietists and nonpietists converge at the same site.

By discussing the experiences of nonpious yet spiritually active ethnic Muslims alongside halalists, I foreground Islam as a repository of *aketic*, or remedial, resources as well as a virtue ethic. This chapter does not seek to delve into an Islamic phenomenology of illness or Muslim healers' experience of therapy, as medical anthropologists and ethnopsychiatrists have masterfully done before (Crapanzano 1973; Boddy 1988, 2013; Pandolfo 2018). Rather, the chapter foregrounds Tatarstani debates and anxieties over the healing of suffering souls/bodies as a locus of tension—but also proximity—between Muslim and nonpietists. The first part of the chapter focuses ethnographically on Islamic spiritual healing (*öşkerü*) for nonpietists at a Kazan mosque; then, via a comparison with Quranic ruqyah, it segues into a discussion of the relationship between *ákesis* and *askesis*. The second part applies this framework to holy spring pilgrimages. The goal of this analysis is to comprehend vernacular devotions such as *öşkerü* and *ziyärät* on their own terms, as well as to better define their relation to ethicized Islam.

Even if in Tatarstan these terms can be applied to forms of experience that are locally framed as standing in tension with each other, it must be emphasized that I do not intend to cast *ákesis* and *askesis* as reciprocally exclusive principles, as I consider them interdependent and mutually compatible. This binomial is analytical: Like "*askesis*," the term "*ákesis*" is meant to function as a loose, unspecific classifier that may be deployed across a spectrum of contexts. As we shall see, both principles can be detected in the experiences of the halal milieu and spiritually active nonpietists—but for the former, *askesis* is hierarchically dominant, while for the latter it is *ákesis* that takes priority.

Öskerü in Kazan: Post-Traditional Healing

Let me begin to unpack the meaning of the term "*aketic* principle" by looking at the spiritual healing sessions carried out at a special mosque in Kazan and exploring the related controversies about the place and proper form of spiritual healing in Islam. The Tatar term "*öşkerü*" or "*öşkertü*," which applies to operations through which the evil eye (*bozım*, *sixer*) and the influence of "unclean forces" are removed, is often used to describe spiritual healing among Volga-region Muslims. Although the term can be used synonymously with Quranic healing (ruqyah), the semantic spectrum of the Tatar word "*öşkerü*" appears broader. For instance, some interlocutors referred to *öşkerü* as synonymous with "exorcism" (*ekzortsizm*) without apparent reference to Islamic theology but rather to the pop-culture (ultimately Christian-derived) meanings carried by that term.

Customarily carried out by village elders or rural mullahs, at the time of my research an "urban" version of *öşkerü* was held every week at the iconic, double-turreted Shamil mosque on the outskirts of Kazan. I attended multiple such ritual sessions in 2014–2015 and during a later visit in 2019. The mosque's social network pages advertise these sessions as "curative/healing prayers" (*tselitel'naya molitva*), but the term "*öşkerü*" is also used by the resident imam and healer-in-chief (Şäräfetdin 2014). These ceremonies feature the recitation of Quranic verses by the mosque personnel and the blessing of water, salt, and dried fruit. In addition, they include chanting formulas of remembrance of God and receiving a "healing puff" from the imam (for an excellent ethnomusicological analysis of the proceedings, see Almazova 2014).

Unlike what one interlocutor described as "more typical" *öşkerü*, which involve one-on-one meetings, healing sessions at the Shamil mosque are attended collectively. Every week, *öşkerü* sessions attract up to eighty to one hundred people. The high turnout has led some (Almazova 2014) to describe healing practices at the Shamil mosque as a veritable "phenomenon." In many respects, this term aptly captures a unique development that bears no resemblance to the ritual activities taking place at other mosques in Kazan. For one thing, the Shamil mosque's prayer hall is furnished with rows of foldable chairs on which participants sit during hour-long *öşkerü* sessions, an arrangement that comes across as unusual in the context of Sunni spirituality (mosques have thick carpets and, at most, a few benches for the elderly, but no chairs or pews). Furthermore, gender separation during the healing sessions is looser than in other mosques, and the majority of *öşkerü*-goers are female, as opposed to what is normally the case with Sunni places of worship in Tatarstan. The dress code at the Shamil mosque is strikingly flexible as well: Most women dress casually and often cover their skin and hair with precariously fastened, see-through shawls. The typical halal milieu stylistic/sartorial statements are nearly absent: Very few female attendees don recognizably Islamic garments, and some do not wear head coverings at all. About two-thirds of the *öşkerü*-goers are middle-aged or older, and many have rural backgrounds. This is also at odds with the demographic composition of the halal milieu, which as we know is made up predominantly of younger, aspirational urbanites. The crowd gathering at the Shamil mosque is described by Almazova (2014, 269) as "secular": Many attendees hail from a late Soviet background, a generation that has little interest in, and even less patience with, the doctrinal strictness of the halal milieu.

Öşkerü attendance is occasional and ad hoc. Those who gather for healing sessions do so predominantly because they seek remedy for specific afflictions. To get rid of "negative energies," a cycle of three sessions is normally required; once the cycle is over, people stop attending, at least until the next affliction emerges. The imam also offers individual sessions for people who book beforehand. The high turnover means that there is a constant flux of people, without *öşkerü* participants forming a stable community. At the time of my visit, however, there seemed to exist a small circle of young males gravitating more stably around the imam. Largely, these came across as individuals cultivating a spiritual interest but hesitant to embrace a high-intensity halal lifestyle. Some of them were attracted to "heterodox" approaches to spirituality. The resident imam, Mahmud-xäzrät, a remarkably charismatic man in his early forties, cultivates a "neo-Sufi" persona. He was initiated into the Naqshbandi-Khalidi brotherhood during his educational sojourn in Turkey but is also influenced by eclectic spiritual/New Age developments such as Universal Sufism (which promotes nonshariatic mysticism). During a conversation I attended, one of his associates declared his admiration for the twentieth-century guru Bhagwan Shri Rajneesh, a.k.a. Osho, who was discussed as "one of the great masters." One last significant difference between the Shamil mosque and typical Sunni mosques is that the prayer hall quickly empties after *öşkerü*, so much so that—at least during my visits—almost none of the attendees would stick around to perform the Islamic prayer at the prescribed time. Other mosques, by contrast, fill up for namaz.

Such idiosyncrasies have earned the Shamil mosque a controversial reputation among pietists and pushed it to the margins of Kazan's halal milieu. When I quizzed some pious interlocutors, including individuals of ecumenical views and (scripturally oriented) Sufi practitioners, about the goings-on at the Shamil mosque, most respondents rolled their eyes, expressing disapprobation or suspicion of the "Shamil phenomenon." One friend dismissed the Shamil mosque healing prayers as a combination of "village superstitions" and "New Age rubbish." I was, in fact, advised against attending the ritual on the grounds that people there were "wasting time with nonsense" (*zanimayutsya erundoy*), which might even be spiritually harmful.

But the Shamil phenomenon also has its supporters. The ethnographic account by respected Tatarstani scholar of Islam Leila Almazova (2014) is noteworthy for its endorsement of the Shamil mosque leadership. Almazova's endorsement should be contextualized within Tatarstan's debate over *traditsionny* and *netraditsionny islam* described in the previous chapter, in which local experts *volens nolens* play a role by lending legitimacy to or withdrawing it from certain spiritual practices (Yusupova 2019). Almazova's piece frames the "Shamil phenomenon," alongside "liberal" Islam, in contraposition to "radical" tendencies (Almazova 2014, 255), and thus as an example of *traditsionny islam* that should be cherished and embraced. By contrast, regular Sunni mosques are characterized as either empty or full of zealots bent on aggressive proselytizing (2014, 267–268). In the spirit of *traditsionny islam*, which places a premium on indigeneity, Almazova opines that the Shamil mosque *öşkerü* originates from prerevolutionary Tatar Sufi rituality (2014, 258). But to make such an argument, some of the objectively "nontraditional" elements of the ritual must be downplayed: The number of attendees, the choreography of the ritual, the unusual utilization of mosque space, the rows of chairs, the casual attire of participants, the partial gender-mixing, the imam's cosmopolitan/eclectic background and its implications for the staging of the *öşkerü*, and so forth. Almazova hypothesizes a connection between today's healing session chants and prerevolutionary Sufi vocalizations, on the grounds that (a) both performances are made without musical instruments and (b) the texts chanted have religious content. Whether such generic resemblances constitute evidence of continuity is perhaps disputable.[1] Almazova herself observes that prerevolutionary Tatar Sufis predominantly performed dhikr silently; however, it is safe to assume that even those who vocalized loudly would have found the choreography, setting, and atmosphere of the Shamil mosque's healing sessions extremely unfamiliar. These healing sessions do not feature or require any of the recognizable elements of Sufism: initiation into a ṭarīqa, transmission of religious knowledge (exoteric and/or esoteric), disciplehood, devotion to a sheikh, bay'ah (pledge of allegiance to a master), regular spiritual exercises, or commitment to a path of self-cultivation.

The characterization of the Shamil mosque's healing prayer as *traditsionny* thus reveals more about the constructedness of this category in Russian/Tatarstani political discourses than about the rite itself or, indeed, the self-understanding of Shamil mosque-goers. When I first approached the mosque staff in 2014, one of the first questions I asked was whether *öşkerü* counted as an example of *traditsionny islam* (at the time, I had not yet grasped the contentiousness of the term). The face of my interlocutor, one of Mahmud-xäzrät's aides, blushed with alarm. He rushed to explain to me that *absolutely no*, what they did had nothing to do with *traditsionny islam*: The mosque's healing prayers were based on the Quran and Sunna, strictly following the example of the Prophet and his followers and so on. The young man clearly knew that the term "*traditsionny islam*," well liked though it was by temporal institutions, carried negative associations—even stigma—among other constituencies.

To mitigate the controversy around *öşkerü* at the Shamil mosque, the Tatarstani Muftiate in 2020 released a YouTube video on the subject of spiritual healing, evidently meant, at least in part, to reassert the doctrinal soundness of the goings-on at the Shamil establishment and confer its institutional backing to the mosque leadership. In the carefully crafted video, a reassuringly "traditional"-looking imam, wearing old-fashioned attire and speaking in Tatar against a "traditional"-looking wooden background echoing village architecture, offered theological justifications for spiritual healing *insofar as* its practitioners stick to orthodox Sunni methods of spiritual healing. In a speech rife with prudent nods to "official" science and medicine and usual references to "our [Tatar] ancestors"—but without a trace of the poisoned terminology of *traditsionny islam*—the practice was described as particularly beneficial for mental health issues such as depression. The speaker expressed satisfaction that "in our age, too," there should be mosques in Kazan—an obvious reference to the Shamil phenomenon—where *öşkerü* is offered to those who need it.[2]

Even though, ultimately, value judgments on this point belong solely to the Kazan ummah, it is my impression that the Shamil phenomenon does not deserve its dubious reputation. While the Shamil healing sessions may be rather distant from what most orthodox Tatarstani Sunnis would consider their ideal, the mosque leadership makes no effort to politicize their experiment and indeed defends it by claiming adherence to the Prophetic example. As a matter of fact, most of the people who flock to the Shamil mosque *öşkerü* seem to operate with a set of concerns that is equally distant from the ideological framework of *traditsionny islam* and the doctrinal stringency of halalists. Their experience is rooted in an existential ground of immanence: a space devoid of the distractions of power and *askesis*. It is a place that resonates with what Badiou (2002) calls "human animalhood": an immediate, nonpolitical (perhaps subpolitical) and nonethical closeness to creaturely experience that may imply heightened vulnerability to suffering. They are individuals who seek healing because and insofar as they are in pain, and neither the protection of the state nor aspirations of piety offer solace in the same way as the spiritual energy mobilized by Mahmud-xäzrät does. The Shamil phenomenon succeeds in its consoling, healing mission. Once that much is acknowledged, a question ensues: What is the relationship between the space of immanence where the *öşkerü* occurs and Islamic orthodoxy?

Ruqyah and Healing Prayers

The Muftiate representative in the video mentioned above had an important point: Spiritual healing is part and parcel of the Islamic discursive tradition to the extent that it conforms to the example of the Prophet (Pandolfo 2018; Rassool 2019). Several of my acquaintances, for example, practice cupping (ḥijāma), a therapeutic technique explicitly mentioned in the hadith. Analogously, Quranic healing is not foreign to Tatarstan's halal milieu: While spiritual medicine is not a particularly prominent aspect of pietists' engagement with Islam, at least in discursive terms (it is not, to my knowledge, a frequent topic in evangelization, sermons, or even everyday conversation between halalists), pietists too are vulnerable to pain and hence liable to seek solace in the curative power of Scripture. The term preferred among pietists is "ruqyah," which has a scriptural basis, rather than the vaguer and folk-sounding "öşkerü."

One of the reasons ruqyah is not a prominent theme among halal-oriented circles may stem from the prophetic saying (Bukhari 6472) according to which those who do not practice ruqyah (in some versions "do not ask to be given ruqyah") will be admitted to Paradise without reckoning. Some interpret this as meaning that while Quranic healing is permissible, greater rewards are granted to those who put their complete trust in God (upovayut na svoego Gospoda). Others interpret this hadith as meaning that Quranic healing should be performed autonomously and privately, without delegating ritual specialists, for ruqyah's efficacy lies exclusively in the power of the Word of God and does not depend on who performs the healing or on how elaborate the ritual is. Furthermore, some observe that harmful jinns are repelled by piety and spiritual discipline, so scrupulous observance of a halal lifestyle prevents the kind of spiritual afflictions that ruqyah cures. Last, many halalists inhabit a modernist, ascetical-rationalist ethos that is not particularly conducive to ritualism or the development of a strongly enchanted picture of the world (Benussi 2020b).

In general, Tatarstani pietists appear to subordinate spiritual healing to the overarching ethical-teleological principle of askesis. On his social media page, one "orthodox" (po Sunne) Quranic healing expert recommends that those who perform ruqyah not only scrupulously follow Islam's doctrinal prescriptions but also incite their patients toward worship (molit'sya) and repentance (pokayanie). The author specifies that "healing should not be the main cause of repentance: [People] should worship God for His dignity only"—that is, not to get something "in exchange." Rāqis (Quranic healers) should not promise healing or "establish a direct link" between treatment (or even prayer) and healing. They "should invite people to put their trust in God, not in healers." Muslims should be clear that if one's illness is willed by God—either as a punishment or as a test of faith, for instance—then no ritual procedure can bring about healing.

Søren Kierkegaard argued that living in an ethical mode implies "resignation" ([1946] 2016, 125–126). Discussing Islamic healing, Stefania Pandolfo has powerfully described the methodical pursuit of capitulation to God's will as "heteronomy of divine command" (2018, 318).[3] At one level, such a spectacular irruption of heteronomy may seem to chafe with the idea of religious discipline as an autonomizing process. And to an extent, such a dissonance is real: when a pietist seeks ruqyah, she might be grappling with a crisis that transcends one's normal abilities to apply Rule and live "by the plan": Faced with one's vulnerable creatureliness, relinquishing one's suffering subjectivity into the hands of God may be the only response. This is something that autonomist theory may prove poorly equipped to capture—proving, if needed, that no single approach can aspire to account for the countless facets of faith. At another level, though, it is helpful to recall that Kierkegaard's "Christian autonomism" did not frame discipline and resignation as incompatible: Autonomy is never to be achieved vis-à-vis God but rather vis-à-vis convention and moral tepidity. Even atheist Alain Badiou's framing of ethics as transcending self-interest and fideliously embracing a higher subjectivity (through love, creative impetus, political enthusiasm, etc.) implies a measure of abandonment, of trust in something bigger and stronger than oneself. This does not imply altogether abandoning the principle of self-preservation—not least because such a move would undermine askesis—but rather keeping it "in its proper place": underpinning, but subordinate to, the ethical imperative.

According to the orthodox rāqi writing on his web page, sufferers should turn to God and reform their lives. Given the circumstances of Russian society, in which many of the people who seek ruqyah are theologically illiterate ethnic Muslims, the author recommends his fellow rāqis to direct patients toward repentance firmly but gently, without excessive pressure. Patients should, however, be asked to drop at once any non-Islamic spiritual healing practices (folk magic, soothsayers, etc.). An orthodox healer's ultimate goal should be to establish continuous, informed religious practice, which is the best guarantee against spiritual misfortunes (see Reinhardt 2016, 85–87, for a Christian analog).[4]

Unlike piety-oriented Quranic healers who place ruqyah within a framework of self-reform, the Shamil mosque approach is premised on "acceptance of oneself for what one is" (Almazova 2014, 265, quoting the resident imam; see Şäräfetdin 2009). Of course, the Shamil mosque is not a norm-free space, and as we have seen its personnel are adamant in claiming Prophetic legitimation. But the Shamil phenomenon's lack of emphasis on fidelity, ritual accuracy, and theological knowledge appears programmatically linked to a logic of "spiritual first help." Mahmud-xäzrät knowingly tailors his approach to individuals who are both unaccustomed and unwilling to embrace "strict observance" (Almazova 2014, 264). His vision seems to be that by purposefully privileging the path of least resistance and accommodating habit over reform, a greater number of individuals may obtain at least some exposure to Islam. This approach is not unreasonable or un-Islamic. As we know, the halal lifestyle is primarily attractive to aspirational, socially mobile, younger individuals. The Shamil mosque's *öşkerü*-goers, by contrast, are by and large "simple working people" (Almazova 2014, 264), most of whom are steeped in the working-class, egalitarian culture of the Soviet province. Socialized in the placid austerity of high socialism, that generation witnessed the traumatic collapse of the paternalist state and the hardship of the 1990s, and now faces inevitable physical decline amid uncertain, turbulent times. Notions of reform, aspiration, and success—material or spiritual—are hardly resonant with their experience of fragility and longing, their ingrained dislike of elitism and individualism, and their existential fears and expectations.

Öşkerü-goers gather at the Shamil mosque because they are afflicted by ailments of various types, including a range of illnesses (mostly mental health issues but sometimes also life-threatening conditions), unfulfilled wishes, the feeling of having been jinxed, or just, as Almazova touchingly puts it, hope to find some "peace for their souls" (2014, 268). Writing on vernacular religiosity among working-class Mediterranean villagers in the 1950s, Ernesto De Martino ([1959] 2015) described rural communities steamrolled by modernization and thrown into a collective uncertainty comparable to that of post-Soviet *öşkerü*-goers. De Martino defined this condition of historically determined existential fragility as a "crisis of presence." The ritual activity of De Martino's Mediterranean peasants, made of exorcisms and invocations tinged with folk Christianity, was less a matter of doctrine (which villagers mostly disregarded as a matter for priests) than an instrument to restore "presence" in the face of historical turmoil. As we shall see shortly, the Shamil phenomenon too can be seen as operating on the level of presence. Mahmud-xäzrät appreciates that the language of piety/reform would not get him very far with his immanence-steeped audience. Ritual practice at the Shamil mosque is deliberately meant to provide relief for the afflicted, not a liturgical framework for ascetical champions. The imam's open, nonjudgmental approach, along with his authority as an imam, his command of the conventions of Tatar vernacular (and official) cultural registers, and his familiarity with popular New Age sensitivities, make him an inspiring, credible figure in the eyes of many spiritually active nonpietists.

Where does this leave us with respect to the allegations of heterodoxy that taint the reputation of the Shamil mosque? Of course, as I mentioned earlier, it is not a foreign anthropologist's business to take sides in local disputes of theological nature. However, I hope that the discussion above bears out my argument that, albeit understandable from a scripturalist angle, such charges miss the point of the Shamil mosque phenomenon.

The arrangement of Mahmud-xäzrät's healing ceremony is indeed unique and eclectic, and only by some stretch of the imagination could it be called "traditional." Many innovative aspects of this assemblage are bound to raise eyebrows.

And yet it could be argued that there is nothing in the Sunna explicitly forbidding the use of, say, chairs during healing. The individual core elements of the Shamil mosque's healing prayer sessions are unequivocally Islamic. Reading specific suras, blowing on afflicted bodies after the recitation of scripture, blessing water, salt, and oil through the Quran—these are all elements of orthodox <u>ruqyah</u> that feature in the Shamil mosque healing sessions, albeit assembled into an idiosyncratic liturgical form. <u>Öşkerü</u>-goers' neglect of Islam's foundational ritual, namaz, will never please pietists (chapter 2). However, the mosque is careful to frame its healing prayer sessions, in orthodox terms, as mere supererogatory supplications and God-remembrance gatherings, not as replacements for namaz. Its leadership merely accepts that most <u>öşkerü</u>-goers will not stick around for prayer: Come—and go—as you are. Last, even though the imam's wide-ranging explorations in religious literature may alarm an orthodox-minded Muslim, there is no doubt that Mahmud-xäzrät would never propound non-Islamic spirituality, let alone discuss Osho's controversial teachings on sexual liberation, in his public capacity as a Muslim spiritual leader.

The Mortal Body: Understanding the *Ákesis* Principle

Rather than trying to assess <u>öşkerü</u> and related spiritual practices in terms of either orthodoxy or traditionality, it is more generative to experiment with conceptual frameworks apt to capture the existential experience of spiritually active Tatar nonpietists, just as the well-oiled Foucauldian-Asadian *askesis* framework captures that of halal milieu pietists. I advance the concept of *ákesis* as such a framework. I derive this term from the Greek word *"akos"*—"remedy, cure, relief" (see the word "panacea")—to define a type of religious praxis whose main drive is the pursuit of remedy from creaturely affliction, of a physical as well as existential nature (the 1990s embodiment turn in anthropology has long revealed the difficulty of drawing a clear-cut line between the two). *Ákesis*, I surmise, constitutes a core principle on which the "lived religion" (Orsi [1985] 2002) of spiritually active ethnic Muslims is based. While, as we have already begun to see, *ákesis* is not antithetical to or mutually exclusive with the *askesis* principle, the relationship between the two is a complex one—not just in Islam but in other Axial traditions as well (B. Meyer 1999, 138–139; Wanner 2020, 92).

Once again, our autonomist framework comes in handy. In chapters 1 and 2, we discussed the halal milieu as a form-of-life rooted in fidelity to a truth. Form-of-life stands in a dialectical relationship with what Agamben (1998) calls "bare life" and Badiou (2002) considers the situational domain of the "human animal."

The notion of bare human animalhood, in this philosophical framework, does not indicate the condition of a brute devoid of intellect or moral resources. Quite the opposite, it indicates human beings' experience as they use intellectual and moral resources in the pursuit of individual or corporate interests—the most basic of which are survival and a modicum of existential security—amid the "various and rapacious flux of life" (Badiou 2002, 12). We are all, at all times, human animals, even though ethical striving, love, art, science, militancy, and so forth enable us to be something else as well. The work of Agamben on bare life dovetails with and qualifies Badiou's argument by emphasizing that the messy domain of interest is riven with power dynamics, with the individuals and groups who are less successful in the race being particularly fragile and exposed to political and economic circumstances. But no matter how successful or unsuccessful one might be in it, Badiou suggests that the domain of human animalhood is inherently infused with vulnerability, pain, and fear. To the extent that they are steeped in human animalhood, observes Badiou, all humans are aware of their finitude and their condition as beings-for-death (2002, 10–11), although love, art, ethics, and so on may lift us above mere mortality.

The notions of human animalhood, bare life, and being-for-death are helpful for framing a religiosity that is not, or is only tangentially, concerned with the pursuit of verities and ethical goods and whose primary locus is fragile bodies and the fissured situations threatened, as De Martino would put it, by a looming crisis of presence. Mixing phenomenology and classical Marxism, De Martino uses this term to define the deterioration of the nexus between self and world under the negative pressure of becoming—that is, unsettling encounters with history at the macro or micro level: conditions of structural vulnerability (poverty, precarity, oppression), cultural catastrophes (uprooting, rapid modernization), personal misfortunes (illness, grief). In his works on the Mediterranean peasantry, he argued that "the power of ceremonial words and gestures [i.e., ritual]" emerges from the need to ward off the "immense power of the negative . . . with its trail of traumas, checks, frustrations" ([1959] 2015, 87). Against this onslaught, the job of ritual is that of mending cracked selves and fixing splintering worlds.

There are manifest similarities between De Martino's case and the lived religion of Tatarstan's ethnic Muslims, not least because of the existential background of the latter group, analogously exposed to the harshness of history. To the predominantly middle-aged women who gather at the Shamil mosque, the new era ushered in by perestroika is rife with uncertainty and bitterness, rather than brimming with opportunities for success and self-development as young urbanites have the luxury to believe. They are attuned to the creatural pain of the human animal, intimately acquainted with worrying, ailing, and the dread of death. This fragile situational self, rather than the robust, capable, immortality-oriented ethical subject, provides the backdrop against which the mundane drama of *öşkerü* takes place: *ákesis*—the pursuit of healing—rather than *askesis* (Şäräfetdin 2009). Again, by foregrounding these two figures, I do not wish to posit starkly opposed alternatives. No one, no matter how steadfast to a truth, can relinquish their animalhood. Islam, like any world religion, speaks to both dimensions, and each religionist may traverse vicissitudes in life during which one or the other principle is more urgently felt: As mentioned earlier, orthodox ruqyah—in which the dimension of divine heteronomy is central—is a case in point. The religious life of pietists may be primarily based on ethical obligations, the rational planning of everyday life, and the reflexive struggle with one's baser self. Yet existential crises may occur in pious milieus too, sometimes experienced as spiritual attacks from malevolent, nameless forces that need to be dispelled through spiritual means (Pandolfo 2018; Rassool 2019).

The relationship between "orthodox" ruqyah and "vernacular" *öşkerü*— bearing in mind that the terms can overlap—may be synthesized by making recourse to a Dumontian "hierarchical opposition" (Parkin 2003) in which two terms are not mutually exclusive but organized hierarchically, with the dominant term encompassing, without annulling, the subordinated one. In orthodox ruqyah, as discussed in the previous section, the ascetic principle encompasses the *aketic* one. Quranic healing is a legitimate option (only) within a framework of self-discipline, assiduous worship, and, for sinners, repentance and reform. Orthodox spiritual healing is accepted as a truth of faith, yet its applicability is limited to specific, well-defined cases—actual spiritual afflictions, not "protection"—and must not contradict the framework provided by scriptural sources. Conversely, in the case of the Shamil mosque *öşkerü* the *aketic* principle encompasses the ascetic one. Spiritual healing, rather than ascetical effort, is central to the experience of *öşkerü*-goers. The ritual may be accessed for protection or even due to curiosity to "try something new" in the landscape of postsecular spirituality, but mostly it addresses experiences of fragility and anguish caused or exacerbated by existential crises (illness, grief, mental health setbacks) that cannot be transcended by embracing unaffordable piety. The ascetic principle might not play a role of great consequence in nonpietists' lives, yet in some respect it remains necessary for the healing ritual to exist. Scriptural Islam furnishes the building blocks of the ritual procedure: Quranic suras, invocations, and chants. *Askesis* "produces" the ritual specialists—that is, the imam and his assistants, who are expected to lead a life of piety. An atmosphere of Muslimness permeates the setting (the mosque), without which the healing would not be possible, and suffuses the proceedings of the ritual.

Rather than on doctrinal or historical-ethnologic grounds, I suggest that the tension between the halal milieu and the Shamil mosque phenomenon lies in the asymmetry between these two structural oppositions, the different emphasis given to *askesis* and *ákesis* in the respective paradigms. As regards the secular mainstream and its institutions, toleration and even encouragement of the Shamil phenomenon under the aegis of *traditsionny islam* can be explained with the fact that *aketic* healing does not give rise to ethical forms-of-life: *Ákesis* does not presuppose adherence to a Rule and the consolidation of ethically intense communities; therefore, it does not constitute a threat to the themitical order. Hence, the ceremony can be benevolently described as an innocuous, culturally authentic practice. Ruqyah as it is practiced by pietists, by contrast, is constantly at risk of being framed by outsiders as yet another obscurantist, foreign-imported *netraditsionny* abstrusity, as is, in general, doctrinal speech about jinns and spiritual agencies, which is indeed hardly heard outside the intimate context of the halal milieu (see chapter 5). At heart, however, the difference between the Shamil phenomenon and Quranic healing is not a matter of orthodoxy or custom, let alone of compatibility with a secular setup. It is a matter of hierarchical primacy given to one or the other of two principles that are equally present in Islam.

"Holy" Water?

Let us explore the interlocking of *askesis* and *ákesis* in another manifestation of ethnic Muslim lived religion: Pilgrimage (*ziyarät*) to healing sites, particularly Tatarstan's "holy springs" (*izge çişmälär*) or "springs of the holy (men)" (*izgelär çişmäse*). The following episode took place in 2017 during a summer fieldwork expedition in the course of which I roamed the Idel-Ural region's holy sites with a good friend, Nurislam, a halal-minded Tatar intellectual. Nurislam and I had made our way to Iske Kazan, a well-known archaeological site some forty kilometers from Kazan, featuring the remains of a medieval city of which almost nothing is left. The site is now home to a museum and a "history park" for tourists inclusive of faux-medieval wooden structures, folk music shows courtesy of sprightly Tatar grannies, and a rather incongruous monument to the Russian poet Aleksandr Pushkin, the main function of which seems to be that of reminding visitors that Tatarstan is Russia. The site is located in a lush, verdant landscape crossed by the meandering Qazansu River and overlooked by a scenic relief, on top of which the holy spring of Mullah Hajji, renowned for its healing water, is perched. A short walk from there, another water source, dedicated to a female figure called Aisha, is ensconced in a shady grove. Although the latter spot is less popular with visitors (perhaps because it lacks a stunning view over the plain), Aisha's water is famed for healing eyesight problems.

A set of devotional infrastructures has developed around Mullah Hajji's spring complex. The main source is protected by a recently erected wooden pavilion with a crescent-shaped entrance. A tiny, beautiful wooden mosque/prayer hut stands a few meters uphill, next to a small birch grove under which devotees have erected what, at first sight, looks like a Muslim cemetery but is, in fact, a set of tombstone-like votive stone slabs. Many of the trees are decorated with white ribbons, although this "pagan" practice is discouraged by a Tatar-written board nearby. The site is often bustling with visitors, especially on summer weekends. Like in the case of the Shamil mosque phenomenon, the demographic makeup of the crowd tends to be characterized by a predominance of middle-aged women, sometimes with husbands and younger family members in tow. On busy days, the scene brims with rustic vivacity, amplified by the casual, unpretentious, sometimes garish attire of visitors. _Ziyarät_-goers climb up and down the rickety metal stairs leading to the spring, carrying plastic containers for the water. Others circumambulate the votive grove, formulating their wishes in silent concentration. No specific prayer, invocation, or fixed set of actions appears to be associated with this procedure: I asked several times on multiple visits, and no univocal answer was produced.

Well-established local narratives assert that the Mullah Hajji site is the resting place of illustrious Muslim holy men (_izgelär_) of yore. These saintly figures catalyze the supplications that Muslim visitors, at least in principle, direct to the Almighty.[5] It bears noting, however, that not all Tatar spring-goers concern themselves with the _izgelär_. On one occasion, for example, I visited the Mullah Hajji site with a self-proclaimed Turkic neo-pagan who only voiced some skeptical remarks about the alleged burials and did not openly offer any Islamic invocations—but still collected the "powerful" water. Furthermore, although the majority of visitors hail from Tatar-Muslim backgrounds, the site is frequented by non-Muslims too (Russians, Chuvash, etc.). Regardless of ethnic or religious allegiances, each visitor may formulate his or her silent supplications according to the respective repertoire or lack thereof. Many tourists simply collect the water and stroll around the site.

On the day of my visit with Nurislam, my friend's feelings oscillated between respectful fascination with his fellow Tatars' nonpietistic devotional practices, on the one hand, and a certain repulsion at the unorthodox aura of the entire business on the other. Come namaz time, Nurislam decided to make his ablutions at the spring before heading to the wooden mosque. As he emerged from the pavilion where the well was located, I noticed that my friend wore an expression of amused bewilderment. Quizzed about what had happened, he burst into laughter and reported a bizarre spiritual misunderstanding between him and a middle-aged, rural Tatar woman who had entered the pavilion during his ablution. Upon spotting Nurislam thoroughly washing his feet, the lady asked him, in a hopeful tone, whether Mulla Hajji's holy water was "particularly good for foot aches." When Nurislam explained to her that he was, in fact, performing *taxarat* (ritual ablution) before prayer, her eyes widened in embarrassment and then narrowed into a perplexed, slightly suspicious look: Perhaps the neat-looking young man was some sort of extremist? Nurislam found the whole episode hilarious. Later, in the prayer hut, he thanked the Almighty for the heartfelt devotion of his fellow Tatars. However, he also implored Him to inject some (correct) faith into their hearts.

Nurislam and the middle-aged woman's understandings and uses of water at the *izge çişmä* are in many ways illustrative of ascetic versus *aketic* approaches to religious life. To my intellectual friend, the site had historical and cultural importance. Unlike hardline scripturalists, who have no time at all for holy springs (Urazmanova et al. 2014, 139–141), Nurislam harbored genuine curiosity for local traditions and respect for the hagiographic narratives about the old masters buried there. To him, however, the spring and the water gushing therefrom was not enchanted, let alone sacred. His engagement with the water was framed within the doctrinally sanctioned, "rational" ritual procedure of ablution. Tellingly, he abstained from circumambulating the grove or tying ribbons, instead making an invocation in a theologically appropriate way, after namaz and in a prayer-dedicated area.

Doctrine-conscious halalists hold that only one water source, the Zamzam Well in Mecca, has a special status in Islam. Drinking Zamzam water is recommended on the grounds of the prophetic Sunna, which informs Muslim narratives about Zamzam's properties and outlines the appropriate code of conduct for its consumption. Besides Zamzam, as a 2019 video clip released online by a young Tatar halal businesswoman-cum-influencer declared, "there is no such concept as 'holy water' in Islam. Sometimes ignorant [*neznayushchie*] people bring about confusion [*vodyat v zabluzhdenie*]. Some claim they have their own [local] holy springs . . . : none of that has anything to do with our religion." The clip passingly mentions the use of water infused with Quranic quotes for ruqyah, but, as we have seen in a previous section, in orthodox Islamic healing the ultimate source of efficacy is the Word of God alone.[6] Writing apropos nature from a scripturalist Christian position, Kierkegaard ([1946] 2016, 225) observed that "nature . . . is the work of God. And yet God is not there; but within man there is a potentiality . . . which is awakened in inwardness to become a God-relationship, and then it becomes possible to see God everywhere." Such words could also apply to Muslim pietists, who as part of their *askesis* endeavor to cultivate their ability to marvel at Creation and discern the majesty of the Most High in the material world but are not intensely drawn to supernaturalism, especially if it exceeds the boundaries of the scriptural.

To the older rural woman, by contrast, Mulla Hajji's water itself had healing power. In an *aketic* mode, if one pours *izge çişmä* water onto one's limbs, that invites the thought that the water gushing forth from such a place of holiness must have inherent, "special" properties related to the wholeness of said limbs. It is implied that the healing force, the resource to overcome bodily affliction, dwells in an enchanted cosmos rather than in scripture—a point that my Turkic neo-pagan interlocutor explicitly expressed—a cosmos organized in a "therapeutic landscape" that, albeit not exclusively available to Tatars, has strong ethnic connotations (Gesler and Kearns 2002; Evered and Evered 2017; see below). Scriptural awareness and theological considerations play little if any obvious role in the constitution of this landscape. Since *aketic* religiosity pertains to the creaturely domain of the vulnerable yet hopeful "human animal," spring-goers do not treat the water's curative power as a verity, a matter of doctrine that invites commitment, as halal milieu pietists do Zamzam water. Their hopes are based on diffused conventions and practices sedimented through a community's history (Di Puppo 2019, 326) and validated by local knowledges and opinions (see chapter 5's discussion of Wittgensteinian "certainties"). These are not anchored to a teleology or code of conduct, nor do they imply textually grounded faith in the water's powers. Rather, *aketic* practices tend to be carried out in an "as if" register ("people say," "legend has it," "there is no harm in trying"), which offers ample room for individual improvisation within an immanent domain that is infused with (the possibility of) the miraculous (Seligman et al. 2008). Make no mistake: It would be problematic to suggest that pietists are entirely foreign to such tentative improvisation ("God knows best"). I reiterate that an *aketic* mode may, and does, manifest itself in the halal milieu. However, rather than being spontaneous and immanence-grounded, pietists' supernatural explorations tend to take place under the aegis of codified divine guidance.

Framing Vernacular Pilgrimage

Ziyarät to *izge çişmälär* has long been one of the most characteristic features of Tatar lived religion, and grassroots interest in holy sites has grown spectacularly since the decline of state atheism. During the warm season, visitors flock to sites such as Iske Kazan's Mulla Hajji and Aisha springs, the Well of Gabdelrakhman in Bolğar, the Hill of the Hojas in Bilär, the Spring of Khasim-Sheikh near Kazan, the Auliya's Spring in Bashkortostan, and many others. They collect water, perform ritualized activities such as the circumambulation of prominent landscape features or monuments, leave coins as small signs of sacrifice, and in some cases—albeit less frequently—slaughter animals (*qurban*) in hope or gratitude.

The growth in holy springs activities coincided with the Islamic boom, engendering a spate of debates (Mukhamedzhanov 2014; Urazmanova et al. 2014; Zagrutdinov and Zavgarova 2018) around _ziyarät_ and related terminology. Particularly contentious are the themes of whether and to what extent the word "_ziyarät_" can be translated into "pilgrimage" (_palomnichestvo_), given that the only doctrinally validated Islamic pilgrimages are the hajj and umrah to Mecca; the problematic notion of "sainthood" in Islam, against the Islamic imperative of tawhīd; the role of the "cult of the saint" and/or of the ancestors in Tatar culture (_ziyarät_ is cognate to the word "_zirät_," which means "cemetery"); and the above-touched issue of local springs' "holy water" versus Zamzam water, which is now distributed in halal shops throughout the region but had never before been locally available to Volga Muslims.

This ferment, in turn, has catalyzed the interest of many students of Islam in Russia and Eurasia, who have shed light on many aspects of shrine devotion (Frank 1996; Rakhimov 2006; Vovina 2006; Karabulatova et al. 2014; Urazmanova et al. 2014; Di Puppo 2019; Seleznev and Selezneva 2019; Schmoller 2020; Henig 2020). While these investigations have brought into sharper focus a wide range of political, geopolitical, discursive, hagiological, or cosmological implications embedded in shrine practices, I would argue that a key existential content that connects devotees to holy sites—that is, the pursuit of healing and well-being—has tended to be taken for granted as an "obvious" feature, often acknowledged but rarely unpacked. By introducing the category of _ákesis_, I hope to offer a theoretically generative, subject-centered, experience-near conceptual framework for _izge çişmä_ activities. This is not to deny the importance of other approaches: There is no doubt, for example, that a political dimension can be discerned when vernacular Islamic practices are co-opted into _traditsionny islam_ narratives, as in the case of holy springs being turned into state-patronized heritage sites (Benussi 2021c). The presence near the Mulla Hajji spring of an incongruous but eloquent statue of Russian arch-poet and national symbol Aleksandr Pushkin is a case in point. Analogously, there is a great deal of merit in exploring localized Islamic cosmologies or unearthing vernacular hagiographical narratives. However, in what follows I seek a different theoretical path to gain insight into the existential content of holy shrine practices.

Despite a variety of intellectual and disciplinarian coordinates informing them, many academic investigations of holy springs tend to share an explicative mechanism based on what might be called the "local-hagiographic dyad." The first component of the dyad indicates a scholarly emphasis on "sacred geographies," regional or national identities, local "Islams," and so forth. The second component implies that importance is allocated to the supernatural beings with which sites are associated, which normally means "saints," mythicized historical figures, sacralized ancestors, or personified natural forces. This is a dyad because, although individual scholars might place a premium on one or another of the two aspects, the local and hagiographic principles tend to reinforce each other.

The problem with the local-hagiographic dyad is its relative distance from the subjects who visit healing sites: their motives, their expectations, and their ways of engaging with holy springs, which might be both simpler and messier than scholars' accounts. All too often, as Jesko Schmoller has observed in a perceptive article on vernacular Islam in the Urals, "the small things that form part of the ritual routines of religious believers or the locations where these practices take place are considered relevant only insofar as they refer to 'something bigger'" (Schmoller 2020, 12). While I could not agree more, Schmoller's own framing of ritual in terms of "banal nationalism," although generative, is not immune to such a risk, as it suggests that people who visit holy springs are actually doing something bigger indeed: declaring an ethnoregional belonging, informally participating in nation-building, establishing transregional allegiances, and so forth. Along similar lines, Ulan Bigozhin (2019, 131) has defined Muslim shrines as "essential pillars of the national spirit" of nations that emerged from the Soviet breakdown; Raufa Urazmanova and her colleagues' study of springs and shrines (2014, 30) invoked Pierre Nora's notion of *lieu de memoire*, which is central to nation studies; while David Henig's (2020) account of discursive tugs-of-war between local and Turkish actors over Bosnian *dovišta* highlights these Muslim holy sites' geopolitical significance. The loco-centric argumentation was pioneered by Allen Frank's (1996) work on pilgrimage practices in Bolğar and the formation of a regional identity based on sacred geographies. Frank himself, however, suggested that the development of regional and subsequently ethnonational identities, which took place between the nineteenth and the early twentieth centuries, was posterior to the emergence of ritual practices performed at holy sites, attested since the Golden Horde period (thirteenth to sixteenth centuries). This suggests that social identities associated with territorial entities are a relatively modern development (see Ross 2020, 59) that gained further traction in the post-Soviet era with the incorporation of pilgrimage sites in heritage-making projects (Urazmanova et al. 2014; Benussi 2020c), but it does not exhaust the entirety of what goes on at healing sites.

Of course, holy sites do play a role in local narratives of identity and geopolitical imagination. The idea of a Muslim land dotted with significant places has, and has long had, communal significance for Inner Russia Muslims (Vovina 2006). During my first visit to the site, in the early 2010s, I noticed Tatar nationalist slogans among the votive messages left as wishes at the Mullah Hajji spring ("Freedom to the Tatar people!"), though over the years the practice of leaving votive messages has been tightly regulated, leaving no room for political content. There is no shortage of visitors who are conversant in discourses on the "ancestral-ity," cultural genuineness, and ethnic significance of holy sites—discourses that are widespread not only among Tatars but in Russia at large (Dashibalova and Bil'trikova 2019; Kormina 2019). Yet this is not the whole story: Other visitors, especially those who are driven by the intention of asking for health, good luck, or consolation, are less easy to pigeonhole as identity tourists hankering after authenticity (Kormina 2010). These pilgrims, who may well make up the major-ity of spring-goers, are invested in the healing power of the place. A smaller but not negligible number of spring-goers are not even Muslim-background Tatars or Bashkirs but Russian, Chuvash, or Udmurt. Such spring-goers are hardly involved in the expression of ethnic or confessional identities. They simply heard that there are places where one's afflictions are mitigated and hopes rekindled.

"Hagiographic" explanations focus less on identity and more on the veneration of supernatural forces. Through this lens, holy spring spirituality is understood as the manifestation of a "cult of saints" (Urazmanova et al. 2014), sometimes glossed as "Sufi" spirituality. The efficacy and indeed the existence of healing sites is attributed to the deeds of Muslim missionaries, masters, and preachers of the past, whose remains are physically located at the sites (Rakhimov 2006). Almaz Zagrutdinov and Fanzilya Zavgarova (2018) have discussed people's "belief that water springs from under the feet of the holy man. . . . The holiness of the person buried in this place spreads into the water, and these [holy] springs, normally, are named after the saints buried nearby." Yet the authors themselves observe that in the case that they discuss, the Khasim-Sheikh spring near Kazan, the physical tomb of the saint is nowhere to be located. In general, although Idel-Ural holy springs are indeed associated with the (idea of) burials of exemplary Muslims, the latter's mausoleums/tombs/remains are rarely physically present.[7] This absence does not detract from the power of the site.

I do not wish to question that burials might have existed at some point in the past—although the actual attribution of burial sites is often contentious (Frank 1996; Rakhimov 2006). But while the burials represent the discursive center of healing sites named after the illustrious or legendary deceased, when it comes to ritual activities carried out thereat, said burials and personages appear to lose relevance. Often, little trace of them exists apart from names—some of which have been forgotten—and faded legends. As Urazmanova and her colleagues report, actually knowing hagiographic stories is not required for accessing heal-ing springs: All one needs to know is that the water is powerful and that the site should not be vandalized or disrespected (2014, 52). These authors even hint at the hypothesis that some saintly burials and cemeteries might have never been there in the first place (31). This all suggests that, leaving aside the vexed question of whether or not the "cult of the saint" is admissible in orthodox Sunni Islam, and how to define it, it is misleading to frame *izge çişmä* activities in such terms, as most visitors do not perform any recognizable "cult," and, in fact, there is little trace of "saints," at least as far as physical features of the sites go.

This argument needs to be nuanced in the case of self-described Sufi pilgrims (Di Puppo and Schmoller 2020; Schmoller 2020). Sufi spirituality tends to have a more positive take on local pilgrimage than do scripturalist approaches to Islam, on account of the centrality of the figure of the sheikh. In some Sufi contexts, the body of a master is understood as a vehicle for divine grace even after death; hence, a physical and spiritual relationship with a buried master can be beneficial insofar as it is framed within a strongly monotheistic framework. To theologically literate Sufis, the spiritual power of a sheikhly burial is subordinate to one's ethical connection to the sheikh as a paragon of Islamic virtue and conduit of God's grace, but not an intercessor or miracle worker. Most Tasawwuf practitioners, in my experience, would be loath to frame such a relationship as the "cult" of a "saint." In any case, it is important to stress that the overwhelming majority of those who visit healing sites in Idel-Ural are not practicing Sufis; furthermore, vernacular practices involving healing water are not "Sufic" in any doctrinal sense.

If Sufism stands as the most scriptural end of the "hagiographic" explanatory mechanism, the other pole is a Durkheimian reading of *izge çişmä* routines as "primordial" religiosity revolving around sacralized ancestors (Urazmanova et al. 2014, 13) or adjacent to animism (Kefeli 2014, 101; Schmoller 2020). While this argument has some merit in terms of "deep history," it appears doubtful that contemporary *ziyarät*-goers would recognize their practices as the worship of ancestors, spirits, or natural forces (except for a minority of self-avowed neo-pagans). Rhetorical references to the moral authority of the ancestors (*predki*) are common in post-Soviet Tatar political and moral discourses, as are New Age ideas about cosmic energies, the powers of nature, the intelligence of water, and so on. But while these motifs may influence a number of *çişmä*-goers, they do not add up to a coherent cosmology and ought not to be romanticized as a pristine, primordial ontological system.

Rather than any Durkheimian "elementary religiosity," I argue that *izge çişmä* practices present us with a bricolage of ideas, borrowings, and justifications (nationalism, New Age, neo-paganism, tourism, heritage, Sufism, revitalized local lore, curiosity) revolving around a shared core—the notion that holy springs are places of healing (Urazmanova et al. 2014, 60, 95). The lowest common denominator shared by most spring-goers is the pursuit of *ákesis*: "In these places, [visitors'] requests will be heard better and faster, and any request can be made—be it about health, luck, or family well-being" (Zagrutdinov and Zavgarova 2018). Tatarstani scholars have noted that springs are classified according to their healing powers: "In the Kukmor district there is the locally well-known spring of Dusay-*babay* (nobody among the locals really knows any biographic detail about Dusay-*babay*). It is thought that that spring's water heals eye diseases. And in the Nyrsy village (Tyulyachy district) there are three unnamed springs. They say that one heals eyesight, another heals hearing, and the third one mental health issues (anxiety, melancholy, stress, and so on)" (Zagrutdinov and Zavgarova 2018). Again, it is noteworthy that Tatarstani ethnographers suggest that the biographies of holy personages, and even their names, are not only unknown but irrelevant to the power of the site. What is known about the legendary owners of the burials, when these holy figures' deeds are remembered, is their thaumaturgical powers. The most illustrative example is the legend around the Well of Gabdelrakhman in Bolğar (see note 7), named after the eponymous saintly man-cum-healer, identified as a Companion of Prophet Muhammed despite the historical incongruence of a Companion present in the Volga region in the seventh century (see Lunde and Stone 2012, xxx). Gabdelrakhman is credited with converting the ruler of the Volga Bulgars, Aydar Khan, after miraculously releasing his daughter Tuy Bike from an incurable illness (Frank 1996, 270–271).

The current popularity of prerevolutionary miraculous tales and legends connected to healing sites, such as the story of Gabdelrakhman or that of the Turkic cultural hero Ural Batyr bringing life and fertility to the land by pouring "living water" onto a mountain in Bashkortostan (Di Puppo and Schmoller 2019b, 143), resonates with the enormous appeal that marvelous stories about miracle-working "holy men" had in prerevolutionary Idel-Ural (Kefeli 2014, 83). Now as then, these narratives attribute the power to heal and perform wonders only to ethical exemplars: individuals who excelled in their piety, devotion, and knowledge. Once again, thus, the ascetic principle is found underpinning and validating sites noted for their thaumaturgical powers. In the next section, we shall look more closely at how Islamic *askesis* intertwines with the "natural spirituality" of healing springs in Tatarstan and other corners of Muslim Eurasia through saintly burials.

Tatar *Ziyarāt*, Eurasian Spirituality, and Islam

In Povolzhye, as in culturally and geographically adjacent Eurasian regions, "most [holy] sites consist of at least a tree, a water source and a tomb" (Abramson and Karimov 2007, 321; see Di Puppo and Schmoller 2019). Strong family resemblances exist between the pilgrimage sites of Volga Tatars and a broader family of religious shrines widespread across Eurasia, often characterized by water springs and trees or groves, sometimes decorated with ribbons. "Therapeutic landscapes" or "enabling places" (Gesler and Kearns 2002; Duff 2012; Evered and Evered 2017) sharing similar characteristics can be found from the Balkans to Mongolia through Ukraine, Siberia, Central Asia, and the Caucasus. They have been observed among peoples of Slavic, Turkic, Mongolic, and Finno-Ugric backgrounds. Communities in which such sites exist might belong to Axial (scripture-based and ascetical) religious traditions such as Islam, Orthodox Christianity, or Tibetan Buddhism, as well as non-Axial ones such as shamanism and other native faiths. Sometimes such sacra are shared by members of different religious groups, as in the Volga region where healing springs attract non-Tatar and non-Muslim visitors too (Bowman 2010; Dubuisson and Genina 2011; Henig 2012; Darieva et al. 2018; Wanner 2020). In Tatarstan and elsewhere across Eurasia, "animated" sites and "places of strength" may attract prayer but require no prescribed ritual routine or performative competence; hence, innovation and individualized practices are common (Wanner 2020, 81).

The analogies between Tatar *izge çişmä* spirituality and other Eurasian natural sacra have led to persistent questions about whether *ziyarät* to *izge çişmä* and related ritual practices are "really" Islamic or, as some scripturalist voices put it, they should be seen as "pagan survivals" carried out by Muslims-in-name-only (Urazmanova et al. 2014, 14). On the other side of the divide, some hail these devotions as "traditionally Tatar" spiritual heritage (Zagrutdinov and Zavgarova 2018). As anthropologists, how are we to situate Tatar *ziyarät* in what appears to be a broader landscape of indigenous Eurasian spirituality without denying its Islamicness? Can we venture into such a minefield without validating one or another emic viewpoint? Only ad hoc comparative research could provide compelling responses to the question, but I would like to briefly outline a hypothesis that may prove equally generative and free from value judgment.

In his classic study of the veneration of saints' statues in vernacular Italian American Catholicism—a practice deemed archaic and heathenistic by many Protestant onlookers—social historian Robert Orsi ([1985] 2002) suggested investigating the practices of religious communities not on the basis of their supposed origin, be it scriptural or prescriptural, but rather through communities' axiological systems. In the case of Italian American Catholic nonpietists, saint veneration has to be understood in the context of a working-class, immigrant, Mediterranean-influenced moral world hinged upon inclusive yet tight family networks that Orsi defined as *Domus*. Healing, solace, and in general the overcoming of crises of presence, to use the De Martinian phrase, were sought through engagement with holy figures who encoded *Domus*-type relationships: the Madonna with her infant; Saints Cosmas and Damian, martyr brothers; Saint Ann, the mother of Mary; or the Holy Family, with Saint Ann (Jesus's grandmother) in the background. To translate Orsi's argument into our framework, the *Domus* functioned as an *aketic* resource owing to its moral preeminence.

Orsi's method may be applied to our case, provided that cultural differences in axiological schemata are taken into account. Vernacular Italian American Catholic devotion does not seem to rely on natural sacra to the same extent as indigenous Eurasian spirituality.[8] Conversely, *Domus*-type personages and relationships do not feature prominently in *izge çişmälär* and analogous sacra. Instead, a central moral and aesthetic role is given to the "native land" (*tuğan yak*, *rodnoy kray*). It could be hypothesized that in Tatarstan, as elsewhere in Eurasia, landscape features are valued as *aketic* resources: The moral centrality of the land among many Eurasian agrarian and seminomadic populations undergirds the spirituality of natural sacra and invests them with *aketic* potential. It could be advanced, in De Martinian terms, that outstanding landscape sites—characterized by the gushing forth of water or the unusual growth of trees—harbor a "surplus of presence" that can be tapped into at times when individual presence becomes fragile and needs restoring. Of course, the wide distribution of therapeutic landscapes across Eurasia does not necessarily imply the existence of a single cosmo-ontological framework, nor does it evince the "survival" of ritual fossils from an ancient common ancestor. Rather, it may imply a loosely shared axiological assemblage characterized by continuities and borrowings as much as innovations and divergencies across historical periods, geographical boundaries, and confessional divides.

Testing such a hypothesis would require separate treatment. However, regardless of how to frame the similarities between *izge çişmälär*, Slavic *mesta sily* ("places of strength"), and Mongolian *arshaan*, what is specific to the former is how the *aketic* potential of natural sacra is linked to and legitimized through an Islamic framework. This occurs through the unique element that sets apart Eurasian Muslims' holy sites from their non-Muslim equivalents: the saintly burials, actual or legendary, of exemplary Islamic figures who embody the ascetical principle of the faith (*äüliya*, *izgelär*) (see Henig 2020). The ethnographer Raufa Urazmanova and her colleagues (2014, 35) have operated a useful conceptual distinction between "sacred" and "holy" items. "Sacred," in their framework, is synonymous with miraculously efficacious. That which heals—which has, in our terms, *aketic* power—is sacred: water, springs, trees, the site itself. "Holiness," by contrast, specifically pertains to Islam and Muslim exemplars; in our terms, it pertains to *askesis*. It is through "the performance of supererogatory [nafil] prayers and good deeds, strict observance of dietary prohibitions (halal and haram), an [Islamically] permissible source of livelihood" that excellent individuals come to emanate "light [nūr] and divine blessing even after death," so that their graves become pilgrimage centers (Mukhamedzhanov 2014).

While Urazmanova et al. use the sacred/holy distinction to venture a binary classification of Tatar healing sites (natural vs. Islamic), I would suggest that all *izge çişmälär*, insofar as they feature natural and hagiological elements, possess both qualities. The holiness of *izgelär'* (*askesis*) authorizes the miraculous efficaciousness (*ákesis*) of the landscape. It is beyond the point to try to assess the precise point in time in which *askesis* and *ákesis* converged at specific sites: Although mention of saintly burials appears in written sources as early as the eighteenth century (Frank 1996; Kefeli 2014, 98; Urazmanova et al. 2014, 88), the association between landscape features (springs, trees) and saintly tombs is most likely older. However, let us recall that material signs of the burials are often absent from *izge çişmälär*, without this absence invalidating their power. It can be supposed that in lieu of holy sites having healing power because of the preexistent physical presence of Muslim burials, at least in some cases Muslim burials might have been (retroactively? legendarily?) associated with places already recognized as having *aketic* power.

Like in the case of *öşkerü* and *ruqyah*, the combination of *ákesis* and *askesis* on the ground yields two symmetrical Dumontian hierarchical oppositions. In one scenario, the ascetic principle is dominant: *ziyarät* to a holy site is framed as an endeavor to establish a relationship with an ethical exemplar through doctrinally validated methods. It is through the master's enduring spiritual presence that divine healing force (glossed, scripturally, as *barakat*) is accessed: through a holy site, but in a context of personal *askesis*. In the second scenario, the *aketic* principle is dominant. Enchanted landscape features are seen as inherently powerful, while Islam constitutes a justifying framework that, albeit important, needs not be subjectively engaged with to tap into a sacred site's healing power. In contemporary Tatarstan, an ascetic approach is practiced by a minoritarian proportion of visitors, typically practitioners of orthodox Sufism (Di Puppo and Schmoller 2020; Schmoller 2020). The second scenario corresponds to the approach of a large if often overlooked number of contemporary spring-goers: spiritually active nonpietists motivated by the desire to overcome existential crises of varying magnitudes through *aketic* practices.

Askesis and Ákesis in Muslim Experience

In this chapter, I have argued that the vernacular practices of spiritually active Tatar nonpietists can be understood as motions directed toward *ákesis*: an overcoming of the fragility of presence through ritual means. The practices we have discussed are often described in problematic terms, such as "cult of the saints," which lend themselves to misinterpretations or polarized readings casting them as either unorthodox, even pagan, or culturally authentic and "traditional." By advancing *ákesis* as a framing device, I hope to have contributed to an understanding of phenomena like *öşkerü* or *ziyarät* to holy springs both in their own terms and in their intertwinement with the Islamic *askesis* of the halal milieu.

Inasmuch as it pertains to the domain of the fragile "human animal," *ákesis* is "below good and evil" (Badiou 2002)—that is, extraneous to an ethic of virtue that identifies the good with a (scripturally defined) teleology. It does not require commitment, it is not exclusive (thus, it allows the sharing of sacra), it does not promise salvation, and it does not engender ethical forms-of-life. Of course, *aketic* religiosity is not amoral—simply, it identifies the good, situationally, with the health and existential well-being of practitioners: their bare life. An ethic of fidelity, conversely, subordinates well-being to the ascetical principle of the Rule (without necessarily denying it). While this helps comprehend fidelious pietists' mixed-to-negative feelings toward *aketic* practices, it is important to emphasize that pietists never cease to be "human animals" confronted with their own crises of presence. In fact, scriptural Islam does include *aketic* dimensions, as we have seen in the case of ruqyah and the consumption of Zamzam water, but personal *askesis* remains central, and healing is understood as dependent on God's agency: In this mode, to overcome a crisis one must trust God and acknowledge him as the ultimate Presence.

Despite pietists' disapprobation, altogether denying the Islamicness of non-pietists' spiritual healing practices would be problematic: Urban *öşkerü* utilizes scripturally validated techniques, while *izge çişmälär*'s "holiness" derives from the exemplarity of legendary spiritual masters who embody an ideal of Islamic askesis. Thus, rather than as mutually exclusive possibilities, I have suggested considering *ákesis* and *askesis* as terms in a Dumontian hierarchical couple, in which either may take a dominant position and encompass the other depending on historical circumstances. This allows us to explore vernacular practices without declaring them either "pre-Islamic" (religiously inauthentic) or "traditional" (culturally authentic).[9]

I emphasize once again that the concepts of *askesis* and *ákesis* are not meant to encode a "sociological" contraposition of city and countryside, or Great versus Little Tradition. Nor are they supposed to exhaust the variety of nuances that could be discerned in the panoply of Islamic practice. Rather, this conceptual couple highlights the coexistence, within the same framework, of a truth-oriented mode that pertains to the perfectioning of the "fidelious subject" and a situational one that pertains to the wholeness of the "human animal." These modes should be understood as autonomous yet liable to interact. In the context of Islam, *ákesis* should not be framed as a "lack" of *askesis* or as its negation: It is far more fruitful to recognize it as its *precondition*—the living human being the "support" of the fidelious subject—and investigate how the two principles combine in concrete situations. In vernacular Islamic spirituality, the ascetic principle still plays a vital role in structuring the forms in which wholeness can be achieved, providing the building blocks of ritual (*öşkerü*) or anchoring sacred sites to an Islamic horizon of holiness (saintly burials at holy springs).

The sequence of ruptures that took place in the twentieth century, especially the eradication of grassroots Muslim institutions, might have widened the gap between *ákesis* and *askesis*, creating a less hierarchically organic and more horizontally antagonistic opposition between the two, mirroring the well-known ideological antagonism between tradition/religion and progress/secularity. Hence, to some of the ethnic Muslims who now visit holy springs, Islamic *askesis* may feel remote, even foreign or threatening. Among halal milieu Muslims, conversely, some may be tempted to disqualify vernacular healing practices such as *öşkerü* and *izge çişmälär* spirituality as misguided, superstitious, or spiritually harmful. However, ideological antagonism obscures the extent to which the ascetical and *aketic* principles, as I have attempted to show, remain profoundly embedded in each other.

ON THE SHOULDERS OF GIANTS
Extraordinary Speech, Truth, and Intensity

A few days after _Uraza Bäyräm_ was celebrated in Akmaş, an east Tatarstani industrial town known for its strong scripturalist community, I was invited by the respected community member Alimdzhan-äfände, a Central Asian man who had long been living in the city, to his Soviet-era apartment for tea. A handful of male guests, all belonging to the local mosque community, joined us as we sipped tea and chatted on, sitting on a thick, industrially made Uzbek rug in Alimdzhan's living room. Before long, the topic of our conversation turned to religion. Among us was Amir, an energetic young man who had recently grown out of a turbulent adolescence and now divided his time between studying religious matters with a Salafi _ustaz_ and exploring business opportunities with fellow halalists.

Amir's above-average proficiency in scriptural matters made his voice authoritative among our host's circle of friends. At one point, my acquaintances began discussing the lives of ancient prophets. "Is it true that Prophet Adam, peace be upon him, was much taller than men are today?" Master Alimdzhan asked. "Of course, he was about thirty meters tall—just a bit less," Amir confidently replied, followed by a round of nods and expressions of mild amazement ("Mashallah!"). As if in response, Alimdzhan-äfände added, "Men were much larger back then, and they also lived much longer. We have been shrinking since." "Yes," another man interjected casually, "he lived a thousand years." That was a very long time indeed, everybody agreed. "And Prophet Nuh [Noah], peace upon him, reached 950 years," explained Amir, prompting another attendee to lament that humankind had shrunk not only in size but also in lifespan. Again, the other attendees eagerly joined in with personal observations and remarks about humans' transformation from long-living giants to the more diminutive beings that we are now. The tone of the exchange, at once matter-of-fact and enthusiastic, struck me.

As the conversation progressed, I caught myself feeling ill at ease. While at the beginning of the meeting I had felt comfortable, actively participating in the conversation, now I just hoped I was managing to camouflage my puzzlement. Over the months, I had acquainted myself with the sermons of local imams, attended classes on halal business or Islamic family life at the local mosque, and come to feel that I had learned to navigate my interlocutors' ethical world, yet at that moment I found myself uncomfortably distant from them. What they were saying was just . . . preposterous. My acquaintances, whom I knew as reasonable, pragmatic, competent individuals who had received enough schooling and mainstream information to master the basics of biology and archaeology, must have been aware of how outlandish such claims would have sounded to most people outside of that living room. So where did their self-satisfied assuredness come from?

The spread of Islamic piety movements in the post-Soviet era brought about a new way of "speaking Islamic piety" in Povolzhye. This meant fresh theological and ideological discursive registers, from Salafism to neo-Sufism and beyond, as well as a specific "sociolect" that incorporates Arabic terminology into the Russian medium, which on account of its plasticity and its status as a world language has overtaken ethnic tongues such as Tatar (Bustanov and Kemper 2013; Bustanov 2017). But the encounter above suggests that piety transforms not only discourse and language but speech as well. This chapter attempts to address this question of how ethical intensity manifests itself in speech events by focusing on a family of utterances pronounced in contexts of *askesis*—that is, the speech environment of ethical forms-of-life.

In retrospect, I realize that my uneasiness during that conversation with my acquaintances in Akmaş was meaningful and could be framed as a successful ethnographic encounter. Speech events like those are not unique to Tatarstan and in fact occur in Islamic reform settings across the globe. Consider the following passage, gleaned from an English-language web page:

> [A] Muslim is obliged to believe in every idea for which there is evidence in the Qur'aan or saheeh Sunnah from the Messenger of Allaah (peace and blessings of Allaah be upon him). . . . A believer is required to believe with firm faith in everything that we are told by Allaah and by the Prophet (peace and blessings of Allaah be upon him), if it is proven to be soundly reported from him (peace and blessings of Allaah be upon him). He must believe in it with firm faith that leaves no room for the slightest doubt. He must accept it in general and specific terms,

whether he understands it or not and whether he finds it strange or
not. . . . Allaah says . . . : "Only those are the believers who have believed
in Allaah and His Messenger, and afterward doubt not but strive with
their wealth and their lives for the Cause of Allaah. Those! They are
the truthful." The basic principle here is to accept the absolute power of
Allaah and to accept what He tells us and what His Messenger (peace
and blessings of Allaah be upon him) tell us, and to say what those who
are well versed in knowledge say: "We believe in it; the whole of it (clear
and unclear Verses) are from our Lord" [Al 'Imraan 3:7].

The author does not deny that aspects of Islamic revelation can be "strange": It
is precisely that which makes them worthy of committing to. Statements about
ancient prophets' superior size and longevity are steeped in Islamic doctrine,
even though interpretations differ.[1] Those utterances made me uncomfortable
because they were *meant* to be extra-ordinary. The matter-of-fact tone in which
they are uttered only adds to their intensity. They do something. By uttering
them, one steps out of the domain of commonsense speech and into the realm of
verity. By partaking in such speech events, "ordinary" subjectivities are unmade,
and *other* subjectivities are brought to life. After uttering this type of statement or
joining the discursive space thereby created, one is not the same as before. This
transformative effect is not limited to individual speakers but extends to communities of utterers that share in the same linguistic "decision-event" (Humphrey
2018; also see Harding 2001, 57–60). Precisely because they are transformative
and put their utterers at odds with ordinary/authorized discourse (Law-vali-
dated), thereby entailing a danger, these speech acts index their utterers' fidelity
to a Rule. By sharing those words with me, my interlocutors had let me into the
"inner" discursive space of their ethical form-of-life, in which things are uttered
that are not necessarily said even in the "outer" discursive space—that of sermons, halal economy seminars, and Quranic classes.

    In what follows, I treat fidelity utterances—which I shall call "fidemes" (mod-
eled on "phoneme")—as units of language that index a commitment (ethically),
manifest a truth-process (historically), and structure a form-of-life (sociologically). Fidemic utterances fall beyond the scope of ordinary speech and can produce consequences. At the personal level, both individual and supra-individual,
their issuance marks the utterer's entrance in a "composition of a subject of truth"
(Badiou 2002, 40). Within a form-of-life, they create a space of discursive sameness—to put it in Tiqqunian terms, they generate "community"; or, to riff on a
famous expression by Michael Herzfeld (2005), they produce something that may
be called "ethical intimacy." Conversely, fidemic speech acts produce a discursive

divide between the utterer's form-of-life and the mainstream. From the outside, fidemes are experienced as counter-doxic, transgressive, even outrageous.

In the following pages, I explore extra-ordinary verity speech through a critical exploration of a series of influential theories of language, truth, and the social power of speech. By touching on several concepts—belief, ordinary language, certainty, illocution, ritual efficacy, excitable speech—we will determine the analogies as well as the differences between fidemes and other forms of speech that have attracted the attention of philosophers and social analysts. This journey, inspired by an ethnographic encounter with giant-talk, can be undertaken only by standing on the shoulders of giants: names of the caliber of Ludwig Wittgenstein, J. L. Austin, Louis Althusser, and Pierre Bourdieu. These thinkers' works will be put in conversation with the autonomist framework that orients this investigation of Islam in post-Soviet Russia. By doing so, I intend to shed light on a dimension of language that has received relatively little attention in previous investigations: the point of encounter of speech, the political, and ethical striving.

After Belief

It would be easy to "explain" pietists' statements about semi-immortal giants as their "beliefs." As the quote offered a few pages ago shows, pietists themselves may use this word in describing their obligation to adhere to revealed truth. But the concept of "belief" is far from innocent, and its analytical purchase has long come under scrutiny. So what do people talk about when they talk about their beliefs?

Anthropology has long concerned itself with systematic efforts to make sense of verbal behaviors that fail to resonate with what the scientific method and post-Enlightenment sensibilities would construe as rational. Both within and outside the discipline, the concept of (religious) belief has been used to that end (Sperber 2009). Belief has been a centerpiece of anthropological thought on religion since Tylor's (1871, 383) definition of the latter as belief in spiritual beings and Durkheim's ([1912] 1995) two-pronged model of religious life as composed of patterns of action (ritual) corresponding to certain states of opinion (beliefs). Between the 1960s and the 1980s, however, compelling reasons were advanced to argue against an irreflexive use of the belief concept (Leach 1966). A vast body of literature has undermined all certainty about the heuristic value of belief as a scholarly category, revealing the numerous unprocessed assumptions behind it. In light of this literature, I argue that it would be myopic to content ourselves with superficially pigeonholing unsettling statements as "beliefs."

Let me briefly summarize the main arguments. Rodney Needham's (1972) paradigm-changing denunciation is a good starting point. The British anthropologist vocally questioned the idea that people's verbal behavior constituted evidence of inner mental conditions, as it had been assumed before: he felt that the concept of belief had allowed scholars of religions to fraudulently claim access to the psychic experience of individuals or collectives as if they were transparent to external inquiry. But not only is the grammar of belief-talk in Western languages opaque and ambiguous (does it indicate an inner state, received doxa, scriptural dogma, or something else?), it is also untranslatable to and from culturally distant cultural environments. Unlike the experience of having a body, feeling pain, and so forth, belief is not identifiable across linguistic divides. This led Needham to question the existence of a "universal capacity" to believe and declare the belief concept—culture-specific and possibly altogether lacking a referent in the world—unsuitable for social analysis.

Shortly afterward, it was Jean Pouillon's turn ([1982] 2016) to further deconstruct the vocabulary of belief. Pouillon suggested that cosmological differences affect how different cultural groups talk about belief and that the dominant anthropological terminology is marred by an unspoken Christian bias. By comparing European languages and the Dangleat language spoken in his Sahelian research site, Pouillon showed how the Western terminology of belief conflates cognitive, affective, moral, and affiliational implications in highly idiosyncratic ways. Christianity (especially Protestantism) being based on a clear-cut cosmological divide between the immanent and the transcendental, multiple dimensions must be conflated in the Christian experience of believing: the existence of a distant God must be cognitively held as valid at a cosmo-ontological level, humans' relationship with God ought to marked as one of trust, and God's existence must be accepted collectively as a dogma or creed. The animistic cosmology of Pouillon's Dangleat-speaking interlocutors, however, did not rest on a neat divide between the natural world and the divined or spiritual domain. The agency of spirits was framed as intimately interwoven with human experience, so there was no need to conflate cognitive, affective, and moral-affiliational experiences into a single linguistic-conceptual node. One would not have to make a strong cognitive or affective investment or declare a formal creed to engage with the spirits. Such cosmology thus afforded the possibility of using a more nuanced, more diversified, and richer terminology than the one-size-fits-all post-Christian concept of "belief" to talk about humans' relationship with the spiritual realm.[2]

Pouillon's call to problematize belief is mirrored by a contribution published in the same year by Malcolm Ruel. Ruel set out to "sketch in outline the monumental peculiarity of Christian 'belief'" ([1982] 2005), parochializing Western assumptions and challenging their exportability into other contexts. He did so by tracing a broad-brushed historical and lexicological analysis of how Christians have talked about belief over the past two millennia. This parable traces Christian "belief" across multiple iterations: from enthusiastic participation in a charismatic movement, to an initiatory declaration, to a corporately declared and institutionally enforced orthodoxy, to an inwardly organized experience, to private opinion. Ruel ended his article by outlining four fallacious assumptions in scholarly belief-talk: (1) that belief is central in all religions in the same ways as in Christianity, (2) that belief forms the basis of social behavior and can be cited as a sufficient explanation for it, (3) that belief is an interior state, and (4) that determining behavior as being motivated by belief is more important, consequential, or explanatory than actually engaging with the content of what is "believed" (emic cosmologies, axiologies, etc.).

To be sure, these works, however influential, did not rid anthropology of belief-talk. Cognitive anthropologists (Luhrmann 1989, 309; 2012; Boyer 2002; Severi 2007) and students of religious identities (Lindquist and Coleman 2008), among others, have reclaimed the concept of belief, although no contemporary anthropologist of religion would argue that this concept can be used innocently. In our case, anyway, we are better served heeding Needham's, Pouillon's, and Ruel's words of warning. Using the category of belief to explain the kind of utterances discussed in this chapter would obscure more than it reveals.

Povolzhye's halal milieu exists in a multilingual environment where different belief-words circulate. Yet they all resist direct translation into the ambiguous, one-size-fits-all concept as "belief." The Tatar language uses distinct (though related through the stem *ışan-*) verbal compounds to (a) express "trust/faith in," with the related moral-affiliational implications ((*Allağa) ışanırğa*: "to believe (in God)"; *ışanuçı*: "believer"), and (b) express a cognitive fact such as conviction, conjecture, or supposition (*dip ışanırğa*).[3] Russian, the dominant language, strongly differentiates between believing as a moral-affiliational stance (*verit'*, "to have faith," and related terms) and believing as "supposing/assuming/reckoning" (*polagat'*, *schitat'*). Finally, Arabic—which is not actively spoken among halalists but exercises an influence as Islam's liturgical language—differentiates between believing in a cognitive sense (*iqtinä'*) and belief as faith (*īmān*). In short, regardless of the language used, it is safe to say that when committed Muslims in Povolzhye exchange statements about prophets' height, age, worthiness, and so forth, they are firmly in the domain of moral/affiliational/creedal statements (*ışanırğa*, *verit'*, *īmān*), not in that of conjectures, opinions, or cognitive activities (*dip ışanırğa*, *polagat'*, *iqtinä'*). The vaguer Western vocabulary of "belief" risks obscuring this crucial distinction.

Of course, pietists may conjecture over articles of faith that invite speculation. For example, Islamic online forums abound with opinions, arguments, and tentative explanations on whether the gradual decrease in humans' height and age may be related to, say, changes in the earth's gravity or, perhaps, the varying composition of the atmosphere. People might become attached to their hypotheses and defend them vigorously. Yet engrossing as they might be, there is a strong understanding that such conjectures are less important than the articles of faith themselves—and indeed, according to some, they are entirely irrelevant. Unlike committing to articles of faith, entertaining secondary opinions or hypotheses is not required of Muslims and may even be seen as unwelcome. During one of our conversations, my good acquaintance Umar (whom we have encountered before in this book) expressed his negative opinion of a tendency among some Muslims to reinforce commitment to a truth of faith by conjecture—for instance, by using the argument that the divine proscription of pork meat is based on its inherent insalubriousness or revolting taste. Such talk is a sign of "weak" faith, my friend reasoned: While one might "opine/reckon" (*predpolagat'*) that pork meat is distasteful, there is no scriptural basis to such thought. What doctrine says about animals is that they all, including spiritually polluting ones like swine and dogs, worship God. Pork meat might well be nutritious and tasty after all, but since God commanded abstention, keeping away from it is a matter of following a divinely decreed Rule, a truth that does not need extra validation.

While a committed religionist will pledge her fidelity to one single truth, the post-Tiqqun collective Invisible Committee has argued that "truths are multiple, but untruth is one, because it is universally arrayed against the slightest truth that surfaces" (2017, 13). These thinkers-cum-activists consider truth a function of ethical intensity—which can go in different, even discordant directions, hence its multiplicity—and untruth a function of conformity and regimentation under the single, oppressively harmonious framework that they gloss as "Empire." Their position resonates with the Kierkegaardian proto-autonomist dictum that "the truth of a proposition . . . is relative to the intention of the asserter and depends ultimately upon what the preposition is asserted against" (Bretall [1946] 2016, 282). Autonomist theory thus offers us an analytical vantage point that (a) does not bind us to the specific truth of this or that form-of-life, and indeed allows for the existence of a great variety of truths, and (b) links verity to the nexus between speech, conduct, and power, enabling us to avoid the shortcut of fact and opinion that is presupposed by the concept of "belief."

From Ordinary Language . . .

The emergence of skepticism toward the analytical power of the belief concept coincided, at least in Anglophone anthropology, with a phase of deeper engagement with the philosophy of Ludwig Wittgenstein (Leach 1966; Needham 1972; see chapter 1), who also famously embraced a nonfactual theory of truth in his latest works (Wittgenstein 1986).

Disillusionment with, if not open hostility to, the social sciences' explanatory, sociologizing tendencies was a recurrent theme in Wittgensteinian philosophy (Wittgenstein 2018), which resonated with the developments of poststructuralist and postmodernist anthropology. Particularly poignant for the purposes of this chapter is Wittgensteinianism's critique of the "stupid" (2018, 72), even "perverse" (Mulhall 2005, 14) ambition of explaining belief through reasoning, which to Wittgenstein meant misrecognizing a truth when faced with one (2018, 72; see Palmié 2018). Unsurprisingly, Wittgenstein's influential critique contributed to the downfall of the belief concept described in the previous section.

If taken to its extreme consequences, Wittgenstein's antirationalism might be incompatible with anthropology as an intellectual project (or indeed with academia itself).[4] Notwithstanding this, Wittgenstein's philosophy of ordinary language and his call for epistemological humility have exerted on the discipline a persistent fascination—which is not surprising considering anthropology's investment in the everyday and its predilection for immersive comprehension over cold dissecting, complexity over exactitude.

Wittgensteinianism's relationship with radical theory is also complicated. While Agamben and the Tiqqun collective (in particular their later avatar, the Invisible Committee) have drawn extensively on Wittgenstein's terminology,[5] Alain Badiou (2019) dismissed Wittgensteinianism as an "antiphilosophy" (see also Norris 2009), in a scathing critique at the heart of which there lies a radically different framing of truth.

Wittgenstein viewed ordinary language (encompassing ethics, aesthetics, faith, etc.) as the realm of "nonsense"—that is, of nonfactual statements. "Nonsense" is not derogatory in a Wittgensteinian framework. Nonsense is not only unavoidable in human language; it is also valuable and worthy of respect (1965, 12): It is through nonsensical language-games that humans can form a relationship with a world devoid of obvious meaning and develop "certainties" about what makes it worth living in. That God loves us, that good deeds shall be rewarded in the Hereafter, and that a given prayer will ease our pain are examples of such worthwhile, consolatory nonsense.

In Wittgenstein's understanding of religion, certainties are formed situationally, through apprenticeship and conventional action (Wittgenstein 1972; see Pitkin 1972; Diamond 2003; Mulhall 2005). Hence, it is through attunement to collective "language-games" and attention to the "borders of language" (Wittgenstein 1972, 12), rather than explanations, that observers may contemplate the "general principles" of religious life (Wittgenstein 2018, 38–40).[6] According to Wittgenstein, religious certainties are impermeable to external analysis and rationalization: There is no Archimedean point outside of language from which to access it. Analytical, scholarly language is therefore, to Wittgenstein, no less nonsensical than any other language-games, but, in its pretense of facticity and exactitude, it is in actuality more misguided. From a Wittgensteinian viewpoint, the harder social analysts attempt to make sense of what they investigate, especially in the case of religion, the more alienated from it (and from genuine human experience in general) they become. Rather than falling into the hubristic and "impossible" position of the analyst, then, one should "only resort to description . . . , and say: such is human life" (Wittgenstein 2018, 34; see also Mulhall 2005, 94).

It is easy to see that such anti-analytical maximalism makes an uneasy bedfellow for any project of social investigation. But in a diluted, less maximalist version, Wittgenstein's framing of religious certainties as rooted in conventional, self-sustaining ordinary language-games can enrich anthropological attempts to understand religious life. Let us return to the healing practices at "sacred" springs that we discussed in a previous chapter. Such practices pertain to certain historically resilient language-games that have to do with restoration through special substances (*lechebnaya voda*, "healing water"), the curative powers of the land (*mesta sily*, "places of strength"), and less directly the holiness associated with saintly burials (*svyatie*, "holy (men)"). Interestingly, if one looks at the "borders of language," no explicit creedal-affiliational speech emerges in association with sacred springs: Despite their remedial connotations, these are not places of "faith" (*vera*, īmān). It is telling in this respect that non-Muslims also gather at Muslim sacred springs. Even cognitive statements about the facticity of the powers involved in healing are hard to come by in ordinary interactions: Spring-goers do not argue for or against places of strength, and the healing process does not require them to voice, defend, or propagate specific opinions. I have never heard anyone say things like "I *believe* that such and such water has curative effects for such and such reasons"; if at all, the language-game of holy springs is likely to produce statements such as "people say that," "people do like this," and so on. Efforts to bring external framings to bear on these language-games, for instance by describing such practices as a "cult of the saints," run the risk of saddling the actual language-game with the foreign grammar of social-science scholarship.

The same applies to other manifestations of vernacular Islam in Povolzhye. The "minimal religion" of "ethnic" Muslims (Epstein 1999a; see chapter 2), based on a privatized, nearly unarticulated but unshakable hope in a benevolent God, can be understood as relying on certainties about language-games that Soviet policies never managed entirely to break up. These were the language-games of early childhood, old age, village custom, the rural household: Corners of ordinary life that, being at the margin of the productivist domain the Soviet authorities most concerned themselves with, were not as efficiently brought under the discursive matrix of the real-socialist language-game. It is worth observing that, according to Wittgenstein (1972, 1986), childhood is a crucial phase, during which conventional frames of reference are fixed and patterns of practice acquired. It is through intergenerational contact in the interstices of Soviet ordinary life that the certainties of minimal religion consolidated themselves at a time in which the official language-game of institutional religion was strictly regimented. The inarticulate quality of ethnic Muslims' "minimal Islam"—a near-wordless profession of the love/power of God—reveals its position in a zone of near-silent wonder where people found solace from the frustrations of a disenchanted mainstream.

. . . To ("Extra-Ordinary") Fidemic Speech

In contemporary Tatarstan, the truth of giant-talk does not proceed from convention. Rather, it indexes a disruption of ordinary language-games, even the "customary" language-games of enchantment. However, these speech events' disruptiveness does not proceed from the *content* of said speech in a linear fashion. In other Muslim settings, where the public sphere has been less thoroughly purged of doctrinally derived religious elements, the extraordinary biologies of Prophets Adam and Nuh may be a source of well-established, "ordinary" wonderment: For example, pious stories about the miraculous age and height of the ancient prophets, or wondrous encounters with jinns, and so on, appear to be customarily exchanged in working-class Middle Eastern communities, where they are considered commonplace components of vernacular religiosity.[7] In post-Soviet and postatheist Tatarstan, "ordinary" enchantment finds expression, besides the ethnically marked pockets of holy springs and *öskerü*, through the all-Russian pop culture language games of magic, New Age spirituality, and alternative medicine (Lindquist 2005). This pervasive kind of enchanted pop culture might be scoffed at by intellectual urbanites, but it is considered harmless and quaint. By contrast, giant- or jinn-talk, anchored as it is onto specific (Islamic) doctrinal sources, is not stably part of these conventional language-games: In the context of Povolzhye, it amounts to "extra-ordinary" speech that circulates almost exclusively within circles of pietists.

Extra-ordinary Islamic utterances may belong to a cosmo-ontological register, pertaining to things that exist, have existed, or will exist (extraordinarily long-lived giants as well as jinns, miracles, apocalyptic portents, etc.), or to a moral register, pertaining to how one should live one's life. Consider the following example. One early autumn afternoon toward the end of my fieldwork, I joined a quartet of old-timers from the Akmaş mosque community for some outdoorsy downtime at the cabin that one of them, Ayrat-abıy, owned in the woodland out of town. The atmosphere in the birch grove was jovial and comradely as we stewed and ate _uxa_ (soup) made with freshly caught river fish. After dinner we availed ourselves of our host's rustic _munça_ (sauna). My burly, bearded companions and I sat amid the resin-scented steam, panting slightly, wearing felt hats to protect our heads from overheating and knee-length swimming shorts to protect our bodies from immodesty. Before long, our conversation shifted to religion, particularly the possibility of interfaith dialogue. "In Russia they say they're Christian, but these 'Christians' don't truly respect Jesus," Ayrat-abıy told us with a tone of conspiratorial gravitas. He then added emphatically, almost like he was speaking to himself, "If you ask me, I am prepared to die at any moment for the sake of Prophet Jesus, peace be upon him. How many of _them_ can say the same?" The other guests joined in with calm intensity: "By all means, one should be ready to lie one's life for the honor of Prophet Jesus, peace be upon him," and other remarks to that effect. The moral gravity of these words made me uncomfortable. These men had just uttered serious words, changing the atmosphere from relaxedly convivial to solemn and almost ominous. I was left unsure as to what to say: I fretted, nodded nervously, and waited for the conversation to change pace.

Even after months in the field, I was taken by surprise: Martyrdom and the merest mention of the possibility of faith-related violence are seldom voiced in the Tatar mainstream. To my knowledge, utterances about martyrdom (which in other Muslim-majority cultural contexts might be more commonplace than here) are especially rare in the official Islamic moral discourse advanced by the Spiritual Directorate, bent on framing Islam as "moderate" and "rational" by the standards of the post-Soviet secular majority and the state. As we have seen, there is a great deal of ethical diversity within the Muftiate, but to the extent that a unitary strategy can be discerned, it seems evident that potentially jarring speech events mentioning martyrdom have no part in it.

The Wittgensteinian concept of "ordinariness" would fail to resonate with such speech events, nor indeed would it successfully describe the ethical form-of-life from which such utterances issue forth. What makes such speech simultaneously compelling and perturbing is precisely its defiant, anti-doxic clarity. Most importantly, unlike Wittgensteinian ordinary language, extra-ordinary and ethically intense speech acts do not hint at _consolation_, the pacifying if illusory experience of meaningful nonsense in a world that does not make sense, but imply the possibility of _salvation_ within a divine plan that possesses a discernible if higher logic anchored in Holy Writ. It is by voicing scriptural truths that one performs one's commitment to Islam and thus accesses the faith's transformative and soteriological dimensions (more on this below).

Autonomist approaches to verity and fidelity are uniquely suitable to interpret such speech events. Badiou distinguishes between the ordinary/conventional domain of situations, to which opinions, debates, agreements, and so forth belong, and the extra-ordinary domain of truth. Badiou's verities come into being through practical processes of fidelity enacted by those who constitute themselves as subjects of truths: Through these processes, verities both transcend and "fix" the conjunctural realm of situation, bringing about changes in political arrangements as well as subjectivities. To better understand how autonomist theory complements Wittgensteinianism and sheds light on areas of language that lie beyond the narrow perimeter of the ordinary, let us clarify the conceptual and terminological differences between ordinary language certainties and Badiousian verities.[8]

Wittgensteinian certainties are doxic and world-anchoring (Severi 2007). In our ethnographic setting, statements such as "A benevolent God exists," "Sacred springs can heal," and "Elders must be honored," express such certainties. Badiousian verities, by contrast, are counter- or extra-doxic, "outrageous" and "critical" in the literal sense of coming from beyond ("ultra") a situation, marking a separation from and establishing a new relationship with it. Truths are therefore inherently, at least potentially, disruptive. Statements such as "Ancient humans were dozens of meters tall" or "I am ready to die for the sake of a Prophet" position the utterer as a *very specific*, pious subject and exist within a sequence of ethical intensity at variance with the themitical and doxic order. They give shape to an ethical form-of-life. Verities are born of a fidelity that manifests itself in action and speech; hence, I define utterances reproducing a truth through speech as fidemic speech acts.

When it comes to religious speech, it is important not to see doxic/ordinary certainties and fidemic speech acts as mutually exclusive, just as it would be unhelpful to consider vernacular and scripturalist ways of living Islam as polar opposites. A living tradition is made of multiple aspects and affords multiple ways of inhabiting it. In Povolzhye, Islamic speech practices include both ordinary and extra-ordinary utterances, although different groups may lean toward one or the other speech habit—pietists' ethical experience being oriented toward fidelity. Furthermore, a historical dimension should be considered in assessing what counts as "ordinary." The utterance "Humans have shrunk since creation" is seen as counter-doxic in post-Soviet Povolzhye, where the sensus communis has been shaped by secularization. In other situational settings, such a statement might be or have been less contentious or indeed entirely doxic. By contrast, a phrase such as "There is but one God" is doxic among contemporary Tatars, even nonpietists, but it might have sounded extra-ordinary when Islam was taking hold among polytheistic populations, both in Inner Russia and in other parts of today's Muslim worlds. What makes an utterance fidemic is not its abstract content but its embeddedness in a *processus de vérité* that is always historically situated.

Performativity and Fidelity

Fidemic language can be "outrageous" even to pietists, but being able to utter it is an essential component of cultivating a pious subjectivity (Davies 2002, 158). My acquaintance Izmail, a language teacher in his mid-late twenties and one of my most candid interlocutors in the field, would sometimes share with me his inner struggles with religious narratives that struck him as "obscurantist"; and yet, when performing his piety, he would still partake in fidemic speech events no matter how their content may trouble him. One day, for example, Izmail invited me to join him and our common acquaintance Ramil, a university student a few years Izmail's junior, at a halal café in Kazan. I knew that Ramil struggled with his religious commitment and sometimes sought Izmail's advice. Izmail, in turn, was concerned about the young man's unsteady religious commitment and careful to hide his own struggles from him. It was against this delicate ethical entanglement that, after a casual chat, our conversation shifted to the topic of the importance of seeking religious knowledge (*znaniya*). My friend Izmail gave an example of such knowledge by reporting a literalist rendition of the creation of the world in six days—one of the "obscurantist" notions that not only puzzled the recalcitrant Ramil but also, as I knew, troubled Izmail for being at odds with his scientific rationality. To my surprise, however, during that conversation Izmail launched into an eloquent spiel that adhered strictly to the Quranic narrative, leaving very little wriggle room for interpretation or critical exegesis. Ramil was left contemplating two options: either disavow the religious truth advanced with calm but seemingly unshakable assurance by Izmail or adhere to it. Confronted with this choice, Ramil aligned with Izmail's utterance, thus confirming his commitment. Emboldened, Izmail later proceeded to invite Ramil to a mosque class on the following day. After we bid goodbye to our acquaintance, Izmail gave me a knowing look. On our subsequent meetings, he would return to his religious quandaries.

I never thought of challenging Izmail on the "lecture" he gave Ramil. It would not have made much sense. I realized that in the pedagogical framework of that speech event, words of piety were offered as a salvific "gift" (P. Anderson 2011, 14), the power of which lies precisely in their "Kierkegaardian" paradoxicality (see below). What mattered was not what exactly to make of a puzzling passage of the Quran (perhaps "days" in the context of divine creation corresponds to cosmic eras or eons, as my friend wondered on other occasions) but the *effect* of stating a fideme, an utterance manifesting one's fidelious engagement with a truth, on the subjectivities of both Izmail and Ramil. This "ethical one-upmanship" reinforces the intensity of commitment on both sides of the speech act. Through it, Izmail became an exemplar of piety, and Ramil was encouraged to encounter a Quranic truth on its own terms and submit to the majesty of a God that transcends human intellect, rather than trying to explain it on external scientific grounds.

For a synthetic formulation of this principle, consider the following statement, extracted from an online debate over the age of Adam: "Allah can do whatever He chooses. Whether Adam was 90 feet or not, it is largely meaningless to our current lives and beliefs. Adam could have been 200 ft. and lived for a million years . . . [that would be] still irrelevant." What is noteworthy here is this pietist's self-aware rejection of attempts to render an article of faith—God's omnipotence—"sensical" or "relevant" by the yardstick of situational sensus communis ("our current beliefs"). In this commentator's view, to bring the latter to bear on the former is not so much *im*pertinent as *not* pertinent. As we shall see in the next section, fidemic speech operates autonomously from the discursive Law of doxic speech.

Fidemic speech events thus have an effect on the situation within which they occur. To paraphrase J. L. Austin, fidemic utterances are performative/illocutionary speech acts, even though they exceed the model originally devised by Austin (1962).[9] Austin's work focuses on utterances that, rather than describing or constating anything, produce a socially binding effect: declarations, proclamations, baptisms, bets, and so on. Austin's theory of illocution can be put in conversation with a Badiousian framework and applied to the utterances discussed in these pages. I argue that in the context of Tatarstan's piety milieus, to state that the world was created in six days is not, as it might superficially appear, a constative pronouncement concerning (one's opinion on) facts; and similarly, to declare one's readiness for martyrdom is not a mere description of one's internal states or "beliefs": Rather, such speech acts are performative utterances concerning subjectivity—in the sense of performing a fidelity, disrupting a doxic situation, and enjoining utterers and listeners alike into an ethical form-of-life. The performativity of fidemic speech acts is linked to the utterer's commitment to a verity whose content is bound up with a broader truth-process. As Søren Kierkegaard put it, in ethical religion only "subjectivity is truth, subjectivity is real" ([1946] 2016, 231).

Fidemes are in some important aspects different from "classic" Austinian illocutions. These tend to be formulaic utterances pronounced in ritual or formalized settings such as liturgies and ceremonies. In Austinian terms, for example, the Islamic profession of faith would count as a "classic" ceremonial/ritual conventional speech act (1962, 19) capable of producing lasting effects on both the utterer and his or her audience—namely, given the right conditions, making one into a (publicly recognized) Muslim. It may be further qualified as an expositional illocution, characterized by the combination of a transparently performative element ("I bear witness that . . . "—the part of the statement that does the transformative job) and a seemingly constative one (" . . . there is no deity other than God"—apparently a factual statement about the world[10]) (Austin 1962, 85–87). However, the ritual context in which they are uttered clarifies, at least in an Austinian analyst's eye, that the point of formulaic creedal performatives like the shahada is not that of being verifiable factual statements (of course, for a committed Muslim, the shahada is factually correct). Unlike ritualized credos ("I testify that . . . ," "I believe in . . . "), by contrast, fidemic speech acts derive their illocutionary force precisely from *not* looking like recognizable ritual formulas and therefore tend to masquerade as constatives.

Fidemic utterances are issued matter-of-factly, posing as factual statements. Locutors do not say things like "I hereby declare that God created the world in six days, thereby pledging myself to the truth of the Islamic tradition and vowing to live accordingly"; they merely say, conversationally, that God made Creation in six days. Matter-of-factness is crucial because it is by uttering these words as a "mere" constative that the speaker performs conviction, thereby indexing the intensity of his or her adherence to the anchoring verity and generating either heightened ethical intimacy among fellow truth-subjects or outrage among outgroups. In other words, ceremonial-creedal utterances and fidemes perform distinct illocutionary functions. While the former's performativity pertains to the speaker's formal belonging in a moral-jural community bound by ritual, the former's illocutionary effect acts at the level of the speaker's fidelity to a truth-process—linking the subjectivities of persons like Izmail and Ramil to an ethical form-of-life.

Like other illocutions, however, fidemes tend to be uttered given the right conditions. Izmail, for example, was perfectly capable of moving from a fidemic register to a philosophical-intellectual one according to the situation (pedagogical conversation, introspective chat, etc.) and interlocutor (ethical mentee, anthropologist, etc.).

Two corollaries ought to be discussed at this point. One concerns the relation between formulaic illocutions and fidemic speech. As we have seen in chapter 2, a Muftiate source described the illocutionary effect of the profession of faith—a "classic" Austinian illocution—as the "passport" to Islam. But we have also seen that holding that "passport" does not, at least in the eyes of some pietists, offer sufficient information about one's standing within the Muslim community—that is, the intensity of one's commitment. In certain cases—for instance, to access a religious wedding ceremony—one might utter the shahada opportunistically, without any ethical commitment attached to the act. This move, however, would not be devoid of dangers: As Austin notes, ritual illocutions risk being nullified unless they are validated by subsequent conduct (1962, 44; also see Hirschkind 2001, 640). The "Wahhabi" wedding scandal described in chapter 2 suggests that weddings not validated post factum by both spouses' assiduous practice of namaz may in extreme cases be contested and even annulled, at least within the form-of-life of pietists. In "ideal" faith communities, fidemic utterances complement and reinforce ritual illocutions: These two forms of performative speech preferably operate in tandem, making moral community and ethical form-of-life coincide in the same linguistic space. In postsecular settings such as Tatarstan, however, this coincidence cannot be taken for granted on account of the historical drift between moral convention and doctrinal integrity.

The second, related point concerns the "extra-ordinariness" of fidemic speech. Fidemic speech proceeds from and rests on a historically recognizable *processus de vérité* (in Tatarstan's context, Islam's discursive tradition); hence, it does possess a citational, internally "conventional," dimension. Yet the truths that inform such processes exceed the realm of ordinary language. The possibility of a disjuncture between the conventions of the situation and the conventions of a truth-process is therefore always given. This, arguably, has occurred in Povolzhye with the secularization of ordinary life in the twentieth century and the emergence of an "ethnic Muslimness" removed from scriptural foundations. When the conventions of a situation and those of a truth-process differ, fidemic speech may find its way into language in outrageous, unsettling ways.

Outrageous Illocutions

In our digital ecumene, it is not surprising that the internet should be a platform not only for the production, reproduction, and circulation of fidemes but also for their spillover beyond the boundaries of ethical forms-of-life and into a public sphere in which their disruptive potential becomes explicit. In late 2020, a North Caucasian Islamic site published a polemical article titled "Will Non-Muslims Be Saved in the Afterlife?" ("*Spasutsya li v Akhirate nemusul'mane?*") which argued, inflexibly but competently relying on theological foundations, that non-Muslims cannot be saved in the afterlife and are destined to everlasting fire. The document included a stern rebuttal of ecumenical Muslim voices suggesting otherwise (it is not difficult to guess that the writer was thinking of Muftiate officials and mainstream Islamic popularizers—see chapters 3 and 6). The author argued that a lenient doctrine of salvation not only is based on arbitrary interpretations of Holy Writ, which in itself is a sin, but also risks legitimizing rank-and-file Muslims' deviations from correct faith to the point of disbelief (kufr).

Islamic soteriology being a complex matter beyond this volume's scope, I will dwell not on the theological soundness of this communiqué but on its social life. Following this text around Russian-language social media, I noticed that it had garnered many approving comments from pious users in in-group channels but also that the document had become a matter of contention on a popular, open-to-all Russian question-and-answer website. The thread, opened by a Russophone Muslim user in a crisis of faith (and unrelated to the North Caucasian website), asked fellow religionists how a just God could keep righteous, decent, and devout people in Hell just on account of their religious backgrounds. An observant Muslim respondent sought to soothe the original writer's spiritual pain with arguments from within the Islamic tradition to the effect that inclusive understandings of the afterlife were possible, and after all God, who is merciful, "knows best." At that point another user, an ethnic Russian who identified as Orthodox Christian, polemically jumped into the discussion with a link to, and extensive quotes from, the North Caucasian article, in order to prove that the Islamic doctrine of salvation was indeed not only "wildly unfair" (*diko nespravedlivo*) but also "unreasonable" (*nerazumno*), thereby implying that the original writer's spiritual quandaries were justified and that the Muslim respondent was either contradicting his own religion or disingenuously trying to downplay a socially unacceptable Islamic teaching.

In that exchange, the Russian user capitalized on the "outrage potential" of the article. Being from the beginning framed as a high-intensity internal intervention within an Islamic theological dispute, not meant for a wide readership but explicitly addressed to fellow pietists (*dorogie musul'mane*, "dear Muslims"), the article was doomed to come across as at odds with the values of pluralism, inclusivity, and tolerance of the themitical mainstream. Ontological fidemes about Hell and moral ones about who will end up there tend to sound alarming and even offensive to secular ears. Like giant-talk or martyrdom-talk, damnation-talk has a great potential to unsettle onlookers (even those who don't "believe" in an afterlife!). And yet there is no denying that even in the most ecumenical Islamic interpretations, salvation is not taken for granted: Damnation and punishment for disbelievers and reprobates are part of the truth by which pietists live, and awareness of such spiritual dangers underpins their ethical efforts. These things, however, are not easily sayable in the secularized public arena without attracting charges of extremism.

What is sayable in public is defined and authorized by institutions, groups, and power-wielding agents. Fidemic speech, however, is liable to defy these power arrangements, in what Jacques Rancière has called "disturbances of life by speech" (1994, 68–70). It has long been observed that truth and institutional power stand in an awkward relationship. The influential Foucauldian notion of parrhesia indicates verbal events in which the speaker, often speaking from a subordinate position, addresses a powerful interlocutor by voicing a strongly held position, even when this may put him or her at risk (Foucault 2001, 2011). Foucault characterizes frank speech not just as a public act but also as an ethical technique of the self, capable of bringing into being a certain type of subject. To an extent, fidemic speech—defiant, subject-forming, integral to ethical practice— can be framed as parrhesiastic, yet there are important points of dissimilarity. In particular, Foucault's conceptualization of veridiction differs substantially from the theory of truth underpinning fidemic speech. Foucault's truths are located in the speaker's mind (2001, 13–14) and are made manifest dialogically, through asymmetrical power relations within a situation: "If there is a kind of 'proof' of the sincerity of the *parrhesiastes*, it is his *courage*. The fact that a speaker says something dangerous—different from what the majority believes—is a strong indication that he is a *parrhesiastes*" (15). By contrast, fidemic speech stems from a relation with a truth that exceeds both the utterer's opinion and the situation within which is it uttered.

Furthermore, although fidemic speech can *become* parrhesiastic when it "spills over" into the themical mainstream, in relation to which fidelious subjects occupy a subaltern position, its circulation may remain within the boundaries of what may be called, adapting Michael Herzfeld's concept, "ethically intimate" forms-of-life in which utterers and listeners partake in the same fidelity project. In post-Soviet Povolzhye, for example, pietists may assume the role of *parrhesiastes* when they express their religious commitment in secular settings despite the stigma attached to it. In a context rife with state paranoia about Islam and widespread alarm over "extremism," even simple acts such as growing a beard or wearing a hijab require a certain amount of "courage"—all the more so for utterances that lend themselves to charges of radicalism. But the deliberate pursuit of confrontation with Russia's themical apparatuses is not the main purpose of the halal milieu's fidemic speech. Tellingly, the North Caucasian article on non-Muslims was framed not as a public declaration but as a warning for fellow pietists within the ethical form-of-life. It did include parrhesiastic elements in attacking the popular position of Islamic ecumenists acting "for the sakes of office and money" (*za dolzhnosti i den'gi*), but the text's purpose was not primarily to stand up to secular power.

In another important contribution on the politics of speech, Pierre Bourdieu has argued that efficacious speech events have force not because of an "inherent" power of language (as Austinian or Wittgensteinian scholarship tends to frame it) but because—and insofar as—they are invested in authority enshrined in the institutional order (1991, 107–111). Bourdieu dwells extensively on "rites of institutions," a term whose semantic ambivalence serves to emphasize, on the one hand, the act of instituting an individual into a given role/identity/group and so on, and on the other, the institutional power that validates said transformation. Thus, ritual speech acts establish and reinforce "social destinies" and boundaries (1991, 122). A Povolzhye-based example of this is the Islamic life-cycle rituals that ethnic Muslims normally undergo (circumcision, wedding, etc.): Through such ceremonies, a group's ancestrally given social identity is confirmed.

Although the two speech acts are not mutually exclusive, fidemic illocutions stand in tension with the ritualistic, institutional speech acts that Bourdieu discusses. Fidemes are not an index of institutional belonging but of the intensity of *ethical* belonging—a dimension that remains at the margins of Bourdieu's work. Rather than the acquisition of an identity or the fulfillment of a social destiny, uttering fidemes verbally realizes one's partaking in an ethical form-of-life, thereby unlocking a potential for "self-institution through alterity"—becoming *other* than one is or is meant to be—which is one of the figures of autonomy (Lynteris 2021, 13). As we shall see in some detail below, fidemic speech may exist within, be co-opted by, or even be amplified through institutional frameworks, but it is not inherently institutional and indeed, to the extent that it runs counter to majoritarian values and wisdom, tends to be anti-institutional. Fidemic speech thus may be juxtaposed to another category advanced by Bourdieu, which the French social theorist calls "heretical" speech acts. Such linguistic events have the ability to (a) "sever the adherence to the world of common sense by publicly proclaiming a break with ordinary order" and (b) "produce a new common sense" (1991, 128–129). This is possible by virtue of such statements' "theory effect" (135)—that is, the unveiling of hitherto-hidden categories and the naming of previously unsayable social realities. Bourdieu's "heretical discourse" is extraordinary and anti-doxic, and endowed with transformative potential.

In important ways, Bourdieu's position dovetails with an autonomist framework of fidelious ethical speech. His concept of heretical speech has more than passing correspondences with Badiou's concept of truth-process, which simultaneously breaks with a situation (the established doxa), makes it legible (ripping through the "veil of silence" around the doxa), and makes a fresh situation possible (a new doxa). Bourdieu offers the example of Marxian class analysis as a new language endowed with such paradigm-changing potential:[11] Arguably, the language of religious reform movements (including Islamic ones) operates analogously, by disorganizing dominant categories and bringing into being hitherto unexplored modes of being. As the Greek theorist Cornelius Castoriadis put it, with an outrageous utterance such as "Our laws are unjust, our gods are false"—the type of piercing cry with which Muslim pietists denounce the morally corrupt, unfaithful, hell-bound mainstream—an altogether "new type" of individual and community must emerge that may lead to an alteration of "the social institution" (1991, 166–167). However, Bourdieu's exclusive focus on collective societal transformation blinded him to a key component of the equation—that is, the *uttering subject* and the transformative/autopoietic dimension of extra-ordinary speech on the latter (Butler 1997[12]). An autonomist-Badiousian perspective allows us to see fidemic speech as enabling the creation, support, and expansion of novel subjectivities (including that of the "militant") and collective forms-of-life. To repurpose an Althusserian expression, by uttering fidemic speech individuals self-interpellate as subjects (Althusser 2014, 262); only, unlike in Althusser, this kind of Logos does not produce heteronomous individuals ideologically subjected to or by Law ("Hey, you there!") but self-Ruling forms-of-life who partake in the "immortality" of a verity ("Hey, we are here!"). Bourdieu's work, however, helps us appreciate with greater clarity what makes certain speech acts "outrageous" and unsettling. Fidemic speech is the application of a Rule in language: autonomous, doxa-defying, indifferent to the norms of ordinary speech. It is not an expression of mere opinion but one of commitment and subjectivity. And perhaps most dangerously, it holds the promise of an alternative theoretical and political arrangement.

Søren Kierkegaard wrote that in contexts of heightened ethical intensity, religious speech often comes across as "absurd" and "offensive" to the uninitiated. Kierkegaard's absurd is "not identical with the improbable, the unexpected, the unforeseen"; rather, it is knowing that something is impossible yet embracing it because "with God all things are possible" ([1946] 2016, 126), in the proverbial leap of faith. Owing to its "paradoxical" quality, faithful speech exercises a cognitively "repellent" influence ([1946] 2016, 221) on the prudent, doxa-bound, "bourgeois" majority. Kierkegaard's intellectual "paradox" finds a moral analog in the related idea of "offense," which goes beyond the cognitive domain and affects personhood globally (Bretall [1946] 2016, 373). To Kierkegaard, it is precisely its absurd and offensive qualities that make (religious) speech redemptive—that is, transformative at the subjective level. To the extent that this transformation requires a break from the discursive norms that enjoy affective validation in or through a Kantian-Arendtian sensus communis, of course, it might hurt or "feel wrong" at the societal level (Bens et al. 2019, 92).

Different varieties of outrageous speech may be considered jarring and treated as censurable because of their bending, subverting, or challenging the "rules of the game." However, I argue that fidemic utterances represent a special case: They are predominantly indifferent to the norms of doxic speech rather than deliberately opposed to them—or, more precisely, they operate on different levels: those of Rule and Law. Rule-bound fidemic speech is unsettling because it exceeds the doxic Law of institutionally regulated ordinary language. Yet as we know, forms-of-life do not exist in a void—to the contrary, they are necessarily if obliquely intertwined with the same situational landscape that they try to transcend. The trouble with fidemic speech begins when it escapes the "ethically intimate" contexts of a form-of-life and gets caught in the broader themitical forcefield.

Fidemic Knowledge Between Form-of-Life and Institution

Autonomous, fidemic speech is bound up with learning to be a pietist. As Castoriadis put it, "*paideia*, education from birth to death, is a central dimension of any politics of autonomy" (1991, 173). Acquiring Islamic knowledge (*znaniya*, ğ*ılem*, 'ilm) is not about the mere acquisition of religion-related content from an academic standpoint (if it were, there would be no difference between a pietist and a competent practitioner of Islamic studies as a secular discipline): "Real" knowledge is that which "brings man closer to Allah" (Tahir-ul-Qadri 2007, 23; also see Hirschkind 2006; Berliner and Sarró 2007; Bowen 2012, 11–41)—that is, it is imbued with ethical intentionality and fidelity. Absorbing (Islamic) *znaniya* is a matter of cultivating one's ability to encounter the Islamic discursive tradition as a transformative, emancipatory truth. To propagate this truth, over the past thirty years post-Soviet Povolzhye pietists have been increasingly active in circulating religious knowledge. Such knowledge is distributed in formal (classes, lectures) as well as informal (social media, youth meetings) settings. Pious topics provide much conversational fodder in the halal milieu's social life, with exemplary stories, Quranic verses, and sayings of the Prophet being regularly discussed over tea or pilaf, after communal prayer, and at mosque gatherings. A modicum of mastery of the Quran, hadith, tafsīr (Quranic interpretation), sīrah (prophetic biographies), and Islamic jurisprudence is expected of pietists. A telling formula I encountered in the field is that a "proper" Muslim should know "at the very least 15 Quranic verses, 50 hadiths, and 5 invocations." Moreover, and crucially, this discursive content must be acted on, shared (P. Anderson 2011), and used to heighten ethical intensity, thereby "becoming" fidemic speech.

Religious knowledge constitutes a domain in which the existential distance between the halal milieu and the mainstream manifests itself with great clarity. Nonpietists are not typically invested in the pursuit of Islamic learning. Most secular Tatars tend to command what pietists consider, at best, a rudimentary and piecemeal catechism. Furthermore, Islamic knowledge has long been and remains a source of friction between Muslim pietists the Russian state: The practice of outlawing Islamic literature, discussed in chapter 3, provides a good example of how "outrageous," anti- or non-doxic fidemic speech is suppressed as extremist.

But as it can be imagined, alongside negative, suppressive tools the Russian state regiments doxa through more subtle action of governmental institutions. As early as in the late imperial era, the schooling of Muslim children as an instrument of Russification emerged as a contentious question fiercely debated by Tatar traditionalists, Islamic modernist reformers, Orthodox missionaries, and Russian nationalists (Campbell 2015; Tuna 2016). Today, the state provides mandatory secular education infused with patriotic overtones that, though in line with mainstream moral sensitivities, do not always go down well with Muslim citizens (Lisovskaya and Karpov 2010). While the USSR authorities successfully implemented ambitious education reforms and established mass literacy in Tatarstan through secular institutions that have perdured into the post-Soviet era, Islamic piety movements challenge, to an extent, the primacy of secular knowledge that the state takes for granted. As a Kazan-based preacher declared to me, "Secular knowledge is like a medicine, while religious knowledge is like food. Both are necessary, but only the latter is indispensable."

Piety and Schooling

Of course, pious Muslims in Tatarstan do appreciate the need for good-quality school curricula (Islamic modernist movements have advocated a positive engagement with scientific disciplines and nonreligious knowledge since the prerevolutionary times: see J. Meyer 2014, 107–129). Nonetheless, they realize that state schools are apparatuses where the Law of the secular order is inculcated: As an "autarkist"-leaning interlocutor put it, "Schools have an incredibly strong influence on our [Muslim] boys, often a negative one—full of random people [children of nonpietists] and unnecessary [un-Islamic] stuff, like New Year celebration and so on,[13] not to mention the problem of skipping namaz."

In Akmaş, in the mid-2000s, pietists took measures to bring halal food into kindergartens and primary schools and lobbied the local authorities and education board for the implementation of "spiritual-moral education" (ädäp-äxlaq törkemnäre, literally "education-morality groups") for the children of pietists. The community was careful to couch their requests in the state-compatible language of "traditional Tatar upbringing" and "high quality standards" rather than sharia, thereby tapping into mainstream moral narratives about traditsionny islam, ethnic identity, and middle-class aspirations: "We don't ask for much—halal food, a bit of sex separation in school activities, and a bit of moral guidance," preferably from observant Muslim pedagogists.

As regards later stages of education, during my stay in 2014–2015, I had the opportunity to visit state high schools in Kazan, Akmaş, Bay Sabası, and Tübän Kama, among others, and they all offered halal food to their pupils. The most prestigious schools carried the imprint of the Hizmet movement's secular but religiously inflected Tatar-Turkish Lyceums. Even though the movement was banned (see chapters 1 and 3), its schools had managed not only to set high standards of excellence for republican institutions to adhere to but also to train scores of competent teachers, many of whom were religiously observant, who went on to teach in state schools. State school curriculums remain, however, firmly secular, and in my conversations with and observation of teachers, including pietists, I ascertained that proselytism and open displays of piety were absent from pedagogical contexts (praying, for example, is performed with great discretion). Fidemic speech was absent from secular state schools. The question of whether pupils and students can wear the hijab at schools remains prickly: The Tatarstani authorities have taken a noninterventionist stance that delegates decisions on this matter to individual schools, resulting in periodic outbursts of "conflict" and "scandals" (Rubtsova 2013; Vasileva 2019; Perepechenova 2020).

In the face of a secular educational system and despite the leeway that that system affords to Muslim parents and students, some autarkist-leaning pietists remain skeptical of the ethical salubriousness of state schools and opt for homeschooling instead (Karimova 2021). One of these parents described the advantages of this option to me in these terms: His eleven-year-old son begins his day studying Quranic recitation, tafsīr, and Classical Arabic under his mother's supervision. "Only then, only *after* religious subjects, does he move on to secular ones—maths, history, Russian, and English." Although the hierarchy is clear, the importance of secular subjects is not denied: The kid is enrolled in a certified online schooling program offered by a serious private institution in St. Petersburg. Reportedly, more than ten families in this community decided to pursue this option. When I asked my interlocutor how he envisaged his son's higher education, he answered that he hopes to send him to a Muslim country, preferably Saudi Arabia, to obtain at least two years' worth of solid religious education. Should his son then decide to pursue a secular degree, "he would pursue secular knowledge through the prism of religious knowledge."

My acquaintance's mention of Medina as an ideal place of learning reveals another source of concern among pietists: the state of Islamic learning within the Russian Federation, which is considered insufficient by many. Fidemic speech circulates horizontally within the halal milieu, among circles of friends, mosque communities, and families, but whether Russia's state-patronized Islamic institutions possess the ethical intensity that gives religious knowledge with the right subject-transformative potential remains a matter of discussion.

Institutionalizing Fidemic Knowledge

In 2014, I attended a public panel about the state of Islamic education in Tatarstan. One of the speakers—a religiously observant intellectual in his early thirties—

assessed the case of the Russian Islamic Institute (also known as "Islamic University") in Kazan, founded in the late 1990s as a groundbreaking institution devoted to the professional training of Tatar spiritual leaders through degrees in Islamic journalism, linguistics, and theology. By differentiating religious education from theology as an academic discipline, the speaker highlighted a paradox that illuminates the institute's ambiguous reputation among the pietists who see it as less "Islamic" than centers of religious learning in the Muslim world:

> In a sense, theology [*teologiya*] risks replacing religious education; i.e., students go to the Institute expecting to learn sharia, but have to go through theology instead in order for their degree to be recognized by the state. Through theology, the Institute manages to be compliant with and get funding from the state. Of course, funding is not a matter of scarce importance. But this way theology stands in the way of properly religious education for future imams. . . . We have ended up with a hybrid thing, which is neither fully religious nor fully secular. They let students obtain a degree of religious training, meaning sharia, plus they fed them theology as an academic subject, and other secular subjects. On the other hand, to the extent that they cast themselves as a religious [not merely professional/academic/secular] institution, the Institute cannot frame theology as an exclusively academic discipline, but rather use it as a way to legitimize themselves [before the state] and legalize their curriculum. They are stuck in the middle.

By "religious education," the speaker meant the pedagogical process that produces pious Muslims: in this book's terminology, *fidemic knowledge* meant to be not just acquired intellectually but ethically acted on. "Learning sharia," in this sense, means learning to act according to sharia and enjoin others to do the same. "Theology," however, is ambiguously suspended between fidemic knowledge and a doxic academic discipline that exists at the same level as Tatar linguistics and journalism.

Kazan's Russian Islamic Institute is aligned with the Tatarstani Muftiate: not only because the latter is one of its founders (alongside the Tatarstani Academy of Science and the federal-level Council of Muftis) but also because the republic's Islamic officialdom is the ideal employer for the institute's trainees. Not coincidentally, the theology curriculum contains, alongside courses such as Rules for Quranic Reading, Introduction to Islamic Jurisprudence, and History of Sufism, courses with an explicit governmental slant including State-Confessional Relations, New Religious Movements, Political Sciences, and Administration of the Muslim Community (*Upravlenie musul'manskoy obshchiny*). A heavy emphasis is given on localism through courses such as History of Tatarstan and the Tatars,

Tatar Theological Heritage (*bogoslovskoe nasledie*), Spiritual Area Studies (*Dukhovnoe kraevedenie*), and Tatar language. Remarkable is also the presence of subjects such as Science and Religion, Modern Natural Sciences, and Methods of Scientific Research, which, at least in principle, should dispel any notions about giants and six-day Creation from authorized Islamic discourse. The latter set of subjects appears in line with the Muftiate-approved discourse of Hanafism as an especially "rational" and science-compliant school of thought within Islam. However, interlocutors who are critical of the institute tended to stress what they perceived as a lack of depth in religious subjects (limited to "foundations of," "introduction to") and an overemphasis on secular subjects and the training of administrators.

To address the problem, the Tatarstani authorities, in the persons of Tatarstan's President Rustam Minnikhanov and the respected Tatar national leader Mintimer Shaimiev, with the explicit support of Vladimir Putin and in partnership with Russia's Islamic officialdom (the two main federal Muftiates and Tatarstan's Spiritual Directorate) as well as the federal Ministry of Education, inaugurated the Bolğar Islamic Academy in 2017. This institution, named after the ancient city in the vicinity of which it is located, aspires to offer higher-level training in "pure" Islamic sciences, with the goal of domestically training Russia and Tatarstan's 'ulama as full-fledged religious scholars, not "mere" confessional administrators. Part of the training takes place in Arabic, and the academy attracted teachers from respected centers of learning in the Muslim world, in particular Cairo's Al-Azhar, in order to curb the flow of pietists pursuing learning outside of Russia and "importing" so-called non-traditional Islam. In other words, the project seeks to "nationalize" global Islamic knowledge and place the circulation of such highly "mobile" fidemic speech under state control (Almazova 2021).

Like in the case of Kazan's Islamic Institute, this brings about predictable ambiguities. As Alfrid Bustanov (2019) put it, the Bolğar Academy exists in an equivocal discursive space where three threads intersect: the doctrinally shaped "theological discourse" of pure Islamic science; a "state security" discourse, emanating from governmental structures and oriented toward the themes of Muslim loyalty and the fight against "radicalism"; and an "ideological" discourse establishing the need for an "enlightened" and modern (read secular-compatible) "Tatar Islam." As a result of the forcing of Islam's fidemic knowledge into a securitarian-secularist discursive scaffolding, some segments of the piety milieu continue to see the Muslim world beyond the borders of Russia as a preferable option to pursue undiluted Islamic knowledge.

Yet, despite mixed feelings in some quarters, the Russian Islamic Institute and the Bolğar Islamic Academy appear to fulfill their function within Tatarstan's Islamic educational landscape (for context, see Kemper et al. 2010), attracting people with a genuine interest in the faith. Most trainees and many teachers aspire to be more than administrators and mouthpieces for state ideology, having a sincere commitment to Islam and being resolved to pursue it within the situational framework available to them. Kazan's Islamic Institute, for example, plays a role in promoting the spread of Islamic knowledge among ethnic Muslims, engaged through free-of-charge, open-to-all courses on the Foundations of Islam. The course, which I attended, does not presuppose heightened ethical intensity and is largely free from topics that could come across as "outrageous" to secular ears, but in the context of postatheist Tatarstan it offers one entry point into a lived engagement with religion.

Like the Islamic bureaucracy that patronizes them (see chapter 3), Tatarstan's Islamic educational institutions are therefore suspended between ethical form-of-life and Law-enforcing temporal apparatus. As manifestations of Islam's truth-process in post-Soviet Russia, they embody a transformational force that, being impossible to ignore or suppress, has "forced" a systemic update in the situation's political order and its pedagogical instruments. As embodiments of the state, on the other hand, they reveal a strategy of co-optation geared toward the "confining" of fidemic speech and ethical intensity into a heteronomous governmental framework established by the state. Whether or not this middle path will be able to bridge the gap between state structures and doctrinally oriented religionists remains to be seen.

Thinking Through Truth

In this chapter, I have advanced the notion of fidemic speech to indicate a form of religious speech that manifests faithfulness to a verity. Developing Badiousian intuitions, I have explored how fidemic speech tends to generate a sense of ethical intimacy among Muslim pietists through the "extra-legal or illegal solidarity of a universal truth" (Hallward 2002, xxviii). Beyond the halal milieu's discursive environment, Islamic fidemic speech "punches a hole in [ordinary] knowledges, is heterogeneous to them" (Hallward 2002, 70); as such, it is therefore apt to unsettle listeners who do not partake in the same form of ethical intensity as the utterers. Unlike ritual formulas (uttering a profession of faith or declaring "belief" in a corporately held opinion), fidemic utterances involve a riskier and more radical stance and can be felicitously uttered only from a place of ethical commitment (one's resolution to live in accordance with the precept of a truth). Fidemic speech is, then, a form of speech that pertains specifically to forms-of-life: the upholding of a truth-of-Rule, a fortiori in opposition to Law-enforced doxa. That giants once roamed the earth and humankind has shrunk since is a matter of commitment, not one of archaeology.

In Povolzhye's halal milieu, the claim is often made that a genuine pietist is "one who thinks," who "knows how to think." It is interesting to observe that Badiou views thinking as an activity pertaining to the field of verities, the "ethics of truth" (Hallward 2002, 1; see Marcuse [1964] 1972, 86–87). Proceeding from a different set of assumptions, the late Paul Rabinow has expressed a view that points in a similar direction—namely, that thinking happens in *milieus* (literally, "between places") and is intimately related to discordance. Thinking happens in a "space of . . . contingency that emerges in relation to (and forms a feedback situation with) a more general situation," through the interplay of "institutionally legitimated claims to truth [and] one or *another type of sanctioned seriousness*" (2003, 19–20; emphasis added).

Giant-talk, martyrdom-talk, or any other form of speech sanctioned by a verity other than institutional doxa might come across as outlandish or perturbing, but it can still be taken "seriously" if considered part of an ethical truth-process the goal of which is to produce fidelious subjects. These subjects are not insulated from the "general situation," the domain of sensus communis and shared knowledge. By uttering fidemic words, they open a discursive space autonomous from, and potentially at odds with, this domain—and purposefully step therein. Rather than taking fidemic speakers as factually ignorant, ideologically extremist, or obnubilated by irrational "beliefs," then, the concept of fidemic speech allows us to locate ethically effective utterances within the context of a form-of-life's dialectical interplay with the doxic mainstream. The grating quality of fidemic speech does not proceed from its utterers' *un*thinking—to the contrary, it emanates from the discordant quality of autonomous thought.

THE BLESSED SHARE

Biznes and Halal Chrematistics

On a snowy evening in early spring 2015, I attended a meeting in an elegant, discreet prerevolutionary building in Kazan's Old Tatar District. Black SUVs converged in the building's slushy, dimly lit parking lot, and a handful or two of suit-clad businessmen and skullcap-wearing clerics climbed up slippery steps. They shook the muddy snow off their leather shoes before entering a spacious attic converted into a working area. The attendees—the cream of the crop of Povolzhye's Muslim entrepreneurial class, a couple of them still carrying faint traces of 1990s hardness in their appearance and demeanor—vigorously shook hands, exchanged hearty salaams, and took their place around a table crammed with teacups, notepads, and a projector. The goal of that private meeting was to bring Russia's Association of Muslim Entrepreneurs (APM—Assotsiatsiya Pred-prinimateley-Musulman' Rossii) into existence. In an excited atmosphere, plans for the future were made, tea drunk, *çäk-çäk* (Tatar pastry) eaten, invocations offered, and technicalities discussed by the about a dozen attendees who would go down as the association's founding members.

One of the technicalities discussed with particular heat was what motto should be chosen to represent the activities and philosophy of APM. After a pro-tracted back-and-forth, the final choice raised unanimous enthusiasm: "Hand in our profits, heart with our beloved God" (*ruka v pribyli, a serdtse s lyubimym Allakhom*) was eventually welcomed as the perfect encapsulation of the associa-tion's concerns and agenda.[1]

The juxtaposition of devout love for God and the Uncle-Scroogeish image of a hand rummaging in dosh gave me pause at the time. My uneasiness revealed something about myself, the assumptions I harbored about the "proper" relationship between profit-making and spirituality: I found something unsettling in such an blend of righteousness and capitalism—particularly in a milieu, that of Tatarstani halalists, the very existence of which marked a departure from "Veblenesque," Pharaoh-like material interest (see chapter 1) and whose members were vocal about the moral evils of materialism, injustice, and inequality. At first sight, such concerns were not shared by my pious interlocutors, at least not outwardly. Yet similar misgivings are not absent from the overall context of post-Soviet Tatarstan, where working-class nonpietists look with ambivalent feeling at the socioeconomic dynamism of the halal milieu, oscillating between admiration and disapprobation, emulation and resentment. Further probing among pious entrepreneurs revealed that despite the matter-of-factness of the APM motto, the pull of worldly success does come with many spiritual and ethical strings attached. How halalists navigate this intertwinement of piety and money is the topic of this chapter.

The APM motto captures a well-recognized aspect of global religious effervescence in an era of capitalist expansion: faith revivals' overlap with material wealth and entrepreneurship in Muslim settings (Osella and Osella 2009; Rudnyckyj 2009, 2010, 2019; Mittermaier 2013; Schielke 2015a, 105–127; Tobin 2016; P. Anderson 2018, 2023) and beyond (Coleman 2000; Harding 2001; Wiegele 2007; Lauterbach 2017). The nexus between piety and capitalism has long puzzled social analysts. It could be argued that views positing a tension between profit and godliness (Weber [1905] 2002, 25), or exchange and grace (Davies 2002, 62–70), manifest culture-specific anxieties rooted in the "categorial forms" of the Greco-Roman and Judeo-Christian moral economies, which cannot be generalized (see Rudnyckyj 2019, 75). Islam, it could be argued, has included elements of economic theory since its inception and is thus ab origine well equipped in terms of economic/financial regulations and concepts (Rodinson 1978; Pellicani 1994, 33–34, 94–97; Tripp 2006; Sagitova 2014). James Hoesterey, in particular, has warned that anthropological approaches to late-modern Islamic capitalism should be mindful of the *longue durée* rather than focus on latter-day neoliberal developments (2016, 5, 102). This applies to our case too: In the Volga region, numerous eighteenth- and nineteenth-century mosques erected by wealthy Muslim merchants stand as testimonies of a long regional history of the intertwinement of affluence and devotion (Khalitov 2012, 78–146). And after all, late-tsarist-era fatwas by renowned Tatar sheikh Rizaeddin Fakhretdin (Galyautdin 2014, 25) reveal that concerns about economic/business conduct were already rife more than a century ago and had no doubt been current among Muslims for a long time before that.

On the other hand, something arguably new is afoot in contemporary religious movements' consumption and moneymaking practices. Over the past few decades, Muslim societies have been investing unprecedented intellectual and ethical efforts in coming to terms with the transformative power of global capitalism, displaying creativity in adapting to the challenge of the times (Maqsood 2014; Marsden 2016; Retsikas 2018). This is even more the case in a postsocialist setting such as Povolzhye. Russia's transformation into a neoliberal autocracy (Kagarlitsky 2002, 2007)[2] has had profound effects, accelerating free-market reforms and mass consumerism. The number of Tatarstani Muslims engaged in market activities has expanded drastically—along with the range and interconnectedness of said activities—swelling the ranks of the aspirational middle class (chapter 1; Benussi 2020b). Pietists purchase services in halal fitness and touring, debate corruption and ethical banking, and attend business seminars in which skullcap-wearing motivators using corporate lingo quote Steve Jobs alongside Quranic verses. Such practices would have certainly befuddled Tatar merchants and intellectuals of earlier eras.

Of course, these challenges are far from exclusive to Povolzhye. Across the globe, capitalism has been both decried by Muslim thinkers as an existential threat to Islamic civilization (Miri and Byrd 2018) and saluted for its transformative potential as "an opportunity for Muslims to re-inscribe themselves into world history" (Tripp 2006, 6; see Rudnyckyj 2019; Abdou 2022). This ambivalence haunts Tatarstan's halal milieu as well. The piety movement is rife with class anxieties, spiritual concerns, and aspirations to achieve the good Rule-abiding life within Russia's turbulent, cutthroat capitalist lifeworld, molded by the cruel Law of rapacious accumulation of which the old guard of reformed Pharaohs have vivid memories, or at least a "spirit of careerism" generating novel anxieties (Yurchak 2003).

The following pages explore how pietists in the halal milieu deal with affluence—its acquisition, management, and loss. Rather than on halal consumption, an issue I have covered in other contributions (Benussi 2020b, 2021a, 2022b), the bulk of this chapter focuses on pietists' moneymaking and the aporias of Islamic business in Russia. The question of consumption will, however, take us to what I call the halal milieu's "moral chrematistic"—that is, pietists' art of managing excess wealth. Once again, I mobilize our familiar autonomist interpretive scaffolding: I argue that by experimenting with ethical entrepreneurship, pietists seek to realize or at least prefigure the realization of their potential while attempting to subtract themselves from the exploitative dynamics of wage labor. The realization (partial or substantial) of economic autonomy, however, comes at a price: ethical unease over Rule-compliant management of surplus money—which the heterodox French theorist Georges Bataille ([1991]

2019) calls "the accursed share"—but also exposure to the formidable pressure of the Law of the market.

Framing the Halal Milieu's Moral Chrematistic

Anthropologists working in Muslim-majority societies have long been investigating Islam's crisscrossing with moneymaking, productivity, and neoliberal capitalism. In the mid-2000s, Daromir Rudnyckyj studied the "assemblage" of Islamic spirituality and Euro-American corporate culture in Indonesia, analyzed through his concept of "spiritual economies" (Rudnyckyj 2009, 2010)—that is, mechanisms of neoliberal subject formation that make use of Islam-derived discursive, rhetorical, and affective tools to forge the ideal late-modern worker. In a more recent monograph, based on his work with Islamic finance experts, Rudnyckyj has investigated Islamic finance in Malaysia as "a means of enhancing the ability of Muslims to live in a pious manner" through economic action (2019, 11). The question of Islamic banking is also discussed in Sarah Tobin's (2016) volume about middle-class Jordanians, in which finance, alongside other expressions of what she dubs, intriguingly if somewhat nebulously, "neoliberal piety," are explored in all their messiness and promise. Practices as diverse as "fasting for Ramadan, wearing the hijab, working at an Islamic bank, or using an 'Islamic' credit card" (2016, 192) are shown as being connected to neoliberal developments in the Middle East. Compared to Rudnyckyj's sanguine assessment of spiritual economies' enabling potential, Tobin dwells more on the combination of optimism and skepticism that surrounds economic products and activities branded as Islamic.

In another important contribution, Samuli Schielke (2015a) has investigated the nexus of revivalist piety and "lived capitalism" in contemporary Egypt, advancing the intriguing contention that revivalist Islam is neither an alternative to nor a corrective for capitalism—rather, revivalist Islam is "an especially compelling way to live capitalism, and vice versa" (2015a, 119). Schielke identifies capitalism as a specific lifeworld or "sensibility of being in the world" (2015a, 16) that perforce conditions the existences of virtuous and less virtuous Muslims. In conversation with Schielke and further developing this line of inquiry, Amira Mittermaier (2013) has contrasted two "economic theologies" among Cairene pietists: one more "neoliberally" inclined, focused on capitalizing spiritual rewards through an almost mercantilist take on piety (Retsikas 2018), and one focused on disinterest, generosity, and a welcoming acceptance of divine blessings. As we shall see, the terminology of reward and blessing is also current in Muslim Povolzhye. Recently, Paul Anderson (2018, 2023) has intervened in this discussion by arguing that the "neoliberal" aspect in the economic practices of latter-day reform-minded Muslims, while not negligible, ought to be considered in, and is counterbalanced by, the broader context of nonopportunistic solidarity, social effervescence, and moral imagination that he documented in prewar Syria. Paul Anderson and Magnus Marsden (2023), who works on Afghan Muslim merchants' trade practices, have argued that an exclusive focus on exchange risks obscuring the ethical and relational dimensions of commerce, an argument that also applies to Tatar *biznesmeny*'s engagements with the market.[3]

Though Central Eurasian Muslims have been less represented in the anthropology of Islamic economy, fresh studies have cast new light on the enmeshment of Islam and capitalism in the formerly socialist world. Aisalkin Botoeva (2018), in a Weberian vein, has for instance explored the "capitalist spirits" (nation-oriented, prosperity-oriented, and spirituality-oriented) of practitioners of halal business in urban Central Asia, while Iwona Kaliszewska (2020) compellingly described the "halal landscapes" of Muslim entrepreneurs in the North Caucasian republic of Dagestan. David Henig's work in Bosnia (2020) also detailed how the concept of halal becomes vernacularized at the grassroots, but in a different way than the abovementioned works (and my own): In the rural communities where he did fieldwork—somewhat removed from the transactional, urban domain of *biznes*—"halal" is synonymous with forgiveness, mutuality, the remission of debts. But all these cases point to a common trend: In all these settings, the recourse of the theological terminology of halal signals a yearning for fairness in the face of a morally fraught economic landscape, on the one hand, and a desire to tame, subdue, or harness the volcanic forces of marketplace capitalism, on the other.

In both explicit and implicit ways, all the contributions mentioned above channel as well as challenge classic anthropological concerns about moral economy (Rudnyckyj 2009, 116; 2018, 9–10; Tobin 2016, 112; Schielke 2015a, 119; Green 2011, 2015; Osella and Rudnyckyj 2017; P. Anderson 2018). Moral economy is a time-honored anthropological notion that carries the double meaning of (a) economic patterns or systems embedded in "traditional" customs, values, relations, and social norms and (b) endeavors to accumulate and distribute wealth in ways perceived as socially just and equitable (Thompson 1971, 1993; Scott 1976; see Edelman 2012). On the whole, scholars of Muslim encounters with the market have maintained a certain ambivalence vis-à-vis the venerable yet cumbersome Thompson-Scottian conceptual framework, attempting to reframe the nexus of morality and economic action in novel terms.

There are good reasons for ambivalence vis-à-vis the classic formulation: the semantic slipperiness of the moral economy concept; its normative anti-capitalist baggage, which chafes against late-modern Muslims' optimistic engagement with the market; and, perhaps chiefly, the fact that Islamic business and consumption practices exist *within* late capitalism rather than in a "traditional" domain outside of it. And while some have passionately vouched for Islamic economy as an anti-capitalist paradigm (Abdou 2022), "really existing Islamic economy" has not (yet) emerged as a viable systemic alternative to the regnant setup. Most of the studies and conceptual formulations mentioned above (spiritual economy, neoliberal piety, economic theology, etc.) are in fact particularly successful in highlighting the unresolved ambivalences that persist in the zone of entanglements of Islam and late capitalism, the "*not-quite-moral* economies" that Muslims in different corners of the globe finds themselves enmeshed in.

And yet, persistent and well documented anxieties over the ills of capitalism, as well as Muslims' desire to tame the market economy by bringing Islam's normative-juridical tradition to bear on it, point to an undiminished intensity of a "moral" dimension of Muslim economic activity. This suggests that the moral economy concept does retain a degree of heuristic vitality. In what follows, I attempt to hone and develop this heuristic by zooming in on a specific, narrower aspect of ethicized economic life that I call "moral chrematistics." The term "*chremastitiké*," introduced by Aristotle, stands in contraposition to "*oikonomia*" (the effective management of the household's resources) to indicate a doctrine, theory, and/or practice of wealth (Sørensen 2018, 100). Chrematistics comprises what Aristotelian moral philosophy, along with most moral teachings including Islamic ethics, considers especially problematic about economic action: The accumulation of money, manipulation of property, maximization of profit, and conspicuous consumption. As Bataille ([1991] 2019, 12) put it, "It is not necessity but its contrary, 'luxury,' that presents [hu]mankind with their fundamental problems." Even without defining it in those terms, anthropologists have long been interested in chrematistics in the context of religious and economic transformation—witness, for example, Girish Daswani's (2016) discussion of the tension between "rich" (moneyed) and "wealthy" (ethically moneyed) in a Ghanaian Protestant community. In the following pages, I hope to illustrate the heuristic viability of this concept by applying it to the "art" of moneymaking among Tatar halalists. I advance the notion of moral chrematistics to identify a set of "affluence techniques" that include both strategies to attract wealth and operations aimed at neutralizing or at least limiting the ethical risks associated with it, be these spiritual (sin) or social (disapprobation) in nature.

As we have seen in earlier chapters, Alain Badiou posited a fundamental tension between an ethics of truth and the domain of "the interest of the human animal," between fidelity and "plenitude." If unattended to, this tension may result in "betrayal" (Badiou 2002, 49–59, 71–80). Yet this danger cannot be completely eschewed, as ethical subjects are human animals immersed in situations: Self-disinterest cannot be total, or it would become self-destruction; and no truth-process could exist in isolation from concrete, interest-ridden situational domains. There is much to Badiou's framework that resonates with Islam's doctrine of wealth and the art of moneymaking, with its outspoken disapprobation of interest (ribā), selfishness, and excessive worldliness. Agamben's philosophical readings of Christian cenobitism highlight a similar tension: Monastics vow to adhere to the "highest poverty" while also engaging in productive, wealth-generating economic activity, under an ethical regime that emphasizes the use of resources and goods over their ownership (Agamben 2013a, 123–124). Despite Islam's rejection of monasticism, Agamben's framework resonates with Islam's insistence on the ultimate sovereignty of God, believers' economic obligations, and redistributive mechanisms. Our autonomist interpretation of Povolzhye Muslims' moral chrematistics will be integrated by including Bataille's intuitions about the dangerous power of "the accursed share" ([1991] 2019). If the French philosopher's Orientalist treatment of Islam has aged poorly,[4] his overall intuitions about the moral sensitivity of excess/surplus of wealth that must be purified—subtracted from the capitalist cycle of accumulation—by means of religiously mandated expenditure or sacrifice remain worthy of serious consideration.

By combining these conceptual strands, I argue that insofar as the truth-process of post-Soviet Islamic piety is born of and within late-modern capitalism with Russia's transition to a market economy, it is inescapably immersed in a capitalistic order. Indeed, postsocialist pietists embrace the tools of capitalism to emancipate themselves from wage labor, heteronomous disciplining, and the shackles of scarcity. Povolzhye's halal milieu strives to reorder the capitalist lifeworld they live in through fidelity to scriptural command. While to an extent this endeavor succeeds, pietists remain nonetheless subject to the overarching norms of the market. The related moral dangers are therefore never completely removed from the lived experience of halal wealth-seekers. In other words, the halal milieu is an ascetical form of capitalist life, necessarily suspended between the Law of self-interest and the Rule of ethical-religious obligation. To understand the practical paradoxes of halalists' moral chrematistics, let me take you through an exploration of the juncture between Islam and the market in Muslim Povolzhye.

The Ethical "Trillionaire"

Perhaps the best embodiment of the halal milieu's engagement with a neoliberal ethos is Shamil-xäzrät Alyautdinov. Born in 1974 to a Moscow-based Mishar (Western Tatar) family, from 1992 to 1998 Shamil Alyautdinov studied Islamic law at Cairo's Al-Azhar University, after which he took up his current position as khaṭīb (preacher and leader) at Moscow's Memorial Mosque and became not only Russia's Muslim trainer/life guru/prosperity televangelist in chief (Bustanov 2012;see Hoesterey 2016, 94–97; Retsikas 2018 for comparable figures) but arguably one of the most resounding Muslim voices in the entire post-Soviet world. Throughout the 2010s, Alyautdinov ran Russia's trendiest Islam-themed website and produced a steady flux of popular literature tailored for a nonspecialized Muslim audience alongside more traditional theology treatises.[5] Alyautdinov's books, translated into Chechen, Tajik, Tatar, and English, cover a range of topics, from romantic life to parenting to managing one's finances. Alyautdinov's "Trillionaire" multi-installment series (2013a, 2013b, 2014a, 2014b, 2015a, 2015b, 2017), exploring the question of how to obtain success "both in this world and the next," is his most popular product.

The figure of the Trillionaire (*trillioner*) is the embodiment of all the qualities needed to become a "person of unlimited possibilities"—that is, a spiritually and materially successful Muslim. Becoming a Trillionaire is not (only) about making money; it also means embarking on a project of self-refashioning into a physically and mentally fit, disciplined, morally and spiritually aware, emotionally fulfilled, and achievement-bound individual. During our conversation, Shamil-xäzrät's right-hand man, Zenur, illustrated this project in the following terms: "To success-seeking Muslims, the Trillionaire trope is captivating—the idea that there are infinite possibilities. The Trillionaire embodies some of the qualities of the Most High: generosity, wealth, love for all things good, the will to call others to the good. We attract young people who are prepared to work hard to obtain these things, who want to get to the best [*luchshego dobit'sya*], increase their income, widen their existential, intellectual, and emotional repertoires." Shamil-xäzrät goes deliberately easy on the Islamic side of his works, simplifying theological language and avoiding formulaic prose. He also allows himself some liberties in terms of scriptural sources (Bustanov 2012, 147–154): For instance, translated quotes from the Quran are rife with interjections and explanations, square-bracketed into the text by Alyautdinov himself. One of the most distinctive features of his oeuvre is a mixture of theological and non-Islamic sources—ranging from globally famous names, such as Steve Jobs, to popular psychologists and neuroscientists like Candace Pert and Philip Zimbardo, to new-age figures such as Carlos Castaneda and Mark Vicente, to self-improvement writers and corporate trainers of the caliber of Ben-Shahar, Daniel Amen, and Jack Canfield.

Although some scripturalist voices criticize Shamil-xäzrät's books as theologically weak, his approach has inspired many imitators. In Kazan, for example, I encountered the work of Abdulla-xäzrät Adygamov, considered by his supporters Tatarstan's "Shamil Alyautdinov to be." In 2015, Adygamov published a book titled *The Golden Rules of Success: One Ayat and Three Hadiths About How to Make It*, promoted by the Association of Muslim Entrepreneurs. I attended Adygamov's book launch in Kazan, during which he explained that he wanted to make an explicitly and uniquely Islamic contribution to the literature on successfulness. Referring to a Sunni theological principle, Adygamov argued that the Quran contains as a matter of course the answers to all quandaries, including the "success question." This remark was perhaps a jibe at his predecessor Alyautdinov, whose habit of referencing non-Islamic sources raised eyebrows in scripturalist quarters. In his presentation, Abdulla-xäzrät listed several spheres in which success is to be pursued by Muslims: the first should be spiritual life, followed by business, family, and fitness/health. The Quranic verse on which his oeuvre was based is 13:11, "Verily never will God change the condition of a people until they change it themselves"—the implication being that one's relational sphere is predicated on one's inner world and one's ability to navigate and intervene on it (see Pandolfo 2018, 327).[6]

Beyond self-help literature, the trope of "success in both worlds" lies at the heart of consulting agencies such as Uspeshny Muslim (Successful Muslim), tailored to aspiring Muslims who want to enter halal business and need managerial or theological advice. I became acquainted with the agency's founder, Idegey, a young man who had been in business since the 1990s when, at just fourteen, he started pitching makeshift garages in his hometown in southeast Tatarstan:

> A Muslim has to be strong—physically, spiritually, financially, and in terms of moral fiber. He should itch for action. Aspire to be an athlete, a businessperson, a public activist. A believer has to be better than other people. One has to be the best at work, the best in his town, the best in his family life. In all regards. One has to change his life, to throw himself into new enterprises. If you work, then you have to work at full blast. . . . A Muslim doesn't work like everybody else does, but ten times better, better, better. Our Prophet (SAS) and the Quran say that you have to push hard [*prokachat'sya*]. Muslims should think big, be ambitious. A halal culture cannot be detached from a culture of entrepreneurship.

I encountered the same ethos during my fieldwork with the scripturalist-leaning mosque community in Akmaş. Azat, one of the community members, told me how the local imam had managed to purge the city's business sphere of its post-Soviet "criminal aspects" (*kriminal'nost'*), at least as far as Muslim business was concerned. The mosque leadership had cultivated a puritan ethos of rigor, honesty, transparency, and hard work among the community, to the point that Azat called the imam "our own Steve Jobs." It is worth noting that references to Steve Jobs were quasi-omnipresent in my field site. The Californian entrepreneur had been apocryphally incorporated into the host of exemplars (Humphrey 1997) whom my Muslim interlocutors regarded with admiration and would cite frequently—along with less surprising figures such as Turkish president Erdoğan and seventh-century military leader Khalid ibn al-Walid.

"Islam develops [*razvivaet*] people, pushes them forward": This is how my acquaintance Azat described the transformation people experience upon conversion. The notion of "development" (*razvitie*) recurred almost obsessively during my ethnography, Islam being described as a "developmental factor" for society at large as well as in terms of personal development. This trope appears to be part of a broader, pan-Russian narrative of moral advancement (Zigon 2010a, 60–61, 216) but is particularly pronounced among young Muslims that seek to optimistically engage with the market economy.

Biznes and Autonomy

The examples above illustrate the huge demand for tools of self-improvement among Povolzhye's Muslim middle class. On one level, it could be said that these projects have a distinct neoliberal character—in the sense that one of their goals is to "overcome the divide between the intimate man and the entrepreneur" (Feher 2009, 33; see Boltanski and Chiapello 2002; Long and Moore 2013, 2; Rose [1989] 1999; Rose and Miller 2008; cf. Abdou 2022 for an alternative reading). Such a reading would be entirely legitimate. In the context of post-Soviet Povolzhye, however, embracing neoliberal transformation implies a withdrawal from the heteronomous domain of the industrial labor regime—and the implications of this withdrawal need to be considered in the context of the formation of an Islamic form-of-life.

Many pietists hail from working-class backgrounds. Their parents and grandparents worked in the Soviet industry or, for the numerous new urbanites who trace their ancestry to the countryside, state-run kolkhozes. In the general economic collapse that followed the USSR's breakup, Tatarstan fared better than other regions and retains strong manufacturing and agricultural sectors. Yet by and large, my interlocutors do their active best to avoid factories and farms and try their hand at *biznes*. Manual/industrial wage-earning jobs are considered respectable in theory, but, de facto, the shop floor is seen as something to escape from. Even in Tatarstan's industrial strongholds, a good part of mosque communities appear to be composed of tertiary-sector workers,[7] with people from the lower professional strata eager to dissimulate their employment situation or stress its temporariness.

While the growing halal industry—halal meat factories, shops, and so on— absorbs an unspecialized Muslim workforce, the service sector appears to exercise a stronger pull. If the younger generation of pietists tend to seek higher levels of education and specialization, older Muslims often prefer self-employment and petty entrepreneurship as *chastniki* (from *chastny*, "private," as one that privately owns and runs a small business). As my friend Alina told me with a generalization that may be overstated but is nonetheless illustrative, "The average mosque-goer here has his own hustle, drives his van around running errands." Some *chastniki* have a transport business, others work as private taxi drivers, others yet as technicians and computer repairers. Several of my participants are, or wish to become, active in spheres such as trade, including retail, logistics, and distribution; services, including halal leisure (gastronomy, tourism, entertainment); technology and innovation; fashion (primarily in the case of female pietists) and design; or cognitive labor, journalism/media, and intellectual work (including in the Islamic bureaucracy). High-level business—national and international commerce, management, real estate, and (halal) finance/consultancy—possesses an aura of extraordinary prestige. But in reality, given a volatile economic environment, even in relatively prosperous Tatarstan, many lower-middle-class Muslims at the time of my research would make do by precariously juggling multiple hustles and projects at a time.

The dreamworld of *biznes* tallies with the middle-class orientation of the halal milieu, its aspirations to success and Weberian "capitalist spirit." But alongside class dynamics, embracing *biznes* also implies securing control over one's body and temporality, both of which are crucial to Muslim pietists' ethical projects. Alina explained that "running your own hustle mean[s] you have control of your time, you are your own master [*khozyain*], you can stop to pray wherever you want and nobody can tell you what to do." Indeed, several self-employed respondents who had previously been wage-earners spoke about the pain of not being able to perform namaz on account of the constraints of the workplace's time discipline (Thompson 1967; see Marcuse [1964] 1972, 18). Industrial clockwork often interferes with the Islamic time discipline of prayer, the ritual foundation of the halal milieu's form-of-life. Hence, numerous halalists considered self-employment, despite its uncertainties, a better option than heteronomous discipline. In another telling example, my acquaintance Usman, the Salafi electrician we met in chapter 1, reported feeling constrained during his stint as a security guard because he was not allowed to grow a beard—thus having to forsake an important element of the cultivation of male Sunni bodily selves—and his appearance and attire had to conform to the company's dress code.

To pietists like Usman, transitioning out of wage-earning and toward self-employment means literally removing their bodies from a regime of appropriation (Agamben 2013a, xiii) that hinders the development of an ethical subjectivity, and wrestling back control of their temporalities from heteronomous ownership. It is, in other words, an emancipatory move. Of course, the astute reader might object that such a move does not ultimately liberate Muslim *chast-niki* from the systemic tyranny of capital. While this is a sensible observation, in the context of post-Soviet Russia *biznes* remains one of the most attractive among the viable options (on the autonomizing pull of self-employment, however precarious, see Millar 2014; Troccoli 2022; on the experience of autonomous self-making among Muslim traders—a demographic that partly overlaps with sectors of Povolzhye's halal milieu—see P. Anderson and Marsden 2023, 782–784).

The pursuit of moderate prosperity, advocated by Shamil-xäzrät and the other champions of "success in both worlds," is similarly conducive to the realization of the halal milieu's ethical form-of-life. In a postsocialist setting in which competition for resources remains intense, achieving above-subsistence income guarantees, for instance, the means to have a large family, which is considered meritorious in Islam. Furthermore, relative affluence enables alms-giving and patronage, which are necessary to fund the halal milieu's spiritual infrastructure—mosques, religious services, and so forth—at a time in which it has become autonomous from foreign aid (D. Garaev 2017). As Bataille wrote, "Wealth changes meaning according to the advantage we expect from its possession" ([1991] 2019, 118, 125–126). In capitalism, the "advantage that matters most" at the systemic level is endless, self-replicating accumulation of capital ("Money can beget money"). Its uncanny, destructive vitality is what makes the accursed share dangerous. But, notes Bataille, endless growth is *not* normally the "final purpose" of concrete individuals and groups at the system's ground level: Some people pursue wealth for leisure, others for social standing, others yet to create a family, and so on. In Muslim Povolzhye, socially mobile Muslim pietists frame wealth as a matter of personal "development," self-worth, a functional household, and personal autonomy from wage work—all of which are seen as conducive to a fulfilling spiritual life—rather than ostentatious extravagance or selfish accumulation, which are strongly condemned. Alyautdinov's Trillionaire metaphor must not be taken at face value: As we shall see, affluence entails financial responsibilities before God and the ummah alike. Granted a combination of wise, prudent expenditure and charitable redistribution, moderate wealth is seen by halalists as nourishment for the biological "support" of Islam's truth-process: the bodies, individual and collective, that compose Islam's form-of-life. Religion, in turn, offers ways to "purify" any dangerous surplus, any "accursed" share, and turn it into a blessing.

Making *Barakat*ful Money

Making money is not considered a religious obligation by Povolzye pietists, yet many see achieving a degree of affluence as a *duty* toward themselves as well as the community. A much-quoted maxim goes, "There can be poor Muslims and rich Muslims, but a rich Muslim is better than a poor one" (see Osella 2017). In the halal milieu's moral chrematistic, material aspirations are not only accepted but actively incentivized—provided certain conditions are met. Theological justifications are drawn from the exemplar repertoire of Sunnism, for instance by referring to the experience of the Prophet and his wealthy first wife, Khadijah, who were business partners:

> A rich Muslim is better than a poor Muslim—although they are both equally Muslim. Why? Because a wealthy Muslim can donate generously. That is why I believe that making halal money is Sunna. One has to strive for riches in order to use his wealth on the path of God [*na puti Allakha*]. (Umar, thirty-one, web entrepreneur, Yar Çallı)

> The Quran does not forbid affluence, to the contrary, it praises it [*eto tolko privetstvuyetsya*]. I think the more wealthy Muslims [there are], the stronger our ummah gets. It benefits Islam. (Ilnur, thirty-three, cadre of the Association of Muslim Entrepreneurs, Kazan)

Like other sectors of the new global bourgeoisie, Tatarstan's halalists operate under a "morality of quality"—a desire to live by higher standards than previous generations on the grounds that comfort and even luxury are both a "right" and a "necessity" in keeping with "middle-class romanticized ideas of 'the good life'" (De Solier 2013, 17, 80, 105). One of the recurring phrases within Alyautdinov's following is that successful Muslims "are worthy of the best" (*dostoyny luchshego*) (Alyautdinov 2013b, 215). One of my friends argued that "it is permissible for Muslims to desire beautiful things, be it with regards to apparel, accommodation, cars . . . Prophet Muhammad (SAS) said that a Muslim should look tidy. You definitely ought to look respectable, neat. People will judge you as a Muslim accordingly." Another, inserting herself in an aspirational global landscape of Islamic modernity, insisted that "there is nothing shameful about being rich. God does not prevent us from being rich—absolutely not. If you go to the Emirates, Malaysia, or Turkey, those countries are doing pretty well!" Superficially, the halal milieu might appear to retain "Pharaonic" traits—a Veblenesque leisure class preferring conspicuous consumption to ascetic austerity (Veblen [1899] 2008). However, the quotes above show that being a "better" (i.e., wealthier) Muslim means shouldering greater responsibility vis-à-vis the community and having specific financial obligations.

Veblenesque markers such as idleness, frivolity, and ostentatiousness are anything but welcome in the halal milieu. An affluent life does not come without strings attached: According to my pious interlocutors, there are strict rules in terms of making, managing, and even losing worldly possessions—while mis-handling the fruits of success might cause one's expulsion from the fold of the saved. Treating wealth "as an end rather than a means"[8] or as an "idol" worthy of "worship" is both spiritually destructive and socially disgraceful in the eyes of the ummah of the righteous. The following pious story circulated in one social media group dedicated to Muslim business: "The Prophet, interrogated about the deterioration of Islam in the dark times before the Last Day (a period that many pietists identify with our era), foresaw that 'People's God shall be their bellies, . . . money their faith, and wealth their honour.' Interrogated as to whether Muslims shall abandon monotheism for idolatry, Muhammad replied, 'So it will be, and their idol shall be money.'" This reference to idolatry resonates with Badiou's concept of betrayal: a capitulation to "pressure from the demands of interest" or the pursuit of a "simulacrum"—such as success in this world—that takes the place of a truth (2002, 78–79). To avoid these dangers,

> Muslims must remain within the framework [*ramki*] of Islam, and not trespass the boundaries of what is permissible. Then business will be halal, whatever it is—restoration, education, trade, anything. As an example, halal business implies the absence of interest loans. If I lend you money and ask for exactly the same amount of money back, and we seal the deal preferably in front of witnesses, then we are doing halal business. If I buy a car for you and tell you exactly how much you are going to pay in advance, that is halal business, too. (Zakir, twenty-nine, halal food entrepreneur, Akmaş)

As the quote above mentions, interest (<u>ribā</u>) occupies a particularly central place in Islam's economic ethos (Rudnyckyj 2019; Abdou 2022): Consider Badiou's dictum that interest is incompatible with ethical conduct. Wealth accumulated in illicit ways—for instance, by stealing or gambling, but also by trading non-halal goods such as alcohol and immodest clothes, or through inadmissible or speculative transaction such as usury or pyramid schemes—is understood as lacking *barakat* (<u>barakah</u>) (i.e., God's blessings):

> Halal money is money earned by working hard, it's got *barakat*, which means that it will give you pleasure, but will also benefit others around you. But money obtained in unlawful ways will not bring you real pleasure. It's empty money [*pustye den'gi*]. The whole point is that wealth is not a goal in itself, but a means to achieve certain moral and spiritual life goals. (Rinat-abıy, thirty, translator, Kazan)

> If a business is halal, God will give barakah [<u>xäläl bulsa, Allah bäräkät birä</u>]. God blesses you. As soon as you stop keeping halal, the party is

over, my dear, it's over. It's too late already. Remember the 1990s? People died every day because of their dirty deeds—drugs, alcohol. But if you stick to halal, you'll get spiritual reward [*acir*]. (Rustem-äfände, forty-four, businessman, Yar Çallı)

To obtain *barakat*, Muslims should not only earn their money in Islamically permissible ways but also accept the financial obligations that God bestows on his ummah—namely, that of mandatory (zakāt)[9] and voluntary (sadaqah) charity:[10]

> If one has worldly possessions [*imushestvo*], and does not share part of these, then this capital loses its *barakat*. One should share with their family, to start with. Then the close ones. Then the needy. Once your basic and spiritual needs are fulfilled, when you have a home and your family is fed, then it's your responsibility to care for those around you. For instance, I recommend that my clients check their neighborhoods for widows, families struggling with financial problems, or elderly people in need. This is voluntary charity. Then there is obligatory zakāt, which is 2.5% of one's income. Zakāt is an obligation, if you don't pay it your religion spoils. You won't be a full-fledged [*polnotsenny*] Muslim anymore. However, it is proven that the more you give, the more you get as a reward. (Bulat, thirty-five, halal financial consultant, Akmaş)

In this moral chrematistic, excess wealth ought to be funneled toward the sustainment of the "human animal" in order for it to be able to adequately support the truth of Islam: one's bodily self, family, and community—particularly vulnerable members. As a prominent advocate of Islamic economics put it, "'Rationality' in Islamic economics does not get confined to the serving of one's self-interest in this world alone; it also gets extended to the Hereafter through the faithful compliance with moral values that help rein self-interest to promote social interest" (Chapra 2013, 23). Specific redistributive mechanisms are in place to "neutralize" the spiritual danger and turn it into a blessing: Not coincidentally, the word "zakāt" means "that which purifies," cleansing "empty money" of its impurity (P. Anderson 2018, 616; Retsikas 2018, 661)—through it, the Bataillean "curse" that lingers about excess wealth.

In sum, the *barakat* idiom implies a balancing act between striving for prosperity and cultivating disinterest. This moral chrematistic applies not only to individuals but also to collective entities. As my acquaintance Amir articulated, Tatarstan is considered a *barakatny* region: "God gifted us gas and oil because we are Muslim, even though a majority are just ethnic Muslims. What to do with this gift—this choice lies with us, now. We need to couple financial and material development with spiritual growth."

The Preordained Chance

A crucial theological component of halalists' moral chrematistics is *rizk/rızık* (rizq), or the worldly "provision"—in the form of means of subsistence but also, as a consequence, one's social standing—that the Most High, one of whose names is the Sustainer, ar-Razzāq, allocates to humans before birth according to His sovereign, unknowable will. Just as the duration of each human life, this ration is divinely predetermined and cannot be changed. As one of my participants explained to me, "When it comes to how long we are going to be around, and how well we are going to do, our will plays a very little role—no role at all in fact." In Islam, God is the ultimate owner of all wealth, while humans are just beneficiaries and stewards of their worldly possessions—hence the religious obligation to share. But how does a seemingly fatalistic doctrine of foreordainment (qadar) square with the halal milieu's entrepreneurial drive toward development and *barakat*ful wealth?

The doctrine of predestination is not interpreted by post-Soviet pietists as necessarily synonymous with passive acceptance of one's condition. Many halalists are drawn to Quranic passages and hadiths suggesting that God repays righteous conduct by bestowing material riches.[11] On these grounds, the notion that human activity *may* increase rizq is considered compatible with qadar. In this reading, what is foreordained is the *possibility* of an increase, within foreordained limits, and conditionally on individual believers' correct conduct upon encountering foreordained opportunities. What matters, then, is recognizing these opportunities, seizing them, and managing them in keeping with Islamic norms and injunctions.

Many pietists are aware that doctrines of predestination, especially if interpreted in ways typically associated with Sufi mysticism or vernacular religiosity, might lend themselves to acceptance or even valorization of poverty. It is telling that in some Muslim-majority regions, the Arabic word for "poor" (faqīr, see Tatar *fäkıyr* "indigent, miserable, beggar") has expanded its semantic field to encompass the meaning of "holy man." Halal milieu religionists, however, tend to distance themselves from such interpretations. Mysticism-informed pauperism is dismissed as "sluggish Sufis wasting their time in mosques" as a Salafi interlocutor put it, while fatalist moral tendencies are actively countered, as exemplified by the following remark by Shamil Alyautdinov's assistant:[12]

> You know the Quranic expression "Kun fayakūn" [Ar. "Be!, and it is"—referring to God's command for His creatures to come into existence],[13] right? So, some people in certain Muslim countries say, "I am who I am—a humble truck driver, a farm laborer, or a factory worker—because this is what God has decreed, kun fayakūn. So what should

I work hard for? It's already decided." But Shamil-xäzrät says to these people, "No, listen, it's down to you really! If you work hard, God shall say 'Be!' once again, and you'll no longer be a mere factory worker, but a company manager." Can you see? Two different understandings of the same Quranic scripture.

Tellingly, in the quote above a negatively connoted fatalistic attitude is associated with wage-earning, heteronomous jobs. I witnessed numerous conversations around the question of whether or not it would be legitimate for a Muslim to lead a pious but passive life ("just sitting at home and praying") and still expect _rızık_ to reach him or her. To most pietists, the answer is negative. Pietists should not lead an exclusively contemplative existence; to the contrary, they have a series of duties toward themselves, their close ones, and their communities—their forms-of-life—that can be fulfilled only through active engagement with the world. Deliberately missing chances to "develop" and thereby fulfill those duties would have to be accounted for in the afterlife, because these chances are sent by God himself. God's intervention in his worshippers' biographies unfolds in the shape of opportunities to grasp and brave choices to make—and it is one's ethical duty to be receptive to these epiphanies:

> Our _rızık_ is predetermined, right. But when it comes to actions, then it's down to us—us only—and you'll receive according to your actions. To make the right choice, you are given clear instructions. So you are going to get precisely what you earned—no more, no less. That is why jihad [effort] is important. Jihad in Arabic means to apply enhanced efforts in the pursuit of given goals. So <u>mujahīd</u> means a person who keeps their goals constantly within their sight [*imeet pered glazami svoyu tsel'*], and devises plans to achieve them [*stroit' plany dlya nee dostizheniya*]. (Robert-äfände, forty-eight, manager, Kazan)

A particularly important idiom through which this dyad of predestined provision and individual initiative is expressed is that of "making a cause" for _rızık_ to be delivered. My good acquaintance Umar articulated this sophisticated theory of halal economic action in the following terms:

> Alhamdullillah we live a decent life, keeping out of financial straits. It's not that I expect to be fed my *rizk* by God, just like this. The Prophet (SAS) said: "I lead my camels, and rely on God." The two things are connected. One has to make a reason [for *rizk* to get to one]. The reason [*prichina*], <u>sabab</u>, is absolutely key.[14] You should make a reason [*delat' prichinu*], first, and then rely on God [*polagat'sya na Allakha*]. God wants to give you [your *rizk*], but you have to make a reason, even just a

little one. In order to get my *rizk*, say, I go to work. And not that alone: I also deepen my knowledge of Islam, attend religious lectures—only for the sake of God. We have to rely on God alone: not on ourselves, not on other people. God alone.

You make a reason, and rely on God—make a reason, and rely on God. If you work hard but don't rely on God, then you won't get *rizk*. You may get something, but then it will lack *barakat*. Similarly, if you remain motionless and only rely on God, then *rizk* won't reach you. It will pass above your head, so to speak. You need to make a cause—extend your hand—to grab it. It's a twofold movement.

The idiom of "making a reason" is widespread in scripturalist-oriented religious literature across Tatarstan. A Russian-medium pamphlet on halal economy reads, "To acquire worldly possessions, it is necessary to make a reason for this to happen. Humans [as opposed, for instance, to angels] were created in such a way that they have to find their own livelihood. All people, righteous and sinful, are busy with this search. After the Friday prayer, the righteous disperse across the land in pursuit of their livelihood,[15] and this quest for God's blessing is a commendable action" (Galyautdin 2014, 6). However, the author warns us, sincere believers are not allowed to crave riches "with their hearts and souls" (6), for souls should be filled with love for God alone. The pursuit of wealth remains praiseworthy insofar as these riches will be used for noble purposes "on the path of God." These notions can be found transversally across most sectors of the halal milieu. In a lecture on *rizk* delivered to members of the Association of Muslim Entrepreneurs, Abdulla-xäzrät Adygamov insisted with similar words on the importance of individual undertaking and the intersection of human initiative and sincere trust in God:

If a person believes the little they have is enough, then they will not take any step to obtain more. Ambitious people have to be dissatisfied—*not* with what God bestowed upon them, *not* with what is predestined onto them, but with their own inability to attain their potential in full, their own lack of initiative. This way, they create a sense of purpose. God the Most High, in His Book, explicitly commands us to seek His grace, after finishing our prayers. He says, "Go out of the mosque and find yourself sustenance, work, move, get a job!" It is well known that Umar ibn al-Khattab would push lazy men out of the mosque after worship with the words, "Go and earn yourself something, don't idle about." So, the Quran and the Sunna tell us that we have to make efforts! Only *after* making those efforts, only *after* deciding, planning, and undertaking, *only then* can we rely on God. *First* action, *then* reliance on God.

Working hard to "make a reason" and putting one's trust in the divine Ruler, scanning one's worldly path for divinely sent opportunities for development, are not, however, infallible recipes for wealth. Humans can never know the extent of their *rizk*, just as they cannot know the length of their lives. Islamic notions of predestination, then, leave room for failure in business. Fiascos and bankruptcy may be attributed to a lack of *barakat*, especially in the case of non-Muslim economic actors. Nonetheless, believers are forbidden to pass spiritual judgment when it comes to fellow Muslims' financial misfortunes. Unlike in the well-known Weberian case, prosperity is not a sign of election,[16] and economic failure might be a test benignly delivered by God on a devout Muslim rather than a form of punishment or a sign of disfavor. This principle is dearly held in a volatile and changeable economic environment such as post-Soviet Russia. Several respondents shared with me their experiences of and thoughts about financial trouble:

> A Muslim frames failure as a test. We know that God made mankind diverse. Some people are richer than others, some smarter, some prettier. So, when we experience disappointments, we lose money, or our love life fails, we have to think that these are tests—and what really matters is how you endure hardship. For instance, will you keep your dignity, or will you humiliate yourself? Will you stick to the rules, or will you start sinning? Will you trust God, and ask for His help, or will you look for sinful shortcuts, like getting into shady business? We *know* that we will be tested on our faith. It's easy to be a Muslim when everything goes fine—but that does not mean much. I am *happy* that we face such testing in this life—it is much better than suffering in the other. I was tested on money myself, I lost a significant sum weeks after the beginning of a promising business. Now I know that helped me improve my financial skills. And there are things we do not know—perhaps a failure will lead us to some greater success we wouldn't achieve otherwise. Plus, hardships help us improve our sabr [forbearance, a key Islamic virtue]. (Fatima, twenty-six, fashion designer, Kazan)

> Failure is, in fact, a gift from God. Once you have mulled it over, you realize that God doesn't want you to embark on that given project. Or that He knows that, in the long term, that project would have harmed you. We don't have a clear picture of all causes and effects, as He does. Disappointment with one's fate is the worst of all sins. (Ravshan-abıy, forty-four, businessman, Tübän Kama)

> Big money is a test. More money, for instance, means more possibilities to sin. Here's a danger. On the other hand, if you don't get what you want

despite real efforts, you mustn't despair—because this means that God has something else in store for you. God doesn't just send trials upon believers like that. Trials are either ways to test one's faith and prompt spiritual growth, or perhaps punishments. Either way, despair is always a sin. One should always be content with what God sends upon him. But, on the other hand, in case of misfortune one should also ask oneself whether God might be displeased with his actions. (Umar, thirty-seven, petty entrepreneur, Tübän Kama)

One popular religious anecdote is frequently cited by pietists in business. In this story, a group of merchants sit together under a tent and talk over tea. At a certain point, a distraught messenger bursts into the tent, telling the wealthiest merchant, in a choked voice, that his fleet is shipwrecked, the sailors have drowned, and his riches are lost to the bottom of the sea. Pale-faced, yet without losing his composure, the formerly wealthy merchant simply utters, "Alhamdulillah" (praise be to God), and resumes drinking his tea. Shortly afterward, a second messenger throws himself into the tent, beaming at the merchant: There was a miscommunication—his fleet has, in fact, successfully reached its destination! All is well! Maintaining complete imperturbability, the merchant looks up and again simply replies, "Alhamdulillah." The moral, as one of my acquaintances put it, is that "a Muslim is always content. In case of a windfall, he thanks the Most High. If he suffers a loss, he should say 'everything belongs to the Most High and everything returns to Him—a misfortune is just a misfortune.'" Put in Badiousian terms, achieving ethical subjectivity implies, at least in the ideal scenario, transcending the self-interest of the human animal and learning to see worldly vicissitudes through the lens of immortality.

Making It Possible

Halalists see Islamic business as more stable, honest, and socially responsible than non-halal business. Despite of their optimism, however, large numbers of Muslim entrepreneurs struggle to keep up with Islamic norms while moving in the rugged terrain of Russia's economic landscape. As the imam of a Salafi-oriented mosque in eastern Tatarstan told me, "Doing business in Russia without trespassing somewhere haram is almost impossible. Haram is connected to business in many ways—[interest-based] banking, [chance-based] insurance, secular laws. There is almost always some illicit profit [likhva] somewhere, some subterfuge [ulovka]." Several respondents who are active in business candidly shared with me the difficulties that hinder efforts to "halalify" economic activity. Ravshan-äfände, for example, is a respected forty-five-year-old pious entrepreneur from eastern Tatarstan who runs a number of businesses in Kazan. Commenting on the halalness of his various activities, Master Ravshan painted a picture in shades of grey:

> My first sector of activity is real estate. I think things should be all right halal-wise here . . . but then again, I rent out to a shopkeeper who sells alcohol, which makes me wonder, is that his sin or mine, too? Well, there is jurisprudence suggesting that that sin falls upon him only, so that sector should be halal, although I know that it could be questioned [*pod voprosom*].
>
> Second, I own a haberdashery, which is 100% halal alhamdulillah.
>
> Third, I co-own a fashion shop that is a source of great concern for me, because the ladies' clothes we sell don't cover female `awrah [immodest parts].[17] Honestly I don't think that can be halal. But I cannot just drop it right now. I have responsibilities towards my partners, even though they are not observant Muslims.
>
> Finally, I own a halal café—that is the apple of my eye. It is going really well, and it feels great to feed people the halal way.
>
> I think the Most High gives you time to figure things out halalwise, it's not just that you have to drop all things haram at once. It's a slow process, you progress step by step [*postepenno*]. A few years ago, I thought that a woman in a bikini is no big deal, now I am more conscious. But consciousness develops slowly. In my case, after three `umra pilgrimages. Some people drop haram business at once, abruptly, but I've rarely seen that myself. Money is the problem, it attracts you, attracts your soul.

It is telling that Ravshan-äfände, who went on the lesser `umra pilgrimage to Mecca three times, had not yet performed hajj, as he confided to me on a separate occasion. Hajj is a religious obligation incumbent on Muslims who, like him, can afford the journey. He explained to me that he had "spiritual reasons" to extend the preparatory phase, possibly—so I gathered—due to a process of atonement for past sins, or in relation to the uncertain status of his income. It is, however, accepted knowledge within the halal milieu that extricating oneself from haram is a messy process, as my acquaintance Aynar, a young pietist attracted to Salafi teachings who makes a problematic living working in Tatarstan's music industry, explained to me:

> I can confirm that in many cases rejection of haram does not happen suddenly and abruptly. I mean, certain things dawn upon you immediately, but more often than not this happens through a protracted pro-

cess of coming to-know [*dlitelny protsess ososnaniya*] and mortification [*smirenie*] of your passions. You have to pray a lot to reject sin. So it is a gradual process, every day you prune a bit—you prune, you prune, you prune. Until what's left is so little that you look at it and think, "Well, it shouldn't be too hard to renounce [this last bit] after all." Sometimes I think that quitting something sinful too abruptly risks hurting you, harming you, even though yes, it is sinful. So I think that the Most High actually expects of you that you act gradually.

A specific obstacle to halalness in business is corruption, a widespread practice in free-market Russia as well as an illicit one under sharia. As one of the imams I interviewed commented, "We all know that in Russia there is corruption. Now, there exists a counter-corruption programme, but it is nobody's secret that there is a lot of corruption in this country. This, too, makes it almost impossible to carry out halal business in Russia." Consider the following excerpts:

> I have discovered only relatively recently that corruption is a sin. To give or accept bribes [*vzyatki*] is a sin, even just to grease the wheels—it's a sin. I didn't know that. And you can find it everywhere in this country. I guess one can refuse to take part in it. Luckily in my business this is not a big issue, rogue state organs never paid us a visit, nor did other "comrades" [the mafia]. I guess that's because our landlord is a respected man in town. Before knowing that it's a sin, yes, I was involved with corruption. But now I will be more cautious. (Ali, thirty-eight, halal café owner, Idelsk)

> I'll tell you in all honesty, Teo—not greasing the wheels is simply *impossible*. I personally try to minimize my involvement in graft as much as possible, and to abstain from the other sins. But avoiding corruption completely is not feasible in this country. Now, some people hold it that giving "presents" to certain people in certain cases is halal, but obviously that is contentious. However, the point is that we do not live in an ideal world. We have to "command good and avoid wrong,"[18] of course, but starting from real-life conditions. And here everybody steals, it's not something you can change, as honest Muslims are too few. We are still a very chaotic country. (Ayup-abıy, forty-seven, large entrepreneur, Kazan)

In the picture drawn by my interlocutors, wishful aspirations of a halal-friendly, corruption-free business environment in Russia cannot be, at this stage, much more than that: wishful aspirations. Given the economic environment's "real-life conditions," 100 percent halal entrepreneurship is understood as being "impossible" (see Laidlaw 1996). As in the case, discussed in chapter 3, of the Law of the land encroaching on and conditioning the unfolding of Rule in an ethical form-of-life, in the economic domain, too, the Laws of capitalism "with Russian characteristics," including pervasive non-Islamic and/or illicit practices (as is well documented, in the post-Soviet space the Laws of moneymaking are not congruent with the official legislative framework), encroach on and condition pietists' economic Rule-following.

It must be emphasized that, to my interlocutors, an inflexible rejection of these Laws on theological grounds would foreclose any possibility of material and ethical "development," thereby preventing pietists from fulfilling their obligations toward themselves, their communities, and God, ultimately harming pietists' form-of-life and hindering the unfolding of Islam's truth-process. Critical compromise is felt to be the most ethically consistent conduct, in a prefigurative logic by which Islamic business will gradually contribute to the reform of Russia's amoral capitalism. Put otherwise, economic success can be in service of ethical-spiritual advancement. Badiou helpfully distinguishes selfish, base interest from the "disinterested interest" that enables and sustains human individuals' perseverant pursuit of their fidelity (2002, 49). Islamic entrepreneurship in Povolzhye can arguably be framed as a delicate balancing act between base interest and "disinterested," enabling interest. In the navigation of such treacherous waters, halalness is a polar star that, albeit unattainable in the immediate present, orients one's course. Rudnyckyj reported similar dynamics of pragmatic compromise in his study of Islamic finance in Indonesia, where the principle of ḍarūrah (necessity) is invoked when financial operators find it impossible to elude the Law of shareholder value: "Business is business" (Rudnyckyj 2019, 49, 56–57).

Pragmatism, however, is not equal to cynicism. When faced with the necessities of business, as my friend Umar put it, "it is key that one does think only of the bottom line. Muslims must sincerely [*iskrenno*] desire that everything be halal. Intention, _niyat_, is what we shall be judged on in the afterlife." If genuine, pious intentionality can neutralize potential spiritual counterblows. This is not always easy though, and watchfulness is required. Umar elaborated further: "Big money is a test. More money means more possibilities to commit sin, and here lies a danger." The danger, as we have seen above, is that of turning the bottom line into an "idol" and caving under the pressure of interest. We know that sincerity, in contexts of ethical intensity, can be framed as one's ability to bracket self-interest: When it comes to matters of money, interest takes on a literal meaning, and halalists must resist the urge to treat wealth as an end in itself and take control of one's subjectivity.

Sin does not, however, preclude the possibility of redemption. Even money earned by non-fully-halal means can be purged of its impurity (if not fully halalified) by good deeds, such as voluntary charity, patronage, and support of local Muslim communities. For example, during one of my visits to Idelsk in the southern Idel-Ural I heard some interlocutors speak in praise of a local grandee of Caucasian origin, a man "of many flaws" who used to be "a great sinner" in the 1990s—in other words, a regional Muslim oligarch with a history of violent entrepreneurship. Even after reforming, the grandee's economic fortune remained steeped in haram. Yet the man spent lavishly on charitable causes "on the path of God" and was believed to have contributed substantively to the construction of a new mosque in a large Russian city. His local clients and admirers in Idelsk wished for him that these deeds "will earn him the Most High's forgiveness": At least in the eyes of the community, sincerely inspired expenditure for the sake of God can lift the curse from ill-gotten surplus.

Unmoored in the Market

The halal milieu's moral chrematistic provides guidance not just in terms of acquiring wealth but also in terms of surplus expenditure—which, of course, includes halal consumption. Povolzhye's halal infrastructure took shape around food (Benussi 2020b, 2021a). As theological awareness grew among Russia's Muslims—as did the breadth and opulence of consumer choice in the postsocialist market (Barker 1999)—halalness became increasingly relevant to spheres including attire, cosmetics and personal care, leisure, real estate, financial products, and even transportation.[19] Pious consumers' attentiveness came to encompass a variety of subtleties, from companies' sourcing of supplies and capital, to manufacturing methods, to packaging styles. Is a halal café truly halal if the shop owner has taken on a loan from a conventional bank? Is it permissible for believers to buy halal foodstuffs from a company that also processes conventional meat? Are Muslims allowed to purchase biscuits sold in packages carrying human representations or, even worse, depictions of characters from Russian folklore? Should not the latter be interpreted as "elements of polytheism" and avoided as such? Questions like these are routinely discussed within the halal milieu, and avoiding haram is indeed complicated even within the most rigorous households:[20]

> I know some people who avoid buying anything, even bread, from supermarkets—including halal supermarkets. That's because these businesses made their initial money by selling alcohol and cigarettes, before opening their halal branches. In fact, I too get myself bread from the city industrial bakery [khlebzavod] whenever possible. But then again, the khlebzavod too might be involved in ribā [interest-based loan]. To

be 100% safe, one should get flour from Muslim farmers and bake at home. Indeed, there are brothers here who never ever eat out. I've heard of people who bring food with them while travelling and drink only bottled water for days because they don't dare to buy anything. Anyway, excessiveness [*cherezmernost'*] is discouraged in Islam, too. This is why I mostly get my groceries in halal supermarkets. (Amir, thirty-one, programmer, Kazan)

The quote above does not describe common occurrences, as the mushrooming of a Muslim-dedicated industry in Povolzhye comprising gastronomy, tourism, fashion, and so forth testifies. However, it is indicative of the high spiritual stakes of Islamically compliant consumption. In my work on the subject (Benussi 2019, 2020b, 2022b), I have analyzed the consolidation of mechanisms—from auditing to branding to smartphone apps—composing an "ethical infrastructure" that secures, despite the inevitable critical points, the peace of mind of most observant Muslim consumers in Russia.

One important trend in anthropological scholarship on Muslim consumption has framed halal commodities, and in particular food, as markers of collective identity—ethnic, racial, religious, or a combination thereof (Mandel 1996; McGown 1999; Gillette 2000; Fischer 2011). While this is a respectable approach to the question, this framing leaves out what is most crucial to Muslim pietists, and that is illustrated by the excerpt above: the binding ethical dimension of halal consumption. In Badiousian terms, it focuses on situational particularisms rather than foregrounding the "truth-element" that underpins economic action. Prior to the mass success of revivalist trends, dietary differences did constitute a divide—as well as an interface—between Povolzhye's Tatar and Russian communities,[21] but the abstract concept of "halal" was hardly used to define what Tatars ate (or "should" eat) in the prerevolutionary and Soviet eras. After the 1990s ethnic boom, the word "halal" became current and came to incorporate, in the eyes of many secular ethnic Muslims, the meaning of "Tatar national food." Within the halal milieu, however, understandings of halal as an ethno-confessional identity marker are frowned upon as parochial and doctrinally misled. Even though identity feelings should not be dismissed as irrelevant, it is halal consumption that pietists see as a cornerstone of their form-of-life.

That consumption practices have a central role in ethical self-making has been recognized by anthropologists (De Solier 2013; Caldwell 2014), with some emphasizing that ethical consumption projects may have explicitly religious connotations (Klein 2009; Liu et al. 2015). However, recognizing halal consumption in Povolzhye as a constitutive element of an ethical form-of-life implies dealing with an apparent paradox. A number of participants harbor a scathingly critical opinion of "materialist" modernity—rife, in their view, with unthinking consumerism, greed, ruthless competition, and individualism. Channeling post-Soviet nostalgia for the frugal but humane real-socialist past (Todorova and Gille 2012), and in alignment with a choir of Muslim critics of the West (Tobin 2016, 115; Rudnyckyj 2019), many pietists express contempt for the mammonism of the mainstream market economy. Despite the vitriol cast against consumerism, however, wholesale rejection of marketplace dynamics is not common and may even be frowned upon as religious "excess." In fact, as we know, halalists enthusiastically participate in a market environment, on the grounds that enjoying the fruits of one's labor and seeking to secure dignified living standards is Islamically permitted, even welcome. How are these two seemingly contrasting postures harmonized?

Peter Luetchford (2016, 39) has noted that "if ethics is defined as an ongoing process of constructing the self, then arguably the principal process through which this is done is that of the production and consumption of material culture"—this being particularly true in late-modern capitalist societies in which consumption choices determine individuals' self-constitution. This brings about a very specific "conundrum," in that self- and world-creating meaningful ethical choices are bound up with that very anethical system—the market—against which these choices are pitted. As James Carrier (2012) put it, ethical consumption projects contain precise ideas of what a desirable social realm should look like and place the purchasing individual at the center of this ideal system. Yet this ideal cannot come into fruition because ethical consumption rejects the economic realm in its *goals*, but not in its *means* (Carrier 2012, 18–19).

Luetchford's and Carrier's observations highlight what I have framed in this volume as a contradiction between Rule and Law. What their analysis leaves unaccounted for is that ethical forms-of-life do not require, nor do they advocate, the complete abrogation of situational Law (capitalism, the state, themitical morality, etc.) to thrive. In fact, it is the Rule-Law tension itself that sustains and informs ethical experience. We shall return to this point in the next, concluding section.

A second paradox of ethical consumption is its apparent tendency to reinforce status inequalities. The halal milieu appeals to a nascent Muslim bourgeoisie seeking to distinguish itself from the proletarian, Soviet-era attitudes of the older, provincial, or rural working class. Halal consumption practices mirror this new form of asymmetry. In the first place, halal products tend to be more expensive, owing in the best cases to producers' attention to quality standards and the costs relative to certification, and in the worst cases to deliberate attempts to exploit pietists' willingness to pay more for their peace of mind. In addition to that, there is the "Trillionaire's" aspirational ethos. The halal sector has become increasingly associated with glamorous imagery: Halal leisure/tourism infrastructures ostentatiously project an aura of luxury and sophistication, while glossy magazines on Islamic lifestyle abound with advertisements for fashionable and costly accessories, cosmetics, and clothes. The main halal supermarket chain in Tatarstan caters selectively to the urban middle classes, making these stores not just sites of ethical self-formation but also spaces of distinction (compare Botoeva 2006). Indeed, some respondents from under-privileged economic backgrounds, who shop in cheap *produktovye magaziny*, expressed to me their frustration with the unaffordability of upscale halal retailers. It would be inaccurate to say that Povolzhye's halal market is exclusively oriented toward the well-off,[22] but the aesthetics of Russia's halal market does abound with Veblenesque motifs of conspicuous consumption that might seem to sit awkwardly with Islam's emphasis on social justice and egalitarianism (Salamandra 2004; Tobin 2016, 48).[23]

Pierre Bourdieu reminded us that both luxury and asceticism, apparently "contrasting ways of defying . . . appetite, need, and desire," are both, in fact, assertions of "conspicuous freedom" from the "constraints which dominate common people" and may thus "coexist at different moments or different levels of the same discourse" ([1984] 2010, 252). This resonates with Bataille's even more radical argument that profligacy and sacrifice are secretly coterminous ways to neutralize the accursed share and ultimately achieve "intimacy" with the divine ([1992] 2012, [1991] 2019). To what extent do these thinkers' provocative gestures toward an emancipatory dimension of luxury dovetail with the autonomist framework explored in this volume?[24] I maintain that the family resemblance between luxury and asceticism is at once structural and superficial. It is structural in the sense that, as we have seen, pietists do conspicuously seek "freedom" vis-à-vis the "constraints" of high-modern capitalist relations (including in its Soviet state-capitalist version)—from wage-earning to the limitations that a meager income imposes on self-actualization. Yet it is superficial in the sense that pietists, albeit drawn to conspicuous consumption on account of their middle-class positionality, still subject their desires to intense ethical scrutiny. Halalists' consumption is conditioned by ethical injunctions to respect precise canons of sobriety, shareability, and usability of material wealth "on the path of God" (compare Davies 2002, 196). Furthermore, spending moneys on halal goods, even if they are more expensive, is not understood as mere "luxury": Pietists see it as one's duty as Muslims to direct surplus wealth to Islamically approved expenditures, even if it goes against one's rational economic interest. When it comes to the costliness of halal consumables, Bataille's categories converge with Badiousian ones: The fact that these goods are expensive implies accepting a "sacrifice" of the accursed share on the part of the pious buyer,[25] an acceptance that goes against one's immediate economic "self-interest," thereby confirming his or her piousness.

An Ethical Form of Capitalist Life

Agamben's notion of form-of-life is, again, of help in reconsidering the relationship between religious-ethical traditions, such as Islam, and the realm of capitalism. We know that Rule does not aspire to subvert Law or substitute it. Ethical forms-of-life are not revolutionary social utopias but rather potentially emancipatory existential configurations. At a fundamental level, the "raw matter" constituting forms-of-life—that is, *life itself*—does not elude the situational biopolitical and economic forcefield and infrastructures that inform society at large. The scaffolding on which form-of-life is structuring is a life-ordering, not a biopoietic (life-making) one. While Schielke described revivalist Islam as "a particularly compelling way to live capitalism" (2015a, 119), I suggest that revivalist Islam could be understood as an *ethical form of capitalist life*.

The lifeworld Povolzhye pietists inhabit, together with scores of Muslims worldwide, is defined by late capitalism. Even though Islamic reform movements often articulate a critique of marketplace materialism, in postsocialist Tatarstan as elsewhere in the Muslim-majority world the building blocks of halalists' lives remain anchored to the globally dominant economic order. While halal economic actors in Povolzhye strive to operate under a rigorous ethical system—Islamically permissible consumption, honesty and transparency in business, "making a reason" for opportunities to arise, utilizing money "on the path of God," and policing one's intentions in ambiguous situations—no holistic, organic "Islamic moral economy" appears forthcoming in Tatarstan: The overarching principles and means by which the regnant economic system operates remain untouched (see Tripp 2006; Kuran 2004, 2011; Tobin 2016). Yet this does not mean that Povolzhye pietists give up their resolution to inhabit their economic lifeworld morally—and autonomously.

Neoliberalism cannot be avoided by post-Soviet pietists; in fact, many young, aspirational Muslims appear to consider it richer in opportunities than both socialist-era planned economy and postsocialist wage-earning industrial work. In lieu of advancing a classical "moral economy" argument, therefore, I have zoomed in on what I have called halalists' "moral chrematistics," or the art of handling surplus wealth in money, consumables, and enrichment opportunities—a surplus that post-Soviet pietists enjoy to a degree unparalleled in the history of Povolzhye Muslims—in ways compatible with Islamic standards of ethical conduct.

This surplus comes with a Bataillean "curse": the risk of turning extra wealth into an "idol," thereby betraying, on the simulacrous altar of self-interest, one's obligation to one's community, the broader social good, and, above all, God. Luckily, Islam gives pietists tools to neutralize the curse. For those who manage to balance the Law of profit and the Rule of halal management of wealth, this surplus can become literally one's "blessed share": the *barakat*ful provision allocated by God (*rizk*) through which pietists can "develop" on the path of spiritual, ethical, and political growth. The blessed share can unlock pietists' personal potential, enabling the cultivation of Islamic virtues, self-realization in Islamically approved ways (e.g., family life), and the prosperity of the community, while, ideally, ensuring the avoidance of a heteronomous regime of wage labor that imposes a discipline extraneous to Islamic Rule.

Conclusion

A GRAEBERIAN REFLECTION

In his *Fragments of an Anarchist Anthropology*, David Graeber provided a provisional list of "areas of theory" that a hypothetical anarchist anthropologist may wish to explore (2004, 65–76). They include a theory of nonstate political entities, an ecology of voluntary associations, a theory of political happiness, a theory of alienation, and a theory of capitalism. Graeber made it clear that such an anthropology should not confine itself to the study of radical social movements, collectives, and the like but be open to the many facets of human life and interpret those in radical ways. Proceeding from the bottom up, it should not hasten to achieve "high theory" status or vie for intellectual hegemony with alternative paradigms. Being first and foremost an anthropology rather a political platform, and notwithstanding its proponents' sympathy for (or participation in) specific causes, it ought to refrain from dictating specific programs. According to Graeber, such an intellectual project ought to "look at those who are creating viable alternatives [and] try to figure out what might be the larger implications of what they are (already) doing, and then offer those ideas back, not as prescriptions, but as contributions, possibilities—as gifts" (2004, 12). It is a way to frame the ethnographic encounter so as to be receptive to the emancipative potentiality of social conformations.

I like to think of this book's autonomist reading of Islamic piety in the Volga region as moving in the direction prefigurated by Graeber. It is certainly not a prescriptive project. It seeks not to supplant alternative approaches but to complement them so as to illuminate aspects worthy of deeper consideration. Most importantly, *Restless Quietists* has attempted to contribute to a "space of hospitality" (Abdou 2022) that may enable possible encounters and gift-giving between scholars, believers, and activists.

Many aspects of this volume resonate with the programmatical points envisioned by Graeber. Its Agambenian-Tiqqunian framing of Islamic form-of-life provides a theory of nonstate political entities (localized ethical milieus linked to a transnational, rhizomatic ethical polity, the ummah) as well as an ecology of voluntary associations (the binding energy of Rule innervating and anchoring ethical forms-of-life, and the interplay of forms-of-life in a Law-infused situational domain). It contributes to a theory of the state through the idea of themitical apparatuses geared toward the management of ethical difference, a process that is liable to being unsettled by the evental eruptions of truths. A theory of political happiness logically follows from autonomism's emphasis on joyous self-ruling, "life that coincides with its form" (Agamben 2013a, 99), generating a "rich, independent multilaterality" of subjects (Negri 1991, 190). Relatedly, a fresh understanding of alienation can be found by combining Agamben's classic work on heteronomous ("bare") life, Tiqqun's critique of impoverished, tamed subjectivities (1999, 2012), and Badiou's reflections on the vulnerability of the human animal (2002). Last, by placing our autonomist framework in conversation with George Bataille, this book has sketched a theory of capitalism that, in focusing on withdrawal from the salaried regime and the pursuit of a meaningful excess, agrees with Graeber's contention that "it is in performing wage labor, [rather than] in buying and selling, that most humans now waste away most of their waking hours[,] and it is that which makes them miserable" (2004, 71).

In his *Fragments*, Graeber poignantly observed that the dominant political position running through the anthropological enterprise is one of "broad populism": "We are for the little guys. . . . You must demonstrate that the people you are studying, the little guys, are successfully resisting some form of power or globalizing influence imposed on them from above" (2004, 98–99). Especially in its more Marxian-inspired iterations, this stance may take on a "dark" hue with an emphasis on structural oppression, suffering, and deficient agency (Ortner 2016). This is all very natural, Graeber concedes, and epistemologically generative too—parts of his own work in Madagascar can be read in that way. The book you have just read, with its focus on the restlessness of a faith group that exists and even thrives in a suffocating and confusing moral, biopolitical, and economic environment, makes no exception. However, Graeber warned, this populism is not in itself particularly "radical" and indeed can be often reminiscent of the identity politics frustratingly pervasive in our age (2004,101).

On the one hand, it could be argued that anthropology's "ethical turn" participates in the populist vocation of the discipline, especially considering how it deals with religion. One may say, for example, that Asadian approaches identify faith groups as the underdogs of secular modernity: dethroned, marginalized, misunderstood, colonized. As for "everyday moralities" approaches, they have often focused on underdogs facing difficult circumstances: peripheral communities (Robbins 2004; Marsden 2005; Montgomery 2016), disoriented urbanites (Schielke 2015a), people grappling with affliction (Mattingly 2010; Zigon 2018). On the other hand, the ethical turn did indeed mark a bold, even defiant, departure (Laidlaw 2014): The time has arrived, it declared, to take a serious look at the concrete uses of any modicum of freedom that individuals actually enjoy, the cultivation of desired subjectivities, and people's pursuits of "the good life" (Robbins 2013a).

Radically inclined anthropologists ought not to dismiss the ethical turn as moralistic or "antipolitical" (Kapferer and Gold 2018, cf. Fassin 2014, 433). Even though mainstream anthropologies of ethics may have prioritized liberalism's negative freedom or foregrounded tradition's constraints on agency, this field of study's antistructuralist posture and penchant for liberty have also opened a precious chance to put the inescapably political question of emancipation at the front and center of the discipline's discursive field. In fact, I am convinced that there are multiple points of contact between the anthropology of ethics and Graeber's call for an anarchist anthropology. Graeber (2004) invoked the need for theories of political happiness, voluntary association, pleasure, and nonalienation: All of this is in line with the ethicists' emphasis on "the good." He foregrounded themes of nonstate entities, hierarchy, and knowledges—themes strongly resonant with the ethical turn's investigation of religious-ethical traditions and subject formation.

It seems to me that autonomist theories of ethical life have a significant role to play at the point of intersection of the ethical turn and radical anthropology. Through this book's attempt to advance a conceptual framework illuminating the emancipatory politics of ethics, I hope to have demonstrated the potential of such an engagement, not just for left-leaning anthropologists but for the discipline at large.

This book has attempted to show that experimenting with radical theory may unlock valuable possibilities in terms of how anthropology and related disciplines approach Islam, and perhaps suggest ways to rethink or overcome existing intellectual problems.

In one of the most influential recent contributions on Islamic history, Wael Hallaq (2013) argued that the premodern moral framework of sharia ineluctably chafes with the institutional and juridical scaffolding of the modern nation-state; hence, the Islamist utopia of a modern caliphate is doomed to fail or produce political monsters. Hallaq's work resonates with recent anthropological conversations on Islam. On one side, we have accounts of Muslim oppositional, intractable positionalities, wherein sharia is the foundation of lively but chronically minoritized counterpublics (Mahmood [2005] 2012; Hirschkind 2005; Fernando 2014). On the other, we have investigations of how Islamic jurisprudence becomes "regimented" into positive law, sometimes with paradoxical or precarious results (Agrama 2012; Daniels 2017).

It lies well beyond this book's purview to imagine ways in which Islam's modern predicaments, or indeed anyone's modern predicaments, may be overcome. The challenge I have attempted to address is, rather, how to intellectually and analytically attend to the variety of Muslims' experiences—from radical noncompliance to stern legalism—in original ways. Through the dialectic of Rule and Law, this book's autonomist anthropology of piety has sought to encompass the emancipative ethics of halal living and the heteronomizing power of state apparatuses and the market, thereby illuminating how Islam can be at once, sometimes within one and the same social context, a wellspring for liberative self-management and an institutionally (and/or thematically) powered governmental mechanism.

I am persuaded that autonomist styles of reasoning could be fruitfully mobilized vis-à-vis a variety of topics in the politics of Islam and religion in general, including discussions on governmentalization and secularity (How is ethical intensity suppressed or channeled?), religious nationalism and violence (Whose interests are at play? Is a given sociopolitical sequence directed toward a plenitude? Can a religious truth-process be superseded by a "simulacrum"?), conversion and social change (How is a situation disorganized? What counts as a religious "event"?), and interfaith dialogue or tension (How do different religious and nonreligious forms-of-life interact? How are amity and enmity negotiated?). However, autonomism's intellectual potential cannot be fully tapped unless its proponents are prepared to challenge and decolonize it through more extensive encounters and deeper engagement with Muslim thought (Abdou 2022).

Autonomism's thought on ethics and religion, like most of the theological turn in Marxist and anarchist philosophies, has so far dwelled near-exclusively on Christianity and Judaism. Islam has featured, with rare exceptions (Wilson 1988), almost as an afterthought. Yet there are examples of resonance, only few of which have been explored. Autonomist theory of ethics, for instance, shares many points of contact with the oeuvre of the mid-twentieth-century Iranian revolutionary-cum-reformer Ali Shariati (2002, [1979] 2011). Borrowing from Marxist dialectic as well as Shi'a thought, Shariati contraposed "red" Islamic praxis to "black" clerical-juridical institutions, a distinction that in part overlaps that between Rule and Law. Furthermore, Shariati's concept of Islam as a "school of thought and action," or maktab, is not dissimilar from autonomist ideas of form-of-life. This is but one example. Experiments in intellectual hospitality may include contrapuntal discussions, collaborative social analyses, and radical interpretations of and from voices ranging from Ibn Khaldun (1989) to Mirsaid

Sultan-Galiev (Soltangalicv 1998), Hakim Bey (Wilson 1988), Ziaeddin Sardar (Inayatullah and Boxwell 2003), Michael Muhammad Knight (2007, 2012), and Mohamed Abdou (2022). This is a work in progress. I am sure that there are things I did not see or that I could have thought through better. But reflection cannot be a solipsistic enterprise: I would be honored if this volume stimulated responses, debate, and constructive criticism. There is still so much to do. Let's keep going, together.

Graeber suggested that an anarchist anthropology would, in a sense, bring the discipline to (one of) its (possible) natural intellectual conclusion(s), which he called a "liberation of the imaginary" (2004, 102). Powered by the vertiginous richness of the ethnographic archive, such an anthropology would at a minimum offer a taste of a bold, optimistic, nondogmatic, kaleidoscopic . . . well, *humanism*, and perhaps something even more than that. Crucially, such an endeavor can only rest on anthropology's magmatic repository of fragments, voices, experiences: Communities, subjectivities, ethical worlds from which "we"—I, you, whoever wants and is able to join—have something to learn. This book expresses the certainty that the Volga region's restless quietists deserve a place in this archive, alongside their ethnic Muslim neighbors, the Islamic bureaucracy, and Tatarstan's Russians, as well as the Kremlin and its grim occupiers.

Regardless of conceptual framings and theoretical discussion, it has been an honor for me to add a more nuanced portrait of Povolzhye's Muslim pietists to the ethnographic record, not just as footnotes to the "Russia," "Post-Socialism," or "Central Asia" files but as specific communities and individuals—caught in often painful and challenging circumstances but not defined solely by them. I will be satisfied if this book has achieved just as much. I hope *Restless Quietists* lived up to such a task, and I look forward to more voices from Tatarstan, Muslim Eurasia, the postsocialist world, and a truly decolonizing globe joining the conversation.

Acknowledgments

If this book is so chunky, it is not just because of my penchant for preambles and digressions, which I won't deny (I'm doing it now!) but also because the journey that culminated in its publication has been very long indeed. It is a joy to retrace this itinerary—and it makes for a totally worthwhile, and delightfully lengthy, excursus. The ethnographic engagement that begot this book started almost fifteen years ago at Ca' Foscari University of Venice, as I was an anthropology master's student whose blossoming interest in Central Eurasia was encouraged by a research team working on Turkic and Islamic afterlives. I am thankful to the late Maria Pia Pedani, as well as Antonio Fabris and Elisabetta Ragagnin, for welcoming me to the team and encouraging my first research forays into Tatarstan. In Venice, I was inspired by conversations with the Masaryk Seminar, Aldo Ferrari, and the broader Russian, Eastern European, and Eurasian studies network. None of my early fumbles at autonomous scholarship would have been possible without the training I received from the Venetian anthropological community. As I type these words in Venice now, years later, I cannot express how fortunate I feel to be able to call the people who taught me so much—Gianfranco Bonesso, Gianluca Ligi, Glauco Sanga, Franca Tamisari, Francesco Vallerani— my colleagues and fellow *cafoscarini*.

As I moved to the University of Cambridge's Social Anthropology Department, my interest in the Volga region's inner borderland grew, iteration after iteration, under the priceless tutelage of Caroline Humphrey. I cannot thank Carrie enough, not only for all the guidance and advice but also for believing in me when I needed it the most. The Socanth community, the Mongolia and Inner Asia Studies Unit, the Alwaleed Bin Talal Centre of Islamic Studies, the Cambridge Muslim in Europe Postgraduate Forum, and Clare College offered countless opportunities for intellectual enrichment. James Laidlaw and Magnus Marsden were marvelous mentors and supporting presences throughout. My subsequent stint as a teaching associate unlocked new vistas on anthropology and helped me place my research in a broader intellectual landscape. At and through Cambridge, I met many wonderful scholars and friends whose insights—shared in formal and informal exchanges, sometimes generously given, sometimes surreptitiously gleaned—shaped this manuscript, both directly and in roundabout ways. It would be impossible to give all of these brilliant people the mention they deserve; a tolerable list should include at least Zubair Ahmad, Paul Anderson,

Cenap Aydin, Matt Candea, Taras Fedirko, Mustafa Gundogan, Julian Hargreaves, Yanti Hoelzchen, Nurul Huda, Voula Koutroumpi, Christos Lynteris, Tommaso Manzon, Dom Martin, Chris Moses, Tobias Müller, Sayana Namsaraeva, Karina Palyutina, Beja Protner, Ed Pulford, Marlene Schäfers, Leonie Schiffauer, Sertaç Sehlikoğlu, David Sneath, Kirie Stromberg, Adela Taleb, Caroline Tee, Beth Turk, the late Pnina Werbner, Amin El Yousfi, Sargai Yunshaab, and Moo, Dan, and the Whitechapel anarchists.

I express my gratitude to the Amsterdam-based network of scholars of Islam in Russia, which welcomed me for a brief but unforgettable stint at the University of Amsterdam. Conversations with Alfrid Bustanov, Mansur Gazimzhanov, Michael Kemper, Shamil Shikaliev, and Gulnaz Sibgatullina have vastly enhanced my understanding of Muslim histories in Eurasia. In happier times, the Amsterdam network overlapped with a vibrant research team in Russia, and I acknowledge the lasting import of exchanges with Dasha Dorodnykh, Danis Garaev, Dinara Mardanova, and Anna Matochkina. Within the field of studies of Islam and Muslims in the post-Soviet space, it has been a pleasure to cross paths and trade views with Dmitriy Oparin, Lili Di Puppo, Jesko Schmoller, Fabio Vicini, and Guzel Yusupova.

At the University of California, Berkeley, I found in Charles Hirschkind a most generous mentor. It was a privilege to discuss anthropology, philosophy, and politics at the seminar he chaired. Despite the disruption brought about by COVID-19, I received food for thought and valuable feedback on my work through Cal's Kruzhok, the Kroužek, the Russian Peripheries Working Group, and the Central Asian Working Group. (Also, I am grateful to Berkeley's secondhand bookshops.) Conversations with Oyuna Baldakova, Sophie Lockey, Liza Michaeli, Gašpar Mithans, Stephanie Postar, and Aleksandra Simonova have enriched me during my stay and beyond. Shoutout to the Humanities & Social Sciences Association, Daniel Kim, and the friends who made the pandemic bearable, especially Toto, Oyuna, Nene, Ale, Iskhak, Aray, João—plus Mimi and Al and the girls. This book would have been much worse without the input I received at the manuscript workshop where I was amicably grilled by James Faubion, Mayanthi Fernando, Basit Iqbal, and Stefania Pandolfo. Attiya Ahmad, Yanti Hoelzchen, Ben Kirby, and Daromir Rurnyckyj also offered priceless advice. A special thank-you is in order for Franck Billé, not only for being an extraordinary source of advice but also for dragging me to the Cornell stand at an American Anthropological Association meeting, thereby starting the process that has led to the existence of this exact book in its shape, form, and color. I wholeheartedly thank Jim Lance, Bethany Wasik, Allison Gudenau, and Cornell's editorial team.

My fieldwork would not have worked out without the help of many friends and participants in Tatarstan and Russia at large. Painfully, future developments of this book have become casualties of the Russo-Ukrainian conflict—at least for now. My loss of friendships and research prospects pales against the horrors of war; still, I mourn this abrupt, ugly estrangement and wonder what reconciliation may look like. Bik zur räxmät to Ilkem-apa and Idgey, who welcomed me into their family. I miss those times. I thank Karina, with Sam, for initiating me into the Tatar language, and Zilya, with Zakir, and Adilya, with Murad, for taking me further. I also wish to extend my gratitude to Elza and Iskander, Amal, Mukaddas-xäzrät, Taya, and Yusuf-xäzrät for their hospitality and help fixing things. The Kazan (Volga Region) Federal University (KPFU) gave me institutional support as a visiting academic. Albina, Nail-abıy, Rimma-apa, Jamilya-apa, Lily, Masha, Denis, Alina, Kamil, Ilnar, Lenar, Aynaz, Ildar, Azat, Abdurrashid, Timur, Ahmet, Rinat, Ismail, Ibragim, Ilzam, Tabris, Foat-abıy, Ayrat-abıy, Marat-äfände, Raufa Urazmanova, Rafik Mukhametshin, Valiulla-xäzrät, Guzel Stolyarova, and many others contributed to this book through their advice, company, friendship, curiosity, patience, and, occasionally, succor. I am indebted to my interviewees and all those who tolerated my nosiness. JazakAllah khayran. You have given me so much.

Italy's 2008 Progetto di Rilevante Interesse Nazionale grant on "Le domande degli angeli" provided funds for my first fieldwork trip to Tatarstan. When I was at Cambridge, I received financial support from the Cambridge Home and EU Scholarship Scheme, the William Wyse Fund, the Alwaleed Bin Talal Centre of Islamic Studies, and the Ling Roth Fund. The writing of this manuscript in its current form was made possible by the EU's Marie Skłodowska-Curie funding scheme, grant number 843901.

The last decade and a half has been quite a ride, as I hopped between cities, countries, and continents. This ride would have been utterly miserable without the presence of close friends. Anto (whose fateful question, "What can you tell me about Tatarstan?" started the whole endeavor), the M&O, Fabius, Amanda, Cesare, Ruiyi, Tommy, Dav, Jean, and Cate, who also made the maps, have been great comrades and sources of moral support and intellectual nourishment at crucial junctures of this process. This book would not have even started without the Lucis' support. To them, and to Titti-apa, who first taught me to be curious and restless, goes my deepest gratitude.

Notes

INTRODUCTION

1. My engagement with autonomism is not exclusive, nor is it a settled matter—either politically or intellectually. I am still grappling with this approach and intend to further probe its possibilities and assess its limitations, including by looking beyond Povolzhye's halal milieu.

2. Basit Iqbal (2021) has pointed out that by selectively engaging with Shi'ism, Agamben avoids discussing the extent to which Sunni theology might complicate his reflection on messianism and jurisprudence. In privileging Shi'a Islam, Agamben appears to tap into a well-established Orientalist tradition of anarcho-autonomist fascination with Shi'ism (construed as "radical" and "heretical") and Islamic esotericism that dates at least to Peter Lamborn Wilson (1988) aka Hakim Bey ([1985] 1991).

3. No ideal types can exhaust the entirety of the field of piety studies, nor should the terms I use be mistaken as representing monoliths in irreducible bipolar opposition. The picture is nuanced, with countless points of convergence and divergence, theoretical strands overlapping and influencing each other, and a constant motion of ideas sustaining intellectual tensions even within the oeuvres of singular scholars (Benussi 2022a). However, it may be reasonable to say that the dominance of communitarian and liberal approaches has left little room for engagement with theories from the left (for exceptions, see Dave 2012; Fassin 2009, 2015; Benussi 2022a; and this book's conclusion).

1. PHARAOH'S CONVERSION

1. This chapter features and considerably expands materials and arguments first published in Benussi 2022.

2. See Sibgatullina and Kemper 2019 for a discussion of Tatar-Muslim Eurasianism.

3. "Bulgarists" linked present-day Tatars to medieval Volga Bulgars, even proposing to change the ethnonym, or at least add "Bulgar" to Russia's official list of ethnonyms alongside "Tatar." Their "Tatarist" opponents contended that the Tatars emerged via direct ethnic filiation from the Golden Horde, which had superseded Bulgaria as regional hegemon in the thirteenth century. The latter group opposed any name change and internal fragmentation within the Tatar-speaking community. Bulgarists' mythology pits "civilized," urban, fundamentally "white" Volga Bulgars against "Asiatic" Mongol invaders, claiming that the Golden Horde had little influence on Bulgar civilization from which they claim descent. Tatarists, by contrast, claim the Genghisite Golden Horde as their own, declaring that the Bulgars had assimilated into the Golden Horde, leaving no traces behind (Shnirelman 1996; Frank 1998). Politically, Bulgarists embraced a Eurocentric, relatively pro-Russian stance vis-à-vis the more autonomy-minded, even independence-leaning, Tatarists. Some maintain that the putatively "white" genetic heritage of the Bulgars survived the Mongol colonization and can be found nowadays in the many European-looking, blue-eyed, and blond-haired Tatars.

4. Hizmet-inspired Tatar-Turkish lyceums (*tataro-turetsky litsei*) have become renowned for their high educational standards. Unlike other regions such as Central Asia (Tee 2016), Tatarstan's Gülenist lyceums have offered exclusively secular curricula,

maintaining a low religious profile. Co-optation into Hizmet happens with the utmost discretion, on a very selective basis, and on pupils' own initiative. Thanks to their high quality, Tatar-Turkish boarding schools have proved inspirational even for the Tatar secular elite. The Hizmet movement was formally outlawed by Moscow's authorities in 2008, but many of its members are still discreetly active in Tatarstan (apart from the Turkish nationals working as teachers, who were repatriated). As of 2015, several Tatar-Turkish lyceums remained operative under the aegis of Tatarstan's government. Over time, new schools of excellence had been opened in the republic based on the model of the Tatar-Turkish lyceums, sometimes employing the same personnel. During my stay in Tatarstan, I visited three Tatar-Turkish lyceums, one Gülenist university student residence, and two republican schools inspired by Hizmet's educational methods.

5. Sufi brotherhoods active in Russia include Sheik Nazim's Naqshbandi branch, Zulfiqar Ahmad's Naqshbandi branch, and al-Ahbash. It is important to remark that indigenous Sufism was almost annihilated by the Soviets in the Idel-Ural region (Bustanov 2016). Post-Soviet brotherhoods, therefore, are branches of transnational networks that span central Eurasia—for example, I have met a secretive but influential Sufi pir of Uzbek origin in Bashkortostan. By contrast, indigenous Sufism is still strong in the Northern Caucasus—which some informants have defined as a "barony of Sufi brotherhoods" (*tari-karskaya votchina*). On Sufism and neo-Sufism in Povolzhye, see Di Puppo and Schmoller 2020.

6. There is a range of institutions and individuals propagating Salafi doctrines both transnationally and locally. These actors tend to make sure that the methodology they advocate is maximally accessible. For instance, although Salafi literature in Tatar does exist, most material catering to Russia's Muslim readership is in the Russian language, which is better understood among the urban Tatar youth.

7. Several Tatarstani mosques feature, are connected to, or had previously featured sports facilities. I observed cases of gyms located in proximity to places of worship or, in some instances, featuring fitness equipment within the mosque premises themselves. In part, this is explicable on the grounds of the halal milieu's emphasis on physical fitness (see chapter 6). However, Vadim Volkov has noted that the earliest cohorts of Russia's criminal underworld were formed by athletes and ex-athletes (*kachki*) sporting "short haircuts, intimidating physical proportions, and brand-name sportswear" (2002, 6, 61). To this day, sportswear and *kachok* style remain associated with the underworld. This style is also popular with the Muslim youth, especially of Caucasian background.

8. On the convergences and differences between Badiou and Rancière, see Bassett 2016.

9. Following Boltanski and Chiapello (2002, 2), by spirit of capitalism I mean the "ideology that justifies people's commitment to capitalism, and which renders this commitment attractive." Max Weber clarified that a distinction is to be made between a "capitalist spirit"—that is, the values and attitudes informing conducts of life compatible with capitalism—and capitalism as an "economic form" stricto sensu ([1905] 2002, 225).

10. It is worth observing that discourses about "progress" have a long history among Volga Muslims, in particular the early twentieth-century Jadid movement (Tuna 2016). While Jadid progress was couched in sociopolitical terms, post-Soviet discourses of "development" (*razvitie*) appear more materially and economically oriented, while retaining a "neoliberal" self-development tinge.

11. The acronym *ZOZh* (*zdorovy obraz zhizni*, "healthy way of life") indicates a movement that discourages alcohol, tobacco, and recreational drugs—seen as scourges that afflict Russian society—and promotes fitness and sobriety (*trezvost'*).

12. This Brazilian telenovela, a family drama partly set in Morocco, features references to Islam and Muslims and reached immense popularity in Russia in the mid-2000s, thus

playing a role in generating interest in Islam among Tatar viewers. *O Clone* had a similar pop culture effect in Central Asia as well (McBrien 2015; Montgomery 2016, 164).

13. This may be partly due to the popularity of Salafi interpretations that discourage musical performances, and partly to a lower pervasiveness of ethnically or racially connoted underground scenes (my acquaintances in the straight-edge scene were more the exception than the rule). On the convergence of race, hip-hop, and Islam in the United States, see Khabeer 2016; for punk-derived genres and taqwacore, see Dougherty 2017.

14. Herding resorts to the notion of "hybridity" to juxtapose Islam and pop culture, but this has its own analytical drawbacks. The language of hybridity implies the preexistence of pristine units in the process of merging, which not only reinforces the idea that Islam is a thing in itself—belonging to the lofty realm of spirituality or civilization, whereas subcultures belong to a lower, frivolous domain—but also fails to define the original units and assess their commensurability. Moreover, in Herding's account youth cultures are framed as something inherently "western," for there "is no [such] autonomous category" in Islam (2013,30), a slippery argument that runs the risk of essentializing Muslim-majority societies. Another problem in Herding's work is her failure to deal with scripturalist segments of Muslim juvenile milieus on the grounds that these are too austere to be "cool"—even though her own ethnographic material, like mine, suggests that Salafis' coolness is amply recognized by many of their peers. Her exclusive focus on youth, in addition, is potentially misleading, given that both in her case and in mine, adult members play an important role in the social life of Muslim networks. Lastly, the category of subculture itself is problematic as its heuristic potential has been subjected to intense criticism by sociologists (Muggleton 2000; Bennett and Kahn-Harris 2004).

15. Sociologists who speak of extreme underground cultures as "surrogates" of religion (Stewart 2019) point in a promising direction, despite relying on problematic language: How can the concept of surrogacy bridge the gap between vastly different areas of experience such as style and spirituality? I propose that it is the experience of subject-affirming consistency—think of a punk rocker who stays true to the DIY imperative and the stylistic tenets of the genre—that undergirds both ethical and aesthetic fidelities.

16. There is insufficient space here for a discussion of Soviet sociology's use of the categories of "way of living"/"style of life" (Tolstikh 1975; Isutkin and Tsaregordtsev 1977; Efimov 1982; also see Beginin 1993; Kulyutkina and Tarasova 1999), a body of literature of intrinsic interest but with little bearing on the use of this expression in this volume.

17. The halal *obraz zhizni* can include choosing Muslim first names for one's children and/or adopting Muslim nicknames (Fatima, Abdurrashid) for oneself instead of Turkic (Aygul, Edigey) or European (Marsel, Rafaelya) options, which are widespread in Tatarstan. Muslim names bear a direct connection to Islam's discursive tradition: They may be the names of prophetic figures (especially Muhammad) or signify a commitment to Islam (e.g., 'abd, "slave" + one the names/attributes of God).

18. Parallels between monastic *regula* and halal Rule may be pointed out: (1) Halal temporalities, like monastic temporalities, are punctuated by prayer; (2) pietists, like monks, keep track of "'every action, great or small' . . . with care" (Agamben 2013a, 23); (3) halal labor, like monastic labor, corresponds to a "spiritualization of the work of the hand"; and (4) halal wealth, as is shown in detail in chapter 6, entails conceptions of nonownership and temporary use of resources that resonate with analogous Franciscan notions (Agamben 2013a, 125): In Islam, God is the sole owner of the universe's riches and the sole master of human fortunes. Despite these analogies, it must be pointed out that orthodox Sunnism forbids monasticism (Quran 27:57, 31:9, 34:9). Pious traditions testify to Muhammad's familiarity with early Christian monks and his acknowledgment of their zeal in the path of God; despite his respect, however, Muhammad viewed monks' celibacy and world-renunciation as spiritual excess. All members of his Islamic ummah were to

share identical obligations, with no groups or individuals claiming privileged relations with God. The sole legitimate form of Islamic "monasticism" (rahbaniyyah), in the eyes of the Islamic Prophet, amounted to namaz, fasting during the prescribed time, pilgrimage, and spiritual struggle—that is, the fulfillment of ritual duties that are imposed on all believers. Muhammed's rejection of the "excesses" of monasticism was meant to annul the distinction between "simple believers" and "monastics," in a spirit of inner-worldly asceticism comparable to Luther's Reformation nine centuries later (Weber [1963] 2023). For more detail, see Shi'i theologian Naser Shirazi's (2006, entry 33) account of Islamic perceptions of monasticism.

19. See Wittgenstein 1986; Winch [1958] 2003; Taylor 1989, 1995; see Clarke 2023 for a survey of the concept of "rule" in the anthropology of Islam and beyond.

20. Michael Herzfeld (2021) works with communities he defines as "subversive archaists." The halal milieu does not invest in archaicity or autochthonism—to the contrary, it sees itself as cosmopolitan. Pietists might agree with characterizations of Islam as an (ethical) tradition in the Asadian sense, and they cherish its history, but they reject localist or indigenist interpretations, focusing instead on this ethics' universality and future-orientation. Nonetheless, their quietist yet inherent subversiveness can be likened to the "cultural forms-of-life" discussed in Herzfeld's account.

2. BECOMING FIDELIOUS MUSLIMS

1. This chapter features and considerably expands materials first published in Benussi 2018.

2. For the sake of anonymity, and since I could not independently verify the details of the story, which may have been subjected to sensationalization by a hostile Tatarstani press, I shall not reference these media reports.

3. Saudi Sheikh Muhammad Ibn Saleeh Ibn al-Uthaimeen (1925–2001) issued an influential fatwa on this subject. Under Hanbali-Salafi jurisprudence, civil marriage is irrelevant a priori.

4. Musa-xäzrät serves as both *imam-khatib*—principal preacher—and *muhtasib* for the Akmaş *muhtasibat*, in which capacity he oversees a regional religious subdivision (*muhtasibat*) comprising dozens of mosques and communities (*mahallas*) scattered throughout the territory. Tatarstan is divided into forty-four *muhtasibats*.

5. Musa-xäzrät preaches in Tatar and advocates the use of Tatar in both the religious sphere and everyday life. Several of Musa-xäzrät's associates are committed to the "spiritual rebirth" of the Tatar nation, some being quasi-professionally engaged in historical and philological research on the biographies and works of prerevolutionary Tatar religious figures. One of their main sources of inspiration is Rizaeddin Fakhretdin (1859–1936), an influential intellectual and theologian who embraced scriptural Islamic modernism.

6. One of the major learning centers for the Salafi movement, carrying the legacy of Sheikh al-Albani, an inflexible advocate of theological pristineness and political quietism (Olidor 2015).

7. Several Russians and one ethnic Jew are members of this group alongside a majority of Tatars. Many Arabic expressions and interjections pepper the parlance of this community: Knowledge of Arabic, even at a basic level, is highly prized.

8. Tatarstani prayer halls do get crowded for Friday prayers. As of 2020, in Kazan there were about seventy mosques catering to a Tatar population of over half a million. In Yar Çallı, Tatarstan's second-largest city, there are fourteen mosques for about 240,000 Tatars. Communal worship on Fridays is a religious obligation for male Muslims, but women are not required to attend in person. However, many mosques in Povolzhye feature spaces for female worshippers. The Tatar-majority rural township of Urta Äläzän in southwestern

Povolzhye (Sagitova 2014) boasts eleven recently built places of worship for a population of about 9,000 people, making it a uniquely lively rural piety hub—which retains, however, vital business and cultural connections with the region's main urban centers.

9. See Furman and Kaariainen 2000 for statistics on belief in God among older people and the rural population in Tatarstan.

10. The notion of God is often rendered by ethnic Muslims through the Russian word "*Bog*." Pietists, by contrast, prefer to use the word "Allah" or circumlocutions such as "the Lord of Worlds" or "the Most High."

11. Historian Devin DeWeese (1994) identified profound connections between religious, dynastic, and regional identities in premodern Inner Eurasia. In a longue durée perspective, it could be conjectured that contemporary ethnic-Muslim identities are influenced by these communalistic-genealogical understandings, whereby religious and communal identities are interlinked (see Kefeli 2014). Genealogy remains a salient cultural motif among Volga Turks to this day.

12. Some scholars have contrasted ritual's "subjunctive mode," based on playfulness, open-endedness, and the principle of "as if," with piety's "sincerity mode," based on earnestness, doctrine, and the principle of "ought" (Seligman et al. 2008). However, this contrast does not appear to hold if applied to Islamic prayer, which at least in theory is supposed to be performed in a sincerity mode. As we shall see in chapter 4, a subjunctive mode might apply to the open-ended healing devotions favored by ethnic Muslims.

13. On this point, I am grateful to James Faubion for his observation that asceticism and *askesis* are not synonymous, asceticism being closer to commitment to a spiritual discipline and *askesis* indicating a "training" in virtue that often includes renunciation as a form of "capacitating limitation." Although this distinction must be acknowledged, in this book I deliberately subsume asceticism under *askesis* in light of the unity of spiritual commitment and ethical discipline in the eyes of most halalists.

14. The notion of jāhiliyyah is part of the repertoire of Islamist and jihadi groups (Nasr 1996, 59–60, 110; Calvert 2009, 217; for a detailed account of this concept in the thought of the founder of contemporary Islamism, Sayyid Qutb, see Khatab 2006).

15. The rate of sadaqah al-fitr is four double handfuls (sā') of rice, grain, or dates per capita. In 2015, members of the mosque community were divided on the issue of how to manage almsgiving. Members closest to a Salafi approach held it preferable to donate saqakah al-fitr in person to recipients of their choice and deliver it exclusively in the form sanctioned by the scriptural sources (foodstuff). Others considered it permissible to donate its equivalent in money and funnel alms through the mosque administrative structure, which designates a team of alms-collectors for this purpose. This team would subsequently redistribute this money to the needy. This is permissible under Hanafi jurisprudence but discouraged by Salafi scholars. This choice on the part of the mosque committee suggests that, despite the prestige of Salafi teachings, Hanafi fiqh was treated as a primary source of guidance.

3. (NOT QUITE) MANAGING MUSLIM MORALITIES

1. This chapter features and significantly expands materials and arguments first published in Benussi 2017 and 2020a.

2. The Yarovaya Package established that missionary activity can be carried out only within religious buildings, forbidding proselytising in residential areas, and only by authorized members of officially registered organizations. In addition, the law is aimed at facilitating surveillance of individuals and groups and further expands the power of law enforcement organs.

3. Pakistan is, in reality, a global partner of NATO and a major non-NATO ally of the United States.

4. Historians of the prerevolutionary Volga region Muslims paint a picture of remarkable moral cohesion within the Volga region's "Muslim domain" (Tuna 2016; Frank 1998, 2012; Kefeli 2014): a world held together by the transmission of religious knowledge and devotional stories, pilgrimage routes (local and transregional) and "sacred geographies," trade, ritual, and custom. The model of society at play here seems in line with the MacIntyrean ([1981] 2007) before-the-fall narrative implicitly or explicitly endorsed by communalist scholars: a world yet untouched, or only marginally touched, by the disaggregating effects of modernity, in which individual and collective subjectivities were organized around a stable teleology, in turn anchored to revealed texts of unparalleled authority. A world, in short, in which action was oriented toward salvation and the norms of humans were (at least ideally) modeled after God's laws: "Islamic governance" as an "organic way of existence" (Hallaq 2013, 3–4). These reconstructions do not dwell on differences and conflict among prerevolutionary Muslims: Without denying them, they frame these as mere wrinkles of little consequence in an otherwise tightly woven moral fabric. Such a picture of organic moral worlds risks downplaying the "wrinkles" therein—for instance, the differences between the dignified puritanism of rich merchants (Gabdrafikova 2013), the thirst for self-reform of petty craftsmen, and the elusive spirituality of peasants, which occasionally veered on "animism," or this society's inner tumults, such as Mahdist disturbances in the countryside or the bourgeoning of modernisms and nationalism in the cities (Kefeli 2014; Tuna 2016). If taken with a pinch of salt, however, these studies' argument is persuasive. Until the turn of the twentieth century, the Spiritual Assembly presided over a world thoroughly infused with Islam, where religion was a core matrix of moral guidance and identity for most Volga region Muslims, despite differences in opportunities, aspirations, and worldviews.

5. This perception of insularity was compromised when the tsarist authorities, during the nineteenth century, ratcheted up attempts to "modernize" Russia's Muslims and end their "isolation" by incorporating them into the civic life of the Empire only to become inordinately paranoid when confronted with Muslim modernism and civic participation projects. See Campbell 2015; Tuna 2016.

6. An early generation of pioneers in the study of Islam in the former Soviet space (Dannreuther 2010; Verkhovsky 2010; Rasanayagam 2011; Pelkmans 2017) approached the "traditional Islam" discourse with skepticism but without addressing head-on this terminology's political implications in their full complexity.

7. Historian and political scholar Gulnaz Sibgatullina (2025), for example, has identified three prevalent "discourse clusters" in Muftiate activity—namely, "loyal," "liberal" (secular, folk, or humanist), and "correct" Islam.

8. While pilgrimage to holy sites has resumed in great numbers since perestroika, it is important to bear in mind that in the context of postatheist Povolzhye only a fraction of the spiritual tourists who flock to these places are animated by Sufi discipline, the vast majority having a more casual or interest-driven motivation (compare Kormina 2019 and Wanner 2020 for analogous observations in non-Muslim post-Soviet settings).

9. Batrov's transition toward Renovationism coincided with his departure from the Tatarstani Muftiate, which is orthodox Sunni and "theological *traditsionny islam*" in orientation. For a grassroots reaction, see Ike Lenar 2018.

10. For a response to some problematic aspects of Almazova and Akhunov's article, see Benussi 2021c.

4. SEEKING HEALING

1. Such features are shared far and wide across countless Islamicate contexts. They are so generic that they could even apply to, say, Roman Catholic Gregorian music.

2. YouTube, June 1, 2020, DUM RT, "Qor'an belän öşkerü," https://www.youtube.com/watch?v=PnLu7rJU3p4.

3. Pandolfo's Moroccan interlocutor, a healer and imam, does not frame spiritual malaise as a disturbance located within an "interiority": Rather, Pandolfo speaks of the nafs as "intimate exteriority" (2018, 318). Among my Tatarstani acquaintances, by contrast, there seemed to be greater emphasis on modernist, psychologized models of selfhood, understood as endowed with an inner forum (Benussi 2020b). The prevalence of such a model might be due to impact of European-modernist patterns of personhood mediated by hegemonic Russian (and Soviet) cultures.

4. Rukya. Lechenie po Sunne, "Lechenie ot koldovstva, sglasa, dzhinnov." Facebook, January 5, 2017, https://www.facebook.com/734843253331914/posts/755987111217528/.

5. Scriptural Islam excludes, at least in principle, intercession and worship or supplications directed to beings other than the Almighty (and the Prophet Muhammad on the Day of Judgment).

6. Po vkusu – po kormanu, "Zam-Zam – voda ispolneniya zhelanii!? Gde ee vzyat?" alif TV, April 27, 2019, https://alif.tv/zam-zam-voda-ispolneniya-zhelanij-gde-ee-vzyat/. For the folk notion of local "pseudo-Zamzam" water springs in the Volga region, see Guseva 2013, 41.

7. The Bolğar complex, which includes a holy spring called the Well of Gabdelrakhman, is said to be the resting place of the three legendary figures who brought Islam to the Bulgar people in the wake of the predication of Muhammad in Arabia. The three are identified as Companions of the Prophet (ṣaḥābah), which is historically implausible since the conversion of Bulgaria took place about two centuries after the first Islamic generation. Legend has it that one of the travelers, named 'Abd al-Rahman, would perform miracles, while another, Zubair, would then marry the daughter of the Bulgar ruler, thereby becoming an ancestor. No actual tomb from the Companions' age has been located: The mausoleums currently standing in Bolğar are too recent to be associated with these legendary events (Frank 1996, 275). The holy spring in Bilär is associated with saintly burials and the martyrdom of twelve, or sometimes forty, virgins (Urazmanova et al. 2014, 88; Kefeli 2014, 186), but again, no physical structure or remains lend concreteness to this story. Iske Kazan's holy spring, as we have seen, is noteworthy for the presence of gravestone-shaped votive slabs, erected there in recent years, but no ancient burials remain.

8. A famous exception is the Catholic sanctuary of Lourdes, in France, which features a healing spring.

9. Such an approach can be applied not only to contemporary controversies but also to historical ones. As early as the nineteenth century, intransigent modernist-scripturalist voices condemned the devotional practices of rural Volga Muslims (Tuna 2016; Di Puppo and Schmoller 2019, 139). Yet those devotions—local pilgrimage, Quranic amulets, healing prayers—played an important role in furthering rural Islamic reform movements. Rural reformers and wandering preachers who peddled miraculous healing techniques were better equipped than elite mullahs to engage with the ákesis-centered value orientation of the Tatar peasantry. Tapping into the axiological schemata of the rural populations, these reformers circulated narratives about miraculous healings, divinely enhanced fertility, the thaumaturgical power of "living water," and the wonder-working burials of saintly figures. By doing so, they championed Islamic orthodoxy against both animism and forced Christianization (Kefeli 2014).

5. ON THE SHOULDERS OF GIANTS

1. Some Muslims understand the hadithic notion that Adam was 60 cubits tall (90 feet/27.4 meters) as a description of the first man's appearance in Paradise, not on Earth.

2. To Pouillon, the Western concept of "belief" conflates different nuances: One is convinced that God exists, one makes suppositions about what God expects of them ("I believe that this is the right thing to do"), one puts one's trust in God, and one affirms the Christian creed, identifying with a specific community. Pouillon compares this with the vocabulary of belief among the Dangleat-speaking Hadjerai people of Chad. Hadjerai religion revolved around deities called margai. Pouillon identifies four verbs expressing people's relation with the margai: (1) *ibiné*, to believe that something (here, the margai) exists; (2) *pakkine*, to suppose/guess something (the margai's will); (3) *amniye*, to trust in somebody (the margai will behave benevolently); and (4) *àbidé*, to worship (the margai as a follower of Hadjerai religion). In sum, the Hadjerai use four different verbs instead of one word with different nuances. Islam complicates Pouillon's argument: It has a strongly monotheistic ontology, yet its liturgical language, Arabic, features—like Dangleat—different verbs to express "to believe" in a religious sense (āmana), opinion/conviction (iqtinā'), and confidence/trust (thiqah). However, this does not invalidate Pouillon's core argument about the nonuniversality of European belief-talk.

3. The converb *dip* makes it clear that the verb refers to an "intellectual activity" (Galieva and Elezarova 2019) sans moral and affiliational connotations.

4. Socio-anthropological engagements with Wittgenstein's thought tend to downplay Wittgenstein's critique of *any* social-scientific epistemology, mellowing the Austrian thinker's project into a call for epistemological reflexivity and methodological relativism, viz., better anthropology. Wittgensteinians such as Hanna Pitkin (1972), Stanley Cavell (1979), and Cora Diamond (2003) have argued that something deeper is at stake in Wittgenstein: the claims of reason itself. In this reading, any pretension of knowledge, any adoption of a skeptical epistemology—i.e., *all* hypothesizing, analysing, sociologizing—expresses a perverse explanatory tendency that alienates its utilizers from ordinary life and the truths that lie therein (Macarthur 2014). Rather than a call for better anthropology, pure Wittgensteinianism would amount to a negation of the anthropological endeavor itself.

5. The influence of Wittgensteinian philosophy on autonomism is not negligible. In both perspectives, (1) truths are not a matter of facticity, even less of factuality, but of existential positionality; hence, (2) they cannot be apprehended/communicated through explanation alone; furthermore, (3) truths pertain to a supra-individual dimension, a form-of-life; and (4) truths are connected to practice. Tiqqun is arguably the most Wittgensteinian of the authors I have engaged in this volume. The French collective's concept of form-of-life progressively shifted from an Agambenian, ethics-based one (Tiqqun 2011b) to a Wittgensteinian one (Invisible Committee 2015): Echoes of the Austrian philosopher are unmistakable in their more recent framing of ethical truths as "not truths about the world, but truths on the basis of which we dwell therein. . . . Truths are what bind us, to ourselves, to the world around us, and to each other. They give us entry into an immediately shared life, an undetached existence" (Invisible Committee 2015, 46–47). Compared to Agamben and Badiou, and on account of their spontaneist and anarchist sensitivities, Tiqqun/Invisible Committee's vision of emancipatory ethics is less explicitly connected to fidelity/discipline/Rule, prioritizing an insurrectionary exposé of the weakness of Law.

6. There is a bleak side to the Wittgensteinian philosophy of religion—namely, what Stephen Mulhall (2005) has defined as a "myth of the Fall of Man" devoid of a coherent prospect of redemption. To Mulhall, the Wittgensteinian picture of humans' epistemological confusion amounts to a secularized version of the Judeo-Christian doctrine of loss of grace. To Wittgenstein, any attempts to increase knowledge by intellectual means would mire us in error. A glimpse of solace lies "on the border of human experience" (Mulhall 2005, 11)—whence the truths of religion emanate—but our inherently opaque relationship with language and therefore with our ordinary selves means that "any coherent prospect of achieving thoroughgoing redemption" is foreclosed (123). It is worth observing

that Wittgenstein, for all his respect toward faith, had a troubled relationship with religion. Tellingly, his remarks on "ethics" (1965) have more to do with mythology, the miraculous, or supernaturalism than with commitment/ascetical striving.

7. I thank Charles Hirschkind for raising this observation and sharing his ethnographic insight about the currency of wonderment-inducing pious stories in Egypt and other MENA countries. On jinns and popular devotion, see Taneja 2017.

8. While in Wittgensteinian ordinary-language philosophy "it makes no sense to suppose the existence of truths beyond those that fall within the range of our present epistemic, cognitive, conceptual or . . . linguistic-expressive capacity" (Norris 2009, 41), such a conception of truth constitutes the cornerstone of Badiou's philosophical edifice. For the Wittgensteinians, the ordinary is a source of harmony—cognitively enigmatic, to be sure, but also soothing in its conventional beauty. Badiou, by contrast, views the domain of situations as tumultuous, disputatious, an arena where different moral and intellectual arguments are made and sometimes collide. Complexity, changeability, and relativity are constitutive characteristics of this realm, which therefore presents an insurmountable challenge to any positivistic claim to analytical exactitude. Situations, however, are not opaque to the intellect. An extrasituational standpoint does exist and is provided by truth, through which the terms of a given situation become philosophically legible and open to intervention.

9. Some commentators consider Austinian philosophy of ordinary language as inherently incompatible with Badiou's activist theory of extra-ordinary truths (Norris 2009, 3, 16). However, Badiousian truths' illocutionary power, their ability to engender effects (Humphrey 2018), point to a significant degree of overlap.

10. This statement, however, is not a verifiable one: a complication that Austin, on account of his commitment to a factual theory of truth, found "irritating" (1962, 86, 139–150). Though half-heartedly, Austin could not avoid positing a distinction between utterances that are happy/unhappy (illocutions) and utterances that are true/false (constatives). The problem with this is that by doing so Austin reluctantly replicates the habit of equating truth to sound knowledge (of facts) or justified opinions (about facts) (1962, 141). In light of Badiou (and Wittgenstein), however, we can adopt a nonfactual theory of truth that transcends both knowledge and opinions. Adam's age and height, for example, pertain not to the realm of facts but to the subjective one of truth; hence, any statement about this matter indexes the utterer's ethical positionality vis-à-vis Islam. Austin's commitment to a facticity theory did not, however, prevent him from noting that "what we have to study is not the sentence but the issuing of an utterance in a speech situation" (1962, 138).

11. Bourdieu's example focuses on the Marxist dictum that "there are two classes" (1991, 134). Such a statement is both constative—as a sociological analysis/Marxian description of wage relations—and performative, in the sense of bringing about novel, hitherto unthinkable ways of envisioning the social, thereby inaugurating new praxes, and ultimately bringing about the very societal arrangements—class struggle with all its ramifications—that it "discovered" in the first place.

12. In conversation with Foucault and Bourdieu, but also Austin and Derrida, Judith Butler (1997) has written an influential reflection on intractable, insurrectional, or offensive speech events including phenomena as diverse as discriminatory slurs, pornography, rap lyrics, and gay self-declarations; however, Butler's book does not touch on speech events animated by commitment to an ethical fidelity.

13. Not being an Islamic festival, New Year is frowned upon by many pietists.

6. THE BLESSED SHARE

1. The APM motto is modeled after a rhyming phrase in Ottoman Turkish with the same meaning—*el kârda, gönül yarda*—that is connected with the Naqshbandi Sufi tradi-

tion. This phrase is not, to my knowledge, current in Turkey's mainstream, but it appears in Islamic-themed social media and web pages. In the Tatarstani context, the APM motto's connection to Sufism is largely (and maybe deliberately, given Sufism's poor reputation among Salafi-influenced pietists) lost in translation.

2. Scholars of different orientations disagree over the extent to which today's Russia can be called neoliberal (Yurchak 2002, 2003; Rutland 2013; Matveev 2016; Ovsyannikova 2016; Zigon 2010b). With many others (Harvey 2005; Ong 2006), I take the view that neoliberalism is a complex phenomenon that accommodates—and indeed relies on—various forms of exception. Neoliberalism "with Russian characteristics" combines cronyism, widespread graft, and an authoritarian political culture, on the one hand, with privatization, deregulation, self-entrepreneurship, and the expansion of bourgeois values, on the other.

3. For a discussion of the anthropological debates on moral and "sacrificial" economies in prosperity Christian settings, see Coleman 2011.

4. Bataille depicted Islam as averse to expenditure/prodigality/sacrificial action, which is an untenable proposition to anyone with an understanding of Islamic economics. The philosopher, who was not a scholar of Islam, ignored crucial elements, some of which are discussed in this chapter, such as (1) the main Islamic festival being called "feast of sacrifice" and involving the gifting of sacrificed goods; (2) substantial charity being both compulsory and strongly encouraged; (3) the expenseful practice of hajj being a religious obligation; (4) an overall major emphasis on redistributive justice, for which numerous juridical and ethical mechanisms exist; and not least (5) the fact that the acceptance of the risk of loss or bankruptcy (hence the possibility of wasteful expenditure) is an inbuilt feature in the theory of Islamic finance, albeit one that is imperfectly applied in practice (Mittermaier 2013; Retsikas 2018; Rudnyckyj 2019, 178–179). Apart from his treatment of Islam, Bataille can also be criticized for his obscurity, pretensions to establish grand universal laws of human conduct, and frequent usage of vague concepts such as "energy" and "force." But he was a product of his time, and if read charitably, many of his intuitions remain good to think with.

5. In a study of charity and Christian institutions in Russia, Melissa Caldwell (2010, 338) mentions a Muscovite Orthodox church providing self-improvement educational programs for parishioners. Similarities between Caldwell's case and Alyautdinov are likely indicators of broader trends across ethical-religious paradigms in Russia.

6. This quote is popular with Muslim corporate trainers worldwide—compare with Hoesterey 2016, 105.

7. In Tübän Kama at the time of my fieldwork, industrial work was associated with the Soviet period and older generations, or with the sizeable local immigrant population of factory laborers from Turkey. Only rarely did the latter make an appearance at the mosque, so it was believed that they had "their own _cämäğat_" (community).

8. "Khadisy o materialnom sostoyanie i bogatstvo," Umma.ru, May 25, 2017, https://umma.ru/hadisy-o-materialnom-sostoyanii-i-bogatstve.

9. Zakāt is a religious obligation for those who possess wealth above a minimum amount called niṣāb (excluded from taxation). While I cannot focus on the subtleties of zakāt in the context of Povolzhye/Russia and related debates, Shamil Alyautdinov's volume on Islamic everyday financing features a solid explanation of zakāt within a Hanafi juridical framework along with several practical examples derived from everyday experiences of Russia-based Muslims that can be read ethnographically (2015a, 39–59).

10. On charity in Islam, see Benthall 1999; Benthall and Bellion-Jourdan 2003; Clark 2004; Mittermaier 2013; Martens 2014; Retsikas 2014; P. Anderson 2018. This is comparable with Evangelical Christianity's rediscovery of tithing, a comparable practice that also bridges the "secular economy and the godly world" under advanced capitalism (Zaloom 2015, 326).

11. See Quran 2:261, 34:39, 71:2–3, 71:10–12. Numerous publications, in Russian (http://islam-today.ru/veroucenie/12-sposobov-uvelicit-svoj-udel/) as well as other languages (Qadhi 2002), describe ways for believers to increase their rizq.

12. Shamil Alyautdinov's own theological discussion of Islamic predestination, in which he disproves fatalistic interpretations of qadar, can be found in his book *A Trillionaire's Finances* (2015, 340–362).

13. Kun fayakūn is a phrase cherished in Sufi mystic contexts, but it has also been taken on by the Indonesian Islamic televangelist Yusuf Mansur, the propagator of controversial theories of Islamic prosperity (Retsikas 2018, 663).

14. The Russian word *"prichina"* can be translated as "reason" or "cause." While the Arabic equivalent "sabab" (mentioned by my interviewee) is routinely translated as "cause," I choose "reason" in this passage so as to (1) avoid ideas of direct causality and (2) emphasize the "reasonability" of the human actions involved. In mainstream Sunni Islam, humans do not have the power to *cause* God to act according to their will but might give the Most High reasons to intervene in their lives in certain (desirable, understandable) ways. Century-old theological debates around the relation between divine will and human agency exist within the Islamic sciences, and I do not have the space to engage in these discussions. My lexical choice is intended to convey a certain shade of meaning formulated within a cultural world that attributes ultimate mastery over existence to the Godhead alone.

15. The author here is referring to Quran 62:10: "And when the prayer has been concluded, disperse within the land and seek from the bounty of God, and remember God often that you may succeed."

16. The topic of divine predetermination and its reverberations in business ethics has been discussed by Max Weber ([1905] 2002) in the context of Calvinism. Early modern Calvinist religiosity, in Weber's account, was haunted by uncertainty about believers' belonging in the slim and exclusive host of the elect, foreordained by God in accordance with a logic unfathomable by humans. To cope with this uncertainty, vernacular Calvinism developed a tendency to see "good works"—that is, a believer's successful engagements with the economic realm—as *signs* of (but not cause for) election ([1905] 2002, 79). This tendency, Weber argues, extended to the *fruits* of economic enterprise, determining a "comforting assurance that the unequal distribution of this world's good was the special work of the providence of God" ([1905] 2002, 119). A detailed comparison between the two religious traditions lies beyond this book's scope. It is safe to say, however, that Sunni soteriology is more optimistic: God wishes salvation for the whole of humanity, not just a preselected few, and through his prophets he has furnished mortals with clear instructions on how to attain it. Of course, mainstream Islam sets strict requirements that must be followed to achieve the goal. However, compared to Calvinism, Islam's community of the saved is perceived as numerous, open, and inclusive, membership depending on pious individual action. As a result, despite the positive emphasis on wealth in the halal milieu, it is more difficult for Povolzhye pietists to imagine a link between the fruits of enterprise and salvation.

17. In mainstream Sunnism, female ʿawrah includes the whole body besides face, feet, and hands, while male ʿawrah the region between the navel and knees (included).

18. This remark references the Quranic "commandment" of enjoining what is right and forbidding what is reprehensible (al-amr bil-maʿrūf wan-nahy ʿanil-munkar).

19. I have been informed about attempts to set up taxi companies catering to Kazan's Muslims. According to these accounts, such business experiments involve the preservation of vehicles' purity from polluting contact with impure animals (such as dogs) and substances (alcohol). Said attempts were, however, short-lived, and I did not come across any such services during my stay in Povolzhye.

20. My Salafi-leaning acquaintance Umar, usually quite careful to avoid exposure to human representations, admitted to me (with a nonchalant smile) the contradiction of allowing his kids to play with Lego figurines.

21. My elderly interlocutors would recall how, in the Soviet-era countryside, Tatar villagers would trade their meat and dairy products with Russian farmers from nearby villages, in exchange for vegetables, greens, and fruits that rural Tatars would not grow.

22. Modest shops selling halal products in the vicinities of neighborhood mosques tend to keep prices low, without seeking to tap into the same imagery of high-quality consumption and refined cosmopolitanism.

23. A tension between ethical universalism and status exclusivity haunts ethical consumption contexts informed by non-Islamic religious traditions as well, as exemplified by Liu, Cai, and Zhu's study of Buddhist vegetarian eateries in Guangzhou, China. The authors note that the devout Buddhist customers operate under a distinct class logic, seeking to "distance themselves from immoral nouveaux riches, working classes, and rural residents, and confirm their identities as moral urban middle-class individuals" (Liu et al. 2015, 561). Secular ethical consumption contexts can be equally riddled with mismatches between inclusive, egalitarian ideals and class/status disparities: see Julie Guthman's (2003, 2008) analysis of organic food consumption in the United States, where class issues are made more acute by the failures of well-meaning food activists to "bring good food" to underprivileged communities. Other relevant scholarship dealing with wealth, distinction, class, and democracy in ethical consumption contexts includes Starr 2009; Johnston and Bauman 2010; Zhang 2010; De Solier 2013; Orlando 2012.

24. Some protagonists of the golden age of Italian autonomism in the 1970s dared to declare, departing from orthodox Marxism's ethos of frugality, that "luxury is a right."

25. In the case of halal meat, sacrifice is inbuilt in the sourcing of the good itself, as animals are ritually slaughtered.

References

Aarons, K., and I. Robinson, eds. 2023. "Destituent Power." Special issue, *South Atlantic Quarterly* 122 (1).

Abashin, S. 2007. *Natsionalismy v Sredney Azii: V poiskakh identichnosti.* Aleteiya.

Abdou, M. 2022. *Islam and Anarchism: Relationships and Resonances.* Pluto.

Abramson, D., and E. Karimov. 2007. "Sacred Sites, Profane Ideologies: Religious Pilgrimage and the Uzbek State." In *Everyday Life in Central Asia: Past and Present,* edited by J. Sahadeo and R. Zanca, 319–338. Indiana University Press.

Abu Ibrakhim Tatarstani, R. [2012?]. "Ozhivlenie yazicheskikh obryadov Bulgara—nachalo kontsa tatarskogo naroda." Self-published pamphlet.

Adygamov, A. 2015. *Zolotye pravila uspekha, ili odin ayat i tri khadisa o tom kak ego dostich.* APM.

Agamben, G. 1998. *Homo Sacer: Sovereign Power and Bare Life.* Stanford University Press.

Agamben, G. 2000. *Means Without Ends: Notes on Politics.* University of Minnesota Press.

Agamben, G. 2009. *What Is an Apparatus? and Other Essays.* Stanford University Press.

Agamben, G. 2013a. *The Highest Poverty: Monastic Rules and Form-of-Life.* Stanford University Press.

Agamben, G. 2013b. *Opus Dei: An Archaeology of Duty.* Stanford University Press.

Agrama, H. 2012. *Questioning Secularism: Islam, Sovereignty, and the Rule of Law in Modern Egypt.* University of Chicago Press.

Ahmad, A. 2017. *Everyday Conversions: Islam, Domestic Work, and South Asian Migrant Women in Kuwait.* Duke University Press.

Ahmad, I. 2017. *Religion as Critique: Islamic Critical Thinking from Mecca to the Marketplace.* University of North Carolina Press.

Ahmed, S. 2016. *What Is Islam? The Importance of Being Islamic.* Princeton University Press.

Aitamurto, K. 2021. "Patriotic Loyalty and Interest Representation Among the Russian Islamic Elite." *Religion* 51 (2): 280–298.

Akhmetkarimov, B. 2020. "Common Sense Is Not So Common: Integration and Perceptions of 'Traditional Islam' in Russia's Volga-Ural Region." *Contemporary Islam* 14:179–202.

Alagha, G. 2016. *Salafism in Lebanon: From Apoliticism to Transnational Jihadism.* Georgetown University Press.

Alexeev, I., and S. Ragozina. 2017. "From 'Good' to 'Right' Islam: The Categories and Concepts in the Modern Russian Analytics and Ideology Language." *Islamology* 7 (1): 89–109.

Alimov, T. 2018. "Igrat s religey—prestuplenie." *Rossiiskaya Gazeta,* August 23, 2018. https://rg.ru/2018/08/23/reg-pfo/kak-musulmane-tatarstana-ponimaiut-tradicionnyj-islam.html.

Almazova, L. 2014. "Fenomen kazanskoy mecheti Shamil: Sufiiskie istoki tselitel'noy praktiki." In *Islam v mul'tikul'turnom mire: Islamskie dvizheniya i formirovanie musul'manskoy ideologii v sovremennom informatsionnom prostranstve*, edited by D. Brilov, 253–272. Izdatel'stvo Kazanskogo Universiteta.

Almazova, L. 2021. "Mobile Actors in the Islamic Education of Post-Soviet Tatarstan." In *Cultures of Islam: Vernacular Traditions and Revisionist Interpretations across Russia*, edited by M. Laruelle and J. Schmoller, 21–36. Central Asia Program, George Washington University.

Almazova, L., and A. Akhunov. 2020. "In Search of 'Traditional Islam' in Tatarstan: Between National Project and Universalist Theories." In *The Concept of Traditional Islam in Modern Islamic Discourse in Russia*, edited by R. Bekkin, 17–56. CNS.

Althusser, L. 2014. "Ideology and Ideological State Apparatuses (Notes Toward an Investigation)." In *The Anthropology of the State: A Reader*, edited by A. Sharma and A. Gupta, 86–111. Blackwell.

Äl-Xänäfi, N. M. 2009. *Min—möselman, çönki min—tatar?* N.p.

Alyautdinov, S. 2013a. *Trillioner dumaet*. Dilya.

Alyautdinov, S. 2013b. *Trillioner slushaet*. Dilya.

Alyautdinov, S. 2014a. *Stan' samym umnym I samym bogatym*. Dilya.

Alyautdinov, S. 2014b. *Ezhednevnik: Raspisanie trillionaera*. Dilya.

Alyautdinov, S. 2015a. *Finansy Trillionera*. Dilya.

Alyautdinov, S. 2015b. *Trillioner deystvuet*. Dilya.

Alyautdinov, S. 2017. *Podsoznatel'nye bednost' i bogatstvo*. Dilya.

Amiraux, V. 2006. "Speaking as a Muslim: Avoiding Religion in French Public Space." In *Politics of Visibility: Young Muslims in European Public Space*, edited by G. Jonker and V. Amiraux, 21–52. Transcript Verlag.

Anderson, D. G., D. V. Arzyutov, and S. S. Alymov, eds. 2019. *Life Histories of Etnos Theory in Russia and Beyond*. Open Book Publishers.

Anderson, E. 2020. "Compelled Silence and Compelled Sound in the Uyghur Genocide." *Georgetown Journal of International Affairs*, December 15, 2020. https://gjia .georgetown.edu/2020/12/15/compelled-silence-and-compelled-sound-in-the -uyghur-genocide/.

Anderson, P. 2011. "The Piety of the Gift: Selfhood and Sociality in the Egyptian Mosque Movement." *Anthropological Theory* 11 (1): 3–21.

Anderson, P. 2018. "'An Abundance of Meaning': Ramadan as an Enchantment of Society and Economy in Syria." *HAU: Journal of Ethnographic Theory* 8 (3): 610–624.

Anderson, P. 2023. *Exchange Ideologies: Commerce, Language, and Patriarchy in Preconflict Aleppo*. Cornell University Press.

Anderson, P., and M. Marsden. 2023. "The Ethics of Commerce and Trade." In *The Cambridge Handbook for the Anthropology of Ethics*, edited by J. Laidlaw, 760–790. Cambridge University Press.

Anjum, O. 2007. "Islam as a Discursive Tradition: Talal Asad and His Interlocutors." *Comparative Studies of South Asia, Africa and the Middle East* 27 (3): 656–672.

Asad, T. (1981) 2009. "The Idea of an Anthropology of Islam." *Qui Parle* 17 (2): 1–30.

Asad, T. 2003. *Formations of the Secular: Christianity, Islam, Modernity*. Stanford University Press.

Asad, T. 2020. "Thinking About Religion Through Wittgenstein." Unpublished manuscript. https://misr.mak.ac.ug/sites/default/files/events/Thinking%20about%20 Religion%20through%20Wittgenstein.pdf.

Aslamova, D. 2011. "Rossii nuzhen suverenny islam?" *Komsomolskaya Pravda*, April 26, 2011.

Austin, J. L. 1962. *How to Do Things with Words*. Harvard University Press.

Badiou, A. 2002. *Ethics: An Essay on the Understanding of Evil*. Verso.

Badiou, A. 2003. *Saint Paul: The Foundations of Universalism*. Stanford University Press.

Badiou, A. 2010. *The Communist Hypothesis*. Verso.

Badiou, A. 2011. *Polemics*. Verso.

Badiou, A. 2019. *Wittgenstein's Antiphilosophy*. Verso.

Badiou, A., and N. Truong. 2009. *In Praise of Love*. Serpent's Tail.

Barker, A. M., ed. 1999. *Consuming Russia: Popular Culture, Sex, and Society Since Gorbachev*. Duke University Press.

Bassett, K. 2016. "Event, Politics, and Space: Rancière or Badiou?" *Space and Polity* 20 (3): 280–293.

Bataille, G. (1991) 2019. *The Accursed Share*. Vol. 1. Zone Books.

Bataille, G. (1992) 2012. *Theory of Religion*. Zone Books.

Bayat, A. 1996. "The Coming of a Post-Islamist Society." *Critique: Critical Middle East Studies* 9:43–52.

Bayat, A., ed. 2013. *Post-Islamism: The Changing Faces of Political Islam*. Oxford University Press.

Bayat, A., and L. Herrera. 2010. *Being Young and Muslim: New Cultural Politics in the Global South and North*. Oxford University Press.

BBC. 2015. "Rossiiskie musul'mane v Turtsii: Protiv Moskvy, no ne v IGIL." BBC News Russkaya Sluzhba, December 18, 2015. https://www.bbc.com/russian/international /2015/12/151218_muhajirs_islam_russia_turkey.

Beginin, V. I., ed. 1993. *Sotsiologiya obraza zhizni*. Saratovsky Universitet.

Bekkin, R. 2020a. *People of Reliable Loyalty: Muftiates and the State in Modern Russia*. Södertörns högskola.

Bekkin, R. 2020b. "The Renovationist Movement in Contemporary Russian Islam." In *The Concept of Traditional Islam in Modern Islamic Discourse in Russia*, edited by R. Bekkin, 87–114. CNS.

Bellah, R. (1970) 2010. "Civic Religion in America." In *A Reader in the Anthropology of Religion*, edited by M. Lambek, 509–518. Blackwell.

Belyaev, M., and A. Sheptitsky. 2015. *Banditsky Tatarstan*. Idel.

Bennett, A., and K. Kahn-Harris, eds. 2004. *After Subculture: Critical Studies in Contemporary Youth Culture*. Palgrave MacMillan.

Benningsen, A., and C. Lemercier-Quelquejay. 1981. *Les musulmans oubliés: L'Islam en Union soviétique*. Maspero.

Bens, J., A. Diefenbach, T. John, A. Kahl, H. Lehmann, M. Luthjohann, F. Oberkrome, H. Roth, G. Scheideker, G. Thonhauser, N. Ural, D. Wahba, R. Walter-Jochum, and M. Zik. 2019. *The Politics of Affective Societies: An Interdisciplinary Essay*. Transcript Verlag.

Benthall, J. 1999. "Financial Worship: The Quranic Injunction to Almsgiving." *Journal of the Royal Anthropological Institute* 5 (1): 27–42.

Benthall, J., and J. Bellion-Jourdan. 2003. *The Charitable Crescent: Politics of Aid in the Muslim World*. Bloomsbury.

Benussi, M. 2017. "The Weight of Tradition: 'Traditional' vs. 'Non-Traditional' Islam in Russia's Volga Region." In *Muslims in the UK and Europe III*, edited by P. Anderson and J. Hargreaves, 9–23. Centre of Islamic Studies.

Benussi, M. 2018. "Ethnic Muslims and the 'Halal Movement' in Tatarstan." *Anthropological Journal of European Cultures* 27 (1): 88–93.

Benussi, M. 2020a. "'Sovereign' Islam and Tatar 'Aqīdah': Normative Religious Narratives and Grassroots Criticism Amongst Tatarstan's Muslims." *Contemporary Islam* 14:111–134.

Benussi, M. 2020b. "Public Spaces and Inner Worlds: Emplaced Askesis and Architectures of the Soul Among Tatarstani Muslims." *Ethnicities* 20 (4): 685–707.

Benussi, M. 2021a. "Living Halal in the Volga Region: Lifestyle and Civil Society Opportunities." In *Rethinking Halal: Genealogy, Current Trends, and New Interpretations*, edited by L.-L. Christians and A. U. Yakin, 265–293. Brill.

Benussi, M. 2021b. "Pietaskapes of Halal Living: Subjectivity, Striving, and Space-Making in Muslim Russia." *Ethnic and Racial Studies* 44 (10):1821–1843. .

Benussi, M. 2021c. "Discussing Tradition: A Response to Two Tatarstani Colleagues." *Context: Časopis za interdisciplinarne studije* 8 (1): 125–132.

Benussi, M. 2021d. "The Golden Cage: Heritage, (Ethnic) Muslimness, and the Place of Islam in Post-Soviet Tatarstan." *Religion State and Society* 49 (4–5): 314–330.

Benussi, M. 2022a. "Emancipating Ethics: An Autonomist Reading of Islamic Piety in Russia." *Journal of the Royal Anthropological Institute* 28 (1): 30–51.

Benussi, M. 2022b. "Ethical Infrastructures: Halal and the Ecology of Askesis in Muslim Russia." *Anthropological Theory* 22 (3): 294–316.

Benussi, M., and T. Manzon. 2023. "Two Ways of Being the Body of Christ: Toward an Anthropology of Church Forms, with Reference to Baptist and Roman Catholic Polities in Italy." *HAU Journal of Ethnographic Theory* 13 (3): 672–686.

Berliner, D., and R. Sarró. 2007. "On Learning Religion: An Introduction." In *Learning Religion: Anthropological Approaches*, edited by D. Berliner and R. Sarró, 1–19. Berghahn.

Bernstein, A. 2013. *Religious Bodies Politic: Rituals of Sovereignty in Buryat Buddhism*. University of Chicago Press.

Bey, H. (1985) 1991. *T.A.Z.: The Temporary Autonomous Zone, Ontological Anarchy, Poetic Terrorism*. Autonomedia.

Bialecki, J. 2010. "Angels and Grass: Church, Revival, and the Neo-Pauline Turn." *South Atlantic Quarterly* 109 (4): 695–717.

Bigozhin, U. 2019. "Sacred Geographies in the Eurasian Steppe: The Aqkol Shrine as a Symbol of Kazakh Ethnicity and Religiosity." *Journal of Ethnology and Folkloristics* 13 (2): 131–133.

Bikbov, A. 2016. "Two Different Paths: How the Economies of Tatarstan and Russia Diverge." *RealnoeVremya*, October 28, 2016.

Boddy, J. 1988. "Spirits and Selves in Northern Sudan: The Cultural Therapeutics of Possession and Trance." *American Ethnologist* 15 (1): 4–27.

Boddy, J. 2013. "Spirits and Selves Revisited: Zār and Islam in Northern Sudan." In *A Companion to the Anthropology of Religion*, edited by J. Boddy and M. Lambek, 444–467). Wiley Blackwell.

Boltanski, L., and E. Chiapello. 2002. "The New Spirit of Capitalism." Paper presented to the Conference of Europeanists, Chicago, March 14–16, 2002.

Borbieva, N. 2009. "Islam and the International Sector: Negotiations of Faith in the Kyrgyz Republic." *Notre Dame Kellogg Institute Working Papers Series*, no. 364.

Borbieva, N. 2012. "Islam in the Nation's Service: Religious Women, the State, and Civil Society in the Kyrgyz Republic." *Slavic Review* 71 (2): 288–307.

Boterbloem, K. 2023. *A History of Tatarstan: The Russian Yoke and the Vanishing Tatars*. Rowman and Littlefield.

Botoeva A. 2006. "Contentious Discourses Surrounding Supermarkets in post-Soviet Bishkek." *Anthropology of East Europe Review* 24 (2): 44–53.

Botoeva, A. 2018. "Islam and the Spirits of Capitalism: Competing Articulations of the Islamic Economy." *Politics and Society* 46 (2): 235–264.

Bourdieu, P. (1984) 2010. *Distinction: A Social Critique of the Judgement of Taste*. Routledge.

Bourdieu, P. 1991. *Language and Symbolic Power*. Harvard University Press.

Bowen, J. 2008. *Why the French Don't Like Headscarves: Islam, the State, and Public Space*. Princeton University Press.

Bowen, J. 2012. *A New Anthropology of Islam*. Cambridge University Press.

Bowman, G. 2010. "Orthodox-Muslim Interactions at 'Mixed Shrines' in Macedonia." In *Eastern Christians in Anthropological Perspective*, edited by C. Hann and H. Goltz, 163–183. University of California Press.

Boyer, P. 2002. *Religion Explained: The Evolutionary Origins of Religious Thought*. Basic Books.

Boyer, P. 2008. "Evolutionary Perspectives on Religion." *Annual Review of Anthropology* 37:111–130.

Bracke, S., and N. Fadil. 2012. "'Is the Headscarf Oppressive or Emancipatory?' Field Notes from the Multicultural Debate." *Religion and Gender* 2 (1): 36–56.

Bretherton, L., V. Lloyds, and V. Napolitano. Forthcoming. *What Is Political Theology?* Columbia University Press.

Bretall, R. (1946) 2016. Introduction to *A Kierkegaard Anthology*, by S. Kierkegaard, edited by R. Bretall, xvii–xxv. Princeton University Press.

Broz, L. 2009. "Conversion to Religion? Negotiating Continuity and Discontinuity in Contemporary Altai." In *Conversion After Socialism: Disruptions, Modernisms and Technologies of Faith in the Former Soviet Union*, edited by M. Pelkmans, 17–39. Berghahn Books.

Brunaska, Z. 2017. "Understanding Sociopolitical Engagement of Society in Russia: A View from Yaroslavl Oblast and Tatarstan." *Problems of Post-Communism* 65 (5): 315–326.

Bulliet, R. 1994. *Islam: The View from the Edge*. Columbia University Press.

Bustanov, A. 2012. "Beyond the Ethnic Traditions: Shamil' Alyautdinov's Muslim Guide to Success." In *Islamic Authority and the Russian Language: Studies on Texts from European Russia, the North Caucasus and Siberia*, edited by M. Kemper and A. Bustanov, 143–164. Uitgeverj Pegasus.

Bustanov, A. 2016. "Sufizm v Rossii: Pro et contra." *Real'noe vremya*, October 31, 2016.

Bustanov, A. 2017. "The Language of Moderate Salafism in Eastern Tatarstan." *Islam and Christian-Muslim Relations* 28 (2): 183–201.

Bustanov, A. 2019. "Vokrug BIA slozhilsya klubok iz trekh vzglyadov na islam v Rossii." *Biznes Online*, September 29, 2019. https://www.business-gazeta.ru/article/440616.

Bustanov, A., and M. Kemper. 2012. "From Mirasism to Euro-Islam: The Translation of Islamic Legal Debates into Tatar Secular Cultural Heritage." In *Islamic Authority and the Russian Language: Studies on Texts from European Russia, the North Caucasus and Siberia*, edited by M. Kemper and A. Bustanov, 29–54. Uitgeverj Pegasus.

Bustanov, A., and M. Kemper. 2013. "Valiulla Iakupov's Tatar Islamic Traditionalism." *Asiatische Studien/Études Asiatiques* 67 (3): 809–835.

Bustanov, A., and V. Usmanov. 2022. *Muslim Subjectivity in Soviet Russia: The Memoirs of 'Abd al-Majid al-Qadiri*. Brill.

Butler, J. 1997. *Excitable Speech: A Politics of the Performative*. Routledge.

Butler, J. 2001. "What Is Critique? An Essay on Foucault's Virtue." In *The Political: Readings in Continental Philosophy*, edited by D. Ingram, 212–228. Basil Blackwell.

Caldwell, M. 2010. "The Russian Orthodox Church, the Provision of Social Welfare, and Changing Ethics of Benevolence." In *Eastern Christians in Anthropological Perspective*, edited by C. Hann and H. Goltz, 329–350. University of California Press.

Caldwell, M. 2011. *Dacha Idylls: Living Organically in Russia's Countryside*. University of California Press.

Caldwell, M. 2014. "Gardening for the State Cultivating Bionational Citizens in Post-socialist Russia." In *Ethical Eating in the Postsocialist and Socialist World*, edited by Y. Yung, J. A. Klein, and M. Caldwell, 188–210. University of California Press.

Calvert, J. 2009. *Sayyid Qutb and the Origins of Radical Islamism*. Oxford University Press.

Campbell, E. 2015. *The Muslim Question and Russian Imperial Governance*. Indiana University Press.

Candea, M. 2016. "De deux modalités de comparaison en anthropologie sociale." *L'Homme* 218 (2): 183–218.

Carrier, J. 2012. Introduction to *Ethical Consumption: Social Value and Economic Practice*, edited by J. Carrier, and P. G. Luetchford, 1–36. Berghahn.

Castoriadis, C. 1991. *Politics, Philosophy, Autonomy: Essays in Political Philosophy*. Oxford University Press.

Cavell, S. 1979. *The Claim of Reason: Wittgenstein, Skepticism, Morality, and Tragedy*. Oxford University Press.

Chapra, M. U. 2013. *Islamic Trade, Export-Import Laws, and Regulations Handbook*. Vol. 1. International Business Publications.

Clark, J. 2004. *Islam, Charity, and Activism: Middle-Class Networks and Social Welfare in Egypt, Jordan, and Yemen*. Indiana University Press.

Clarke, M. 2013. "Integrity and Commitment in the Anthropology of Islam." In *Articulating Islam: Anthropological Approaches to Muslim Worlds*, edited by M. Marsden and K. Retsikas, 209–227. Springer.

Clarke, M. 2023. "Rules." In *The Cambridge Handbook for the Anthropology of Ethics*, edited by J. Laidlaw, 508–535. Cambridge University Press.

Coleman, S. 2000. *The Globalisation of Charismatic Christianity*. Cambridge University Press.

Coleman, S. 2011. "Prosperity Unbound? Debating the 'Sacrificial Economy.'" *Research in Economic Anthropology* 31:23–45.

Crapanzano, V. 1973. *The Hamadsha: A Study in Moroccan Ethnopsychiatry*. University of California Press.

Daniels, T. 2017. *Living Sharia: Law and Practice in Malaysia*. Washington University Press.

Dannreuther, R. 2010. "Russian Discourses and Approaches Towards Islam and Islamism." In *Russia and Islam: State, Society and Radicalism*, edited by R. Dannreuther and M. March, 9–25. Routledge.

Darieva, T., F. Mühlfried, and K. Tuite, eds. 2018. *Sacred Places, Emerging Spaces: Religious Pluralism in the Post-Soviet Caucasus*. Berghahn.

Das, V. 2012. *Life and Words: Violence and the Descent into the Ordinary*. University of California Press.

Das, V. 2015. "What Does Ordinary Ethics Look Like?" In *Four Lectures on Ethics*, by M. Lambek, V. Das, D. Fassin, and W. Keane, 53–126. Hau Books.

Dashibalova, I., and A. Bil'trikova. 2019. "Etnokul'turny turizm v Buriatii: Vozmozhnosti i ogranicheniya." *Gumanitarny nauchny vestnik* 6:1–6.

Daswani, G. 2016. "A Prophet but Not for Profit: Ethical Value and Character in Ghanaian Pentecostalism." *Journal of the Royal Anthropological Institute* 22 (1): 108–126.

Dave, N. 2012. *Queer Activism in India: A Story in the Anthropology of Ethics*. Duke University Press.

Davies, D. 2012. *Anthropology and Theology*. Berg.

De Martino, E. (1959) 2015. *Magic: A Theory from the South*. HAU Books.

De Solier, I. 2013. *Food and the Self: Consumption, Production and Material Culture*. Bloomsbury.

Deutscher, P. 2016. "'On the Whole We Don't': Michel Foucault, Veena Das and Sexual Violence." *Critical Horizons* 17 (2): 186–206.

DeWeese, D. 1994. *Islamization and Native Religion in the Golden Horde: Baba Tükles and Conversion to Islam in Historical and Epic Tradition.* Pennsylvania State University Press.

DeWeese, D. 2016. "It Was a Dark and Stagnant Night ('til the Jadids Brought the Light): Clichés, Biases, and False Dichotomies in the Intellectual History of Central Asia." *Journal of the Economic and Social History of the Orient* 59: 37–92.

Di Puppo, L. 2019. "The Paradoxes of a Localised Islamic Orthodoxy: Rethinking Tatar Traditional Islam in Russia." *Ethnicities* 19 (2): 311–334.

Di Puppo, L., and J. Schmoller. 2019a. "Introduction: Sacred Geographies and Identity Claims." *Journal of Ethnology and Folkoristics* 13 (2): 124–127.

Di Puppo, L., and J. Schmoller. 2019b. "The Revival of Sacred Sites in the Urals: The Local and Beyond." *Journal of Ethnology and Folkoristics* 13 (2): 143–145.

Di Puppo, L., and J. Schmoller. 2020. "Here or Elsewhere: Sufism and Traditional Islam in Russia's Volga-Ural Region." *Contemporary Islam* 14 (2): 135–156.

Diamond, C. 2003. "The Difficulty of Reality and the Difficulty of Philosophy." *Partial Answers* 1 (2): 1–26.

Dinç, D. 2021. *Tatarstan's Autonomy Within Putin's Russia: Minority Elites, Ethnic Mobilization and Sovereignty.* Routledge.

Dinkevich, M. 2014. *Obraz Zhizni/Lifestyle.* Common Place.

Dougherty, M. 2017. "'Taqwacore Is Dead. Long Live Taqwacore' or Punk's Not Dead? Studying the Online Evolution of the Islamic Punk Scene." In *The Web as History: Using Web Archives to Understand the Past and the Present*, edited by N. Brügger and R. Schroeder, 204–219. UCL Press.

Dubuisson, E.-M., and A. Genina. 2011. "Claiming an Ancestral Homeland: Kazakh Pilgrimage and Migration in Inner Asia." *Central Asia Survey* 30 (3–4): 469–485.

Duff, C. 2012. "Exploring the Role of 'Enabling Places' in Promoting Recovery from Mental Illness: A Qualitative Test of a Relational Model." *Health and Place* 18 (6): 1388–1395.

Durkheim, E. (1912) 1995. *The Elementary Forms of Religious Life.* Free Press.

Dyer-Witheford, N. 2015. *Cyber-Proletariat: Global Labour in the Digital Vortex.* Pluto.

Eagleton, T. 2018. *Radical Sacrifice.* Yale University Press.

Edelman, M. 2012. "E. P. Thompson and Moral Economies." In *A Companion to Moral Anthropology*, edited by D. Fassin, 49–66. Wiley Blackwell.

Efimov, N. I. 1982. *Sovetsky obraz zhizni.* Novosti.

Elridge, A., and B. Iqbal. 2022. "A Tropics of Estrangement: *Ghurba* in Four Scenes." *Diacritics* 50 (1): 112–140.

Epstein, M. N. 1999a. "Minimal Religion." In *Russian Postmodernism: New Perspectives on Post-Soviet Culture*, edited by M. N. Epstein, A. A. Genis, and S. M. Vladiv-Glover, 163–171. Berghahn Books.

Epstein, M. N. 1999b. "Post-Atheism: From Apophatic Theology to 'Minimal Religion.'" In *Russian Postmodernism: New Perspectives on Post-Soviet Culture*, edited by M. N. Epstein, A. A. Genis, and S. M. Vladiv-Glover, 345–393. Berghahn.

Evered, K., and E. Evered. 2017. "Therapeutic Landscapes and Nationalism: Turkey and the Curative Waters of Kemalism." *Landscape History* 38 (2): 77–96.

Fadil, N. 2011. "Not-/Unveiling as an Ethical Practice." *Feminist Review* 98:83–109.

Fadil, N., and M. Fernando. 2015. "Rediscovering the 'Everyday' Muslim: Notes on an Anthropological Divide." *Hau: Journal of Ethnographic Theory* 5 (2): 59–88.

Falkenberg, G. 1988. "Insincerity and Disloyalty." *Argumentation* 2:89–97.

Faller, H. 2011. *Nation, Language, Islam: Tatarstan's Sovereignty Movement*. Central European University Press.

Fassin, D. 2009. "Moral Economy Revisited." *Annales* 2009/6:1237–1266.

Fassin, D. 2014. "The Ethical Turn in Anthropology: Promises and Uncertainties." *HAU Journal of Ethnographic Theory* 4 (1): 429–435.

Fassin, D. 2015. "Troubled Waters: At the Confluence of Ethics and Politics." In *Four Lectures on Ethics*, by M. Lambek, V. Das, D. Fassin, and W. Keane, 175–210. Hau Books.

Faubion, J. 2001. *The Shadows and Lights of Waco: Millennialism Today*. Princeton University Press.

Faubion, J. 2011. *An Anthropology of Ethics*. Cambridge University Press.

Féaux de la Croix, J., and M. Reeves, eds. 2023. *The Central Asian World*. Routledge.

Federici, S. 1998. *Caliban and the Witch: Women, the Body and Primitive Accumulation*. Autonomedia.

Feher, M. 2009. "Self-Appreciation; or, The Aspirations of Human Capital." *Public Culture* 21 (1): 21–41.

Fernando, M. 2014. *The Republic Unsettled: Muslim French and the Contradictions of Secularism*. Duke University Press.

Finkelde, D. 2017. *Excessive Subjectivity: Kant, Hegel, Lacan, and the Foundations of Ethics*. Columbia University Press.

Fischer, J. 2011. *The Halal Frontier: Muslim Consumers in a Globalized Market*. Palgrave Macmillan.

Flathman, R. 2003. *Freedom and Its Conditions: Discipline, Autonomy, and Resistance*. Routledge.

Foucault, M. 1997a. *Ethics: Subjectivity and Truth*. New Press.

Foucault, M. 1997b. *The Politics of Truth*. Semiotext(e).

Foucault, M. 2001. *Fearless Speech*. Semiotext(e).

Foucault, M. 2010. *The Government of Self and Others: Lectures at the Collège De France, 1982–1983*. Palgrave MacMillan.

Foucault, M. 2011. *The Courage of the Truth: The Government of Self and Others II: Lectures at the Collège de France, 1983–1984*. Palgrave MacMillan.

Frank, A. 1998. *Islamic Historiography and "Bulghar" Identity Among the Tatars and Bashkirs of Russia*. Brill.

Frank, A. 2012. *Bukhara and the Muslims of Russia: Sufism, Education, and the Paradox of Islamic Prestige*. Brill.

Friess, N., and K. Kaminskij, eds. 2019. *Resignification of Borders: Eurasianism and the Russian World*. Frank and Timme.

Froese, P. 2010. *The Plot to Kill God: Findings from the Soviet Experiment in Secularization*. University of California Press.

Furani, K. 2019. *Redeeming Anthropology: A Theological Critique of a Modern Science*. Oxford University Press.

Furman, D., and K. Kaariainen. 2000. "Tatary i russkiye—veruyushchiye i neveruyushchiye, staryye i molodiye." In *Starie tserkvi, noviye veruyushchiye: Religiya v massovom soznanii postsovetskoi Rossii*, edited by K. Kaariainen and D. Furman, 209–236. Letny Sad.

Gabdrafikova, L. R. 2013. *Povsednevnaya zhizn' gorodskikh tatar v usloviyakh burzhuaznykh preobrazovanii vtoroy poloviny XIX–nachala XX veka*. Akademia Nauk.

Galieva, A., and Y. Elezarova. 2019. "Grammatikalisatsiya rechevogo konverba dip v tatarskom yazyke (na korpusnykh dannykh)." In *Korpusnaya Lingvistika*, 103–111. Izdatel'stvo Sankt-Petersburgskogo Gosudarstvennogo Universiteta.

Galyautdin, I. 2011. *Pokazukha*. Tauba.

Galyautdin, I. 2014. *Bogatstvo*. Iman.

Gambetta, D., and S. Hertog. 2016. *Engineers of Jihad. The Curious Connection Between Violent Extremism and Education*. Princeton University Press.

Garaev, D. 2017. "Musul'manskaya blagotvoritel'nost v Kazani: Mezhdu moral'noi ekonomikoy i simvolicheskim kapitalom." Paper delivered at the Islam and the City Muslims in the Urban Space of Contemporary Russia workshop, St. Petersburg, December 14, 2017.

Garaev, R. 2020. *Slovo patsana: Kriminal'ny Tatarstan 1970–2010-x*. Individuum.

Garipova, R. 2013. "The Transformation of the Ulama and the Shari'a in the Volga-Ural Muslim Community Under Russian Imperial Rule." PhD diss., Princeton University.

Garipova, R. 2016. "The Protectors of Religion and Community: Traditionalist Muslim Scholars of the Volga-Ural Region at the Beginning of the Twentieth Century." *Journal of the Economic and Social History of the Orient* 59 (1–2): 126–165.

Gellner, E. 1960. *Words and Things: A Critical Account of Linguistic Philosophy and a Study in Ideology*. Beacon Hill.

Gellner, E. 1986. *Relativism and the Social Sciences*. Cambridge University Press.

Gesler, W., and R. Kearns. 2002. *Culture/place/health*. Routledge.

Ghodsee, K. 2009. *Muslim Lives in Eastern Europe: Gender, Ethnicity, and the Transformation of Islam in Postsocialist Bulgaria*. Princeton University Press.

Gier, N. 1980. "Wittgenstein and Forms of Life." *Philosophy of the Social Sciences* 10:241–258.

Gillette, M. 2000. *Between Mecca and Beijing: Modernization and Consumption Among Urban Chinese Muslims*. Stanford University Press.

Göle, N. 2015. *Islam and Secularity: The Future of Europe's Public Sphere*. Duke University Press.

Golubev, A., and O. Smolyak. 2013. "Making Selves Through Making Things: Soviet Do-It-Yourself Culture and Practices of Late Soviet Subjectivation." *Cahiers du Monde Russe* 54 (3): 517–541.

Graeber, D. 2004. *Fragments of an Anarchist Anthropology*. Prickly Paradigm.

Graeber, D. 2016. *The Utopia of Rules: On Technology, Stupidity, and the Secret Joys of Bureaucracy*. Melville House.

Graney, K. 2009. *Of Khans and Kremlins: Tatarstan and the Future of Ethno-Federalism in Russia*. Rowman and Littlefield.

Green, N. 2011. *Bombay Islam: The Religious Economy of the West Indian Ocean, 1840–1915*. Cambridge University Press.

Green, N. 2015. *Terrains of Exchange: Religious Economies of Global Islam*. Oxford University Press.

Guseva, Y. 2013. "Sufiiskie bratstva, 'brodyachie mully' i 'svyatie mesta' Srednego Povolzhya v 1950–1960-e gody kak proyavlenia 'neofitial'nogo islama.'" *Islamovedenie* 2:35–43.

Guthman, J. 2003. "Fast Food/Organic Food: Reflexive Tastes and the Making of 'Yuppie Chow.'" *Social and Cultural Geography* 4 (1): 45–58.

Guthman, J. 2008. "Bringing Good Food to Others: Investigating the Subjects of Alternative Food Practice." *Cultural Geographies* 15: 431–447.

Gvosdev, N. 2001/2002. "Managing Pluralism: The Human Rights Challenge of the New Century." *World Policy Journal* 18 (4): 51–58.

Hallaq, W. 2013. *The Impossible State: Islam, Modernity, and Modernity's Moral Predicament*. Columbia University Press.

Hallward, P. 2002. Translator's introduction to *Ethics: An Essay on the Understanding of Evil*, by A. Badiou, vi–li. Verso.

Halverson, J., S. Corman, and H. Goodall. 2011. *Master Narratives of Islamist Extremism*. Palgrave Macmillan.

Handman, C. 2015. *Critical Christianity: Translation and Denominational Conflict in Papua New Guinea*. University of California Press.

Hannerz, U. 1992. *Cultural Complexity: Studies in the Social Organization of Meaning*. Columbia University Press.

Harding, S. 2001. *The Book of Jerry Falwell: Fundamentalist Language and Politics*. Princeton University Press.

Hardt, M., and A. Negri. 2017. *Assembly*. Oxford University Press.

Harvey, D. 2005. *A Brief History of Neoliberalism*. Oxford University Press.

Henig, D. 2012. "'This Is Our Little Hajj': Muslim Holy Sites and Reappropriation of the Sacred Landscape in Contemporary Bosnia." *American Ethnologist* 39 (4): 751–765.

Henig, D. 2020. *Remaking Muslim Lives: Everyday Islam in Postwar Bosnia and Herzegovina*. University of Illinois Press.

Herding, M. 2013. *Inventing the Muslim Cool: Islamic Youth Culture in Western Europe*. Transcript Verlag.

Herzfeld, M. 2005. *Cultural Intimacy: Social Poetics in the Nation-State*. Routledge.

Herzfeld, M. 2021. *Subversive Archaism: Troubling Traditionalists and the Politics of National Heritage*. Duke University Press.

Hirschkind, C. 1996. "Heresy or Hermeneutics: The Case of Nasr Hamid Abu Zayd." *SEHR Stanford Electronic Humanities Review* 5 (1): 463–477.

Hirschkind, C. 2001. "The Ethics of Listening: Cassette-Sermon Audition in Contemporary Egypt." *American Ethnologist* 28 (3): 623–649.

Hirschkind, C. 2006. *The Ethical Soundscape: Cassette Sermons and Islamic Counterpublics*. Columbia University Press.

Hirschkind, C. 2020. *The Feeling of History: Islam, Romanticism, and Andalusia*. University of Chicago Press.

Hobsbawm, E. (1965) 2012. *Primitive Rebels: Studies in Archaic Forms of Social Movement in the 19th and 20th Centuries*. Abacus.

Hoesterey, J. K. 2016. *Rebranding Islam: Piety, Prosperity, and a Self-Help Guru*. Stanford University Press.

The Holy Qur'an. 2001. Translated by Abdullah Yusuf Ali. Wordsworth Edition.

Humphrey, C. 1997. "Exemplars and Rules: Aspects of the Discourse of Moralities in Mongolia." In *The Ethnography of Moralities*, edited by S. Howell, 25–47. Routledge.

Humphrey, C. 2002. *The Unmaking of Soviet Life: Everyday Economies After Socialism*. Cornell University Press.

Humphrey, C. 2017. "Loyalty and Disloyalty as Relational Forms in Russia's Border War with China in the 1960s." *History and Anthropology* 28 (4): 497–514.

Humphrey, C. 2018. "Reassembling Individual Subjects: Events and Decisions in Troubled Times." In *Recovering the Human Subject: Freedom, Creativity and Decision*, edited by J. Laidlaw, B. Bodenhorn, and M. Holbraad, 24–52. Cambridge University Press.

Humphrey, C., M. Marsden, and V. Skvirskaja. 2009. "Cosmopolitanism and the City: Interaction and Coexistence in Bukhara." In *The Other Global City*, edited by S. Mayaram, 202–231. Routledge.

Ibn Fadlan. 2012. *Ibn Fadlan and the Land of Darkness: Arab Travellers in the Far North*. Penguin.

Ibn Khaldun. 1989. *The Muqaddimah: An Introduction to History*. Princeton University Press.

Ike Lenar. 2018. "Borets za traditsionny islam okazalsya sektantom." *Ansar*, August 24, 2018. http://www.ansar.ru/analytics/borec-za-tradicionnyj-islam-okazalsya-sek tantom.

Inayatullah, S., and G. Boxwell, eds. 2003. *Islam, Postmodernism and Other Futures: A Ziauddin Sardar Reader*. Pluto.

Ingold, T. 2017. "Anthropology Contra Ethnography." *HAU: Journal of Ethnographic Theory* 7 (1): 21–26.

Insarov, M. 2003. "O passivnosti proletariata." *Samizdat*, December 22, 2003.

Invisible Committee. 2009. *The Coming Insurrection*. Semiotext(e).

Invisible Committee. 2015. *To Our Friends*. Semiotext(e).

Invisible Committee. 2017. *Now*. Semiotext(e).

Iqbal, B. 2021. "The Messiah and the Jurisconsult: Agamben on the Problem of Law in Sunni Islam." *Journal of Religion* 101 (3): 351–370.

Iskhakov, D. M., ed. 2006. *Tatarskaya natsiya v XXI veke: Problemy razvitiya*. Institut istorii im. Sh Mardzhani Akademii naurk RT.

Iskhakov, D. M. 2010. *Tatarlar: Xalık isäben alu häm säyäsät*. Tatarstan kitap näşriyatı.

Isutkin, A. M., and G. T. Tsaregordtsev. 1977. *Sotsialistichesky obraz zhizni i zdorovie naseleniya*. Meditsina.

Ivanets, O. 2015. *Anarkhiya i khaos: Kriminal'naya revolyutsiya v Rossii 1990 godov. Isto-riya ekspropriatsiyy i razboev*. Common Place.

Jaeggi, R. 2018. *Critique of Forms of Life*. Harvard University Press.

Johnston, J., and S. Bauman. 2010. *Foodies: Democracy and Distinction in the Gourmet Foodscape*. Routledge.

Kagarlitsky, B. 2002. *Russia Under Yeltsin and Putin: Neo-Liberal Autocracy*. Pluto.

Kagarlitsky, B. 2007. *Empire of the Periphery: Russia and the World System*. Pluto.

Kaliszewska, I. 2020. "Halal Landscapes of Dagestani Entrepreneurs in Makhachkala." *Ethnicities* 20 (4): 708–730.

Kamalova, L. 2015. "Muftii RT prinimaet uchastie v Mezhdunarodnoy bogoslovskoy konferentsii v ingushetii." *Tatar-Inform*, May 14, 2014. https://www.tatar-inform .ru/news/muftiy-rt-prinimaet-uchastie-v-mezhdunarodnoy-bogoslovskoy-kon ferentsii-v-ingushetii-454761.

Kapferer, B., and M. Gold, eds. 2018. *Moral Anthropology: A Critique*. Berghahn.

Kappeler, A. 2001. *The Russian Empire: A Multiethnic History*. Routledge.

Karabulatova, I., E. Ermakova, and G. Shiganova. 2014. "Astana the Capital of Kazakh-stan and Astanas in Siberia as a Linguistic-Cultural Aspect of the National Islam of Eurasia." *Terra Sebus* 2014:15–30.

Karimova, L. 2021. "Re-Appropriating Traditional Tatar Educational Culture or Building Their Own: Homeschooling Practices Among Observant Muslims in Tatarstan." In *Cultures of Islam: Vernacular Traditions and Revisionist Interpretations Across Russia*, edited by M. Laruelle and J. Schmoller, 47–59. Central Asia Program, George Washington University.

Karpov, V. 2010. "Desecularization: A Conceptual Framework." *Journal of Church and State* 52 (2): 232–270.

Karpov, V. 2013. "The Social Dynamics of Russia's Desecularisation: A Comparative and Theoretical Perspective." *Religion State and Society* 41 (3): 254–283.

Karpov, V., E. Lisovskaya, and D. Barry. 2012. "Ethnodoxy: How Popular Ideologies Fuse Religious and Ethnic Identities." *Journal for the Scientific Study of Religion* 51 (4): 638–655.

Kaylan, M. 2014. "Kremlin Values: Putin's Strategic Conservativism." *World Affairs* 177 (1): 9–17.

Keane, W. 2006. *Christian Moderns: Freedom and Fetish in the Mission Encounter*. University of California Press.

Kefeli, A. 2014. *Becoming Muslim in Imperial Russia: Conversion, Apostasy, and Literacy*. Cornell University Press.

Kemper, M. 2012. "Mufti Ravil Gainutdin: The Translation of Islam into a Language of Patriotism and Humanism." In *Islamic Authority and the Russian Language: Studies on Texts from European Russia, the North Caucasus and Siberia*, edited by M. Kemper and A. Bustanov, 105–141. Uitgeverj Pegasus.

Kemper, M. 2019. "Religious Political Technology: Damir Mukhetdinov's 'Russian Islam.'" *Religion State and Society* 47 (2): 214–233.

Kemper, M., R. Motika, and S. Reichmut, eds. 2010. *Islamic Education in the Soviet Union and Its Successor States*. Routledge.

Kemper, M., and G. Sibgatullina. 2021. "Liberal Islamic Theology in Conservative Russia: Taufik Ibragim's 'Qur'ānic Humanism.'" *Die Welt des Islams* 62 (2): 279–307.

Khabeer, S. A. 2016. *Muslim Cool: Race, Religion and Hip Hop in the United States*. NYU Press.

Khakimov, R. 2003. *Gde nasha Mekka? Manifest Evroislama*. Magarif.

Khakimov, R. 2004. "Vyzovy vremeni i modernizatsiya islama." *Sova*, February 17, 2004.

Khakimov, R. 2013. "Gde nasha Mekka? Versiya 2.0." *BiznesOnline*, March 11, 2013. https://www.business-gazeta.ru/article/79936.

Khalid, A. 2007. *Islam After Communism: Religion and Politics in Central Asia*. University of California Press.

Khalitov, N. Kh. 2012. *Tatarskaya mechet' i ee arkitektura*. Tatarskoe Knizhnoe Izdatelstvo.

Kharkhordin, O. 1999. *The Collective and the Individual in Russia: A Study of Practices*. University of California Press.

Khatab, S. 2006. *The Political Thought of Sayyid Qutb: The Theory of Jahiliyyah*. Routledge.

Kierkegaard, S. (1843) 1994. *Fear and Trembling and The Book on Adler*. Knopf.

Kierkegaard, S. (1843) 2004. *Either/Or: A Fragment of Life*. Penguin Books.

Kierkegaard, S. (1845) 1988. *Stages on Life's Way*. Princeton University Press.

Kierkegaard, S. (1946) 2016. *A Kierkegaard Anthology*. Edited by R. Bretall. Princeton University Press.

Kishik, D. 2008. *Wittgenstein's Form of Life (To Imagine a Form of Life, I)*. Continuum.

Kishik, D. 2012. *The Power of Life: Agamben and the Coming Politics (To Imagine a Form of Life, II)*. Stanford University Press.

Klein, J. 2009. "Creating Ethical Food Consumers? Promoting Organic Foods in Urban Southwest China." *Social Anthropology* 17 (1): 74–89.

Knight, M. M. 2007. *The Taqwacores*. Telegram.

Knight, M. M. 2012. *William, S. Burroughs vs. The Qur'an*. Soft Skull.

Kormina Zh. 2010. "Avtobusniki: Russian Orthodox Pilgrims' Longing for Authenticity." In *Eastern Christians in Anthropological Perspective*, edited by C. Hann and H. Goltz, 267–286. University of California Press.

Kormina Zh. 2019. *Palomniki: Etnograficheskie ocherki pravoslavnogo nomadizma*. VShE.

Kovalskaya, K. 2024. "(Not-So-) Radicals: Debating Moderate Salafism in Russia." *Problems of Post-Communism* 72 (2): 140–151.

Kravchenko, M. 2018. *Inventing Extremists: The Impact of Russian Anti-Extremism Policies on Freedom of Religion or Belief*. United States Commission on International Religious Freedom.

Kulyutkina, Y. N., and S. V. Tarasova, eds. 1999. *Mirovozpriyatie i obraz zhizni*. Obrazovanie-Kul'tura.

Kuran, T. 2004. *Islam and Mammon: The Economic Predicaments of Islamism*. Princeton University Press.

Kuran, T. 2011. *The Long Divergence: How Islamic Law Held Back the Middle East*. Princeton University Press.

Laclau, E. 2007. *Emancipation(s)*. Verso.

Lagalisse, E. 2019. *Occult Features of Anarchism*. PM Press.

Laidlaw, J. 1996. *Riches and Renunciation: Religion, Economy and Society Among the Jains*. Clarendon.

Laidlaw, J. 2007. "A Well-Disposed Social Anthropologist's Problems with the Cognitive Science of Religion." In *Religion, Anthropology, and Cognitive Science*, edited by H. Whitehouse and J. Laidlaw, 211–246. Carolina Academic Press.

Laidlaw, J. 2014. *The Subject of Virtue: An Anthropology of Ethics and Freedom*. Cambridge University Press.

Laidlaw, J. 2018. "Fault Lines in the Anthropology of Ethics." In *Moral Engines: Exploring the Ethical Drives in Human Life*, edited by C. Mattingly, M. Dyring, M. Louw, and T. Schwarz-Wenter, 174–195. Berghahn.

Lambek, M. 2007. "On Catching Up with Oneself: Learning to Know That One Means What One Does." In *Learning Religion: Anthropological Approaches*, edited by D. Berliner and R. Sarró, 65–81. Berghahn.

Lambek, M. 2010. *Ordinary Ethics: Anthropology, Language, and Action*. Fordham University Press.

Lambek, M. 2012. "Religion and Morality." In *A Companion to Moral Anthropology*, edited by D. Fassin, 341–358. Wiley Blackwell.

Laruelle, M. 2007. "The Struggle for the Soul of Tatar Islam." *Current Trends in Islamist Ideologies* 5:26–39.

Laruelle, M. 2016a. "How Islam Will Change Russia." Jamestown Foundation Paper, September 2016.

Laruelle, M. 2016b. "Russia as an Anti-Liberal European Civilization." In *The New Russian Nationalism: Between Imperial and Ethnic*, edited by P. Kolstø and H. Blakkisrud, 275–297. Edinburgh University Press.

Lauterbach, K. 2017. *Christianity, Wealth, and Spiritual Power in Ghana*. Palgrave MacMillan.

Leach, E. 1966. "Virgin Birth." *Proceedings of the Royal Anthropological Institute of Great Britain and Ireland* 1966: 39–49.

Lindquist, G. 2005. *Conjuring Hope: Magic and Healing in Contemporary Russia*. Berghahn.

Lindquist, G., and S. Coleman. 2008. "Introduction: Against Belief?" *Social Analysis* 52 (1): 1–18.

Lisovskaya, E., and V. Karpov. 2010. "Orthodoxy, Islam, and the Desecularization of Russia's State Schools." *Politics and Religion* 3 (2): 276–302.

Liu, C. X. Cai, and H. Zhu, 2015. "Eating Out Ethically: An Analysis of the Influence of Ethical Food Consumption in a Vegetarian Restaurant in Guangzhou, China." *Geographical Review* 105 (4): 551–565.

Long, N., and H. Moore, eds. 2013. *The Social Life of Achievement*. Berghahn.

Louw, M. 2018. "Haunting as Moral Engine: Ethical Striving and Moral Aporias Among Sufis in Uzbekistan." In *Moral Engines: Exploring the Ethical Drives in Human Life*, edited by C. Mattingly et al., 83–99. Berghahn.

Luehrmann, S. 2011. *Secularism Soviet Style: Teaching Atheism and Religion in a Volga Republic*. Indiana University Press.

Luetchford. P. 2016. "Ethical Consumption: The Moralities and Politics of Food." In *The Handbook of Food and Anthropology*, edited by J. Klein and J. L. Watson, 387–405. Bloomsbury.

Luhrmann, T. 1989. *Persuasions of the Witches' Craft: Ritual Magic in Contemporary England*. Harvard University Press.

Luhrmann, T. 2012. *When God Talks Back: Understanding the American Evangelical Relationship with God*. Vintage Books.

Lukes, S. 1982. "Relativism in Its Place." In *Rationality and Relativism*, edited by M. Hollis and S. Lukes, 261–305. MIT Press.

Lunde, P., and C. Stone. 2012. Introduction to *Ibn Fadlan and the Land of Darkness: Arab Travellers in the Far North*, xiii–xxxiii. Penguin.

Lynteris, C. 2021. *Human Extinction and the Pandemic Imaginary*. Routledge.

Macarthur, D. 2014. "Cavell on Skepticism and the Importance of Not-Knowing." *Conversations* 2:2–23.

MacIntyre, A. (1981) 2007. *After Virtue: A Study in Moral Theory*. University of Notre Dame Press.

Maevsky, K. 2014. "Letter from: Halal Haircuts in the Capital of Tatarstan." *Calvert Journal*, September 23, 2014.

Mahmood, S. 2001. "Feminist Theory, Embodiment, and the Docile Agent: Some Reflections on the Egyptian Islamic Revival." *Cultural Anthropology* 16 (2): 202–236.

Mahmood, S. (2005) 2012. *Politics of Piety: The Islamic Revival and the Feminist Subject*. Princeton University Press.

Malashenko, A., and A. Starostin. 2015. *The Rise of Nontraditional Islam in the Urals*. Carnegie Moscow Centre.

Mandel, R. 1996. "A Place of Their Own: Contesting Spaces and Defining Places in Berlin's Migrant Community." In *Making Muslim Space in North America and Europe*, edited by B. D. Metcalf, 147–166. University of California Press.

Maqsood, A. 2014. "Buying Modern: Muslim Subjectivity, the West and Patterns of Islamic Consumption in Lahore, Pakistan." *Cultural Studies* 28 (1): 84–107.

Marcuse, H. (1964) 1972. *One Dimensional Man*. Abacus.

Marsden, M. 2005. *Living Islam: Muslim Religious Experience in Pakistan's North-West Frontier*. Cambridge University Press.

Marsden, M. 2016. *Trading Worlds: Afghan Merchants Across Modern Frontiers*. Oxford University Press.

Marsden, M., and K. Retsikas, eds. 2013. *Articulating Islam: Anthropological Approaches to Muslim Worlds*. Springer.

Martens, S. 2014. "Muslim Charity in a Non-Muslim Society: The Case of Switzerland." *Journal of Muslims in Europe* 3 (1): 94–116.

Matsuzato, K., and F. Sawae. 2010. "Rebuilding a Confessional State: Islamic Ecclesiology in Turkey, Russia and China." *Religion State and Society* 38 (4): 331–360.

Mattingly, C. 2010. *The Paradox of Hope: Journeys Through a Clinical Borderland*. California University Press.

Matveev, I. 2016. "Russia, Inc." *OpenDemocracy*, March 16, 2016.

Mazzarella, W. 2017. *The Mana of Mass Society*. Chicago University Press.

McAllister, C., and V. Napolitano. 2021. "Political Theology/Theopolitics: The Thresholds and Vulnerabilities of Sovereignty." *Annual Review of Anthropology* 50:109–124.

McBrien, J. 2006. "Listening to the Wedding Speaker: Discussing Religion and Culture in Southern Kyrgyzstan." *Central Asian Survey* 25 (3): 341–357.

McBrien, J. 2015. "Watching Clone: Brazilian Soap Operas and Muslimness in Kyrgyzstan." *Journal of Objects, Art and Belief* 8 (3): 374–396.

McBrien, J. 2017. *From Belonging to Belief: Modern Secularisms and the Construction of Religion in Kyrgyzstan*. University of Pittsburgh Press.

McCarthy, L. 2020. "Managed Civil Society and Police Oversight in Russia: Regional Police–Public Councils." *Europe-Asia Studies* 72 (9): 1498–1522.

McClure, K. M. 1990. "Difference, Diversity, and the Limits of Toleration." *Political Theory* 18 (3): 361–391.

McGown, R. 1999. *Muslims in the Diaspora: The Somali Communities of London and Toronto*. University of Toronto Press.

McLennan, G. 2015. "Is Secularism History?" *Thesis Eleven* 128 (1): 126–140.

Merzlikin, P. 2019. "Crushing the Anarchists." *Meduza*, April 18, 2019. https://meduza.io/en/feature/2019/04/19/crushing-the-anarchists.

Meyer, B. 1999. *Translating the Devil: Religion and Modernity Among the Ewe in Ghana*. Edinburgh University Press.

Meyer, J. 2014. *Turks Across Empires: Marketing Muslim Identity in the Russian-Ottoman Borderlands, 1856–1914*. Oxford University Press.

Millar, K. 2014. "The Precarious Present: Wageless Labor and Disrupted Life in Rio de Janeiro, Brazil." *Cultural Anthropology* 29 (1): 32–53.

Minnullin, I. 2014. "Sunflower and Moon Crescent: Soviet and Post-Soviet Islamic Revival in a Tatar Village of Mordovia." In *Allah's Kolkhozes: Migration, De-Stalinisation, Privatisation and the New Muslim Congregations in the Soviet Realm (1950s–2000s)*, edited by S. A. Dudoignon and C. Noack, 421–446. Klaus Schwarz.

Miri, D., and S. Byrd, eds. 2018. *Ali Shariati and the Future of Social Theory: Religion, Revolution, and the Role of the Intellectual*. Brill.

Mittermaier, A. 2012. "Dreams from Elsewhere: Muslim Subjectivities Beyond the Trope of Self-Cultivation." *Journal of the Royal Anthropological Institute* 18:247–265.

Mittermaier, A. 2013. "Trading with God: Islam, Calculation, Excess." In *A Companion to the Anthropology of Religion*, edited by J. Boddy and M. Lambek, 274–398. Wiley Blackwell.

Moad, E. 2022. "Islamic Wittgensteinian Fideism?" *European Journal of Analytic Philosophy* 18 (2): 5–28.

Montgomery, D. 2016. *Practicing Islam: Knowledge, Experience, and Social Navigation in Kyrgyzstan*. University of Pittsburgh Press.

Montgomery, D. W., and J. Heathershaw. 2016. "Islam, Secularism and Danger: A Reconsideration of the Link Between Religiosity, Radicalism and Rebellion in Central Asia." *Religion, State and Society* 44 (3): 192–218.

Mouffe, C. 2005. *On the Political*. Routledge.

Muggleton, D. 2000. *Inside Subculture: The Postmodern Meaning of Style*. Bloomsbury.

Mukhamedov, A. R. 2011. "Parallelnye miry: 'Soblyudayushchie' i 'nesoblyudayush-chie.'" *Ansar*, August 19, 2011.

Mukhamedzhanov, A. 2014. "Avliya: Sovsem ne 'svyatie.'" *Islam Segodnya*, December 26, 2014. https://islam-today.ru/blogi/ildar-muhamedzanov/avlia-sovsem-ne-svatye/.

Mukhametrakhimov, A. 2020. "Kamil' Samigullin: 'Gde segodnya mozhno pogovorit' na rodnom yazyke? Eto mecheti.'" *Duslyk*, June 11, 2020. https://tatar-duslyk.ru/kamil-samigullin-gde-segodnya-mozhno-pogovorit-na-rodnom-yazyke-eto-mecheti/.

Mukhametshin, R., ed. 2010. *Islam i musul'manskaya kul'tura v srednem Povolzhe: Istoria I sovremennost*. Akademia Nauk RT.

Mulhall, S. 2005. *Philosophical Myths of the Fall*. Princeton University Press.

Müller, D. 2019. "Appropriating and Contesting 'Traditional Islam': Central Asian Students at the Russian Islamic University in Tatarstan." *Central Asian Survey* 38 (3): 400–416.

Nasr, S. V. R. 1996. *Mawdudi and the Making of Islamic Revivalism*. Oxford University Press.

Nazarova, G. 2016. "Kamil khazrat Samigullin: 'V Tatarstane pyatnichnye propovedy dolzhny byt' tol'ko na tatarskom yazyke.'" *Tatar-Inform*, August 11, 2016. https://

www.tatar-inform.ru/news/kamil-hazrat-samigullin-v-tatarstane-pyatnichnye-pro
povedi-dolzhny-byt-tolko-na-tatarskom-yazyke.

Needham, R. 1972. *Belief, Language, and Experience*. Blackwell.

Nefliasheva, N. 2018. "Kak zhivult v Turtsii 'novie mukhadzhiri' iz Rossii: Migratsiya
rossiiskikh musul'man v 2000-e gg." *Aziya i Afrika Segodnya* 8 (733): 27–34.

Negri, A. 1991. *Marx Beyond Marx: Lessons on the Grundrisse*. Autonomedia.

Newman, S. 2015. *Postanarchism*. Wiley.

Nielsen, K., and D. Z. Phillips. 2005. *Wittgensteinian Fideism?* SCM.

Norris, C. 2009. *Badiou's "Being and Event": A Reader's Guide*. Bloomsbury.

Olidor, J. 2015. "The Politics of 'Quietist' Salafism." In *Project on U.S. Relations with the
Islamic World*, 18. Brookings.

Ong, A. 2006. *Neoliberalism as Exception: Mutations in Citizenship and Sovereignty*.
Duke University Press.

Orlando, G. 2012. "Critical Consumption in Palermo: Imagined Society, Class and
Fractured Locality." In *Ethical Consumption: Social Value and Economic Practice*,
edited by J. G. Carrier and P. Luetchford, 203–233. Berghahn.

Orsi, R. (1985) 2002. *The Madonna of 115th Street: Faith and Community in Italian
Harlem*. Yale University Press.

Ortner, S. 2016. "Dark Anthropology and Its Others: Theory Since the Eighties." *Hau:
Journal of Ethnographic Theory* 5:89–92.

Osella, F. 2017. "'A Poor Muslim Cannot Be a Good Muslim': Islam, Charitable Giving, and Market Logic in Sri Lanka." In *Religion and the Morality of the Market: Anthropological Perspectives*, edited by F. Osella and D. Rudnyckyj, 217–239.
Cambridge University Press.

Osella, F., and C. Osella. 2009. "Muslim Entrepreneurs in Public Life Between India and
the Gulf: Making Good and Doing Good." *Journal of the Royal Anthropological
Institute* 15: S202–S221.

Osella, F., and D. Rudnyckyj. 2017. "Introduction: Assembling Market and Religious
Moralities." In *Religion and the Morality of the Market*, edited by D. Rudnyckyj
and F. Osella, 1–28. Cambridge University Press.

Ovsyannikova, A. 2016. "Is Neoliberalism Applicable to Russia? A Response to Ilya
Matveev." *OpenDemocracy*, May 20, 2016.

Ozyurek, E. 2006. *Nostalgia for the Modern: State Secularism and Everyday Politics in
Turkey*. Duke University Press.

Palmié, S. 2018. "Translation Is Not Explanation: Remarks on the Intellectual History
and Context of Wittgenstein's Remarks on Frazer." In *The Mythology in Our Language: Remarks on Frazer's Golden Bough*, by L. Wittgenstein, 1–28. HAU Books.

Pandolfo, S. 2018. *Knot of the Soul: Madness, Psychoanalysis, Islam*. University of Chicago Press.

Parkin, R. 2003. *Louis Dumont and Hierarchical Opposition*. Berghahn.

Parsons, T. (1964) 2023. Introduction to *The Sociology of Religion*, by M. Weber, xxix–
lxxvii. Beacon.

Pedersen, M. 2011. *Not Quite Shamans: Spirit Worlds and Political Lives in Northern
Mongolia*. Cornell University Press.

Pelkmans, M. 2006. *Defending the Border: Identity, Religion, and Modernity in the
Republic of Georgia*. Cornell University Press.

Pelkmans, M., ed. 2009. *Conversion After Socialism: Disruptions, Modernisms and Technologies of Faith in the Former Soviet Union*. Berghahn.

Pelkmans, M. 2017. *Fragile Convictions: Changing Ideological Landscapes in Urban Kyrgyzstan*. Cornell University Press.

Pellicani, L. 1994. *The Genesis of Capitalism and the Origin of Modernity*. Telos.

Perepechenova, K. 2020. "Upravlenie obrazovaniya Kazani uladilo konflikt s zapretom khidzhaba v shkole." *Tatar-Inform*, September 23, 2020. https://www.tatar-inform.ru/news/upravlenie-obrazovaniya-kazani-uladilo-konflikt-s-zapretom-hidzhaba-v-shkole.

Pina-Cabral, J. 2010. "The Door in the Middle: Six Conditions for Anthropology." In *Culture Wars: Context, Models and Anthropologists' Accounts*, edited by D. James, E. Plaice, and C. Toren, 152–169. Berghahn.

Pitkin, H. 1972. *Wittgenstein and Justice*. University of California Press.

Poe, M. 2003. *The Russian Moment in World History*. Princeton University Press.

Pouillon, J. (1982) 2016. "Remarks on the Verb 'To Believe.'" *Hau: Journal of Ethnographic Theory* 6 (3): 485–492.

Privratsky, B. 2001. *Muslim Turkistan: Kazak Religion and Collective Memory*. Curzon.

Pryce, P. 2013. "Putin's Third Term: The Triumph of Eurasianism?" *Romanian Journal of European Affairs* 13 (1): 25–43.

Qadhi, A. A. Y. 2002. *15 Ways to Increase Your Earnings from the Quran and Sunnah*. Al-Hidaayah.

Rabinovich, T. 2017. "Living the Good Life: Muslim Women's Magazines in Contemporary Russia." *European Journal of Cultural Studies* 20 (2): 199–214.

Rabinow, P. 2003. *Anthropos Today: Reflections on Modern Equipment*. Princeton University Press.

Ragozina, S. 2018. "Zashchishchaya 'traditsionny' islama ot 'radikal'nogo': Diskurs islamofobii v Rossiiskikh SMI." *Gosudarstvo, religiya, tserkov' v Rossii i za rubezhom* 36 (2): 272–299.

Ragozina, S. 2020. "Official Discourse on Islam and Islamic Discourse in Contemporary Russia: Stereotypes and Intertextuality." In *The Concept of Traditional Islam in Modern Islamic Discourse in Russia*, edited by R. Bekkin, 115–134. CNS.

Rajaee, F. 1999. "A Thermidor of 'Islamic Yuppies'? Conflict and Compromise in Iran's Politics." *Middle East Journal* 53 (2): 217–231.

Rakhimov, R. 2006. *Astana v istorii sibirskikh tatar: Mavzolei pervikh islamiskih missionerov kak pamyatniki istoriko-kul'turnogo naslediya*. Gosudarstvennoe ucherezhdenie kul'tury tyumenskoy oblasti.

Rancière, J. 1994. *The Names of History: On the Poetics of Knowledge*. Minnesota University Press.

Rappaport, R. 1999. *Ritual and Religion in the Making of Humanity*. Cambridge University Press.

Rasanayagam, J. 2011. *Islam in Post-Soviet Uzbekistan: The Morality of Experience*. Cambridge University Press.

Rassool, G. H. 2019. *Evil Eye, Jinn Possession, and Mental Health Issues: An Islamic Perspective*. Routledge.

Reinhardt, B. 2015. "A Christian Plane of Immanence? Contrapuntal Reflections on Deleuze and Pentecostal Spirituality." *HAU: Journal of Ethnographic Theory* 5 (1): 406–436.

Reinhardt, B. 2016. "'Don't Make It a Doctrine': Material Religion, Transcendence, Critique." *Anthropological Theory* 16 (1): 75–97.

Religiya Segodnya. 2020. "Evroislam v Tatarstane ukhodit na pokoy." *Religiya Segodnya*, May 29, 2020. https://reltoday.com/news/evroislam-v-tatarstane-uhodit-na-pokoj/.

Retsikas, K. 2014. "Reconceptualising Zakat in Indonesia: Worship, Philanthropy and Rights." *Indonesia and the Malay World* 42 (124): 337–357.

Retsikas, K. 2018. "Multiplication Through Division: Value, Time, and Prosperity in Indonesia." *HAU: Journal of Ethnographic Theory* 8 (3): 656–671.

RFE. 2020. "Ultraconservative Russian Priest Arrested amid Convent Raid." *Radio Free Europe*, December 29, 2020. https://www.rferl.org/a/ultraconservative-russian-priest-arrested-amid-convent-raid/31024660.html.

Robbins, J. 2004. *Becoming Sinners: Christianity and Moral Torment in a Papua New Guinea Society*. University of California Press.

Robbins, J. 2007a. "Continuity Thinking and the Problem of Christian Culture: Belief, Time, and the Anthropology of Christianity." *Current Anthropology* 48 (1): 5–38.

Robbins, J. 2007b. "Between Reproduction and Freedom: Morality, Value, and Radical Cultural Change." *Ethnos* 72 (3): 293–314.

Robbins, J. 2013a. "Beyond the Suffering Subject: Toward an Anthropology of the Good." *Journal of the Royal Anthropological Institute* 19 (3): 447–462.

Robbins, J. 2013b. "Monism, Pluralism, and the Structure of Value Relations: A Dumontian Contribution to the Contemporary Study of Value." *HAU Journal of Ethnographic Theory* 3 (1): 99–115.

Robbins, J. 2020. *Theology and the Anthropology of Christian Life*. Oxford University Press.

Rodinson, M. 1978. *Islam and Capitalism*. Pantheon Books.

Ro'i, Y. 1984. "The Task of Creating the New Soviet Man: 'Atheistic Propaganda' in the Soviet Muslim Areas." *Soviet Studies* 36 (1): 26–44.

Rorlich, A.-A. 1986. *The Volga Tatars: A Profile in National Resilience*. Hoover Institution Press.

Rose, N. (1989) 1999. *Governing the Soul: The Shaping of the Private Self*. Free Association Books.

Rose, N., and P. Miller. 2008. *Governing the Present: Administering Economic, Social and Personal Life*. Main Press.

Ross, D. 2020. *Tatar Empire: Kazan's Muslims and the Making of Imperial Russia*. Indiana University Press.

Rouhani, F. 2003. "'Islamic Yuppies'? State Rescaling, Citizenship, and Public Opinion Formation in Tehran, Iran." *Urban Geography* 24 (2): 169–182.

Rousselle, D. 2012. *After Post-Anarchism*. Repartree.

Rubtsova, E. 2013. "V Tatarstane razgoraetsya skandal iz-za khidzhabov." *MKRU Kazan*, April 10, 2013. https://kazan.mk.ru/articles/2013/04/10/839563-v-tatarstane-razgoraetsya-skandal-izza-hidzhabov.html.

Rudnyckyj, D. 2009. "Spiritual Economies: Islam and Neoliberalism in Contemporary Indonesia." *Cultural Anthropology* 24 (1): 104–141.

Rudnyckyj, D. 2010. *Spiritual Economies: Islam, Globalization, and the Afterlife of Development*. Cornell University Press.

Rudnyckyj, D. 2019. *Beyond Debt: Islamic Experiments in Global Finance*. University of Chicago Press.

Ruel, M. (1982) 2005. "Christians as Believers." In *Ritual and Religious Belief: A Reader*, edited by G. Harvey, 242–265. Routledge.

Rutland, P. 2013. "Neoliberalism in Russia." *Review of International Political Economy* 20:1–52.

Sagitova, L. 2014. "Traditionalism, Modernism and Globalisation Among the Volga Muslims: The Case of Sredniaia Eliuzan." In *Allah's Kolkhozes: Migration, De-Stalinisation, Privatisation and the New Muslim Congregations in the Soviet Realm (1950s–2000s)*, edited by S. A. Dudoignon and C. Noack, 454–493. Klaus Schwarz.

Sagramoso, D., and A. Yarlykapov. 2013. "Caucasian Crescent: Russia's Islamic Policies and Its Responses to Radicalization." In *The Fire Below: How the Caucasus Shaped Russia*, edited by R. Ware, 51–98. Bloomsbury.

Salamandra, C. 2004. *A New Old Damascus: Authenticity and Distinction in Urban Syria*. Indiana University Press.

Salazar, C., and J. Bestard, eds. 2015. *Religion and Science as Forms of Life: Anthropological Insights into Reason and Unreason*. Berghahn Books.

Sal'vadore, D. 2014. "Turtsiya stanovitsya priyutom dlya rossiiskikh musul'man." *GoloSIslama*, September 24, 2014. https://golosislama.com/news.php?id=25003.

Şäräfetdin, M. 2009. *Här avıruğa şifa birüçe doğa*. Şamil mäçete.

Şäräfetdin, M. 2014. *Bik taesirle öşkerü doğası*. Şamil mäçete.

Sartori, P. 2016. "Ijtihād in Bukhara: Central Asian Jadidism and Local Genealogies of Cultural Change." *Journal of the Economic and Social History of the Orient* 59:1–2.

Schielke, S. 2015a. *Egypt in the Future Tense: Hope, Frustration and Ambivalence Before and After 2011*. Indiana University Press.

Schielke, S. 2015b. "Living with Unresolved Differences: A Reply to Fadil and Fernando." *HAU: Journal of Ethnographic Theory* 5: 89–92.

Schmoller, J. 2020. "The Talking Dead: Everyday Muslim Practice in Russia." *Nationalities Paper* 48 (6): 1036–1051.

Schmoller, J., and M. Laruelle, 2025. "What Does the Mufti Say? Internal and Public Debates about Islam in Russia." *Problems of Post-Communism* 72 (2): 113–118.

Scott, J. C. 1976. *The Moral Economy of the Peasant: Rebellion and Subsistence in Southeast Asia*. Yale University Press.

Scott J. C. 1986. *Weapons of the Weak*. Yale University Press.

Scott, J. C. 2008. *Seeing Like a State: How Certain Schemes to Improve the Human Condition Have Failed*. Yale University Press.

Secor, A. 2007. Afterword to *Women, Religion, and Space: Global Perspectives on Gender and Faith*, edited by K. M. Morin and J. K. Guelke, 148–158. Syracuse University Press.

Seleznev, A., and I. Selezneva, 2019. "Kontsept astana v evraziiskom kul'turnom-istoricheskom prostranstve." *Istoriya* 10 (1), https://sochum.ru/s207987840002382-9-1/.

Seligman, A., R. Weller, M. Puett, and B. Simon. 2008. *Ritual and Its Consequences: An Essay on the Limits of Sincerity*. Oxford University Press.

Severi, C. 2007. "Learning to Believe: A Preliminary Approach." In *Learning Religion: Anthropological Approaches*, edited by D. Berliner and R. Sarró, 21–30. Berghahn.

Shagaviev, D. 2020. "The Ahl al-Sunnah wa-l-Jama'ah and the Grozny Fatwa." In *The Concept of Traditional Islam in Modern Islamic Discourse in Russia, Sarajevo*, edited by R. Bekkin, 57–86. CNS.

Sharafutdinova, G. 2014. "The Pussy Riot Affair and Putin's Démarche from Sovereign Democracy to Sovereign Morality." *Nationalities Papers* 42 (4): 615–621.

Shariati, A. 1979. *Red Shiism*. Shariati Foundation and Hamdami.

Shariati, A. 2002. *Where Shall We Begin? Enlightened Thinkers and the Revolutionary Society*. Citizens International.

Shariati, A. (1979) 2011. *School of Thought and Action*. Abjad.

Shirazi, N. 2006. *180 Questions. Enquiries About Islam*. Vol. 2, *Various Issues*. World Federation of KSIMC.

Shnirelman, V. 1996. *Who Gets the Past? Competition for Ancestors Among Non-Russian Intellectuals in Russia*. John Hopkins University Press.

Shterin, M., and D. Dubrovsky. 2019. "Academic Expertise and Anti-Extremism Litigation in Russia: Focusing on Minority Religions." *Soviet and Post-Soviet Review* 46 (2): 211–236.

Sibgatullina, G. 2025. "The Muftis and the Myths: Constructing the Russian 'Church for Islam.'" *Problems of Post-Communism*. 72 (2): 119–130.

Sibgatullina, G., and M. Kemper. 2017. "Between Salafism and Eurasianism: Geidar Dzhemal and the Global Islamic Revolution in Russia." *Islam and Christian -Muslim Relations* 28 (2): 219–236.

Sibgatullina, G., and M. Kemper. 2019. "The Imperial Paradox: Islamic Eurasianism in Contemporary Russia." In *Resignification of Borders: Eurasianism and the Russian World*, edited by N. Friess and K. Kaminskij, 97–124. Frank and Timme.

Sidło, K., and M. Benussi. 2020. "Criticism or Compliance? The Syrian Crisis Viewed by Russia's Muslims and MENA Christians." In *Russia in the Middle East and North Africa: Continuity and Change*, edited by C. Lovotti, E. Ambrosetti, C. Hartwell, and A. Chmielewska, 127–154. Routledge.

Slezkine, Y. 1994. "The URSS as a Communal Apartment, or How a Socialist State Promoted Ethnic Particularism." *Slavic Review* 53 (2): 414–452.

Sloterdijk, P. 2009. *You Must Change Your Life*. Polity.

Smith, J. 2013. Form-of-Life: From Politics to Aesthetics (and Back)." *Nordic Journal of Aesthetics* 23 (44–45): 50–67.

Soltangaliev, M. 1998. *Saylanma xezmätlär / Izbrannye Trudy*. Ğasır.

Sørensen A. 2018. *Capitalism, Alienation and Critique: Studies in Economy and Dialectics (Dialectics, Deontology and Democracy, Vol. I)*. Brill.

Sperber, D. 2009. "Culturally Transmitted Misbeliefs." *Behavioural and Brain Sciences* 32:534–535.

Starr, M. 2009. "The Social Economics of Ethical Consumption: Theoretical Considerations and Empirical Evidence." *Journal of Behavioral and Experimental Economics* 38 (6): 916–925.

Stavrakakis, Y. 1999. *Lacan and the Political*. Taylor and Francis.

Stavrakakis, Y. 2000. *The Lacanian Left: Psychoanalysis, Theory, Politics*. Edinburgh University Press.

Stephenson, S. 2015. *Gangs of Russia: From the Streets to the Corridors of Power*. Cornell University Press.

Stewart, F. 2019. *Punk Rock Is My Religion: Straight Edge Punk and "Religious" Identity*. Routledge.

Strathern, M. 1987. "An Awkward Relationship: The Case of Anthropology and Feminism." *Signs* 12 (2): 276–292.

Sulakshin, S. S., V. E. Bagdasaryan, M. V. Vilisov, Y. A. Zachesova, N. K. Pak, O. A. Seredinka, and A. N. Chirva, eds. 2006. *Natsional'naya identichnost' Rossii I demograpfichesky Krizis: Marerialy Vserossiisky nauchnoy konferentsii*. Nauchny Ekspert.

Suleiman, Y. 2013. *Narratives of Conversion to Islam in Britain: Female Perspectives*. Centre of Islamic Studies.

Suleiman, Y. 2015. *Narrative of Conversion to Islam in Britain: Male Perspectives*. Centre of Islamic Studies.

Suleymanova, D. 2009. "Tatar Groups in Vkontakte: The Interplay Between Ethnic and Virtual Identities on Social Networking Sites." *Digital Icons: Studies in Russian, Eurasian and Central European New Media* 1 (2): 37–55.

Sultanova, R. 2011. *From Shamanism to Sufism: Women, Islam and Culture in Central Asia*. I. B. Tauris.

Sunier, T. 2012. "Beyond the domestication of Islam in Europe: A reflection on past and future research on Islam in European societies." *Journal of Muslims in Europe* 1 (2): 189–208.

Suny, R. G., and T. Martin, eds. 2001. *A State of Nations: Empire and Nation-Making in the Age of Lenin and Stalin*. Oxford University Press.

Tahir-ul-Qadri, M. 2007. *Islamic Concept of Knowledge*. Minhaj-ul-Quran.

Taneja, A. 2017. *Jinnealogy: Time, Islam, and Ecological Thought in the Medieval Ruins of Delhi*. Stanford University Press.

Tarlo, E. 2010. *Visibly Muslim: Fashion, Politics, Faith*. Bloomsbury.

Tatar-Inform. 2019. "Muftii Tatarstana v Mekke vstretilsya s glavoy Vsemirnoy islamskoy ligi." *Tatar-Inform*, May 28, 2019. https://www.tatar-inform.ru/news/muftiy -tatarstana-v-mekke-vstretilsya-s-glavoy-vsemirnoy-islamskoy-ligi.

Taylor, C. 1989. *Sources of the Self: The Making of the Modern Identity*. Harvard University Press.

Taylor, C. 1995. *Philosophical Arguments*. Harvard University Press.

Tayob, S. 2017. "Islam as a Lived Tradition: Ethical Constellations of Muslim Food Practice in Mumbai." PhD diss, Utrecht University.

Tee, C. 2016. *The Gülen Movement in Turkey: The Politics of Islam and Modernity*. I. B. Tauris.

Thompson, E. P. 1967. "Time, Work-Discipline, and Industrial Capitalism." *Past and Present* 38:56–97.

Thompson, E. P. 1971. "The Moral Economy of the English Crowd in the Eighteenth Century." *Past and Present* 50 (1): 76–136.

Thompson, E. P. 1991. "The Moral Economy Reviewed." In *Customs in Commons*, 259–351. Penguin.

Tiqqun. 2010. *Introduction to Civil War*. Semiotext(e).

Tiqqun. 2011a. *Conscious Organ of the Imaginary Party/Exercises in Critical Metaphysics*. samizdat.

Tiqqun. 2011b. *This Is Not a Program*. Semiotext(e).

Tiqqun. 2012. *Theory of Bloom*. Creative Commons.

Tobin, S. 2016. *Everyday Piety: Islam and Economy in Jordan*. Cornell University Press.

Todorova, M., and Z. Gille, eds. 2012. *Post-Communist Nostalgia*. Berghahn.

Tolstikh, V. I. 1975. *Obraz zhizni: Poniate, real'nost' problemy*. PolitLit.

Tomba, M. 2013. *Marx's Temporalities*. Brill.

Tonner, P. 2017. "Wittgenstein on Forms of Life: A Short Introduction." *E-Logos Electronic Journal for Philosophy* 24 (1): 13–18.

Toshchenko Zh. 2012. "Mankurtizm kak forma istoricheskogo bezpamyatstva." In *Planarnoe zasedanie "dialog kul'tur i partnerstvo tsivilisatsii: Stanovlenie global'noy kul'tury*, 224–231. RAN.

Treiber, G., and T. Christiaens. 2021. "Introduction: Italian Theory and the Problem of Potentiality." *Italian Studies* 76 (2): 121–127.

Tripp, C. 2006. *Islam and the Moral Economy: The Challenge of Capitalism*. Cambridge University Press.

Troccoli, G. 2022. "The Ambivalence of Autonomy: Skills, Trust, Tactics, and Status on a Construction Site in Belize." *Anthropology of Work Review* 43 (1): 38–48.

Tuna, M. 2016. *Imperial Russia's Muslims: Islam, Empire, and European Modernity, 1788–1917*. Cambridge University Press.

Turoma, S., and K. Aitamurto. 2016. "Renegotiating Patriotic and Religious Identities in the Post-Soviet and Post-Secular Russia." *Transcultural Studies* 12 (1): 1–14.

Tylor E. B. 1871. *Primitive Culture: Researches into the Development of Mythology, Philosophy, Religion, Art, and Custom*. Vol. I. John Murray.

Urazmanova, R. K., G. F. Gabdrakhmanova, F. K. Zavgarova, and A. R. Mukhametzyanova. 2014. *Musul'mansky kul't svyatikh u tatar: Obrazy i smisly*. Institut Istorii im. Sh. Marzhani/Akademii Nauk Respubliki Tatarstan.

Usmanova, D., I. Minnullin, and R. Mukhametshin. 2010. "Islam and Religious Education in the 1920–1930s." In *Islamic Education in the Soviet Union and Its Successor States*, edited by M. Kemper, R. Motika, and S. Reichmut, 21–66. Routledge.

Van der Veer, P. 1996. *Conversion to Modernities: The Globalization of Christianity*. Routledge.

Vasileva, N. 2019. "Strasti po khidzhabu: V Mordovii—nelzya, a v Tatarstane—mozhno?" *Vechernyaya Kazan'*, April 9, 2019. https://www.evening-kazan.ru/articles/strasti -po-hidzhabu-v-mordovii-nelzya-a-v-tatarstane-mozhno.html.

Veblen, T. (1899) 2008. *The Theory of the Leisure Class*. Dover.

Verkhovsky, A. 2010. "Russian Approaches to Radicalism and "'Extremism' as Applied to Nationalism and Religion." In *Russia and Islam: State, Society and Radicalism*, edited by R. Dannreuther and L. March, 26–43. Routledge.

Virno, P., and M. Hardt. 2006. *Radical Thought in Italy: A Potential Politics*. Minnesota University Press.

Volkov, V. 2002. *Violent Entrepreneurs: The Use of Force in the Making of Russian Capitalism*. Cornell University Press.

Vovina, O. 2006. "Islam and the Creation of Sacred Space: The Mishar Tatars in Chuvashia." *Religion State and Society* 34 (3): 255–269.

Wanner, C. 2020. "An Affective Atmosphere of Religiosity: Animated Places, Public Spaces, and the Politics of Attachment in Ukraine and Beyond." *Comparative Studies in Society and History* 62 (1): 68–105.

Warhola, J. 2007. "Religion and Politics Under the Putin Administration: Accommodation and Confrontation Within 'Managed Pluralism.'" *Journal of Church and State* 49 (1): 75–95.

Weber, M. (1905) 2002. *The Protestant Ethic and the Spirit of Capitalism: And Other Writings*. Penguin.

Weber, M. 1946. *From Max Weber: Essays in Sociology*. Oxford University Press.

Weber, M. (1964) 2023. *The Sociology of Religion*. Beacon.

Whitehouse, H., and J. Laidlaw, eds. 2007. *Religion, Anthropology, and Cognitive Science*. Carolina Academic Press.

Wiegele, K. 2007. *Investing in Miracles: El Shaddai and the Transformation of Popular Catholicism in the Philippines*. University of Hawaii Press.

Wiktorowicz, Q. 2006. "Anatomy of the Salafi Movement." *Studies in Conflict and Terrorism* 29:207–239.

Wilson, P. L. 1988. *Scandal: Essays in Islamic Heresy*. Autonomedia.

Winch, P. (1958) 2003. *The Idea of a Social Science and Its Relation to Philosophy*. Routledge.

Wittgenstein, L. 1965. "A Lecture on Ethics." *Philosophical Review* 74 (1): 3–12.

Wittgenstein, L. 1972. *On Certainty*. Harper and Row.

Wittgenstein, L. (1953) 1986. *Philosophical Investigations*. Blackwell.

Wittgenstein, L. (1931) 2018. *The Mythology in Our Language: Remarks on Frazer's Golden Bough*. HAU Books.

Yadgar, Y. 2015. "Traditionism." *Cogent Social Science* 1:106–134.

Yakupov, V. 2011. *Islam segodnya*. Iman.

Yakupova, V. 2000. *100 istoriy o suverenitete*. Idel.

Yarlykapov, A. 2010. "'Folk Islam' and Muslim Youth of the Central and Northwest Caucasus." In *Religion and Politics in Russia: A Reader*, edited by M. Mandelstam Balzer, 109–129. Routledge.

Yarlykapov, A. 2017. "Islam i traditsiya na Severnom Kavkaze." In *Etnicheskoe i religioznoe mnogobraziye Rossii*, edited by V. A. Tishkov and V. V. Stepanov, 301–315. Rossiiskaya Akademiya Nauk.

Yemelianova, G., ed. 2010. *Radical Islam in the Former Soviet Union*. Routledge.

Youzhuang, G. 2012. "Miracles and Revolutionary Reversals: Terry Eagleton's Theological Turn." *Literature and Theology* 26 (3): 323–337.

Yurchak, A. 2002. "Entrepreneurial Governmentality in Postsocialist Russia: A Cultural Investigation of Business Practices." In *The New Entrepreneurs of Europe and Asia*, edited by V. E. Bonnell and T. B. Gold, 278–323. M. E. Sharpe.

Yurchak, A. 2003. "Russian Neoliberal: The Entrepreneurial Ethic and the Spirit of New Careerism." *Russian Review* 62 (1): 72–90.

Yurchak, A. 2005. *Everything Was Forever, Until It Was No More: The Last Soviet Generation*. Princeton University Press.

Yusupova, G. 2019. "Exploring Sensitive Topics in an Authoritarian Context: An Insider Perspective." *Social Science Quarterly* 100 (4): 1459–1478.

Yusupova, G. 2020. "The Religious Field in a Russian Muslim Village: A Bourdieusian Perspective on Islam." *Ethnicities* 20 (4): 769–792.

Zagrutdinov, A., and Zavgarova, F. 2018. "Kakikh svyatikh pochitayut tatary i kak rodnikovaya voda pomogaet sdat' EGA." *Inde*, July 24, 2018. https://inde.io /article/14455-etnograficheskiy-interes-kakih-svyatyh-pochitayut-tatary-i-kak -rodnikovaya-voda-pomogaet-sdat-ege.

Zaloom, C. 2015. "The Evangelical Financial Ethics: Doubled Forms and the Search for God in the Economic World." *American Ethnologist* 43 (2): 325–338.

Zhang, L. 2010. *In Search of Paradise: Middle-Class Living in a Chinese Metropolis*. Cornell University Press.

Zigon, J. 2007. "Moral Breakdown and the Ethical Demand: A Theoretical Framework for the Anthropology of Moralities." *Anthropological Theory* 7 (2): 131–150.

Zigon, J. 2008. *Morality: An Anthropological Perspective*. Berg.

Zigon, J. 2010a. *Making the New Post-Soviet Person: Moral Experience in Contemporary Moscow*. Brill.

Zigon, J. 2010b. *"HIV Is God's Blessing": Rehabilitating Morality in Neoliberal Russia*. University of California Press.

Zigon, J. 2017. *Disappointment: Toward a Critical Hermeneutics of Worldbuilding*. Fordham University Press.

Zigon, J. 2018. *A War on People: Drug User Policies and a New Ethics of Community*. University of California Press.

Žižek, S. 2014. *Event: A Philosophical Journey Through a Concept*. Penguin.

Zupančič, A. 2000. *Ethics of the Real: Kant, Lacan*. Verso.

Index

1990s, the: as a time of chaos, 21, 24, 39, 92; as a time of hardship, 118; as a time of possibility, 26, 29, 56, 83, 87, 187; as a time of violence, 23, 33–34, 36–37, 81, 163, 177

affliction, 111, 113, 116–119, 121, 125, 128, 194

affluence. *See* wealth

Agamben, Giorgio: on apparatuses 94; on bare life, 119–120; on capitalism, 173, 190; on form-of-life, 10–12, 44–50, 143, 193, 203n18; on monasticism, 47, 65, 84, 169

ákesis, 111, 119–125, 127, 129–135, 144. *See also* healing (spiritual)

Al-Albani, Mohammad Nasir al-Din, 6, 30, 63, 204n6. *See also* quietism, quietists; Salafi

alcohol, 37, 40, 56, 63, 78, 176–177, 183, 186

alienation, 11, 17, 36, 46, 144, 192–193

Althusser, Louis, 139, 155

Alyautdinov, Shamil, 42, 169–171, 175

anarchism, 69, 84; and anthropology, 14, 16, 22, 192–196. *See also* Graeber, D.; and autonomism, 9; destituent and transtituent power, 49; postanarchism, 3, 49

ancestor, 26, 70, 72–74, 115, 126–129, 207n7; ancestral essence 55, 58, 62, 72, 101, 154; ancestral religion 58, 70–73

apparatus, 49–50, 195; ideological, 8, 11, 18, 21, 157, 161; security, 2, 42, 86–87; themitical, 12, 21, 80–82, 93–96, 108–109, 153, 193. *See also* Muftiate

ascesis, 22, 64–73, 124, 169, 175, 189, 205n13; vs ákesis, 112–122, 130–135; and capitalism, 169, 175, 186–191; as source of tensions, 14–19, 49, 80–86, 137. *See also* secularity; sincerity

aspirations: middle-class, 2, 4, 21, 25, 36, 38–39, 42, 157; religious, 106, 115, 184; to worldly and spiritual success, 22, 118, 156, 173, 175, 188

Athari. *See* Hanbali; Salafi

atheism: 60, 72; Badiou's, 15, 117; and postatheism, 27, 70, 90–92, 145, 161; state 3, 5, 24–26, 55, 125

Austin, T. L., 53, 73, 73–79, 139, 148–151, 209n9

authoritarianism: under Putin 5, 26, 38, 55, 85–86, 93, 109, 165. *See also* Putinism; under empire, 91; under Soviet rule, 51, 106

autonomism, 9–12. *See also* Agamben G.; Badiou A.; radical theory; Tiqqun

Badiou, Alain, 10–16, 21, 35–38, 46–51, 79; on the human animal, 115, 119–122, 134; on interest, 68–70, 168–169, 176, 182, 185, 189–190; and Islamic askesis, 64–75, 117; on truth, 11–12, 28–32, 43, 138, 147–151, 176; on void, 25–28, 32–33, 37, 39. *See also* ákesis/aketic

Balkans, 131

Bashkir, 7, 55, 92, 102, 128

Bashkortostan, 7, 20, 92, 97, 125, 130

Bataille, Georges, 22, 165–166, 168–169, 174, 189, 210n4

beard (Islamic attribute), 33, 42, 98, 153, 173

being-for-death, 120

Bolğar (site), 7, 125, 127, 130, 207n7; Holy Bolğar Gathering, 72–74, 125; Bolğar Islamic Academy, 160. *See also* healing (spiritual); pilgrimage

Bosnia, 61, 127, 167

Bourdieu, Pierre, 139, 153–155, 189, 209

bourgeoisie, 17, 36–38, 39, 81, 155, 175, 188

bureaucracy (Islamic). *See* Muftiate

burial (of saint), 102, 111, 123, 128–135, 144; as Islamic practice, 81. *See also* healing (spiritual); pilgrimage

business (economy), 8, 32–33, 68, 72, 164–165, 171–177, 190; and failure or uncertainty, 181–182; halal, 22, 63, 136, 167, 176, 182–190; haram, 24, 68, 184–186

capitalism, 2, 9, 22, 38–39, 174, 185, 188, 192–193; and Islamic piety, 164–168, 190; neoliberal, 11, 38, 166–167, 172, 190, 210n2; spirit of, 36–37, 39, 53, 167, 173, 202n9

Castoriadis, C. 66–67, 154–155, 156

Caucasus (Northern), 63, 90, 103, 131, 151–153, 167, 202n6

www.ingramcontent.com/pod-product-compliance
Lightning Source LLC
Chambersburg PA
CBHW030401270326
41926CB00009B/1211